DEVOTIO ANTINOO:
THE DOCTOR'S NOTES,
VOLUME ONE

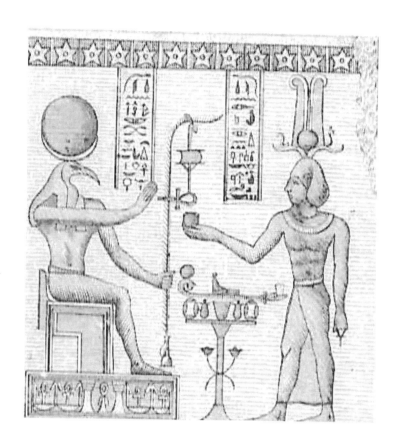

DEVOTIO ANTINOO: THE DOCTOR'S NOTES, VOLUME ONE

P. Sufenas Virius Lupus

The Red Lotus Library

September, 2011

Unless otherwise specified, the illustrations in this book are public domain photographs obtained from the website http://www.antinoos.info/.

The Red Lotus Library is the publication imprint of the Ekklesía Antínoou, a queer, Graeco-Roman-Egyptian syncretist reconstructionist polytheist group dedicated to Antinous, the deified lover of the Roman Emperor Hadrian, and related divine figures.

The Red Lotus Library
Anacortes, WA, U.S.A.

Printed by CreateSpace in the United States of America

DEO HEROIQVE ANTINOO
ET DEIS MVLTIS
ROMANORVM GRAECORVM AEGYPTORVM
PRO POPVLIS ECCLESIAE ANTINOI
P. SVF. VIRI. LVP. HVNC LIBRVM
DED. L.
DIES NATALIS ANTINOI
MDCCCLXXXI P.M.A.
V • S • L • M
HAEC EST VNDE VITA VENIT

To the youthful suicides,
Brandon E. Bitner,
Jamey Rodemeyer;
And to those killed in unspeakable ways
For being who they are,
David Kato Kisulle,
Stacey Blahnik,
Fred/F.C./"Beyoncé" Martinez,
Freddy Roberto Canul-Arguello;
And far too many others...
May their families have strength and peace,
May their spirits have rest and freedom,
May their memories never depart from the earth.

Someone will gather
garlands of lamented names,
and will lament more
the youth of the dying men.

Table of Contents

III. THE *DIVI* AND THE *SANCTI*

Preface and Acknolwedgments

The book you hold in your hands is the culmination of just over nine years' worth of practical devtion to Antinous, on the part of myself as well as a large and varying cast of other players—ritualists, devotees, scholars, event attendees, friends, co-religionists, critics, well-wishers, and a great variety of others—who have helped to suggest, inspire, refine, develop, and encourage these various practices. The resulting book is intended to help those who are just starting out in their practical devotions on this path and with this particular god (and some of his friends), whether they identify with the Ekklesía Antínoou's overall aims in whole, in part, or not at all.

I would like to emphasize that if one considers oneself first and foremost a devotee of Antinous, that is excellent, and a great deal of what follows in the present volume will be useful to you. However, devotion to Antinous is not by any means limited to those who are solely Antinoan in their focus, nor is it limited to people who are in some way connected to the Ekklesía Antínoou. Wherever any devotion to Antinous exists—no matter how large or small-, singular or as part of a larger pantheon—it is a wonderful and beautiful thing as far as I'm concerned. I would hope that this book will end up appealing to and being useful for people who are interested in and devoted to Antinous who are Wiccan, Feri, ADF, Thelemites, Gnostics, Hellenics, Kemetics, *Religio Romana*, Brotherhood of the Phoenix, Radical Faeries, Minoan Brotherhood, reconstructionists of various other types, eclectics of many stripes, and anyone and everyone else who may find Antinous of sufficient interest and attraction to engage in the work of devotion with him.

Over the years since June of 2002, I have written a great deal of material on Antinous, and it was expressed within the Ekklesía Antínoou that a published "dead trees" collection of these materials would be desirable. As I began the work of compiling the best, most interesting, and most helpful of these writings, I soon found that the resulting book would be far too large, and that it would have to be broken down into two smaller books. I decided that to break it into a

1

book of primarily devotional material and primarily theological material would be the best option to take, despite the fact that theology should influence and inspire devotion, and devotion is in turn supported by and prompts theological thinking.

Of these two, the more important one to release first was the devotional volume. Modern paganism, and polytheistic religions generally, are religions of practice, of conduct, and of experience, as opposed to religions of creed. Belief is important, but nowhere near as important as the doing of regular ritual, of conducting one's life in a virtuous manner, and in having direct experiences of divine realities, worlds, worldviews, and entities. Thus, to make the overall emphasis of what it is that we are attempting to do in the Ekklesía Antínoou and with our devotions to Antinous more visible, more viable, and more relevant, as well as more exemplary of this basic stance within a polytheistic religious framework, this book and the practices that it explores was deemed far more essential and urgent to make available for anyone who wishes to examine it.

That is not to say that there isn't theologizing, or discussions of particular understandings of divine encounters (which is what a "belief" is—not something adhered to in absence of definitive proof, but instead an articulation of a particular divine experience, even though the nature of that experience is subjective, not verifiable by conventional means, or beyond the reach of more objective metrics and apprehensions) found in this book—there are, and in fact some postulates in these practices depend upon them. However, as with everything in polytheistic cultures, these are highly individual, even when they are encountered within a spiritual community that shares many ideals in common amongst its various members. Individual theologies and beliefs, as well as individual practices, should be as individualized and particular as can be whenever it is possible for such individualization to occur. The same holds true for anything and everything in the Ekklesía Antínoou. If anything in this book ends up being useful, productive, enlightening, or inspiring to your own practices and your own engagements with life generally and with Antinous and friends in particular, then feel free to use it as you like, or modify it to make it work better for you; if something becomes an impediment or is not interesting or useful to you, then disregard it.

2

Before making my final acknowledgments of particular people for their direct assistance and inspiration in producing this volume, I would like to make one final apology. I strive to very high standards of scholarly discourse and documentation whenever possible. I apologize that I have not included full and thorough references for every single point and idea brought up in the present book. You will find that there are a number of footnotes—perhaps, by some standards, even what would be considered a "large" number!—but I hope that they are not excessive or that their presence detracts from this volume for those who aren't interested in the information they contain. Any ancient text which is directly quoted, as well as any important book, study, or idea which can be tracked directly to a definite source, should hopefully be noted in the course of the chapter in which it is found. There is no collected bibliography for this book, as a result, but there will be a comprehensive one in the second volume of this work.

There are many people to thank for their various contributions to the present volume. First off, I would like to thank the Ekklesía Antínoou collectively, the group for whom this volume was produced, and in whose service I have been for a number of years now. Thank you all for your continued participation, enthusiasm, conversation, and unrestrained dialogue on these matters! In particular, I'd like to single out a few individuals: Quintus Poppaeus Sabinus, Jimmy "Tarik," Shawn Postoff, Sanatani, C. A. Young, Shade, Selene, Jiovanni Minagro, Jay Logan, Kallimachus, Duti, and David. I'd also like to thank the various *Mystai Antínoou*: Aristotimos, Erynn Rowan Laurie, BlackCat, Jimbo, Tristissima *et alia*, Ogam, Michael Routery, Sr. Krissy Fiction, and Michael Sebastian Lux; and also the many "Assistai" we have had over the years who have been essential in performing the Antinoan Mysteries: Lucinda Diann, C. Lee Vermeers, Janet Summerswind, Llynne Merytamon, Joseph Kramer, Nicole Hernandez, Steeleheart, Birch, and Bob Mathis-Friedman. I'd also like to thank the various *Luperci* who have participated with us at PantheaCon in the three years that we have performed that ritual there (apart from those who are already listed above): Sannion, Derik Cowan, Lupa, and S. J. Tucker; and also those who have participated in the Communalia rituals we have held for the last two years: EliSheva, Rabbit, Ember, and Chandra Alexandre. Sannion deserves further recognition as a great inspiration and trusted friend. Nicole Hernandez further merits great appreciation and thanks for her provision of art in various contexts, as does C. A. Young for providing the cover art for the present book, and Shawn Postoff the (*agon*-winning!) art for the back cover. Mick McCoy also allowed me to re-use the piece on p. 206, which originally appeared in *The Phillupic Hymns* as the frontispiece, to illustrate the poem which originally inspired his art. Erynn Rowan Laurie has been an inspiration, a colleague, a multiple co-religionist, and also a generous contributor of her own efforts to the present book (particularly in the form of the ritual for the Festival of the Lion Hunt and the Red Lotus). Professors Mary Beard, John North, Simon Price, and Cambridge University Press are also thanked most graciously for their granting of permission to reprint the Lanuvium *collegium*'s temple constitution in the present book. Patrick Jones was most helpful in the past with translational issues, and David Kraetzer was helpful in this regard as well, in addition to making many texts available to me that I was not able to access myself.

I must insist that the present book is not "academic," despite the footnotes and the index. Royston Lambert's *Beloved and God: The Story of Hadrian and Antinous*, was also stated to not be an academic book, and yet it has been treated as one by both academics as well as general readers ever since it was released. And, while excellent, it is also rather frustrating, as some references are incomplete or confusing, if not altogether lacking. Some modern devotees of Antinous, however, have considered it a "bible" of sorts, and I am especially disparaging of such a notion. The present book should not be cited as an academic resource, but it can most certainly be used as a jumping-off point for pursuit of some of these texts and ideas in an academic fashion. I certainly would never suggest that the present book is in any way a "bible" for devotees of Antinous, or even for the Ekklesía Antínoou specifically, and I am against any such notion in any section of modern paganism and polytheism. We certainly have sacred texts that are cherished, recited, preserved, studied, and discussed, but to suggest that there is a "canon" of such texts to which no more may be added, and in which no changes might be made (which is what "scripture" and "bible" both imply, for good or ill) is nonsensical, since the gods are still revealing themselves to us now, and will continue to do so into the future and beyond. The moment a text becomes "scripture," it loses the ability to adapt to this changing divine reality, and becomes ossified

4

and, if anything, a limit to spiritual exploration rather than an aid to it. I would never wish that to happen to anything associated with Antinous. And, even apart from this, scholarship and translations of texts, and their further understanding, are always prone to change, and we must not resist such improved understandings by any means!

My hope is that this book becomes an aid to your own understanding, a tool for use in your own practice, and a goad toward cultivating an experience of Antinous and the other deities, heroes, *Divi* and *Divae*, *Sancti* and *Sanctae*, and myriad further figures associated with him. Let the research and practices outlined here neither substitute for your own further research, insights, and practices, but also let it not be daunting, or an impediment to your own practice. The most important thing, with all of the gods, is not to think about them, or to consider doing things for them, *but to do them*. Therefore, go forth in practice as a testament to your devotion, to Antinous, and to all of your other gods!

P.Suf.Viri.Lup.
Dies Natalis Antinoi MDCCCI
November 27, 2011

A Note on Language and Pronunciation

In my work with modern Antinoan devotion, I have used a lot of Latin. I enjoy speaking and writing in Latin, and find it to be familiar enough and yet simultaneously unusual enough to put me slightly out of my comfort zone, which is a good position in which to be when doing ritual. The use of a "liturgical language" is intended to have this effect: the Old Japanese used as part of Shinto rituals, for example, which is not the common and everyday modern Japanese language, gives an air of formality and tradition to their ceremonies, and likewise the Sanskrit used in Hindu rituals in comparison to the modern Hindi, Tamil, and other dialects.

However, I am well aware that the language in which Hadrian and Antinous would have most often spoken would have been Greek—it was Antinous' native language, and Hadrian was reputed to have spoken better Greek than formal Latin. Many of the inscriptions and papyrus texts relating to Antinous are in Greek, while a much smaller number are in Latin, and an even smaller number are in late Egyptian. I simply prefer Latin for two reasons: it fits my own aesthetics, and I don't know enough Greek off the top of my head to make it second-nature at this point (though I'm certainly trying to learn!).

All of that having been said, the "official language" of the Ekklesía Antínoou, at this stage, is English, and always will be. It is the language of many of our prayers, and all of our conversations and theological writings. Thus, if you do not have any interest in Latin (or Greek, or Egyptian), or the use of other languages in ritual, it will not be a barrier to participation in Antinoan devotion by any stretch of the imagination.

However, there is one matter that requires some attention to important detail, whether we are using English or any other language for liturgical purposes, and that is pronunciation, particularly of certain important names, the main one being "Antinous." In both Greek (where his name is rendered in English letters "Antínoös") and in Latin ("Antinous"), Antinous' name has four syllables—the final two vowels are separated by hiatus, and are not a diphthong as they can potentially be in English and other languages. Indeed, this is why the Greek version usually has an umlaut over the second "o," in order to indicate that it is a separate syllable. Thus, in Latin, Antinous' name is pronounced "on-TEE-no-us" (with the final "u" like "put" rather than like "bus"), and in Greek it is "on-TEE-no-os" (with the final "o" as in "post"). Antinous has a long history of being pronounced in English, however, for the last century and more, as his name and story was used by various Uranian Poets (including Oscar Wilde), and all of them were classically educated in both Greek and Latin, and thus their pronunciation was influenced by their knowledge of those languages as well. When one says "Antinous" in English, therefore, it should be something like "an-TIN-o-us" (with the same "u" like "put" in the Latin example above).

While this may seem, to some opinions at least, a bit overly fussy, I would invite you to think of it in the following manner. If you were introduced to someone new, and their name was Simon, but you insisted on pronouncing it as if it were French and therefore to the English ear sounded more like "Simone," you might not only annoy the person involved, but you might actually get enmity from them over your refusal to pay them the courtesy of being called what they prefer. The names of the gods are similar: there is heritage and tradition behind the ways they have been invoked, and to ignore established tradition—whether English, Greek, or Latin—is inadvisable at best. Because the exact pronunciation of deity names was important to many Greek and Egyptian magical practices, for example, it is best when the pronunciation of an important name is known to follow in the tradition of observing such rules. One would not expect someone called "Simon" to turn around in a crowd if someone kept yelling "SIMONE!" at them; likewise, when we pray to the gods and perform rituals in their honor, we should do them the courtesy of pronouncing their names correctly so that they will not only know we are addressing them, but will be more likely to hear our entreaties favorably.

It might also be handy to know a little bit about Latin declensions of the name of Antinous as well at this stage. The following forms of Antinous' name would be used in various Latin grammatical contexts:

<u>Nominative:</u> Antinous (when he is the subject of a sentence—"Antinous is from Bithynia.")

<u>Genitive:</u> Antinoi (usually when he is the possessor of something, "Antinous' spear," "the friends of Antinous.")

<u>Dative:</u> Antinoo (when he is the indirect object of a sentence, "We give thanks to Antinous," "we do this ritual for Antinous.")

<u>Accusative:</u> Antinoum (when he is the direct object of a sentence, "We praise Antinous," "Hadrian loves Antinous.")

<u>Ablative:</u> Antinoo (when he is the object of various prepositions or grammatical constructions, "with Antinous," "about Antinous," etc.)

<u>Vocative:</u> Antinoe (when Antinous is directly addressed, "Antinous, hear our prayer," "Hail, Antinous!")

When using Latin, it is important to know that the vowels are "continental" in quality, rather than their typical values in English, so that most of them are like the long versions of the vowel in English—"o" is "oh," "i" is "ee," "a" is "ah," "u" is "oo," and "e" is "eh" (i.e. what Canadians say after many declarative statements, not the New Yorker expression of not being impressed!). The most important cases of Antinous' name, therefore, will be the nominative (pronounced as mentioned previously) and the vocative, which is pronounced "on-TEE-no-eh" (or "on-TEE-no-ay," with "ay" being like the English "hay, say, may," etc.).

There are various schools of modern Latin pronunciation, but one of the advantages of the name of Antinous is that it entirely avoids some of the controversial issues that cause those schools to argue with one another (e.g. how to pronounce "v" and "c," mainly, but also the quality of some diphthongs, e.g. "ae"). However one decides to pronounce the other words one may encounter in the prayers and rituals given below, the name of Antinous in all cases should be something upon which everyone can agree.

Devotio Antinoo:
Devotion to Antinous,
An Introduction

There are a thousand ways to kneel and kiss the ground.

–Rumi

Antinous was born on November 27, c. 110-112 CE in the Roman province of Bithynia, in the city of Bithynion-Claudiopolis, to parents who were descendants of Greek colonists from Mantineia in Arcadia. In one of many tours in the Eastern Empire in c. 123-125, the philhellenic Emperor Hadrian took the boy into his company, and Antinous probably finished his schooling in Rome. In 128, the Emperor and his court underwent a tour of the East once again, and at the outset, Antinous was the acknowledged "imperial favorite," the recognized lover/companion of the Emperor himself. The two toured various important cities, took initiations into the Eleusinian Mysteries in Greece (Hadrian doing so for the second time), probably engaged with Epicurean philosophers in Athens, and participated in various other religious and mystical ceremonies, as the Emperor was always fascinated with religion and the occult. In Alexandria, very likely in the summer of 130, the pair also engaged in Hadrian's favorite pastime of hunting, and slew a particularly dangerous lion that had been ravaging the Libyan countryside, a feat of epic proportions which inspired several poems and was a cornerstone of the later Antinoan mythos. The two met an Egyptian priest/poet named Pancrates/Pachrates, who performed some effective spells for Hadrian.

Soon after, in late October of 130, Antinous disappeared while the imperial barge was traveling up the Nile in the neighborhood of Hermopolis; and on October 30, 130, his body was found washed up on the banks of the Nile, drowned. Some suspected foul play; others said it was suicide; still others said it was a willing sacrificial death on behalf of the ailing Emperor and the Empire; Hadrian's own opinion on the matter was that it was sheer accident. The Emperor's laments were excessive and even unseemly by the standards of his day. However, by Egyptian custom of the time, anyone who had drowned in the holy waters of the Nile was considered deified, was syncretized to Osiris, and was given a minor cult. Hadrian used this opportunity to found a city in Egypt in his honor, Antinoöpolis, which became the seat of his cult; but the Imperial favor did not finish there. Antinous' deification was proclaimed throughout the Empire, games were held every few years in Antinous' honor until well into the fourth century, and temples were established in various places (particularly in the Greek East). His image in the form of statues, coins, and medals was propagated widely; an oracle was set up to him; poems and hymns were composed to him, and Antinoöpolis became a hotbed of religious activity. In the year after Antinous' death, a miracle in the form of an excessive inundation of the Nile followed, which was attributed to his good favor in relief of a several-year drought. A new star in the constellation of Aquila was pointed out to Hadrian in early 131, stated to be Antinous' soul in the heavens, and the astrologers of the second century record the constellation as Ganymede/Antinous in his honor.

Deification of a non-imperial person was unheard of in Rome, and was frowned upon by the Senate; Hadrian was the only one to have ever done this. Yet, Antinous' veneration even took root in the city of Rome itself. Until the final "triumph" of Christianity in the fourth century, Antinous' cult was thriving, and he was syncretized to many gods in different localities, including Hermes, Dionysus, Apollon, Belenus, Osiris, Pan, Adonis, Silvanus, Eros, and others,[1] and he was venerated as a hero, an admirable mortal whose virtues granted him immortality. Some modern commentators say he was the "last pagan god,"[2] and a definite rival for the Christian religion. The fathers of the church censured Antinous' cult from its first appearance, and resented that he was often compared to Jesus—another living human who died

---

[1] See P. Sufenas Virius Lupus, *The Syncretisms of Antinous* (Anacortes: The Red Lotus Library, 2010), for details on all of the attested syncretisms of Antinous.

[2] Though Glykon, the snake-oracle propagated by Alexander of Abonuteichos a decade or so after Antinous' death, is often not taken into account in such assessments. There are bound to be others which emerged as well, whether or not historians have overlooked them, or that we simply have hitherto not had access to information about their cultus.

10

and was said to still live, both fully human and fully divine. This derision continued from the second century through the eleventh with some Byzantine Christians. The dates of Antinous' birth and apotheosis (at very least) were celebrated in his ancient cult.

The Ekklesia Antinoou is the name for the modern re-founded cult of Antinous, organized by P. Sufenas Virius Lupus and Hiram Crespo in mid-2002, and carried on by them after disagreements with earlier groups from mid-2007 onwards. The influences in the modern cult practices, like those of the ancient cult, are varied and highly syncretistic, taking elements from primarily Greek, Roman, and Egyptian religions, but also Gnosticism, Hinduism, Celtic, Platonic, and even Catholic sources (most of the founding members were brought up Catholic, but had since been involved with different forms of paganism). Our focus is on the holiness of the queer sensibility, the wisdom of youth, the beauty and gifts of graceful aging, and the remembrance of our queer spiritual heritage, as well as mystical connection with divinities and the fostering of our own inherent divinity, and continuing the useful practices and devotions found in the ancient world, but adapted for the modern person, in addition to creating new traditions and finding new significances and theologies in the ongoing contact we experience with Antinous and various other deities connected to him. It is, in short, queer Graeco-Roman-Egyptian syncretist reconstructionist polytheism, with a strongly mystical bent, focused on Antinous and related deities and divine figures.

Like most ancient religions, the focus of the Ekklesía Antínoou's practice is not orthodoxy—"belief in Antinous" or any related figure is not required to participate in this group or any ritual put on by it. All one needs is an open, respectful, and spiritual attitude in relation to what occurs. As there are very few dedicated members of the Ekklesía Antínoou, it is not expected that one will find all parts of the rituals and practices detailed in the book which follows here relevant to one's own life; and as we do not proselytize, we also do not suggest that this is "the only way," or is even necessarily the best way, to honor these ideals and these particular divine figures, much less for all queer people, or for all of humanity-in-general. However, by your patronage of this publication, I am personally honored, and we are honored as an organization, and appreciate your attention and interest very much.

Many pagans of various stripes have taken part in our activities before, but also atheists, agnostics, and even a Muslim and an Irish cradle-Catholic (the latter a straight one, no less!) who was adamant in seeing these devotions as one of many expressions of the movement of the Holy Spirit in another cultural context.

The Emperor Hadrian was the consummate and archetypal Hellenophile, witnessed in so many ways, perhaps most readily by his physical appearance in that he was bearded, the Greek signifier of the maturity and wisdom of age. In his own spiritual interests and pursuits, and his interest in oracles and magical practice from a young age, he was highly syncretistic. In the tradition of the *Interpretatio Romana*, well demonstrated by Julius Caesar and others (including Alexander the Great of Macedon, in his encounters with India, and Herodotus—though both of these would be better described as *Interpretatio Graeca*), the deities and beliefs of other cultures were understood not necessarily on their own terms (the Romans were not anthropologists!) but through the comparison of known Roman cognates, often erasing indigenous names and characteristics in favor of a homogenous but common mythic understanding throughout the empire. While this may bear a certain and limited resemblance to modern comparative mythological explorations or the promiscuous eclecticism of many neo-agnostics and new age believers, we can only laud the Roman tolerance and willingness to appropriate foreign beliefs so far. These cultures and the deities in them have an integrity of their own, and should be respected wherever possible. Thus, even though some late antique devotees of Antinous might have been under the impression that Osiris and Dionysos were "the same," nonetheless the separate nomenclature of Antinous-Osiris and Antinous-Dionysos remains. And Antinous himself, while often adopting the characteristics or epithets of other gods, is never seen to replace or overshadow them completely. One should remember this always when dealing with him: he is always himself, even when he is wearing the attributes of some other deity.

Hadrian's foresight and the prevailing polytheistic and syncretistic tendency of late antiquity allowed Antinous to be worshipped as Osiris in Egypt (and elsewhere), as Dionysos in Greece (and elsewhere), as Hermes in Rome (and elsewhere), as himself in concert alongside

Diana in Lanuvium, and innumerable other ways besides. The cultus of Antinous was a localized, highly adapted and adaptable phenomenon, and though some customs seemed to be shared across time and distance, and his particular image was fairly standardized in its essential features in most places, nonetheless Antinous' devotion took root in the hearts of his votaries in each location individually. The same should be true in today's reverence for and worship of the deity. This syncretistic tendency, continued from the past, has allowed the modern Ekklesia Antinoou to explore critically yet piously some myths which did not or may not have been apparent to the classical world—either because inaccessible, antagonistic, ignored, or simply not yet attested. A modern religion can do no less if it wishes to be relevant in the lives of its practitioners.

The following statement from Garth Fowden's *The Egyptian Hermes: A Historical Approach to the Late Pagan Mind*, which includes a quote from a Hermetic text found amongst the Oxyrhynchus Papyri, attached to an aretalogy of Asklepios, puts us perfectly in the milieu in which the texts found in this book were originally written (whether they are the fragmentary remnants from the ancient cultus, or are more modern and recent in origin), and the spirit in which they are offered here as well. "In the ancient world it was customary for gods to demand that accounts of their wonders be composed by their devotees...'every gift of a votive offering or sacrifice lasts only for the immediate moment, and presently perishes, while a written record is an undying deed of gratitude, from time to time renewing its youth in the memory.'"[3]

Something often forgotten in the modern world is that the mere telling of stories and listening attentively to them is not just a form of entertainment, or even a method of education and edification. In many societies of the past—and many which continue today—the telling of a story, a myth, a legend, is itself infused with significance, and great merit attaches to those who can remember the stories and interpret

---

[3] Garth Fowden, *The Egyptian Hermes: A Historical Approach to the Late Pagan Mind* (Princeton: Princeton University Press, 1993), p. 147. The text quoted is *P. Oxy.* 1381, which can be found in Frederick C. Grant, *Hellenistic Religions: The Age of Syncretism* (New York and Indianapolis: The Liberal Arts Press, 1953), pp. 124-127 at 127.

their meanings. Most forms of art recognized in the modern world have their origins in religion and the recounting of narrative: visual arts were icons and representations of stories; poetry and song, drama and dance were all one activity that retold the stories of gods and heroes. As many of these forces which can be marshalled into a modern and creative form of spirituality should be pursued as possible.

Therefore, I offer those who are interested here some of the prayers, the rituals, the feasts, the practices, and the indications of the philosophies underlying them which can create, consist of, and motivate practical devotion to Antinous the God. This practice is above all an individual one, and no one practice or method will appeal to or be useful for any and every adherent. So, these are only an appetizer; individual taste and experimentation with one's available ingredients and their combinations will have to be the daily nourishment of this religious experience.

The basic format of this book is as follows. The first chapters of Part I give some basic ideas about Antinoan devotion, what is needed for it, and some of the ways one can enrich one's knowledge in order to have more effective engagement with Antinous and the gods and figures related to him. The sections which follow are prayers and hymns specifically concerned with Antinous, which can be used in a variety of contexts. With the three hymns/prayers to Wepwawet, Hekate, and Ianus (which are used at the beginning of most major public rituals), we move into Part II, with further devotional explorations of Antinoan practice, rituals for different occasions, calendars and explanations of holy-days, and a number of hymns dealing with specific divine aspects of Antinous' various syncretisms. We then move further in Part III into ways in which the *Divi* and the *Sancti* of the Ekklesía Antínoou can be honored—including Divus Hadrianus and Diva Sabina, Sancta Julia Balbilla, Herodes Attikos and his *Trophimoi* (particularly Polydeukion), and the grouping of Antinous together with Polydeukion and Lucius Marius Vitalis as the *Treískouroi*. Amidst these, and flowing into Part IV, are translations of actual poems, hymns, inscriptions, and other texts dealing with these various figures from the late antique Mediterranean world, as well as Antinous himself, which can be used for a variety of purposes, or simply studied as informational resources or used as inspirational wells from which to

14

draw the water to allow your own devotional impulses to thrive. Finally, the end of Part IV and all of Part V includes several texts which are not directly connected to Antinous, but either give some further color and context to the activities of Hadrian in the ancient world, or that are later texts which can easily be understood as meaningful and useful in an Antinoan setting.

Volume Two of the present book, which should be available in the near future, will have more theological reflections and theoretical essays on Antinous, which might deepen one's understanding of this devotional path and the gods associated with it, as well as giving historical context to aspects of the ancient cultus and how they can be understood in the early twenty-first century.

May all the gods—but especially Antinous and the Divine Hadrian—go with you on your journeys in the following pages, and remain with you when you close these covers!

I.
GETTING STARTED

Basic Antinoan Practice

Now that you've decided to take the stab and wish to practice some sort of devotion to Antinous, the first question is: what to do? Where does one start?

Following on from the previous chapter (which hopefully gave some basic historical background to the original cultus as well as the modern Ekklesía Antínoou), there are a few theological premises, implicit with any polytheistic practice, which should most likely be taken into account as one does this.

Antinous is a god, but this does not mean that he is omniscient, omnipresent, or omnipotent. You can pray to him for whatever you like, but it may not be in his power to help you achieve whatever it is you ask for. Antinous can be anywhere, but he's not everywhere at all times, and thus one must call to him and get his attention. Antinous can know a great deal, but he cannot (and does not!) know everything, and therefore you can't assume that he knows what you want or need, or knows what you're thinking, or that he even knows you at all until you have been introduced to him. This means that in order to pray to him, you actually do need to speak out loud. It can be in a hushed voice, or even a whisper, but it does need to be out loud.[4]

Second, you'll need an image of Antinous. Aniconic spiritual practices can certainly be effective, but the cultus of Antinous (both ancient and modern) is not aniconic. It is my own experience that images of Antinous are helpful, not only in focusing our own efforts, but also in being a physical representation of the presence of the god. The eyes and ears of a statue, a bust, or even a two-dimensional representation

---

[4] In the Lupercalia ritual in February of 2010 held by the Ekklesía Antínoou at PantheaCon, one participant expressed his prayers to Antinous through sign language. I believe this was an effective thing to do. The use of specific hand gestures or postures as *mudras* for Antinoan purposes is a topic which will be addressed later.

(whether a painting, a photograph of a known image, or a coin inscription) are the eyes and ears of the god in the world. So, anything, from a reproduction bust to an image on your computer screen to a postcard, can serve in this fashion. One should do one's devotions to Antinous in front of such an image, or with such an image close at hand, whenever possible. Certain symbols of Antinous (particularly the red Nile lotus) can also function in this fashion in absence of better alternatives.

With those premises in mind, and those material components, what comes next? The following three things have been the basic components to most deity-specific cultic practices through much of the world: praise, offerings, and prayer. Praise can be in the form of hymns, songs, and other verbalized statements which glorify the presence and blessings of the god; this can also be in simple and spontaneous expressions of thanksgiving, gratefulness, and appreciation for the gifts of the god in one's life. Offerings can consist of many different things, including food and water, incense, light (in the form of candles or oil lamps), alcoholic beverages, but also more permanet material things like a shrine, votive jewelry and statues, or works of art, performance (music or dance or other things, including ritual actions themselves!) or poetry. Prayer is communication with the god (often in the form of a request), and as far as the human portion of that communication goes, one should express one's wishes clearly and specifically, leaving it up to the god to act toward carrying them out or otherwise.

Many of the devotional texts given later in this book can be used for praise. Likewise, particular prayers can also be used that are included later in this book, as joining one's own efforts into a similar form and set of words for a group of people builds not only communal bonds and experience, but also strengthens the overall effectiveness of that prayer through shared effort. However, whenever possible, creating one's own forms of praise and of prayer is best, whether these are improvised and different each time, or one develops one's own set forms, texts, and preferred phrases and expressions.

Dancing, singing, sacred drama, and other performative actions can certainly be done, and if done, they should be done "in the sight" of an

18

icon or image of the deity. When one is doing this, one is actually entertaining the deity, along with possibly praying to them or offering them a hymn. With that in mind, don't let the fact that you may not be a world-class singer, dramatist, or dancer restrict you from doing whatever you are able and whatever you feel like you can do (or can handle on a given date!) for the god. Devotional fervor and intent counts for a great deal, but be just as prepared to laugh at yourself if you sing badly as the god may be laughing at you too—and, realize that's not necessarily a bad thing! Demeter needed nothing more than a good laugh at one point on her search for Persephone, and it was a good thing therefore that Iambe and Baubo were there to oblige that need. (Likewise with Re and Hathor!) If you are not a good singer at all, then don't offer a song; but, if you feel you would like to give it a try anyway, do not stint in doing so with every ounce of your talent and your effort, no matter what the outcome may be.

More permanent offerings must be taken care of in particular ways. Votive jewelry offered to the god should not be re-used or given away, it should remain dedicated to the god. Certain material offerings can be replaced on an annual basis: for example, in my own practices a stone is given at the end of the Foundation Day rituals, which is then replaced the following year; but, some people have taken all of these stones from rituals and have made a small herm or sacred cairn in their yard with them. However one chooses to do this is fine. Flowers can be offered, and can be left on one's shrine for lengthy periods, but will eventually need to be replaced—even if one likes the dried/dead flower look!

What to do with food offerings, though? This is a contentious issue, because food offerings were disposed of in different ways in the past based on what cultures were involved, and often which gods were involved. For example, in Greece, offerings to "heavenly" deities were burned, but offerings for "chthonic" deities were placed into an offering pit; further, sometimes part of the sacrificed food was shared with heavenly deities, but chthonic offerings were always given to the gods *in toto*. The same is not true of Egypt, where all food offered was returned to the priests or to the people who offered it. In several polytheistic practices that still persist today (Hinduism and Shinto, for example), food offerings are left on the altar for a short while, and then are given back as *prasad* (Hindu) or *naorae* (Shinto) to worshippers, so that they may share in the blessings and joyfulness of the ritual actions and the presence of the god thereby.

We live in a much different world now, where we are aware of ecological factors and are often concerned with conservation. There are very few dedicated temples and other such ritual sites where offerings to deities can be made, and then burned or buried as necessary; and, not everyone has access to a fireplace, back-yard barbecue, or hole in the ground in which to create the same effects. Also, a number of us are not from economically privileged backgrounds, and the idea of "wasting food" is either abhorrent or simply impossible based on our income. Thus, the methods which one uses to dispose of food offerings may be even more complicated. Work out whatever feels best for you, and in absence of direct instructions from the god (which can occur, so be prepared if it does to act upon them!), do what feels best and most responsible and respectable from your own personal ideals, philosophy, and personality.

Offering of water on a regular basis was part of Egyptian practice, particularly for deceased ancestors. If nothing else, Antinous was a deceased human whom we admire, whether or not one thinks of him as a god, hero, *daimon*, or anything else. Thus, this sort of offering on a regular basis, along with anything else, and on its own in absence of anything else, is a good practice. How should one dispose of it? I suggest that drinking it afterwards, as the final action after one's devotions wrap, is a good idea. Water is a finite resource, more so in some locations than in others, and thus should be respected and not wasted whenever possible. However, some rituals and offerings of water are not just for Antinous, they may be for the *Sancti*, who are our recognized divine and holy ancestors who were once living. If a water offering is for a *Sanctus/a/um*, I would suggest pouring it out into a plant, tree, or something, particularly a plant that serves as one's "offering plant" in one's yard or house. If the offering is for a god or for Antinous, I would suggest consuming it yourself as your physical communion with the god. It is the equivalent of sharing a drink in fellowship to do so.

20

One can also dedicate one's activities in daily life to the god, but this should be prefaced with a prayer of dedication or statement of intention, and then also formally closed with something along the same lines. What types of activity can be offered to Antinous? Anything involving political advocacy for the rights of sexual minorities; study of ancient religions or one's writing and research about them, particularly if it concerns Antinous, Hadrian, or one of the deities related to these; athletic activities, exercise, and anything that benefits one's physical health; hunting (as it was Antinous and Hadrian's favorite pastimes—if you do it, be safe, follow all local regulations, obtain the proper permits, and never abuse the privilege or disrespect the animals who are your prey by being wasteful, etc.), but also conservation activities to keep wild places preserved (Hadrian himself attempted to protect the famed forests of Lebanon); gardening; hiking and forest walks; anything involving horses, from riding or raising them to grooming them, or supporting charities that benefit them (and, indeed, any other animals or wildlife, but horses and dogs in particular); swimming, boating and other aquatic activities—and not drowning while doing them!; being social with others (and maintaining social responsibility while doing so—e.g. not getting raucously drunk and rude, not driving drunk, not breaking any laws); enjoying dramatic and musical performances and artistic events; visiting museums and ancient sites (whether specifically sacred or not); sexual activities between legally consenting adults; and, really, anything which one thinks might be appropriate for Antinous, or that would be pleasing to him.

Let there be a warning with this, though: do not mistake what you like to do—whether it be knitting or watching *Star Trek* episodes—as something which will automatically appeal to the god. It is possible to make anything which one does holy and sacred, mindful and aware, and pleasing to the gods; but, one should realize that some things may not be of interest to some gods. Given that I come from a polytheist viewpoint, this isn't much of a problem, because if Antinous isn't interested in something which one does regularly and enjoys, there's bound to be another god somewhere who is—so go and find that god, and enjoy your activity! Further, there may simply be some activities that don't appeal to any gods, but that's no reason not to do them yourself, it is more a matter of not offering them to the gods inappropriately. Think of the cliché often said at gift-giving holidays: it's the thought that counts. Yes, it is—but make sure you do *stop and think*, because getting something for someone that you know they don't like isn't very thoughtful.

The gods can become involved in almost every aspect of our lives, but a god (and Antinous is no exception) does not need to be involved in every aspect of one's life in order for one's life to be holy or virtuous or useful. Use your discretion and your discernment, and be as aware as possible for any signs or messages from the god that they are not interested in what you happen to be doing. It is possible to give too much to a god, just as it is possible to overly fawn on and smother another human. So, don't get carried away with saying "I offer my getting the mail today to Antinous," "I offer my taking off my shoes to Antinous," "I offer my Nintendo Wii Bowling game to Antinous," and so forth.

Something that should also be kept in mind in considering any of this is that though it may be admirable and worthwhile to aim toward a constant communion with one's deities, it rarely if ever happens automatically. One has to attain a very deep and abiding relationship with a particular deity for their presence and involvement to be continuous in every activity in one's life. Presuming this is the case just because one has made a single prayer to Antinous (or any deity), and one has simply decided that everything in one's life is holy, does not mean that it is automatically so. In polytheism, there is no such thing as "one-stop shopping."[5]

One thing should primarily be of concern in undertaking any devotion to Antinous: the most important thing is to *do something*, and to do it regularly, whether that means once or more a day, once a week, once a month, or even only once a year. For a polytheistic spirituality, the most important thing is always the practice, and the doing of it as best as one is able. There will be times when one gets bored or frustrated; there will be times when something doesn't go quite right; there will be

---

[5] I wrote on this topic in the "Queer I Stand" column at Patheos.com's Pagan Portal: http://www.patheos.com/Resources/Additional-Resources/Dangers-of-the-One-Stop-Shopping-Mentality-P-Sufenas-Virius-Lupus-07-29-2011.html.

22

occasions when it is hard to find enough space, resources, or time to do something as adequately as one would prefer. But, don't let those things block you from not making the best of your available efforts and resources. If you mean to do a big ritual, and something comes up and you're not able to, do a small one instead. If you wanted to spend two hours in meditation and prayer but find you can only spare five minutes, do the five minutes. And, if you miss it entirely or for whatever reason can't do it at all, then at least going before your image of Antinous and saying "I'm very sorry, I wasn't able to do this, I'll try harder the next time, and I still like you!" can go a very long way to maintaining one's connection to the god. Just as you wouldn't fail to show up for an engagement with a good friend without accounting for yourself afterwards, the same should be true of ritual. One cannot assume that "the gods understand," even when dire emergencies occur, because they aren't omniscient and omnipresent. So, keep them informed as much as you can!

And the rest, as they say, is gravy. But, seeing as I have gone to the trouble of writing an entire book, please do read on!

Antinoan Feast of the Senses

The idea of a "Feast of the Senses" was innovated by Sannion, who describes the whole process in his essay of the same name.[6] Incorporating this, whether one does it as a stand-alone ritual in near silence, or if one incorporates these sensual aspects into one's other devotional activities, is an excellent way to stimulate the mind and the spirit to think along these lines. Below, what I'm giving is a list of things that I have used, or that I am suggesting as possibly useful, for the various aspects which Sannion discusses as essential components to the "Feast of the Senses" for Antinoan purposes. As ever, these are only suggestions; one should generate lists of one's own, and see what works for and appeals to one, and see what ends up emerging in one's own relationship with Antinous which would be appropriate to use in this regard.

PRELIMINARIES:

There is a trend in some Antinoan relics and cultic documents which suggests a very particular devotional practice which was associated with him, which is the connection between bathing and Antinous. Remember, first off, that ancient Roman bathing was a very different matter than our modern methods, that it was as much a social thing as a cleanliness matter (partially out of necessity, since few people were well off enough to own their own private baths in their houses), and it was also quite different than the purificatory baths which the Egyptians used—though if one wishes to interpret it in this manner, one certainly is free to do so. The evidence which suggests this connection is the existence of the statue in Leptis Magna of Antinous in a Narcissus-like aspect, which was found in a public bath founded by Hadrian, with Antinous looking downward into the pool, now in Tripoli.[7] In the

---

[6] This can be found in H. Jeremiah Lewis, *The Balance of the Two Lands: Writings on Greco-Egyptian Polytheism* (Eugene: Nysa Press, 2010), pp. 156-168; *Ecstatic (For Dionysos)* (Eugene: Nysa Press, 2011), pp. 60-69; and also at the following web address: http://sannion.livejournal.com/621819.html.
[7] See the image at http://www.antinoos.info/bild/antin720.jpg. Caroline

24

Lanuvium cult, on major holidays like the various *Dies Natalis* of Antinous and Diana, the president of the gathering/feast was also to provide bath oil in the public baths for all participants in the feast. And there is also the profusion of *balsamaria*, small anthropoid bust-shaped containers for oil that are in the shape of crude Antinoi, which were very likely used for bath oil.[8] So, all of this evidence suggests that bathing as, or before, sacred ritual practice was something which was important for some people, and which can be adapted for modern usage. If you are going to do this as a ritual on its own, you can decide whether you want to use it for purification purposes,[9] or whether you'd prefer to do it as its own section of the feast of the senses (perhaps for the "touch" section), in which case I'd suggest getting oneself clean with a shower or in some other way before sitting back to relax in a tub of water for a while and sitting in one's own filth!

Bath salts and oils of various types can be added as one sees fit. If one has access to a private swimming pool or hot tub, this would also be an excellent way to observe this ritual, especially if one's friends in devotion were to be in one's company as well; but one's own humble tub in one's own bathroom is certainly good enough to use as well.

SMELL:

While various other aspects of the Feast of the Senses will also have their accompanying smells, isolating the sense of smell on its own is also a very good idea, as smell is intimately connected to memory and thus can be an important ingredient in creating memorable experiences and associations. Here is what I would suggest for the use of incense and essential oils in this regard.

While in Cork, the only available incense to me at my local shop was

---

Vout discusses the possibility that this statue reflects multiple syncretisms in *Power and Eroticism in Imperial Rome* (Cambridge: Cambridge University Press, 2007), pp. 96-113, which suggests a syncretism to Apollon Lykeios, Dionysos, Narcissus, Hylas, Hyakinthos, and Echmoun (and through the latter to Asklepios).

[8] E.g. this one, from Belgrade: http://www.antinoos.info/bild/antin79.jpg.

[9] A ritual specifically for this purpose, the Inundation, has been developed, and will be further discussed and elucidatied in another chapter below.

Nag Champa; that worked, and indeed anything would work in a pinch, but I didn't think it was in any way particularly connected to Antinous (though having its presence certainly put me into that mindset, as I was using it in my weekly devotional practices there during 2005). At the same time, nothing I ever experienced suggested it was undesirable or forbidden.

As far as actual "attested" things go, there is very little to go on, but certain connections suggest themselves for various reasons. I'd recommend using narcissus oil or incense if it is available (due to the Narcissus connection/comparison with Antinous); while I have not yet been able to use or try kyphi, that would also be a traditional Egyptian incense to use. Due to Antinous' lotus connection, lotus incense is also good, and I've been using that most pleasantly for several years—whether it is from Red Nile Lotuses or not is usually not verifiable, and in any case not as important as the overall lotus association. Another one that I'd highly suggest, as the result of Tony Mierzwicki's PantheaCon workshop that I attended in 2008, is storax—it is mentioned as an accompanying incense in a number of the *Oprhic Hymns* dealing with Dionysos and the chthonic Hermes, so it is indeed very appropriate for Antinoan purposes. It comes from a tree that is only found in Asia Minor, and so there is the further connection that it recalls Antinous' Bithynian homeland. Also, pine incense can also be nice, as the area that Antinous came from was rich in evergreen trees.

TASTE:

What are good foods for Antinous? What is good for offerings on their own, and what is good for feasts? Good questions!

In terms of making drink offerings as part of other, non-feast rituals, I'd suggest a number of things. The ones which we have traditionally used are water, oil (usually olive oil), and wine of various sorts—anything with an Antinoan or Dionysian feel would certainly be appropriate, and anything that is Greek or Mediterranean (or from Asia Minor or Egypt, or Italy...European things in general, even) would very likely work quite well. (One time that I did this, I used Greek wine that was rather inexpensive, because that seemed to be the best thing available by my means at that stage.) I've also offered milk and honey—which was a traditional Greek offering in hero-cultus—either separately or together or with other things as well, on various occasions (e.g. Lupercalia, where milk is part of the various traditional sacrifices on the day). In certain circumstances, I've also used other types of alcohol, including absinthe, Jägermeister (which might be particularly good for the various hunting festivals, even though it is "deer's blood" rather than boar, lion, or bear blood!), and whiskey. A few of the Ekklesía Antínoou members have spoken about icewine as well, and I think that would probably work very well also; but use your own tastes and discretions in this regard. Pomegranate wine or juice,[10] and the fruit itself, is also good, as are figs, apples, and grapes.

There is also the issue of offering sweets and chocolate. I'm entirely in favor of this! I've offered Antinous chocolate on a number of occasions; I have done so on many Foundation Day rituals, and one of our Mystai also made this offering for the Antinoan Mysteries. So, most certainly that works—chocolate is a pleasure food for all times, and I'm sure Antinous would enjoy it greatly if he had the opportunity to taste it! However, if one deposits one's chocolate offerings outside, be careful that neighborhood dogs and cats can't get to them.

We have held full-on feasts for the *Dies Natalis Antinoi*, and we went with the Mediterranean food option when we did so. Foods served included dolmathes (grape leaves wrapped around rice and, in my preferred case, chicken, though I've had beef or lamb ones as well on other occasions), hummus, babaganoush, tzatziki sauce, falafel, lentil soup, and pita bread. When we made this, one of our cooks by mistake used vanilla yogurt for the tzatziki instead of plain yogurt, and it turned out spectacularly! It was so good, it has been decided subsequently that this particular serendipity will always be associated with Antinous, and will be used in his honor whenever possible.

When we had the actual feast, it followed the general pattern of the Greek *theoxenia* quite closely. We had all of the food prepared, and

---

[10] This has been the drink with which the oaths sworn at the Communalia ritual in 2009 and 2010 have been sealed, as if to indicate "this oath is binding until death" because of pomegranates' connection to Persephone.

then when the time came for us to eat, we prepared a place/altar space for Antinous on the table where all the food was. If you have a table that can accommodate food and guests, then set him a separate space and plate, but otherwise work with what you've got. We then processed him in with sung acclamations, seated his image at the table in front of the plate, and dished him up a portion of everything that was being eaten, serving him first as we sang. As the feast went on, and people had dessert, then we always served Antinous first; and when someone suggested having tea, we poured him a cup of that as well (to go with his wine); and when I went for a diet soda (my preferred drink!), I gave him the first can out of a new case of it. The liquid offerings were poured out in the usual spot in the little forested/wooded area behind the apartment complex afterwards, while all of the food offerings were burned in the fireplace (a fireplace that is only used for ritual purposes) after the feast was over. So, all of that went quite well! Whether this is part of your "Feast of the Senses," or if you simply hold a feast for Antinous as part of (or the entirety of) any of your celebrations of the holidays in his honor, this is a good way to do it.

Another food option that I think would suit the Antinoan context quite well is Indian food. As it is a very spicy cuisine which is also highly based in dairy products (milk, butter, yogurt, etc.), it seems like it would very likely appeal to the ancient people. Indian cuisine also does wonderful things with chick peas/garbanzo beans/*ciceronis*, from curries to fudge and other sweets, which would tie in to the Mediterranean use of these legumes in some of the dishes mentioned above.[11] According to the *Historia Augusta*, for the dedication of the Olympeion in Athens, which Hadrian completed after it had been started centuries before, an Indian snake was brought to be displayed especially for the occasion; I can't help but think that those coming back from India probably brought other wonderful things for the

---

[11] I had an idea for an alternative history story in relation to all this—what if Antinous didn't drown in the Nile, and instead he and Hadrian went on to travel elsewhere? I think it's possible that they may have returned to Alexandria and decided, "What the hell—let's do a full Alexander!" and gone onward to India, to explore and see the world, and to encounter other religious expressions. That story will be published soon in Inanna Gabriel and C. Bryan Brown (eds.), *Etched Offerings: Voices from the Cauldron of Story* (Mt. Vernon: Misanthrope Press, forthcoming 2011).

Emperor to enjoy.

Something else which the *Historia Augusta* mentions that Hadrian loved, and which was invented by his first adopted heir Aelius Caesar (Lucius Ceionius Commodus) is the *tetrafarmacum*, a meat pie made up of four ingredients: wild boar, pheasant, ham, and a sow's udder. While the latter ingredient is rather disgusting to contemplate, the entirety suggests that pork and game birds would be very suitable as feast items for anything in honor of Antinous, Hadrian, or any of the hunting deities or other figures associated with them.

SIGHT:

To start with, I'd suggest a few colors associated with Antinous: primarily I'd suggest red, black and white, the three most basic colors in most color systems, which were also the three basic Indo-European colors. As these were the traditional ephebic colors in Greece and Graeco-Egyptian culture, they're also appropriate. I'd also suggest purple, to associate him with the Emperor, but also with Dionysos' grapes and so forth. We've also come to associate a forest green with Diva Sabina, and use green candles in rituals to her. A deep blue is associated with Polydeukion, yellow with Memnon, and red with Achilles.[12]

As far as visual symbolism goes: we have the basic items of the star, flowers (especially the red Nile lotus/*Antinoeia*), and the moon, which are associated in various ways with Antinous in his mythology or his coinage. We also have the *Pamphobeteus Antinous* spider that was named for him, and also the lion from the lion hunt. Other symbolic associations are by deity-type and region, and can vary widely. We've used any red flowers we can get a hold of in the past, both as decorations and offerings for him—the red carnation is cheap and generally easy to come by, and fits in with another slain lover-turned-into-flower, Karneios, so we've been using them since the beginnings of the modern devotion to Antinous in 2002 without complaint. Also,

---

[12] Achilles the *Trophimos* of Herodes Attikos, not to be confused with Achilleus, the hero of the Trojan War. More will be said on him, and the other *Trophimoi*, in a subsequent chapter.

horses and hounds are associated with Antinous in a few depictions, which is in line with his status as a hunter, and with general Greek hero-cultus as well.

But of course, one of the most wonderful aspects of this particular religious devotion is the great profusion of surviving images from the ancient world which depict Antinous. While there are a few reproduction busts and other figures/statues available, these are often misidentified (one that is now known as the Capitoline Hermes is very often still sold as "Antinous"), or are somewhat expensive (since they are considered "classical art reproductions" rather than fairly cheap "devotional art"), so not very many of us have busts for our personal shrines.[13] In absence of something like this, the next best thing is to make an image of your own, in whatever medium and style you wish—whether it "looks like" the Antinous we know from the statues or not is not as important as you feeling that it represents him accurately, whether it is a sketch, a cartoon, a collage, a painting, or a sculpture or even (as Shawn Postoff has most beautifully done) a mosaic![14] If a bust or your own work is not available, then of course the next best thing is to have an image printed out or copied from one of the many photographs of the various ancient statues.

I have compiled a short list (by no means complete!) of some of the major deity-forms to whom Antinous is syncretized here with examples from the statuary, as well as a few that give particular "moods" in my estimation. Have a look at these and others[15] at:

http://www.antinoos.info/antinous.htm

---

[13] However, one has become popular in recent months, which can be found for about $160 US by entering "Antinous bust garden" on your preferred search engine, or going to the following link:
http://backyardgardener.com/gp/Vendors/Garden_Statue_Shop/Garden_St atues/Greek_Roman_Statue/Antinous_Garden_Stat.html.
[14] I'd be interested in seeing an abstract or Cubist Antinous someday...but I probably wouldn't be interested in having such a thing on my own personal shrine...your own opinion may differ!
[15] See the fuller discussion of them as well in P. Sufenas Virius Lupus, *The Syncretisms of Antinous* (Anacortes: The Red Lotus Library, 2010).

DIONYSOS: The most common depiction of Antinous is as this multifunctional and diverse deity. My favorite is the Braschi Antinous located in the Sala Rotunda of the Vatican.[16] There is also another at the Vatican,[17] one at the Banca d'Italia in Rome,[18] one from Naples,[19] the "Lansdowne" head from Hadrian's VIlla, now in the Fitzwilliam in Cambridge,[20] the "Townley" bust now in the British Museum in London,[21] one from St. Petersburg,[22] one from Chalkis, found in the baths of Loutra near Aidepsos,[23] one from Copenhagen,[24] one from Berlin,[25] and a variety of others. There is one from Eleusis, of Antinous as Iakkhos (who was syncretized with or considered to be the same as Dionysos) as well.[26] Pausanias, in his description of the temple to Antinous in Mantineia, says that most of the images portray Antinous as Dionysos, and this small list here certainly proves that assertion correct!

HERMES: Several of the most beautiful Antinous statue depictions are in a Hermetic aspect. The most outstanding, of course, is the Farnese Antinous, now in Naples, which is the first image of Antinous that I ever knowingly saw, in John Boswell's classic *Christianity, Social Tolerance, and Homosexuality*.[27] The view from every angle is splendid![28] Another one, which is often thought to be Antinous as Apollon due to its find-spot at Delphi, is actually Antinous Heros Propylaios (i.e. a Hermetic epithet), and it was commissioned by Flavius Aristotimos, Plutarch's successor.[29] This Hermetic image is also on a number of coins depicting Antinous, particularly those issued by Alexandria, of

---

[16] http://www.antinoos.info/bild/antin58.jpg.
[17] http://www.antinoos.info/bild/antin945.jpg.
[18] http://www.antinoos.info/bild/antin345.jpg.
[19] http://www.antinoos.info/bild/antin477.jpg.
[20] http://www.antinoos.info/bild/antin703.jpg.
[21] http://www.antinoos.info/bild/antin852.jpg.
[22] http://www.antinoos.info/bild/antin1152.jpg.
[23] http://www.antinoos.info/bild/antin65.jpg.
[24] http://www.antinoos.info/bild/antin597.jpg.
[25] http://www.antinoos.info/bild/antin644.jpg.
[26] http://www.antinoos.info/bild/antin187.jpg.
[27] http://www.antinoos.info/bild/antin588.jpg.
[28] http://www.antinoos.info/bild/antin35.jpg,
http://www.antinoos.info/bild/antin34.jpg.
[29] http://www.antinoos.info/bild/antin22.jpg.

which replicas can often be purchased.

APOLLON: The only somewhat secure identification of Antinous with Apollon is one from the Louvre in Paris, the colossal famed Mondragone Head; whether it is actually an Apollonian identification or not is up to your own discretion, but it has certainly been presented that way in much of the literature on Antinous.[30] Antinous is given the epithet *Neos Pythios* on a number of coins from Asia Minor as well.

SILVANUS: the *falx* (vineyard knife), hunting tunic and dog make the depiction from Lanuvium by Antoninianus of Aphrodisias most certainly Antinous in a Silvanian aspect; this would fit his pairing at that location with Diana, making both hunting deities therefore.[31]

AGATHOS DAIMON: The singular depiction under this aspect is now in Berlin. It was probably an Antinous head attached to the body, but it has been this way since Frederick the Great's time, c. 1760 CE.[32] Such depictions are suggestive in themselves, and have their own history, even if they do not date back to the original cultus in late antiquity.

HERAKLES: There is a statue from the Louvre in Paris, which was originally from Hadrian's Villa, and therefore may perhaps portray a "victorious lion-slayer" in the aspect of the hero/demi-god.[33]

OSIRIS: This was the original syncretism of Antinous, based on his manner of death in the Nile in Egypt. There are several examples from the Vatican, including one from the Canopus room in Hadrian's Villa, which is somewhat eroticized in body despite its otherwise austere visage.[34] A further example is now located in Dresden, Germany, but also comes from the Canopus "Serapeum."[35] There is also the only painting of Antinous yet identified or discovered from the ancient world, which is Oseirantinous, as found on the tondo of the two

---

[30] http://www.antinoos.info/bild/antin114.jpg.
[31] http://www.antinoos.info/bild/antin977.jpg.
[32] http://www.antinoos.info/bild/antin779.jpg.
[33] http://www.antinoos.info/bild/antin790.jpg.
[34] http://www.antinoos.info/bild/antin40.jpg.
[35] http://www.antinoos.info/bild/antin68.jpg.

32

Antinoöpolitan lovers.[36] Note the predominance of red, black and white in their clothes,[37] particularly in relation to the color symbolisms and associations mentioned earlier in this section.

ARISTAIOS: Whether this is an ancient original or not, the one depiction of him under this aspect is in the Louvre in Paris.[38]

GANYMEDE: While this particular association would seem to be quite logical for Antinous, it is a comparison only usually found in Christian writings that are derisive of the entire Antinoan cultus, or in allusions in the writings of Lukian of Samosata. The head and torso of the singular statue depicting Antinous as Ganymede have been restored to have this "cupbearer of the gods" aspect. The statue is now in Port Sunlight, U.K.[39]

VERTUMNUS: There are a few of these depictions, including the one in the Vatican,[40] one in Japan,[41] and also possibly the famous Albani Relief.[42]

A YOUTHFUL ANTINOUS: The statue from Olympia may depict him as he was known in his younger days;[43] and also another from a museum in Munich does likewise.[44]

AN OLDER ANTINOUS: The portrayal from the *tondi* on the Arch of Constantine, particularly the Lion Hunt in this case, may depict Antinous as he may have been not long before his death, which is a slight bit older than his most widespread and recognizable images.[45]

---

[36] http://www.antinoos.info/bild/antin880.jpg.
[37] http://www.antinoos.info/bild/antin883.jpg.
[38] http://www.antinoos.info/bild/antin627.jpg.
[39] http://www.antinoos.info/bild/antin209.jpg.
[40] http://www.antinoos.info/bild/antin687.jpg.
[41] http://aediculaantinoi.wordpress.com/2011/09/28/antinous-in-tokyo/
[42] http://www.antinoos.info/bild/antin50.jpg.
[43] http://www.antinoos.info/bild/antin55.jpg.
[44] http://www.antinoos.info/bild/antin76.gif.
[45] See figure 14 in Royston Lambert, *Beloved and God: The Story of Hadrian and Antinous* (New York and London: Viking, 1984).

A "HAPPY" ANTINOUS: The head in Knole, Kent, U.K. (which is, sadly, never displayed), which was from Hadrian's Villa, almost looks to me like he's smiling.[46] Also, the Egyptianizing Antinous,[47] reconstructed from fragments found at Hadrian's Villa, now in the Louvre.[48]

A PENSIVE/CONTEMPLATIVE/MORE SAD ANTINOUS: the Ildefonso group, now in Madrid, Spain (of which very likely only the head of Antinous is original), widely copied and displayed, and known for a great deal of history as "Castor and Pollux," has a very sad and thoughtful expression,[49] particularly as one examines the head closely.[50]

AND ONE MORE: This might have been part of an equestrian statue, now in Astros, Greece, and was found at Herodes Attikos' villa near Loukou at Eva, which is the most recently discovered new Antinous statue (from 1996).[51]

Have a look around at these depictions (and others), and see what you associate each of the statues with, deity-wise and aspect-wise. I think of Antinous the Liberator as the Herakles statue and the Silvanus relief; Antinous the Navigator as the Braschi Antinous (as Dionysos) in the Vatican; and Antinous the Lover as the Farnese (Hermes).[52] But, again, your own perceptions are the most important matters to which you should attend!

---

[46] http://www.antinoos.info/bild/antin322.jpg

[47] As of the first printing of this book in October of 2011, this remains the only statue from the original cultus of Antinous that I have seen with my own eyes, when it was on tour in the U.S.—specifically, at the Seattle Art Museum—in March of 2008.

[48] http://www.antinoos.info/bild/antin705.jpg.

[49] http://www.antinoos.info/bild/antin428.jpg.

[50] http://www.antinoos.info/bild/antin53.jpg.

[51] http://www.antinoos.info/bild/antin306.jpg.

[52] These theological concepts will be discussed in greater depth in *Studium Antinoi: The Doctor's Notes, Volume Two*; some information can also be found at http://aediculaantinoi.wordpress.com/2010/11/01/triads-of-antinous-1-three-aspects-of-antinous/.

TOUCH:

As mentioned above, the bath portion of a ritual or as a ritual on its own would certainly be a tactile and sensual way to do devotions focused on this particular sense. Or, having a massage with scented oil could also work (though don't do this without having tried the oil on yourself in a small experimental amount first, as some of them can burn people's skin or one can be allergic to them, so be careful and cautious with this!). Again, good old olive oil can be used for this purpose, and indeed was used for this purpose in the ancient world, and for many other things (including lamp oil, etc.—and the heat generated from oil lamps, candles, and so forth can be a touch-centered sensation as well).

Massage of different types, and touch in general, is a very powerful and often overlooked thing, so touching yourself (in both its suggestive and non-suggestive senses) is a very good idea; but also doing this with a partner (or others) can also be a wonderful and healing thing, since people in Western society generally don't even touch casually very often. Massage, of the regular and erotic types, can therefore play into this, as can sacred sexuality practices; and if you're on your own and doing this, likewise with mindful masturbation/soloving. However, remember that one should never use ritual to get sex, or think that sexual practices in themselves (when one is just doing them randomly or without any explicit spiritual or devotional sense) can constitute ritual, or replace it. If you are doing sexual ritual, everyone involved should be consenting to it, which means that picking up a random trick or one-night-stand partner from the internet or a bar, and then "using" them for sexual ritual purposes without telling them that's what you're doing, is unethical and manipulative, and should be avoided at all costs.

As far as materials and physical substances which can also suggest different tactile connections to Antinous, here's some possibilities. Get a small piece of marble and feel its smoothness—and remember all the statues of Antinous as you do so. Warm the marble up with your own body heat and imagine the statues of Antinous living and breathing and pulsing with life, and make them come to life like Pygmalion and Galataea (only, you know, gay, so much hotter!). Use leaves of various kinds from different plants (myrtle, ivy, grapes, etc.) as well as other plant products (e.g. pinecones, used in the Dionysian *thyrsus*) and feel these, run them across your skin, etc., and remember Antinous was an outdoorsman and a hunter. Furs of various types (including pseudo- or actual leopard skin, in conjunction with Dionysos) would also be appropriate to wear or experiment with. Egyptian cotton, or linen, would be appropriate to wear or use. Papyrus, if it can be had, would also be enjoyable to experiment with—remember that so many of the words we have from the ancient cult have only survived because of the durability of this material.

While there's nothing wrong with being rather hirsute (Hadrian and all of the Emperors after him were, after all!), if you really want to get into that ephebic feeling, you might consider depilation via your favorite means as a further skin-based thing you can do, whether just on your face or other parts of the body. Also, physical exercise—particularly in the Antinoan case rowing, running, and swimming—as well as horse/equestrian activities, are also good. If you can, perhaps try oiling yourself up and wrestling with someone sometime in the Graeco-Roman fashion! (Hermes invented that sport—so why not do it in Antinous-Hermes' honor?)

And then, of course, there's also just regular old nudity—so many of the Antinous sculptures depict him as such (or in an advanced state of undress!), so you might consider giving that a try on occasion, whether by yourself or with others, as part of ritual or your own regular practices, weather and climate and skin conditions permitting...!

SOUND:

This might be the most difficult of the senses to pin down accurately. While we have tons of words associated with the old cultus—and what are words but sounds symbolized through sight?—it is not currently widespread (or perhaps even desirable!) to have a recording of someone reading these words, whether in Egyptian, Greek, or Latin. But, if you wanted to make such a thing, feel free to do so.

We do know that Egyptians, and some Graeco-Egyptian practices, considered the "seven vowels" important:[53] in Greek, these were a, e, i. o, u, long "e" (*eta*) and long "o" (*omega*). In the various cases of Antinous' name in Greek and Latin, the five vowels of English (a, e, i, o, u) all occur at some point, and thus these can be used and chanted as syllables of power in invocations and at other occasions, as will be detailed later.

We are also uncertain of the music that was used in ancient times, though we do have notation for some of Mesomedes' hymns (some of which have been recorded on YouTube videos),[54] and we know that he wrote at least one hymn for Antinous, so if one is able to get that notation and put it to use with some experimentally-minded, knowledgeable musicians, perhaps progress in this regard can be made in the future.

We are thus left with modern music and things we associate with him, which is going to vary more widely than anything else yet mentioned in this little exercise and list of suggestions. Some of what follows works very well for me, while some of it may seem utterly ridiculous to many of you—I leave it to each of you to make that choice for yourselves.

I've used the tunes from many of Krishna Das' *kirtans* for Antinoan purposes; particularly good albums for this include *Pilgrim Heart*, *Live on Earth* ("Samadhi Sita Ram," "Hanuman Puja/Hanuman Chalisa," and "Sri Krishna Govinda" particularly), *Flow of Grace* ("Halleluja Chalisa"), *Heart Full of Soul*, and *All One*. Try singing "*Antinoe, Antinoe, Ave Ave Antinoe; Hadriane, Hadriane, Ave Ave Hadriane*" to any tune that "Hare Krishna" can be sung to, and it works quite well. I have made YouTube videos of my own original Antinoan hymns in Latin that have been based on some of Krishna Das' tunes, which you can consult if interested.[55]

---

[53] For some discussion of this practice, see Joscelyn Godwin, *The Mystery of the Seven Vowels: In Theory and Practice* (Grand Rapids, MI: Phanes Press, 1991); Tony Mierzwicki, *Graeco-Egyptian Magick: Everyday Empowerment* (Stafford: Megalithica Books, 2006).

[54] E. g. http://www.youtube.com/watch?v=UnRd8fXdR0U.

[55] http://www.youtube.com/watch?v=RzhzPS9l-GA.

Certain soundtracks also can also work well. The soundtracks to *Gladiator*, and to the HBO series *Rome*, have several good songs on them, which give me a more Hadrianic and Imperial flavor than anything. Clodagh Symond's "Be More Obvious" off of *Six Elementary Songs* is in Ancient Egyptian, and is about a "beautiful boy rising in the East"—what could be more Antinoan?

Empire Brass has a recording of Wecker's "Hopper Dance" on their album *Passage: 138 B.C.-A.D. 1611*, which is quite excellent, and has been the "themesong" for the August festival of the Lion Hunt and the Red Nile Lotus for the past few years. "Osiris Lives" from Sharon Knight and T. Thorn Coyle's album *Songs for the Waning Year* is quite ideal for Foundation Day observances. Hildegard of Bingen's "O Euchari" (particularly in the version of it from the album *Vision*) also conjures Antinoan feelings for me.

Certain selections from Orff's *Carmina Burana* are also appropriate. I particularly like "Fortune Plango Vulnera"; "Ecce gratum"; the instrumental following the latter; "Were du werlt alle min"; "Aestuans interius"; "Circa mea pectora"; "Tempus est iocundum"; and "Ave Formosissima"—the latter of which is especially useful for one of our holidays, the Apotheosis of Sabina, as will be detailed later in this book. And, of course, "O Fortuna" is also good, but not necessarily Antinoan in my experience and estimation! Nusrat Fateh Ali Khan's Sufi music, off the one album I've heard (*En Concert a Paris*) is quite good, especially "Hamd" and "Naat." For usage on the Apotheosis of Sabina festival, I'd also suggest a few other songs: The Moors' "*Dea Noctu Imperatrix*" (from their album *The Moors*) is excellent,[56] as well as Gjallarhorn's "*Suvetar* (Goddess of Spring)." That particular festival has often been one in which the contributions of women to spirituality and to music has been highlighted, so any music of this nature would be appropriate. Philip Glass' *Orion*, and particularly the final song, "Greece," also works pretty well as an all-purpose Antinoan mood-setting tune, particularly because it is a work of "musical syncretism," one might say.

---

[56] Sharynne Nic Mhacha, the lead singer of that group, did a live *a capella* version of it for the Apotheosis of Sabina ritual in Cork in 2005, which was AWESOME!

As far as more popular music goes—this is where it gets really ridiculous! Dead Can Dance's music in general can have some good Antinoan reverberations, but particularly useful for this is "Devorzhum," from their album *Spiritchaser*. (Their lead female singer, Lisa Gerrard, did the vocals on the *Gladiator* soundtrack!) Loreena McKennitt's "Dante's Prayer" (from *The Book of Secrets*), as well as several songs from *An Ancient Muse*, are also quite good and Antinoan in their implications and feelings for me. Of course, John Cameron Mitchell's *Hedwig and the Angry Inch*, and particularly the song "The Origin of Love," has Antinoan associations for me to a very large extent.[57] From various years in Eurovision, I rather liked the 2003 offerings by France (Louisa, "Monts et Merveilles") and the winner from Turkey (Sertab Erener, "Every Way that I Can"); from 2004, Sanda's "I Admit," and of course the winner, Ruslana's "Wild Dance" (from the Ukraine!), and Sakis Rouvas' "Shake It" (from Greece); and in 2005, the Turkish entry by Gulseren, "Rimi Rimi Ley," and the Greek winner, Elena Paparizou's "My Number One." In traditional Irish music, there's a beautiful song called "Black is the Color," which reminds me of Antinous in many ways. I also rather like Enya's "May It Be" (from the *Lord of the Rings* soundtrack), as well as Annie Lennox's "Into the West" also from that series. Enya's "Evening Falls" off of *Watermark* is also quite good, I think. P.J. Harvey's "This is Love," from her album *Stories from the City, Stories from the Sea*, has a particular in-yer-face sensuality about it that I quite like, and can work well in certain circumstances (the Bear Hunt/Erotikon or the Boar Hunt, for example). Sarah Brightman's "Deliver Me," and her orchestrally-based cover of Queen's "Who Wants to Live Forever" also bring up Antinoan associations for me. Sarah McLachlan's "Building a Mystery," "Into the Fire," "Possession," "Sweet Surrender," and "Fumbling Toward Ecstasy" also work for me in Antinoan terms.

And then in actual well-known popular music: who else but Shania Twain and "I'm Gonna Getchya Good!" (which was the "theme song,"

---

[57] I had a dream several years back in which Hadrian and Antinous were present and listening to music from various visiting artists, and when it came time for me to present, I sang this song, which in the dream was something I thought they would appreciate despite perhaps not knowing the language; it seemed to garner their approval!

in a sense, to my pilgrimage in Newcastle back in 2004), and Shakira's "Whenever, Wherever" (it's sort of the popular music version of *Vel in limine mundi, Ecce, / Ego semper sum coram te!* which translates as "Even at the edge of the world, behold, I am in your presence!"); if you're asking Antinous for help finding a lover/partner, then why not do so to Abba's "Gimme Gimme Gimme"? And to get into that youthful, ephebic rebellious energy, I rather like Bon Jovi's "It's My Life." And, to get into Hadrian's mindset on a particular Foundation Day ritual in Cork, after doing a liturgical piece we used to do called the Litany of Fire, I sang an *a capella* version of Johnny Cash's "Ring of Fire." (Yes, I am a redneck pagan!)

And to just tap into that "gay vibe," a variety of things can work. Old classics certainly can fill the bill, but favorites of mine would include Madonna's "Like a Prayer." Various European dance music hits can also be good for this, for example O-Zone's "Dragostea Din Tei" is quite good (and reminds me of so much of my time overseas, much of which was spent in devotion to Antinous). And, practically anything by Lady GaGa these days could work as well—I find "The Edge of Glory" to be particularly good.[58]

ANYTHING ELSE?

Because it doesn't fit anywhere else very neatly, I thought I would mention a few other associations that have emerged over the years here:

1) As far as gemstones and crystals are concerned, amethyst is one that is particularly resonant with Antinoan energies.

2) There is the constellation named for Antinous, which is now

---

[58] I have also written some filks based on Lady GaGa's songs for Antinoan purposes, which can be found here: http://aediculaantinoi.wordpress.com/2011/07/04/all-we-hear-is-radio-ga-ga/ (for "Pancrates," based on "Poker Face," and "God Romance," based on "Bad Romance"), http://aediculaantinoi.wordpress.com/2011/02/11/a-little-preview/ (for "*Hadriane*," based on "Alejandro"), and http://aediculaantinoi.wordpress.com/2011/03/09/polydeukion/ (for "Polydeukes," based on "Paparazzi").

called Aquila or Aquila/Ganymede, so finding it in the night's sky or looking at it in relation to one's astrological chart can be useful. Further, the constellation of Aquarius is also considered to be Ganymede, and therefore Antinous-connected. There is also the moon of Jupiter called Ganymede. And, there are asteroids named for Antinous and Hadrian, so seeing any of these in relation to one's birth-chart can also be fascinating.

3) For those who are interested in kabbalistic associations, Antinous can have sympathies with any of the sephiroth, but he's particularly active on the middle ones of the middle pillar—Yesod and Tiphareth.[59]

I'd really be interested to hear what others think in these various sensual categories—what has worked for you, what you think might work or be useful and fruitful, what attracts you, and what you have associated with Antinous (and Hadrian and Sabina and others) thus far or offered to him. If you have any sense of certain things being distasteful to him, or not a good idea to offer, that's also something which would be useful to share with people. (For example, just because I don't want to push my luck, I never go swimming during the Sacred Nights of Antinous, just in case another drowning decides to happen, and *imitatio Antinoi* goes too far for one of his devotees!)

Do feel free to get in touch with me via the Ekklesía Antínoou Yahoo! Group or my blog, Aedicula Antinoi,[60] if you have information or ideas in this regard! I'm really looking forward to hearing what you come up with!

Much love, many blessings, and all the sensual and spiritual presence of Antinous to each of you!

---

[59] Though I would note that because the kabbalah was developed specifically in relation to a monotheistic deity, trying to squeeze anything deity- or spirituality-related into it, especially if one's main spirituality is polytheistic, is using a Procrustean bed. To counter these tendencies, the Ekklesía Antínoou Serpent Path is being developed, which is discussed in various places on the Aedicula Antinoi blog, as well as being a subject to be outlined further in future workshops and publications.

[60] http://aediculaantinoi.wordpress.com/.

Antinoan Feast of the Mind

In addition to the sensual things which one can do to create Antinoan associations with one's own subconscious—for that is what we are ultimately doing when we make attributive associations between deities or ideas and particular concrete objects and experiences, on which more in a few moments—I'd also like to suggest a number of things which one can do as an Antinoan devotional activity involving reading.

Let me first make the caveat, though, that simply reading books or doing research about Antinous can be devotional, but is not devotional automatically. To make such an activity devotional, it can be as simple a matter as beginning by saying "I dedicate this work to Antinous" or "As I improve my knowledge, so too does the knowledge of Antinous improve within me," or what have you, whatever phrase makes the most sense to you and resonates with your intentions the best. When I research and find something particularly wonderful or unknown or ground-breaking, I often stop and thank Antinous for showing himself to me in a new way, through the texts I encounter directly, or through someone's interpretation of those texts.

At particular periods in the past, it has almost seemed as though Antinous has "wanted" to be known more, and is guiding the research process in subtle ways...I wanted very desperately to be able to consult the old Dietrichson book on Antinous, but was uncertain where to find it (other than perhaps the British Library), but I did a search for a laugh on our library catalogue in Cork, Ireland, and they had a copy (which I had to order from deep storage, but still... No one had ever checked it out before!). On other occasions, I went, for example, in the very early days to the volumes of Athenaeus which were on the shelves at our library, and didn't know in which one to begin looking, so I just grabbed one and opened to a random page, and there was the exact information I was looking for. This sort of thing happened a lot in the early days of the modern Antinoan practice (2002-2003), and was great encouragement. Things are getting more and more difficult to find, though, because the trail of evidence often runs out, with few further avenues to pursue, or it ends with an untranslated and fragmentary text that I'm currently unable to make any sense of...but this is also to be expected, and dealt with as necessary.

As mentioned above, the purpose of all of these devotional activities and associations outside of actual ritual is to strengthen one's imagination and inculcate constant presence, awareness, and memory of Antinous. So, if you start doing the practice of the Feast of the Senses, and use storax or lotus incenses, and then at some future point you walk into a building or someone's house or some other location and you smell storax or lotus, and you suddenly think, "Ah, that reminds me of Antinous," then you are given a moment of possible reflection, and you can consider how Antinous is a part of your life and influences things and is "with you" even when you weren't thinking about him directly, or weren't doing things in an Antinoan devotional mode. They're little prompts and opportunities for you to remember him and to acknowledge him in your daily life, until you are able to actually cultivate an awareness of Antinous' presence and love at all times. This will not happen immediately, it is the cumulation of many years of practice. "May I always be in the presence of he who is Beautiful, Just and Benevolent" is the last line in one of our prayers not just because it sounds nice, but because it is a worthy and worthwhile goal, to always remember and be conscious of the fact that we are, and we can be, in the presence of Antinous and many other deities and spirits and non-corporeal beings at all times, and our honoring of them, our awareness of them, and our memory of them improves our lives and causes them to do what they can for our improvement and blessing.

This might be a rather obvious thing to say, and yet because so many people in the modern world aren't in the habit of doing ritual on a regular basis, or understanding what ritual is for (in a theological or a psychological sense), it might just help to have this as one possible interpretation of why these things are important and useful. Other understandings are certainly possible, and if anyone reading this has their own thoughts or opinions on the matter, they should certainly be honored and taken into utmost consideration.

I will eventually have an Antinoan bibliography made up of all the things I actually have in my possession, or have seen, so that those who are interested in pursuing these things and finding the information upon which many of the activities and ideas found in this book and in my wider Antinoan-focused activities has derived, and then making your own interpretations and conclusions from them, will be possible.[61] However, in the meantime, I'd like to just give a "thematic" outline for the twelve months of the year, and suggest particular books and such that might be interesting or useful to read for devotional purposes in a general sense. This present list of suggestions is by no means complete or comprehensive, and in fact I encourage all of you to make your own such lists and fill this one out to a greater extent, and feel free to share your ideas about these things as a result.

Let's take it month by month, according to the secular calendar.

In January, we celebrate two major holidays: the birthday of Hadrian on the 24th and the first appearance of Antinous' star on the 29th. I'd suggest two types of things to read for a "mind feast" this month, therefore: imperial biographies of Hadrian (or of other Antonines, Trajan, and so forth), and astrological texts of any sort. While it is quite scholarly, and perhaps a bit too heavy if you want something easier and less dense, I would highly recommend Anthony Birley's *Hadrian the Restless Emperor*[62] as one possibility; it is the best modern academic biography of Hadrian, and is packed with information (including an excellent chapter on Antinous' death and subsequent cultus). Another excellent and lavishly illustrated volume is Thorsten Opper's *Hadrian: Empire and Conflict*,[63] which is the museum catalogue for a 2008 exhibit at the British Museum, and contains some very important and up-to-date material, as well as providing an overview of Hadrian's life and principate (including a whole chapter on Antinous with some beautiful photos). A very enjoyable book, which is a translation and annotation of several ancient astrological texts (with

---

[61] This will appear in *Studium Antinoi: The Doctor's Notes, Volume Two*, which should be available in the near future; a preliminary version of the bibliography is available at http://aediculaantinoi.wordpress.com/antinous-bibliography/.

[62] Anthony R. Birley, *Hadrian: The Restless Emperor* (London and New York: Routledge, 2000).

[63] Thorsten Opper, *Hadrian: Empire and Conflict* (Cambridge: Harvard University Press, 2008).

info in the notes on Antinous' constellation) is Theony Condos' *Star Myths of the Greeks and Romans: A Sourcebook*.[64] You could also combine the Hadrianic and astrological trends of this month by examining and meditating upon Hadrian's actual horoscopes that survive from the ancient world, which can be found in O. Neugebauer and H. B. Van Hosen's *Greek Horoscopes*.[65] If you're into ancient astrology, though, devote spare reading time this month to boning up on information for that purpose. Use an online program to make your own birthchart, and factoring in either the constellation Aquila/Antinous/Ganymede, or the asteroids Hadrian and Antinous, or the moon of Jupiter called Ganymede, can also be interesting to consider.

In February, the primary celebration is not Antinoan-exclusive, which is the Lupercalia on the 15th. Read up on myths of wolves and humans, werewolves, warriors, and the ancient foundations of the city of Rome. Plutarch's account of Lykastos and Parrhasios (in *Greek and Roman Parallel Stories* §36) would be good, as well as perhaps T. P. Wiseman's book *Remus: A Roman Myth*,[66] and you also might consider something like Daniel Gershenson's *Apollo the Wolf-God*[67] or Kris Kershaw's *The One-Eyed God: Odin and the Indo-Germanic Männerbünde*[68] (which has info on the warrior culture from which the Romulus and Remus/Lupercalia myth originated), or Phillip A. Bernhardt-House's *Werewolves, Magical Hounds, and Dog-Headed Men in Celtic Literature*.[69] Anything devoted to the deities Mars or Vesta would also be appropriate, since Romulus and Remus' father was Mars and their

---

[64] Theony Condos, *Star Myths of the Greeks and Romans: A Sourcebook* (Grand Rapids, MI: Phanes Press, 1997).

[65] O. Neugebauer and H. B. Van Hoesen, *Greek Horoscopes* (Philadelphia: The American Philosophical Society, 1987).

[66] T. P. Wiseman, *Remus: A Roman Myth* (Cambridge: Cambridge University Press, 1995).

[67] Daniel E. Gershenson, *Apollo the Wolf-God*, Journal of Indo-European Studies Monograph 8 (McClean, VA: Institute for the Study of Man, 1991).

[68] Kris Kershaw, *The One-Eyed God: Odin and the (Indo-) Germanic Männerbünde*, Journal of Indo-European Studies Monograph 36 (Washington, D.C.: Institute for the Study of Man, 2000).

[69] Phillip A. Bernhardt-House, *Werewolves, Magical Hounds, and Dog-Headed Men in Celtic Literature* (Lewiston, Queenston, and Lampeter: The Edwin Mellen Press, 2010).

mother was a Vestal Virgin.

In March, there are several occasions of note. At the beginning of the month, we celebrate Herodes Attikos, Polydeukion, and the other *Trophimoi*. Read something, therefore, about the Sophists or the Second Sophistic in the 2nd c. CE, like Philostratus' *Lives of the Sophists*,[70] or other such works. Jennifer Tobin's *Herodes Attikos and the City of Athens*[71] also has a great deal of useful information in it, for those wanting something more academic. Another major Antinoan celebration is the Apotheosis of Sabina on March 21. This could also be a month, therefore, to focus on goddesses, and of the renewal of spring and of life in general. If you're into agriculture or gardening, reading books on those matters is a good thing, or learn some new recipes by studying your favorite cookbooks. As far as more academic and historical/theological reading might be concerned, *The Roman Goddess Ceres* by Barbette Stanley Spaeth[72] is a good one—it actually talks about Sabina on a number of occasions, since this was one of her primary syncretisms after her apotheosis. Late in the month, we celebrate the *dies Sanctae* of Hypatia of Alexandria, so any book having to do with her (or watching the film *Agora*) would be quite appropriate. And, the television serial and book by Sarah Waters, *Tipping the Velvet*,[73] is also relevant, because it not only deals with Victorian-period "Sapphism," but the narrator dresses as Antinous for a costume party at one point!

April, which is taken up by the Megala Antinoeia on the 21st, is a month in which a number of themes can be pursued. Love is certainly a major theme this month, but so is hunting, athleticism, and civic functioning. Turning to the last matter first, one might consider

---

[70] Wilmer Cave Wright (ed./trans.), *Philostratus: Lives of the Sophists; Eunapius: Lives of the Philosophers* (Cambridge: Harvard University Press, 1921).

[71] Jennifer Tobin, *Herodes Attikos and the City of Athens: Patronage and Conflict under the Antonines* (Amsterdam: J. C. Gieben, 1997).

[72] Barbette Stanley Spaeth, *The Roman Goddess Ceres* (Austin: University of Texas Press, 1996).

[73] Sarah Waters, *Tipping the Velvet: A Novel* (London: Virago Press, 1998).

46

looking at Mary T. Boatright's *Hadrian and the City of Rome*,[74] which has sections on the Pantheon, the temple of Venus and Roma, the Arch of Constantine, and the Obelisk of Antinous (for starters!); one might also consider William MacDonald and John Pinto's *Hadrian's Villa and Its Legacy*.[75] If you've been putting off getting to work on some regular workout, exercise or gym regimen since your last New Year's resolution to that effect, why not give it a go now for the Megala Antinoeia, and if you don't actually start going to the gym or doing a workout, then finally pick up that self-help book on diet and/or exercise that someone got you (or you got yourself!) on the bargain table at Barnes & Noble. As far as hunting is concerned, this month commemorates the bear hunts of Hadrian, so one could take that literally and read about hunting, or read about bears (including the Winnie the Pooh and Bernstein variety), or about efforts on conservation and protection of endangered bears—in this regard, I'd recommend a book (and buying this book contributes to a conservational charity) by gay British actor/comedian/writer Stephen Fry called *Rescuing the Spectacled Bear*.[76] Or, one could take "another" interpretation of "bear," and go out and read and look at some good gay bear porn and erotica—why not? Which leads into the next category! Love and eroticism are major things to consider in this month, and there are a number of books I could recommend in that regard on specifically-Antinoan topics: Caroline Vout's *Power and Eroticism in Imperial Rome*[77] is quite good, as is Craig A. Williams' *Roman Homosexuality: Ideologies of Masculinity in Roman Antiquity*.[78] Samuel Delany's *Phallos*[79] is a very strange novella having to do with an ancient esoteric erotic cult, of which Antinous was an unwitting part. Also related to the Hadrianic circle would be Daryl Hine's translation *Puerilities: Erotic Epigrams of The Greek*

---

[74] Mary Taliaferro Boatwright, *Hadrian and the City of Rome* (Princeton: Princeton University Press, 1987).

[75] William L. MacDonald and John A. Pinto, *Hadrian's Villa and Its Legacy* (New Haven and London: Yale University Press, 1995).

[76] Stephen Fry, *Rescuing the Spectacled Bear: A Peruvian Diary* (London: Hutchinson, 2002).

[77] Caroline Vout, *Power and Eroticism in Imperial Rome* (Cambridge: Cambridge University Press, 2007).

[78] Craig A. Williams, *Roman Homosexuality: Ideologies of Masculinity in Classical Antiquity* (New York and Oxford: Oxford University Press, 1999).

[79] Samuel R. Delany, *Phallos* (Whitmore Lake, MI: Bamberger Books, 2004).

Anthology,[80] which was compiled by a court poet of Hadrian's, Strato; and Amy Richlin's translation/edition *Marcus Aurelius in Love: The Letters of Marcus and Fronto,*[81] with the Fronto there concerned being Marcus Cornelius Fronto, the second-greatest Roman orator ever to have lived (apart from Cicero), who was a young contemporary of Hadrian's and a tutor to the future emperor Marcus Aurelius. So, these are just some ideas. Feel free to come up with ones more suited to your own interests in this regard!

The month of May has two foci: the figure of Hermes (whose mother, the nymph Maia, gives her name to the month, and who had a festival therein), and the Boar Hunt on May 1. As far as the Hermes aspects go, I'd suggest as possible titles *Hermes the Thief* by Norman O. Brown[82] and Karl Kerényi's *Hermes, Guide of Souls*;[83] for a more Graeco-Egyptian version, see Garth Fowden's *The Egyptian Hermes.*[84] Again, one can carry over the hunting theme from the previous month, and read things about hunting or boars, or learn some new methods for preparing your favorite pork-based dishes; one might also consider reading various myths devoted to boar hunting, including those of Herakles, and the great Insular Celtic epics on this theme, particularly the Irish *Toruigheacht Dhiarmada agus Ghráinne*[85] (for the Finn mac Cumhaill fans among us!) or *Scéla Mucce Meic Dátho*[86] (for the

---

[80] Daryl Hine (trans.), *Puerilities: Erotic Epigrams of The Greek Anthology* (Princeton: Princeton University Press, 2001).

[81] Amy Richlin (ed./trans.), *Marcus Aurelius in Love: The Letters of Marcus and Fronto* (Chicago: University of Chicago Press, 2006).

[82] Norman O. Brown, *Hermes the Thief* (Great Barrington: Lindisfarne Press, 1990).

[83] Karl Kerényi, *Hermes Guide of Souls*, trans. Murray Stein (Putnam, CT: Spring Publications, 1976).

[84] Garth Fowden, *The Egyptian Hermes: A Historical Approach to the Late Pagan Mind* (Princeton: Princeton University Press, 1993).

[85] Neasa Ní Shéaghdha, *Tóruigheacht Dhiarmada agus Ghráinne: The Pursuit of Diarmaid and Gráinne*, Irish Texts Society Vol. 48 (London and Dublin: Irish Texts Society, 1967).

[86] In John T. Koch and John Carey (eds.), *The Celtic Heroic Age: Literary Sources for Ancient Celtic Europe & Early Ireland & Wales*, Fourth Edition (Andovery and Aberystwyth: Celtic Studies Publications, 2003), pp. 68-75.

Ulidians!), and the Welsh *Culhwch ac Olwen*.[87] Also, as the date given on the "*tondo* of the two lovers" from Antinoöpolis is May 10, one might consider reading about them; I first learned of them in Marilyn B. Skinner's *Sexuality in Greek and Roman Culture*,[88] on a day in London in April of 2005 when lightning literally flashed and wonders ensued...

In June, we celebrate a festival of Antinous as Apollon on the 21st, so perhaps read a book that is Apollon-dedicated, or that is devoted to Delphi or the Pythia and ancient oracles. Michael Pettersson's *Cults of Apollo at Sparta: The Hyakinthia, the Gymnopaidiai, and the Karneia*[89] is a book that might be of interest due to the homoerotic content of the myths associated with those Apollonian figures. Also, as it is usually a month during which Gay Pride festivals occur, one might consider reading books on queer activism or the history of that movement, or more broad titles on queer spirituality generally (things by Mark Thompson,[90] Will Roscoe,[91] etc.). For those who are interested and are following the track of particular *dies Sancti*, Marguerite Porete's day is on June 1, so attempting to read her *Mirror of Simple Souls*[92] (which is difficult at the best of times!) might also be useful for some people who are so inclined.

July has a number of things associated with it. There is the Silvanus and Antinoan Arbor Day festival, which occurs on the 16th. An excellent book on Silvanus in particular that mentions Antinous and Hadrian several times is Peter F. Dorcey's *The Cult of Silvanus: A Study*

---

[87] In Patrick K. Ford (trans.), *The Mabinogi and Other Medieval Welsh Tales* (Berkeley, Los Angeles, and London: The University of California Press, 1977), pp. 119-157.

[88] Marilyn B. Skinner, *Sexuality in Greek and Roman Culture* (Malden and Oxford: Blackwell Publishing, 2005).

[89] Michael Pettersson, *Cults of Apollo at Sparta: The Hyakinthia, the Gymnopaidiai and the Karneia* (Stockholm: Svenska Institutet i Athen, 1992).

[90] Mark Thompson, *Gay Soul: Finding the Heart of Gay Spirit and Nature with Sixteen Writers, Healers, Teachers, and Visionaries* (New York: HarperCollins, 1995).

[91] Will Roscoe, *Queer Spirits: A Gay Men's Myth Book* (Boston: Beacon Press, 1995).

[92] Ellen J. Babinsky (trans.), *Marguerite Porete: The Mirror of Simple Souls* (New York and Mahwah: Paulist Press, 1993).

in Roman Folk Religion.[93]   One might also choose to read on the Etruscans (from whom Silvanus seems to derive), or about Roman Britain generally and Hadrian's Wall (as Silvanus is a "boundary god"), as well as on trees, forests, and conservation efforts. One might also consider volunteering for some such public effort in this month— planting trees, or cleaning up stretches of highway, etc. The rising of Sirius and the festival of Hermanubis is a minor holiday at the end of the month, so one might wish to read myths of dogs, or simply any dog or dog-related books, stories, etc. One such book might be David White's *Myths of the Dog-Man*,[94] which discusses Hermanubis quite extensively; another lighter example might be *Paws and Reflect: Exploring the Bond Between Gay Men and Their Dogs* by Neil Placky and Sharon Sakson.[95] Finally, the death of Hadrian is marked on July 10, so one might consider, in addition to reading his "Animula Vagula Blandula" poem and meditating upon it, looking at Marguerite Yourcenar's *Hadrian's Memoirs*.[96]   Further, for more information on the imperial cult, one may wish to read S. R. F. Price's *Rituals and Power: The Roman Imperial Cult in Asia Minor*[97] (which does also speak of Antinous a bit here and there).

The month of August has two major devotional events of note: the lion hunt and miracle of the red lotus on the 21st/22nd, and the *Dies Natalis Dianae* on the 13th. For the former, reading the sections of Athenaeus, Pancrates, the Tebtynis Papyrus, and other such Antinoan texts is a good idea, and these are available later in this book as well as in *The Phillupic Hymns*.[98] Or, do things like watch *The Lion King* or other such films, or (particulary appropriate) *Masai: The Rain Warriors*,

---

[93] Peter F. Dorcey, *The Cult of Silvanus: A Study in Roman Folk Religion* (Leiden: E. J. Brill, 1992).

[94] David Gordon White, *Myths of the Dog-Man* (Chicago and London: University of Chicago Press, 1991).

[95] Neil Placky and Sharon Sakson, *Paws and Reflect: Exploring the Bond Between Gay Men and Their Dogs* (Boston: Alyson Books, 2006).

[96] Marguerite Yourcenar, *Hadrian's Memoirs*, trans. Grace Frick (New York: Farrar, Straus and Young, 1955).

[97] S. R. F. Price, *Rituals and Power: The Roman Imperial Cult in Asia Minor* (Cambridge: Cambridge University Press, 1986).

[98] P. Sufenas Virius Lupus, *The Phillupic Hymns* (Eugene: Bibliotheca Alexandrina, 2008).

a film about a group of young African tribesmen who go to hunt a lion in order to bring the rains—it's so close to the purpose of our festival, including the victorious warrior dying in the process, as to be practically required! One can also read books that are lion-related, or go to your local zoo if they have lions. And visit your local gardens, parks and so forth, especially if they have water-flowers of any sort. As for Diana, one might consider reading the Lanuvium temple's constitution (which is found translated in Mary Beard, John North and Simon Price's *Religions of Rome, Vol. 2: A Sourcebook*,[99] and also later in this book), or about the wider cults of Lanuvium, including Diana Nemorensis—and therefore Frazer's *The Golden Bough!*[100]—but also more sensible treatments, like C. M. C. Green's *Roman Religion and the Cult of Diana at Aricia*,[101] and the general myths of Diana and Artemis in the ancient world.

September does not have any major important Antinoan festivals that are absolutely required. Our observance of Antinous and Hadrian's participation in the Eleusinian Mysteries takes place then. I'd suggest looking at Kerényi's *Eleusis: Archetypal Image of Mother and Daughter*[102] as one possibility, therefore. (He mentions, and translates, part of the Tebtynis Papyrus on which the Antinoan lotus information is found, but not for that reason!) Read the *Homeric Hymn to Demeter*,[103] and any other myths and literature on underworld mysteries and initiations. Consider the wider cultures of ancient Greece particularly, and of Athens and all of its splendors in architecture and philosophy; read up on Plato, or the Epicureans, or what have you. Why not hold a

---

[99] Mary Beard, John North, & Simon Price (eds./trans.), *Religions of Rome, Volume 2: A Sourcebook* (Cambridge: Cambridge University Press, 1998), pp. 292-294. This text is also included in a subsequent chapter of the present book.

[100] Sir James George Frazer and Robert Fraser, *The Golden Bough: A Study in Magic and Religion: A New Abridgement from the Second and Third Editions* (Oxford: Oxford University Press, 1998).

[101] C. M. C. Green, *Roman Religion and the Cult of Diana at Aricia* (Cambridge: Cambridge University Press, 2007).

[102] Carl Kerényi, *Eleusis: Archetypal Image of Mother and Daughter*, trans. Ralph Manheim (Princeton: Princeton University Press, 1967).

[103] Apostolos N. Athanassakis, *The Homeric Hymns* (Baltimore and London: The Johns Hopkins University Press, 2004), pp. 1-14.

symposium of your own? We also observe Lucius Vitalis' death during September on the 6th, so one might read the inscription mentioning him (translated later in this volume), the sections of Lambert's *Beloved and God: The Story of Hadrian and Antinous*[104] relating to him, and a great deal of Shawn Postoff's material posted on *The Sacred Antinous* website,[105] in which Vitalis is a major (and wonderfully, and furthermore very plausibly, interpreted) character. Another suggestion, which has relevance to Vitalis (and also Polydeukion), and which would serve as a good transition-text into October, is Christopher Jones' *New Heroes in Antiquity: From Achilles to Antinoös*,[106] which is a newer and quite excellent, brief treatment of the Antinoan cultus.

One of our most active months, of course, is October: one of our general recognitions of the *Sancti* takes place on the 11th, for starters, so reading anything of the works of any of our many *Sancti* would be good; also, any of the memorial poetry and literature surrounding Matthew Shepard, who is celebrated on the 12th, could also be read— his mother Judy Shepard's *The Meaning of Matthew*,[107] and the memorial volume *Blood and Tears*[108] are both particularly good. We celebrate a festival of Osiris on the 24th to kick off the Sacred Nights, so reading anything about Osiris, or about ancient Egyptian mythology and religion, and in particular various versions of and works about Coming Forth By Day/the Book of the Dead, would be most appropriate.[109] The general mystery (in the modern novel, rather than ancient religious, sense) of Antinous' death is a topic dealt with in Ben

---

[104] Royston Lambert, *Beloved and God: The Story of Hadrian and Antinous* (New York: Viking, 1984).

[105] http://www.sacredantinous.com/.

[106] Christopher P. Jones, *New Heroes in Antiquity: From Achilles to Antinoös* (Cambridge: Harvard University Press, 2010).

[107] Judy Shepard, *The Meaning of Matthew: My Son's Murder in Laramie, and a World Transformed* (New York: Penguin/Hudson Street Press, 2009).

[108] Scott Gibson (ed.), *Blood & Tears: Poems for Matthew Shepard* (New York: Painted Leaf Press, 1999).

[109] Raymond Faulkner (trans.), *The Egyptian Book of the Dead, The Book of Going Forth By Day: The First Authentic Presentation of the Complete Papyrus of Ani* (San Francisco: Chronicle Books, 1998); Mark Smith (ed./trans.), *Traversing Eternity: Texts for the Afterlife from Ptolemaic and Roman Egypt* (Oxford: Oxford University Press, 2009).

Pastor's novel *The Water Thief*,[110] so that would be some lighter fare fiction to consider; its lavish description of the cults of Antinous in various locations, as they may have been in the late third century, is very well executed. Also, as one of the effects of Antinous' death was Hadrian's foundation of Antinoöpolis, Mary Boatright's *Hadrian and the Cities of the Roman Empire*,[111] which has a section on Antinoöpolis, might also be interesting reading. And, of course, one might simply consider looking at the entire phenomenon of the Antinoan cult by reading (or re-reading) Royston Lambert's *Beloved and God: The Story of Hadrian and Antinous*.[112]

In November, a number of minor holidays take place. One of these is the three-day visit of the imperial party to the colossoi of Memnon, and thus an appropriate book to read on this occasion is the lighter, more for a popular audience biography of the Emperor, Elizabeth Speller's *Following Hadrian*,[113] which especially focuses on the role of Sabina and Julia Balbilla (and in fact each chapter has a telling of events in the voice of Julia)...while it is debatable as to how "accurate" any of this is, it's certainly another interesting viewpoint to consider, and can be fun and enjoyable if taken in its proper context. The *Natalis Antinoi*, on November 27, is also an extremely important holiday that was celebrated widely in the ancient world. Thus, anything having to do with Antinous' life—including anything mentioned previously—could be read in this month for that purpose as well.

Finally, we come to the month of December, which in Antinoan terms primarily involves our celebration of Antinous Epiphanes—an epithet of Dionysos—on the 21st. So, any Dionysian literature would be good to consider: Kerényi's *Dionysos: Archetypal Image of Indestructible Life*,[114]

---

[110] Ben Pastor, *The Water Thief: A Novel* (New York: Thomas Dunne Books/St. Martin's Press, 2007).

[111] Mary Taliaferro Boatwright, *Hadrian and the Cities of the Roman Empire* (Princeton: Princeton University Press, 2003).

[112] Royston Lambert, *Beloved and God: The Story of Hadrian and Antinous* (New York: Viking, 1984).

[113] Elizabeth Speller, *Following Hadrian: A Second-century Journey through the Roman Empire* (London: Review/Headline Book Publishing, 2002).

[114] Carl Kerényi, *Dionysos: Archetypal Image of Indestructible Life*, trans. Ralph Manheim (Princeton: Princeton University Press, 1976).

or Walter Otto's *Dionysus: Myth and Cult*,[115] etc. The possibilities here (and elsewhere) are endless, nearly! Given that World AIDS Day is on December 1, it might also be good to watch a film like *Angels in America* (the HBO miniseries), which not only is an excellent and well-acted adaptation of Tony Kushner's play of the same name, but it also features Hadrian's Villa in the final scenes, and in the scene where Prior has his hallucination toward the beginning, it takes place in a room that has a dome based on Hadrian's Pantheon in Rome.

So, in the process of having generated this list, I've found that a good deal of the books I'd suggest to beginners and those interested in learning a lot about Antinous and Hadrian, who don't have access to or are not interested in doing a lot of shelf-scanning in libraries, have been enumerated. If there are particular holes in your own knowledge that you'd like to fill by looking at some of these books, I'd strongly encourage you to look at them, at whatever is a convenient time for you to do so, or along the timelines suggested above. The world is your oyster with this, and with all things Antinoan, and I want to emphasize that over and over again—all of you have as many options with bringing Antinous into your devotional lives as you can possibly envision, so this is yet another such option for those who are interested. I would also encourage all of you to write in with your own suggestions and ideas on these matters, especially if there are things which were not mentioned above that you think should be (apart from scholarly articles and such—although if you have those to suggest as well, please do! I may not have them myself, and I'm always looking to expand my knowledge!), so please feel free to get in touch with me on these matters.

---

[115] Walter Otto, *Dionysus: Myth and Cult*, trans. Robert B. Palmer (Bloomington and Indianapolis: Indiana University Press, 1965).

Antinoos-Bakchos (no. 12)
Japan. Palais Dresden

55

A Prayer to Antinous

The following is a short prayer, written in Latin in early 2009, which can be used in a variety of fashions. I find it is useful to sing it[116] as a dedicatory prayer before doing any activity that is concerned with Antinous, whether it be reading about him, writing a blog entry or a poem or anything else about him, speaking about him in a workshop or an interview, or as a short preface to anything which may involve him.

Sic semper puero divino orans
Bithyniae Graeculo Arcadi
facior Hadriani amator par tu
Imperator Pacis Mundi

Vince hostem omnem amoris
Mercurii victor filie–gaudete!–
converteque animum odiosi
in pacitore prudente

Oramus[117] *hoc per Hadriano Sabinaque et te.*

Thus praying always to the Divine Boy,
the Arcadian Greek of Bithynia,
I am made more like you, the lover of Hadrian–
Emperor of the World of Peace;

---

[116] I sang this at the beginning of the interview T. Thorn Coyle did with me on her *Elemental Castings* podcast in May of 2011, which can be heard at: http://www.thorncoyle.com/podcasts/ElementalCastings_42_SPIRIT_05061 1.m4a.

[117] This is the form for the first-person plural, "we"; if one is praying it singly because one is by oneself, the proper usage would be *Oro*, "I."

56

Defeat every enemy of love
O victorious son of Hermes–may all rejoice!–
and turn the heart of the hateful one
into a sensible peacemaker.

We pray this through Hadrian, and Sabina, and you!

Ritual Acclamations and Hand Gestures

There are a variety of ritual acclamations—short phrases, usually in Latin—as well as postures and hand gestures used in the Ekklesía Antínoou's practice of modern Antinoan devotion, with which it would be useful to become familiar. Some of the hand gestures and postures are traditional, while others are more novel, or have not been employed in a specifically Antinoan context previously.

Perhaps the most important, basic ritual acclamation is *Ave Antinoe*, "Hail, Antinous!" It is often repeated as *Ave Ave Antinoe*, or is used in conjunction with another short phrase, *Vive Antinoe*, "(Long) Live Antinous!" Many large rituals held in the Ekklesía Antínoou begin with a procession, in which a call-and-response chant of *Ave Ave Antinoe, Vive Vive Antinoe* is repeated several times during a procession that takes place in the ritual space, in which the principal image of Antinous is usually carried to the cardinal directions, and around all of the ritual attendees and participants (sometimes with attendants holding candles, offerings, or other objects) before it is formally installed on the altar or shrine-space for the ritual and presented with offerings.

Haec est unde vita venit, "This is where life comes from," is also used in a variety of contexts, including in the opening chants of many Antinoan ritual processions. This phrase was revealed to me in a dream in the summer of 2003, and has proven to be very versatile in its employment in Antinoan devotional contexts. The "this" of the statement is deliberately left undefined, while simultaneously (and paradoxically!) being an emphatic pronoun, so it serves to draw attention to the "this" concerned, while at the same time not specifying what it is. Thus, the person using the phrase can say it in utter confidence that their own thoughts on the matter are primary. The "this," for my own purposes, can refer to a great many things: devotion to Antinous, devotion to spirituality and the gods generally, homoerotic love, connection to the cosmos...the possibilities are quite endless. So, whatever you think gives origin to your life, or at least is the source of what enlivens you, that is the "this" referred to in this phrase.

And, note something else about this phrase. *Haec* is a Latin demonstrative pronoun, meaning "this," which is always inflected in terms of number and gender, and it is feminine here in order to agree with *vita*, which is the feminine noun "life." Finding or establishing one's own place and direction within the wider universe of "life" is what is prompted by this statement, and that universe is understood as feminine in nature, whether literally and grammatically or in a more cosmic manner. While goddesses and other feminine divine figures (*Divae*, *Sanctae*, heroines, etc.) are certainly a part of the practice of the Ekklesía Antínoou, the focus upon Antinous, Hadrian, and the various deities to whom they were syncretized or related might suggest on a casual glance that this is a "male-oriented" or even "male-dominated" practice, which is far from the truth. Erynn Rowan Laurie has already written on the experience of being a woman in the modern Ekklesía Antínoou.[118] Brandy William's excellent book *The Woman Magician* challenges the reader to envision a universe that is not gendered as male, nor that is non-gendered, but instead one that is specifically and explicitly female,[119] and she provides a myth of cosmogenesis populated by female divinities from Egyptian tradition that is both beautiful and appealing.[120] In absence of one's own preference on these matters, I would suggest this is a brilliant, useful, and justice-making manner in which to consider these matters, and one can very easily do so by one's understanding of *Haec vita*, "this life," which is devotion to Antinous.

Various other lines, in English or in Latin (or Greek or Egyptian!) may emerge in your own reading through this book, outside research, and your own planned and spontaneous devotional practices, which may be used quite effectively in a variety of contexts. Be very willing and open to experiment with these and see what you come up with that ends up being the most beneficial to your resulting practices.

---

[118] Erynn Rowan Laurie, "His Mother's Whole Body Heals: Gender and Ritual in the Ekklesía Antínoou," in *Women's Voices in Magic*, ed. Brandy Williams (Stafford: Megalithica, 2009), pp. 167-173.
[119] Brandy Williams, *The Woman Magician: Revisioning Western Metaphysics from a Woman's Perspective and Experience* (Woodbury: Llewellyn Publications, 2011), pp. 186-187.
[120] Williams, pp. 207-210.

Many religions worldwide have particular *mudras*, the Sanskrit term for hand gestures and postures that has entered common speech (to an extent, at least!), which are used by practitioners to symbolize particular states of being, attributes, or ideas. Ancient Greece, Rome, and Egypt had many of these, and some of them have been adapted into an Antinoan devotional context.

When praying, there are two important hand gestures that are often used. Generally, when calling out to Antinous in prayer, it is best to raise one's arms slightly (with bent elbows), having one's hands at least level with (if not higher) than one's head, with palms flattened and facing outward from oneself. This is similar to the *henu* posture in Egyptian practice, and also reflects the "*orans* position" that occurs frequently in ancient European art and archaeology. It is the position shown on the left below.

If one is specifically addressing the Hero Antinous, or any of his aspects that are more chthonic in nature, one's arms should be at one's side, with elbows bent slightly, and the hands should be slightly cupped and pointing downward, with palms facing outward/upright. Imagine having one's hands filled with sand, for example, and positioning them in such a way that the sand trickles out of them, but not too quickly,

60

for the best results. This is the position shown in the right photo above.

An ancient Roman hand gesture that was done for fertility and good luck, but also to avert evil, was the *mano fico*, the so-called "fig-hand" (though that is an Italian mistranslation of the term that goes back even to Dante). It is made by making a fist, and then putting one's thumb in between one's pointer finger and middle finger.[121] (See the left photo below.) I have found it useful in any context in which I wish to shield myself or to turn back any evil influences I feel I might be encountering in daily life.

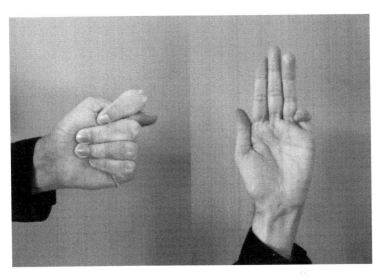

A further ancient hand gesture, this one deriving from a Semitic context, is the "hand of protection," often known now as the *hamsa*. While this appears as a stylized visual symbol in a variety of locations, I have also found it useful as a hand gesture, both in asking for protection from the gods and in offering protection to them (in the sense that sometimes one swears to uphold a particular practice or ideal on behalf of the gods one serves, etc.). It is produced by placing all the finers of the hand together, with the pinky bent at the first joint, and the thumb pointed slightly outward from its joint. (See above,

---

[121] This can be seen in Lesley Adkins and Roy A. Adkins, *Dictionary of Roman Religion* (New York: Facts on File, 1996), p. 140.

right.) When the hand is held with fingers upright and palm facing forward, it is offering protection; when the hand is held so the fingers point downard but the palm facing up, it is asking for protection.

A further hand gesture which ultimately derives from ancient precedent, but which ended up emerging in my practices without knowledge of its connections to particular deities, is one that I associate with Antinous the Liberator in particular. I usually do this with my right hand, but can do it with both hands or only the left on some occasions. One extends the thumb, pointer, and middle fingers, but retracts the ring finger and pinky finger. I also tend to spread my extended fingers slightly, rather than keeping them in tightly or even loosely together. (See below, left.) This gesture is particularly associated with the many votive hands of the god Sabazios,[122] a super-syncretistic deity from Thrace who was eventually worshipped across the Roman Empire, and was syncretized to Dionysos, Zeus, and other deities. (See below, right.) As the Bithynians considered themselves Thracian, it is very likely that Antinous (despite being of Arcadian/Greek ethnicity) may have encountered Sabazios rather frequently during his childhood in Bithynia.

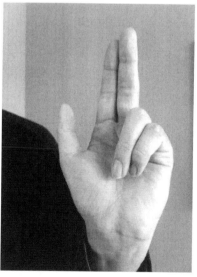

---

[122] An example is shown in Robert Turcan, *The Cults of the Roman Empire* (Oxford and Malden: Blackwell Publishers, 1996), p. 320.

A hand gesture associated with Antinous the Navigator is one that is also attested in Buddhism as a gesture having to do with transmitting the tradition and its teachings, but in the Antinoan context signifies guidance and reassurance. I usually make this gesture with my left hand, but it can be done with both hands or only the right on certain occasions. It is very much like the "A-O-K" gesture for Americans, only the extended pinky, ring finger and middle finger are held more tightly together, while the circled thumb and pointer finger are also held in more tightly to the other fingers. (See below, left.)

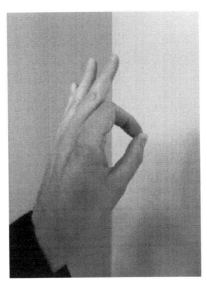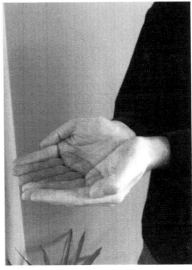

A gesture that I associate with Antinous the Lover is much simpler, and has similarities to the Buddhist and Hindu *mudras* associated with "boon-bestowing." Simply put both hands together, and cup them slightly. (See above, right.) If one wishes to receive the blessings of Antinous the Lover, one should hold one's hands upwards or inclined, as if those blessings are showering down from above. If one wishes, however, to give the blessings of Antinous the Lover to others, one should hold one's hands downwards, as if the blessings are falling from one's own hands onto the ground (and to the world!) beneath.

When I use these gestures, I have an alliterative mnemonic that I use to remember the basic attitude or state of mind which one should attempt to adopt when presenting one of these gestures, which has to do with my basic understanding of what each of the three aspects of Antinous does as a primary activity. Antinous the Liberator **Guards**; Antinous the Navigator **Guides**; and Antinous the Lover **Gives**. Therefore, one's facial expression and demeanor should attempt to convey these ideas. The Liberator's expression need not be fearsome nor intimidating, so much as devoted and vigilant and demonstrative of strength, resolve, and courage. The Navigator's aspect is one of nurturance, of patient correction and benevolent overseeing, as well as gentle encouragement and instruction. The Lover is generous, outgoing, interested, and excited, both to be giving forth to others and to be receiving from them. When doing particular practices during specific parts of the year, or to draw forth specific aspects, syncretisms, or energies from Antinous in ritual, understanding these bodily positions and emotional states can go far in allowing one to feel the movement and embodiment of Antinous through those aspects and syncretisms.

Generally, I stand for most ritual actions and prayers in an Antinoan context. However, on certain occasions, I feel it is proper to kneel in order to show my respect or my humility, particularly when I am entreating Antinous and the other gods for a favor (as one often does in a great deal of prayer). Many modern pagans actively resist and even detest the suggestion of such a posture, as it implies submission and subservience, and thus they will not kneel nor bow their heads or bodies in the honor of any deity. If one happens to feel that way, that's fine. But, one of the things that distinguishes the gods—even those that were formerly human, like Antinous—is that they are by nature beings who are existentially higher, greater, and more powerful than we are. There is no shame nor subservience in admitting this fact. I certainly think that the gods are not interested in their modern devotees bowing and scraping and groveling in front of them; however, a bow of respect, or a posture of humility is indeed in order, in my opinion, if for no other reason than to put oneself into a particular frame of mind as one performs one's devotions. I particularly like the Roman tradition of genuflecting—which is to say, kneeling down on one bended knee—as a show of respect to Antinous, and also in particular to Hadrian, who was due such respect as the Emperor.

The most important concern, of course, in determining what hand

64

gestures and bodily postures should be used in devotional contexts is what one feels is most appropriate and useful. Some people who are not physically able to do some of these postures or hand gestures should not feel excluded by not doing so, as there is no set-in-stone requirement on any of these matters. Therefore, work out what will create the most effective results for yourself, and follow any intuitions or direct instructions you are given by Antinous and the other gods in the process of determining what might work best for you.

Inundation Ritual

Many religions have rituals in which one is ceremonially immersed in water as a form of literal or symbolic purification: Christians have baptism, the Jewish tradition has the *mikveh*, Islam has *wudhu*, and so forth. One of these that has been particularly influential in my own practices is the Shinto ritual practice of *misogi*.[123] The use of water in ritual settings almost has a universal (and obvious!) connotation of purification in some manner.

But, what are the reasons for such a ritual in an Antinoan context?

Apart from the general Roman concern with bathing as both a social and a hygienic activity (which Hadrian certainly shared), there are several indications in surviving materials on Antinous that suggest bathing (at very least), and possible ritual bathing, in association with certain groups or locations in ancient Antinoan devotion. Firstly, there is the mention in the temple constitution of the Lanuvium *collegium* dedicated to Antinous and Diana that the *quinquennalis* of the society, "on the birthdays of Diana and Antinous...is to provide oil for the society in the public bath before they banquet."[124] Second, the oil for such occasions may have been contained in anthropomorphic *balsamaria*, of which several survive that depict Antinous.[125] Third, a multiply-syncretistic statue of Antinous was found in the Baths of

---

[123] See Ann Llewellyn Evans, *Shinto Norito: A Book of Prayers* (Victoria: Matsuri Foundation of Canada/Tenchi Press, 2001), pp. 126-132 for the basics of this ritual.

[124] Mary Beard, John North, & Simon Price (eds./trans.), *Religions of Rome, Volume 2: A Sourcebook* (Cambridge: Cambridge University Press, 1998), p. 294. This text is also given in full in a subsequent chapter below.

[125] Kazimierz Majewski, "Brazowe Balsamaria Antropomorficzne w Cesarstwie Rzymskim," *Archaeologia* 14 (1963), pp. 95-126; Jerome M. Eisenberg and F. Williamson Price, *Art of the Ancient World: Greek, Etruscan, Roman, Byzantine, Egyptian, & Near Eastern Antiquities*. Volume 19 (New York and London: Royal Athena Galleries, 2008), pp. 34-35. One (of twelve) such examples is given at: http://www.antinoos.info/ bild/antin948.jpg.

Hadrian in Leptis Magna (modern Libya).[126] A further line, which is incorporated into the ritual below, is a suggestive one from a hexameter hymn, of which a portion celebrates Antinous and recounts his famed lion hunt and the red lotus which came from it, found in Oxyrhynchus: "Into the Nile he hurried for purification of the blood of the lion."[127]

The reason this procedure is called the "Inundation" ritual is in reference to the miraculous over-abundance of the yearly inundation of the Nile which took place in the year after Antinous' death, during which time it reached levels higher than it ever had in previous Egyptian records.[128] In previous years, it had been painfully inadequate, which not only impoverished Egypt but also threatened a great deal of the Roman Empire, since exported Egyptian grain kept most of the population fed. Therefore, to incorporate this imagery into one's devotions, and to take part in the overabundance of divinity which Antinous' example represents for those who hold him as divine, this ritual has been called the Inundation.

I have performed this ritual in a lake, in swimming pools, and in hot tubs. While I have performed *misogi* in a river, I have not yet had the opportunity to perform the Inundation in a river, nor in the ocean. Any body of water—including one's own bath tub!—would certainly be possible, but when doing so in natural settings, it is best to make sure that the water concerned is safe. Shinto *misogi* is done in places, for example, in which the water does not run too swiftly, nor too slowly. If

---

[126] Caroline Vout, *Power and Eroticism in Imperial Rome* (Cambridge: Cambridge University Press, 2007), pp. 96-100.

[127] J. R. Rea (ed./trans.), *The Oxyrhynchus Papyri* 63 (London: Egypt Exploration Society, 1996), §4352, pp. 1-17 at 8 (ii.10), 9-10, 13 (10). This text is also given below in a subsequent chapter.

[128] James Henry Oliver, *Greek Constitutions of Early Roman Emperors from Inscriptions and Papyri* (Philadelphia: American Philosophical Society, 1989), §88, p. 224; S. Eitrem and Leiv Amundsen (eds.), *Papyri Osloenses* III (Oslo: Jacob Dybwad, 1936), §78, pp. 55-61; Bernard P. Grenfell and Arthur S. Hunt (eds.), *The Oxyrhynchus Papyri* 3 (London: Egypt Exploration Society, 1903), §486, pp. 180-183. Both of these documents give evidence, from both imperial edicts and local legal records, that the inundation of the Nile in 131 was so excessive that it caused a great deal of collateral damage.

you are not a strong and competent swimmer, doing this ritual with the supervision and assistance of others, or in extremely shallow water, is very sensible—it simply will not do to have devotees of Antinous imitating him in every respect, including drowning while they perform rituals for him! In terms of what should be worn for the ritual, do whatever you feel is best, whether that is a full Victorian bathing costume or skinny-dipping; take into account what is legal and permissible in the context in which you are performing this ritual. If you have a particular bathing suit that you want to dedicate especially for this occasion, that can be a potentially useful thing, particularly if you choose a color that is connected to Antinous.

The Inundation ritual takes part in three phases: preliminary prayers, exercises, and then the Inundation itself (which is to say, the immersion in water).

Facing east, one recites the preliminary prayer, which is the Prayer Against Persecution.[129]

The exercises take place in three parts.[130]

1) Antinous the Lover roots the Red Lotus in the Nile. This is a breathing and touch exercise that is designed to get one's energy moving before the rest of the exercises. One takes the flat of one's hand and as one inhales and exhales deeply, moves the hand up and down along the center line of the body, starting from as low on one's torso as one can go (to the top of the genitals) and then up to just above the navel initially. Once the energy is circulating in this area, then one takes longer and deeper breaths and moves the hand from the lowest part of the torso to the level of the heart. Once this is done sufficiently, one moves the hand from the lowest part of the torso to the neck/bottom of the head. This is done at one's own pace. Participants besides myself in this ritual have reported "interesting" effects when this has been done! The purpose of this is to come to alignment and "rootedness" in one's own self, very particularly in one's

---

[129] This is given below in a subsequent chapter.
[130] The names of the exercises were created by Erynn Rowan Laurie.

68

own body.

2) Antinous the Navigator rows the Boat of Millions of Years. This is a physical exercise, in which one stands, with the left foot forward and slightly crouched first. One puts one's arms in a position as if one is rowing a boat, and as one pulls back, one inhales on the syllable/vowel "AAAAAH," then exhales with "IIIII" while pushing forward, then inhales with "OOOOOH" as one pulls back and exhales with "EEEEE" as one pushes forward. As one does this, one is calling out to Antinous as one moves and sweats. The four-part movement and vowel sounding is considered one repetition, and one does twenty of them. Each of the vowels represents the Greek and Latin vocatives of the vowels in the name of Antinous, and so they should be pronounced according to those values rather than what they may appear as in English (so, phonetically, it's "AW," "EE," "OH," "AY"). After doing twenty repetitions of that, one puts the right foot forward, and while using the same motions in coordination with inhalation and exhalation, instead one exhales on "AAAAAH," inhales on "IIIII," exhales on "OOOOOH," and inhales on "EEEEE." One does that twenty times as well. As one accomplishes this exercise, one is rowing and toning in concert with all of the Holy Sailors who have ever been on Antinous' Boat of Millions of Years, thus connecting with the others doing the exercise as well as the wider community and all of one's spiritual ancestors.

3) Antinous the Liberator slays the Lion. From a standing position, one breathes in and out deeply three times, and then inhales one more time, and forcefully exhales with a "HA!" or some other such forceful syllable or sound, and makes a stabbing motion as if one is wielding a spear held in both hands while lunging outward/forward. One does this three times, first to the left, then to the right, then to the center, thus symbolically slaying the lion from all directions and in all dimensions of time (past, present, future). This exercise is to use the aligned self (rooting the Red Lotus in the Nile) and the connections with one's community (rowing the Boat of Millions of Years) in measured and limited manners to clear all obstacles in the exterior world that may interfere with our spiritual work, personally or communally.

Finally comes the Inundation itself. One gets into the water, and says the line "Into the _____ he hurried for purification of the blood of the _____" three times, and then one submerges oneself under the water as completely as possible, then does it again. The blanks are filled in with appropriate river-names and animals to the season of the year. For February through March, it is "Tiber" and "dog," in reference to Lupercalia; for April, it is "Alpheios" and "bear," in reference to the bear hunt; in May, it is "Rhebas" and "boar," in relation to the boar hunt; and from June through January, it is "Nile" and "lion," in relation to the lion hunt. (Though, other rivers and animals are possible, depending on one's own intuitions and understandings and where one is located–if one is doing this in a natural river or lake, and one is aware of the primary prey animal of the area, that would also work as a way to connect one's Antinoan practices with one's actual landscape: "Skagit" and "salmon" would be a possibility, for example.)

This ritual can be part of one's daily practice, or it can be something that one does at the beginning of a day on which another important ritual is being held, or it can be something that one does only once a year (e.g. at Summer Solstice, for example, which is the first time I performed the immersion that eventually became this ritual in 2008). At PantheaCon in 2010 and 2011, the Inundation was performed in the morning before sessions began on one or more days throughout the convention, and likely will be in the future for all Ekklesía Antínoou participants, as well as anyone else who wishes to join us, to "start the day out right" for such an occasion.

Coming Forth By Day

The following piece is a meditation on divinization, created via inspiration from parts of the Egyptian Book of the Dead,[131] the text prepared for the deceased and interred with them to guide them on their way to the otherworld and their experiences therein, in order to bring about the rejuvenation of their soul and its continued existence in the Realms of the Justified Dead. It is an excellent way to contemplate one's own growth in one's divine nature. It also functions well ritually on Foundation Day to express the apotheosis of Antinous, which should be re-enacted every year on that occasion in some manner. Parts of it are unclear in terms of who the speaker is, who it is addressed to, and so forth, but the ambiguity is fruitful, as it allows one to blur the distinction between divinities already acknowledged and those still in the process of becoming.

Behold, the Beautiful Boy rises in the East
from the body of the twelve-chambered dragon
in his boat of millions of years!

Triumphant you will pass over the sky.
You will be associated with the stars.
Praises will be sung to you in your boat;
Hymns will be chanted by the holy sailors.

---

[131] For a full edition of these type of texts, see Raymond Faulkner (trans.), *The Egyptian Book of the Dead, The Book of Going Forth By Day: The First Authentic Presentation of the Complete Papyrus of Ani* (San Francisco: Chronicle Books, 1998); Mark Smith (ed./trans.), *Traversing Eternity: Texts for the Afterlife from Ptolemaic and Roman Egypt* (Oxford: Oxford University Press, 2009).

I sit among the great ones
who dwell in their seats;
I sit down by the side of the Divine Spirit.
I am the moon among the gods;
I am established among the shining ones.

I walk the earth in your footsteps.
I sojourn in the underworld
and come forth again after traversing the tomb.
I dispel the night.

I am your beloved.
I have opened every way in heaven and on earth.
I know your name.
I know forms of you that are not known.
I have risen like a god among humans.

I sit upon my seat on the horizon;
I dwell in the limits of the earth.
I am born renewing myself,
I am made young daily.

I have become a prince,
I have become glorious.
I am the lion coming forth with strides.
I have shot arrows.
I have wounded the beast.

I am the eye of the gods.
I have divided heaven;
I have passed through the horizon.
I am taken possession of by a being beautified and gracious.

Behold, I am provided with your millions of enchantments.
My mouth is opened and my breath is refreshed,
my soul flies like a hawk over the desert.

I am held by the arms of one greater than me,
I am under the protection of him at whose name
the gates of the dead tremble.

Behold, in the East the Beautiful Boy Antinous
rises to give his rays to the shadowed earth.
His face is glory to all who see it!

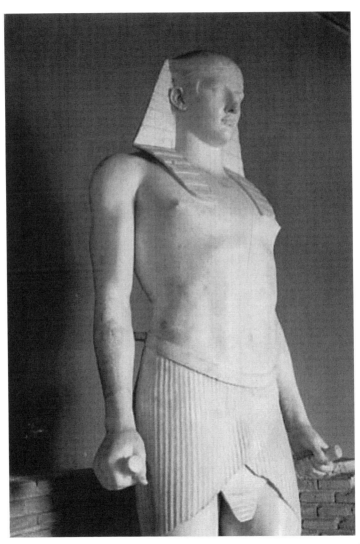

Antinoan Petition

This particular ritual script/text has evolved over the course of the last eight years through several different recensions. The first time it was given was on July 16, 2003, at a short ritual I held in the ruins of a temple in Benwell, a suburb of Newcastle-upon-Tyne in the U.K., on Hadrian's Wall. On that occasion, I was literally working from a piece of scratch paper that had as many names of deities and epithets as I was able to remember on that occasion (and the days preceding it) that were connected to Antinous. A more formalized version of it was then created in the following month. However, a year or two after it was created, I realized that many of the deities or epithets named were actually not relevant to Antinous, and had no connection to him that could be proven outside of some specious conjectures and wish-fulfillment of some of my associates at the time, so I revised it to only include attested deity-names and epithets that I was able to find in one of Hugo Meyer's books on Antinous,[132] plus a few additions that I had picked up in the course of my own modern practices. It had been performed in that fashion of the "third recension" for the majority of my practices.

However, in the most recent year, a few further clarifications, re-additions, and adjustments have been made to it, so that the form you will read below is the most up-to-date recension, as of the final writing and editing process of the present volume in the early autumn of 2011. I expect that it will continue to be in the present form for a number of years, though it is always possible that it may shift once again!

For that matter, those who decide to use it should adapt it to their own needs, and add whatever further prayer intentions one might wish in the latter part of it. If you wish to say it in English, or to subtract some of the deity epithets and names that you are either unfamiliar with or

---

[132] Hugo Meyer, *Antinoos: Die archäologischen Denkmäler unter Einbeziehung des numismatischen und epigraphischen Materials sowie der literarischen Nachrichten, Ein Beitrag zur Kunst- und Kulturgeschichte der hadrianisch-frühantoninischen Zeit* (Munich: Wilhelm Fink, 1991), pp. 163-173.

with which you have no connections, that is also perfectly permissible. It is a modular, adaptive text, and is meant to be used in a way that is both sensible and practical, so however you might wish to accomplish that end is of the utmost concern.

The constant refrain in this prayer is DONA NOBIS PACEM, "Give us peace!" It is in the imperative mood, since it is asking as sternly as possible for its result. The phrase is familiar to many pre-Vatican II-era Catholics as a regular part of the Mass, as well as being known in a musical setting that is often used as a Christmas carol. In the present context, it is asking not only for "peace" in the sense of absence of conflict, but also in the sense of "peace of mind." Though the many petitions expressed in the latter part of the prayer may not come about (through the direct intervention of the gods or otherwise), having peace in oneself about their outcome, and continuing to advocate for them, is something that the god Antinous never fails to instill when he is asked for it. The other prayer, DONA EIS VIRTUTEM, "Give them strength," is also something that Antinous (and the other gods) can equally give in abundance to anyone who asks for it. The strength to do what is necessary, and the peace in one's own mind and heart while dealing with the difficulties of the world, are perhaps some of the simplest prayers that one can do, but also some of the most effective, and the most likely to be granted by the gods.

When I pray this in a ritual setting, I usually take a deep breath in and out during the prayer petitions in the final section before saying "*Dona Nobis Pacem*" with everyone present. As a ritual/prayer-leader, I usually read the line that is listed in regular type below, and everyone present (including myself) responds with the boldface **DONA NOBIS PACEM**.

Many of the deities and epithets in the prayer below are detailed at greater length in *The Syncretisms of Antinous*.[133]

---

[133] P. Sufenas Virius Lupus, *The Syncretisms of Antinous* (Anacortes: The Red Lotus Library, 2010).

In nomine Antinoi Aeterni, Distributoris Pacis,[134]
AVE VIVE ANTINOE!

Antinous Osiris, **DONA NOBIS PACEM**
Antinous Dionysos, **DONA NOBIS PACEM**
Antinous Achilleus, **DONA NOBIS PACEM**
Antinous Adonis, **DONA NOBIS PACEM**
Antinous Agathos Daimon, **DONA NOBIS PACEM**
Antinous Argeiphontes,[135] **DONA NOBIS PACEM**
Antinous Alpheios, **DONA NOBIS PACEM**
Antinous Aristaios, **DONA NOBIS PACEM**
Antinous Apis, **DONA NOBIS PACEM**
Antinous Asklepios, **DONA NOBIS PACEM**
Antinous Attis, **DONA NOBIS PACEM**
Antinous Belenus, **DONA NOBIS PACEM**
Antinous Choreios,[136] **DONA NOBIS PACEM**
Antinous Cydnos, **DONA NOBIS PACEM**
Antinous Kynegetikos,[137] **DONA NOBIS PACEM**
Antinous Daimon, **DONA NOBIS PACEM**
Antinous Deus Amabilis,[138] **DONA NOBIS PACEM**
Antinous Deus Frugiferus,[139] **DONA NOBIS PACEM**
Antinous Endymion, **DONA NOBIS PACEM**
Antinous Ephebos,[140] **DONA NOBIS PACEM**
Antinous Epichorios Theos in Mantineia,[141] **DONA NOBIS PACEM**
Antinous Epiphanes,[142] **DONA NOBIS PACEM**
Antinous Eros, **DONA NOBIS PACEM**
Antinous Ganymede, **DONA NOBIS PACEM**
Antinous Neos Hermes, **DONA NOBIS PACEM**

---

[134] "In the name of the Eternal Antinous, Distributor of Peace."
[135] "Argus-Slayer, a Hermetic epithet.
[136] "God of the Dance," a Dionysian epithet.
[137] "The hunter" (literally "master/leader of hounds").
[138] "The lovely god."
[139] "The fruitful god."
[140] "The youth."
[141] "The Native God in Mantineia."
[142] "The god-who-comes/appears," a Dionysian epithet.

Antinous Herakles, **DONA NOBIS PACEM**
Antinous Heros, **DONA NOBIS PACEM**
Antinous Heros Propylaios,[143] **DONA NOBIS PACEM**
Antinous Neos Iakkhos, **DONA NOBIS PACEM**
Antinous Kastor, **DONA NOBIS PACEM**
Antinous Lunus,[144] **DONA NOBIS PACEM**
Antinous Men, **DONA NOBIS PACEM**
Antinous Musegetikos,[145] **DONA NOBIS PACEM**
Antinous Pan, **DONA NOBIS PACEM**
Antinous Poseidon, **DONA NOBIS PACEM**
Antinous Neos Pythios, **DONA NOBIS PACEM**
Antinous Silvanus, **DONA NOBIS PACEM**
Antinous Vertumnus, **DONA NOBIS PACEM**

Antinous Synthronos ton en Aigypto Theon,[146] **DONA NOBIS PACEM**
Antinous Theos Hermes epi Hadrianou,[147] **DONA NOBIS PACEM**
Antinous Mysterius Maximus,[148] **DONA NOBIS PACEM**
Antinous Homo Deus,[149] **DONA NOBIS PACEM**
Antinous cum Omnis Martyris Fidelis,[150] **DONA NOBIS PACEM**

Antinous with Horus and Set, **DONA NOBIS PACEM**
Antinous with Hylas and Hyakinthos and Narcissus, **DONA NOBIS PACEM**
Antinous with Meleager and Androklos and Eunostos, **DONA NOBIS PACEM**

---

[143] "Hero before-the-gates," a Hermetic epithet.
[144] In reference to Antinous' unsyncretized identification with the moon.
[145] "Leader of the Muses," an Apollonian epithet.
[146] "Enthroned with the Gods of Egypt."
[147] "The God Hermes under Hadrian."
[148] "The Greatest Mystery."
[149] "The Human-God."
[150] "With all the witnesses of steadfastness."

Antinous with David and Jonathan, **DONA NOBIS PACEM**

Antinous with Ba'al and Kinar, **DONA NOBIS PACEM**

Antinous with Melqart and Echmoun, **DONA NOBIS PACEM**

Antinous with Gilgamesh and Enkidu, **DONA NOBIS PACEM**

Antinous with Alexander and Hephaistion, **DONA NOBIS PACEM**

Antinous with Harmodius and Aristogeiton, **DONA NOBIS PACEM**

Antinous with Diana and Persephone and Venus, **DONA NOBIS PACEM**

Antinous with Jupiter and Mars, **DONA NOBIS PACEM**

Antinous with Agdistis and Magna Mater, **DONA NOBIS PACEM**

Antinous with the Divine Hadrian and the Divine Sabina, **DONA NOBIS PACEM**

Antinous with the Divine Nerva and the Divine Trajan, **DONA NOBIS PACEM**

Antinous with the Divine Plotina and the Divine Matidia, **DONA NOBIS PACEM**

Antinous with the Divine Aelius Caesar and the Divine Antoninus Pius, **DONA NOBIS PACEM**

Antinous with Herodes Attikos and Appia Annia Regilla, **DONA NOBIS PACEM**

Antinous with Polydeukion and Memnon and Achilles, **DONA NOBIS PACEM**

Antinous with Lucius Marius Vitalis, **DONA NOBIS PACEM**

Antinous with all of the *Sancti* of the Ekklesía Antínoou, **DONA NOBIS PACEM**

We pray for those of your people who have died at the hands of persecution and hate, like Harvey Milk, Brandon Teena, Gwen Araujo, Billy Jack Gaither, and Matthew Shepard, and far too many others... **DONA NOBIS PACEM**

We pray for those who have died from HIV/AIDS, and for those who have been affected by other sexually transmitted diseases... **DONA NOBIS PACEM**

We pray for those who have been so struck with melancholy, and who have been terribly tormented by bullying, who have taken their own lives in desperation and loneliness... **DONA NOBIS PACEM**

We pray for those who have been the victims of rape, sexual assault, sexual harassment, and sexual abuse... **DONA NOBIS PACEM**

We pray for those whose lives have been destroyed by drugs, alcohol, and other addictions...**DONA NOBIS PACEM**

We pray for those who are closeted, may they be strengthened, *Dona Eis Virtutem*[151]... **DONA NOBIS PACEM**

We pray for those who advocate, campaign, and stand up for the rights of sexual minorities, *Dona Eis Virtutem*... **DONA NOBIS PACEM**

We pray for the young, that they may grow up well, and that we may recognize their gifts, *Dona Eis Virtutem*... **DONA NOBIS PACEM**

We pray for the old, that they may still enjoy life and give us their wisdom, and that we may realize their beauty, *Dona Eis Virtutem*... **DONA NOBIS PACEM**

We pray for all of the women of the world, that they may be free from persecution and abuse, and we pray for and are

---

[151] "Give them strength."

especially thankful for all of the fag-hags, *Dona Eis Virtutem*... **DONA NOBIS PACEM**

We pray for the growing number of straight allies, may they be appreciated and affirmed, may their numbers increase, and may their solidarity with us not be abridged, *Dona Eis Virtutem*... **DONA NOBIS PACEM**

We pray for those of goodwill in many other religions worldwide, may their tolerance become acceptance, and may their acceptance become alliance, *Dona Eis Virtutem*... **DONA NOBIS PACEM**

We pray for all those of past, present, and future, who are your people, the *Populus Antinoi*, who are lesbian, gay, bisexual, transgendered, transsexual, queer, intersexed, genderqueer, and other sexual minorities, *Dona Eis Virtutem*... **DONA NOBIS PACEM**

We pray for the Ekklesía Antínoou, the Aedicula Antinoi, and the *Populus Antinoi*, that we might meet and continue your work in peace... **DONA NOBIS PACEM**

We pray for our allies in the groups Neos Alexandria, AMHA, Hrafnar, Come As You Are Coven, SHARANYA, and the Circle of Dionysos,[152] may our ties of friendship and alliance be strengthened with them, *Dona Eis Virtutem*... **DONA NOBIS PACEM**

---

[152] These are groups which the Ekklesía Antínoou has worked in close relationship with for the duration of its existence on various publishing and internet-based endeavors (Neos Alexandria), or with whom we have put on events (Circle of Dionysos), or with whom we have performed the Communalia ritual at PantheaCon in 2009 (AMHA, Hrafnar, Come As You Are Coven) and 2010 (SHARANYA). It is likely that others will be added in the years to come as more Communalia rituals are performed.

We add the following intentions...
DONA NOBIS PACEM

DONA NOBIS PACEM
AVE VIVE ANTINOE!

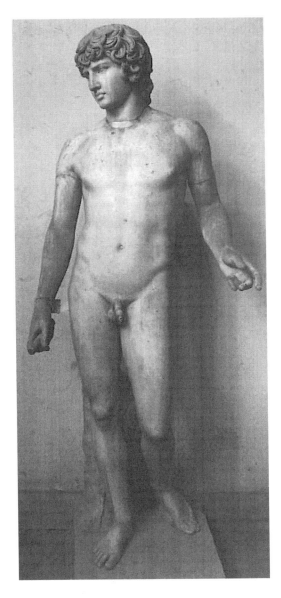

Prayer Against Persecution

This prayer originated in the early autumn of 2007, after I read the *Qu'ran* for the first time in its entirety in preparation for a class I was teaching. I found the book very difficult to read, not because it was hard-to-understand, but because the condemnations on page after page of polytheists, non-Muslims, and "Sodomites" were maddeningly frequent, violent, and hate-filled. It drew my attention to the difficulty which all queer people face in the world today, where our exclusion, persecution, and even violence against us is not only supported by the (infallible) religious scriptures of several major monotheistic religions, but is in fact condoned or even demanded by those scriptures.

(Please understand, I am very well aware that there are Christians, Muslims, and Jews who bear no ill will whatsoever toward polytheists and queer people, and who even are queer themselves. My dissatisfaction and upset in relation to these issues is not at any of those people, but instead the conservative elements in these religions who are of the opinion that their understanding of their supposedly singular and unitary divine being is the only valid religion in existence, and the proscriptions against homoeroticism and gender variance in their sacred writings are binding upon all people.)

This prayer, therefore, was written initially to counteract some of that negative animus, and an earlier recension of it included a short litany to various other deities, including Allah himself.[153] However, soon the prayer was modified, those sections were removed, and I began using it in daily devotions. It was first used publicly at a protest in September of 2007, when a virulently homophobic dominionist Christian group had a large meeting in Washington state, not far from where I was

---

[153] I would note that just because Muslims think he is the only deity, and that he is the same as the deity that Christians and Jews worship, does not necessarily mean that they are correct about this, particularly since the provenance of Allah as one god among many in the Arabian pantheon had centuries of tradition behind it before the Islamic prophet came on the scene in the early seventh century CE.

living at the time. I have made it a part of my practice to, for example, say this prayer before teaching a class or making a public appearance, as well as on many ritual occasions.

The reality of our situation as modern queer and polytheistic peoples is that we will come under fire from hostile forces of a social, religious, and political nature. Asking Antinous for strength in this process, and to moderate our upset at these things so that we do not perpetrate the worst excesses of hatred and vengeance which these hostile forces seem to revel in, is an important concern in attempting to live a spiritual life that is both freedom-enhancing as well as justice-concerned.

Ave Ave Antinoe, Beate, Iuste, Benevolentis...

I cry out in supplication to you, Antinous;
I raise my voice in song and prayer to you, O Bithynian;
I give thanks to you for my trials and my triumphs, O Good God!

I give glory to you,
the Beautiful, the Just, the Benevolent.

It is you who is the sustainer of my life;
it is you who is my protector in the afterlife;
it is you who is the visitor and the rejuvenator and the consoler
in my dreams and my sleep and my rest.

May I rejoice in the successes of both friend and foe;
may I weep with all who are in suffering and travail.

May you give me the strength
to not curse those who would wish me harm;
may you give me the peace to not be troubled
by those who would persecute me.

When I hear the words of those who would condemn me,
may my heart not be hardened towards them;
When they beset me with their hosts of hatred,
may their flood-tide wash over me
as harmless as it was for you on the day of your foundation;
May I never succumb to the temptations
of hatred, spite, and violence.

Though I am not perfect,
I pray that in this affirmation
I may become more perfected.

May my mercy and compassion and forgiveness extend to all,
and may the love of the Beautiful and the Just
pour out over me in my difficulties.

To this god Antinous I have chosen to address my prayer,
and in this god Antinous I take refuge.

May harm never come to those who do good!
May I always be in the presence of he
who is Beautiful, Just, and Benevolent!

Ave Ave Antinoe;
Haec est unde,
Haec est unde,
Haec est unde vita venit!

Ave Ave Antinoe;
Haec est unde,
Haec est unde,
Haec est unde vita venit!

Ave Ave Antinoe;
Haec est unde,
Haec est unde,
Haec est vita venit!

Spell Against Homophobia

The following is a spell I wrote, based on the late antique Greek spell in which Antaura (an atmospheric demon) is confronted by Artemis and told to inflict its headaches elsewhere.[154] It was written in response to the various reactions that culminated in Spirit Day on October 20, 2010 as a way of commemorating all of the recent youthful suicides that occurred because of homophobic bullying and harassment.

These type of spells persisted for many centuries, in many locations, well into the Christian period, where saints replaced the gods in performing the demon-expelling action. Here, I am treating homophobia as a *daimon* that has been created very specifically and propagated deliberately by a lot of religious bigots in this country (and others), and with the help of Antinous, I am wishing that *daimon* to be expelled and sent back where it came from–a small list of some of the people responsible for it (which you can augment as much as you like with further such people, or for particular homophobic bullies and individual you've met personally).

The first part of the spell is an *historiola*, a short myth that explains where the spell comes from and why it works. This phenomenon occurs in many ancient and medieval spells, and in these, spell-writers are able to create new myths that are in line with the actions and attributes of the gods and spiritual beings involved in them. The telling of the tale is essential to the working of the spell, so you should say it aloud at least once while you prepare the spell.

The next part of the spell involves drawing the figures indicated. The

---

[154] A. A. Barb, "Antaura. The Mermaid and the Devil's Grandmother: A Lecture," *Journal of the Warburg and Courtauld Institutes* 29 (1966), pp. 1-23.

one on the left is a glyph representing Antinous in his many syncretized forms, which is the basis of the Serpent Path (which I will be writing more about in the future in other publications). The figure on the right is an image of the god Chnoubis, a syncretistic serpent deity connected to Glykon and who for various reasons is also connected to Antinous, as well as the names "Chnoubis" and "Glykon" in Greek, with the three S-shaped symbols with a line through them that represents Chnoubis, and also the name of IAO, the Greek form of the name of the Hebrew god.[155]

The final part of the spell is pronouncing the *voces magicae*, the "words of power" that empower the spell. Several of these come directly from late antiquity; however, another one is a divine name of Antinous that was revealed to me in my own practices during 2010, specifically in relation to the Hero Antinous, his divine nature which is closest to humanity and most concerned with human's well-being and defense. The first time I spoke the name aloud three times when doing an offering, a vision of a youthful black-clad warrior appeared over my right shoulder. It is a powerful name if pronounced correctly.

I suggest that one draw the rough form of the figure in the air, with one's hand in the gesture of Antinous the Liberator, and say the *voces magicae* formula three times while doing so; if you can't, print it out and trace it with a pen or a wand or your finger while saying it. If you make your own version of the images, carry it with you as a talisman, or make it into a piece of jewelry; in a pinch, write it on your hand or another part of your skin.

The most important thing about magic, in my opinion, is not that one "believes" in it to make it work; it's simply to do the operation with

---

[155] For more on these, see Howard M. Jackson, *The Lion Becomes Man: The Gnostic Leontomorphic Creator and the Platonic Tradition* (Atlanta: Scholar's Press, 1985); Atilio Mastrocinque, *From Jewish Magic to Gnosticism*, Studien und Texte zu Antike und Christentum 24 (Tübingen: Mohr Siebeck, 2005).

86

utmost attention and devotion. As a character in the film *True Stories* advised another character who was doing some Voudun practices was advised, "You don't have to believe, you just need to follow directions."

I do this spell on Spirit Day, as well as on Foundation Day, and I have had many other magicians, pagans, and occultists join me in doing so on these occasions over the last year. Whenever else you might feel it necessary to do the spell, please do not hesitate to perform it.

Spell Against Homophobia

A daimon was going over the mountain one day.

Antinous saw the daimon on its way.

"From whence have you come?" Antinous asked.
 "From Phobos in the dark abyss of the ocean," it said.

"To where are you going?" Antinous asked.
 "To plague the spirits of young and old,
 men and women and those who are neither,
 to make them fear, to drive them insane,
 to force them to take their own lives."

"From whence comes this fear?" Antinous asked.

"From the endless fountain of Fred Phelps,
 from the burbling spring of Joseph Ratzinger,
 from the dead mound of Jerry Falwell,
 from the rotting stone of Pat Robertson,
 from the stunted garden of James Dobson,

from the blasted stump of Boyd Packer,
from the gasping geyser of Michelle Bachmann,
from the whining wind of Anita Bryant,
from the withered reeds of Orson Scott Card,
from the belching volcano of Paul Cameron,
from the spluttering stream of Tom Prichard,
from the tainted well of Peter Sprigg,
from the poisoned lake of Timothy Dailey,
from the wretched rivulet of Tony Perkins,
from the gaseous cloud of Jonathan Katz,
from the hidden vault of Eddie Long,
from the shriveled shoot of Ted Haggard,
from the nefarious nest of Cindy Jacobs,
from the abominable altar of Damon Thompson,
from the twisted horn of Janet Mefferd,
from the feeble pit of George Alan Rekers,
from the mouths that have swallowed the spit
from these other mouths and more."[156]

"Do not come hither, O daimon, but return
    to the depths of the oceanic abyss,
    and take with you the endless fountain,
    the burbling spring,
    the dead mound,
    the rotting stone,
    the stunted garden,
    the blasted stump,
    the gasping geyser,
    the whining wind,
    the withered reeds,

---

[156] Unfortunately, there will never be a shortage of people to add to this list. Substitute ones you are familiar with for ones that you may not be, and feel free to add further lines to it, as long as they are echoed in the response from Antinous which follows.

the belching volcano,
the spluttering stream,
the tainted well,
the poisoned lake,
the wretched rivulet,
the gaseous cloud,
the hidden vault,
the shriveled shoot,
the nefarious nest,
the abominable altar,
the twisted horn,
the feeble pit,
and all the spit
from all these mouths and more![157]
Do not trouble young nor old,
man nor woman nor those who are neither,
do not plague with fear nor insanity,
do not destroy the preciousness of life!"

"I will oppose you," answered the daimon.

"I will resist you!" said Antinous.
    "I will break your wings, o daimon;
    I will crack your skull, o daimon;
    I will steal your arms, o daimon;
    I will drown your limbs, o daimon;
    I will stir up your bowels, o daimon;
    I will confuse your mind, o daimon;
    I will put fear into you, o daimon,
    and into those from whence this fear has come!"

---

[157] If possible, what comes before this as Antinous' response to the daimon
should be said in a single breath.

"Do not flay my skin!
Do not split my knees!
Do not blind my eyes!
Do not block my ears!
Do not cut out my tongue!
Do not slice my entrails!
Do not destroy my health!"

"I will do all of these and more
if you do not return from whence fear has come!"

The daimon went back.

AVE VIVE ANTINOE.
VEL IN LIMINE MUNDI ECCE
EGO SEMPER SUM CORAM TE.
HAEC EST UNDE VITA VENIT.
GRATIAS AGEMUS.

[Say this three times while drawing the figure on the next page:]

HOROI BARBAROU HEROI BORBAROU IA IA IAO IAOAI ACHELEIDG ACHELEIDG ACHELEIDG AIOE AIOE AIOEU

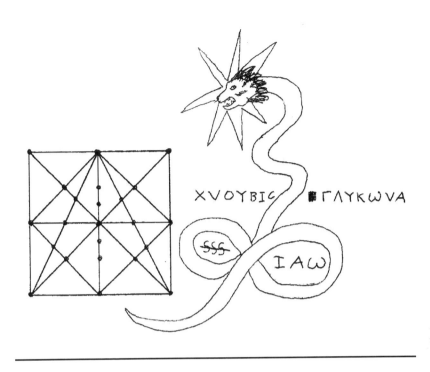

XVOYBIC ▦ ΓΛΥΚШΝΑ

SSS

ΙΑШ

Ave Ave Antinoe

This is a Latin hymn, meant to be sung, which combines elements from many of the ancient devotional texts devoted to Antinous. It was first written in 2003, and it can easily be sung to any tune to which the *Hanuman Chalisa* has been set. It has been a regular part of nearly all of the major rituals for Antinous that I've held, both publicly and privately, since 2003.

The translation provided below is only for the purposes of understanding what is being spoken—the original language of the hymn and its best form should be considered the Latin version. It was published earlier in *The Phillupic Hymns*.[158]

Ave, laudo Antinoe; / Ave, laudo Antinoe;
Ave, laudo Antinoe; / Ave, laudo Antinoe;

Natus in Bithynia, / mortus in Aegypto
In deorum numerum / is vivit laudo;
Erat delicia / amans Hadriani,
Domini Mundi / Caesaris Romani;

Canto laudes tua / omni tuis populis,
In Scapha tua / tu vivis perennis;
Puer aeternus / cum vultu pleno gratia,
Mors tui Hadrianum / plevit cum tristitia;

---

[158] P. Sufenas Virius Lupus, *The Phillupic Hymns* (Eugene: Bibliotheca Alexandrina, 2008), pp. 224-226.

Saeculum ad saeculum / forma tua durens,
In modis sacris tuis / nos purum faciens;
Mantinoeia dicitur / beata tua mater
Hermes, qui appellamus / Mercurius pater;

Flamma Cupidinis / summersum in aqua
Factum est florens tua / pulcher iuventa;
Imperator vidit / in tuis pulchritudine
Bonitatem quam possit / fideliter diligere;

Similiter Herculi / et leone venatio
Potentia tua / magnum transformatio
Accidit quando / leonis sanguis
Transmutus est / in ruborem floris;

Hasta invicta / Hadrianus subvenit
Beneficium qui / mors tua solvit;
Mox peragraveras / adverso flumine
Sacra Nilus flumen / tua Domine;

Tota terra torrida / sine vitae aqua
Locus mortis tuae / urbs Thothis sacra;
Mysteria maximae / in noctes illas
Cognitus est te / altissimas tenebras;

Luna Diana / noctis regina
Occidit Actaeonem / in modo canina;
Eras fidelissimus / canis venaticus
Sublatus est Diana / clarus tuus vultus;

Ave, ave Antinoe / Liberator
Homo Deus, Victor, / pacis Imperator;
Ave Antinoe / Ave Navigator,
Veni, veni Antinoe / Amator;

Stella arderens / tua in Aquila
Donec nautae sanctae / in tua Scapha;
Floris tuae in terra / radices agerens
Dum templa tua / in nostra corda faciens;

Tuum oraculum / dicit clara voce,
Nos reficimur / mirabilibusque;
Nos conservarmur / nostra fidelitas,
Omnes laudis Liberator / te agemus gratias;

Vel in limine / mundi, Ecce!
Ego semper / sum coram te! [iterum][159]

Ave Ave Antinoe; Ave Ave Antinoe; [iterum]
Haec est unde, haec est unde, haec est unde vita venit; [iterum]

Hail Antinous, I praise you!... [repeat]

Born in Bithynia, died in Egypt,
He lives among the gods, I praise you!
He was the favorite lover of Hadrian—
Ruler of the World, Caesar of the Romans.

I sing your praises to all your people;
You live forever in your Boat,
The eternal youth with a face full of grace
(Your death filled Hadrian with sadness)

Your beauty enduring from age to age
Making us pure in your ways.
Your beautiful mother was called Mantinoë,
Hermes (was) your father, whom we call Mercury;

---

[159] "Repeat."

Eros' fire submerged in the water
Made the fair flowering of your youth;
The Emperor saw in your beauty
The goodness which he would be able to love truly.

Like Hercules and the hunt for the lion
By your power a great transformation
Happened when the blood of the lion
Was transmuted into the redness of a flower.

With an invincible spear Hadrian came to your aid—
A favor which your death repaid.
Soon you would have traveled up the river,
The Sacred Nile, your river, O Lord!

The entire land was parched without the water of life;
The place of your death was the holy city of Thoth.
The greatest mystery in those nights
Was known by you, the deepest obscurities.

Diana Luna, queen of the night
Killed Aktaion in a bitchy way;
You were the most faithful hunting-hound:
Your glorious face was elevated by Diana.

Hail, hail Antinous the Liberator!
Man-God, Victor, Emperor of peace!
Hail Antinous, Hail the Navigator!
O come, O come, Antinous the Lover!

Your star burning in the Eagle
While the holy sailors are in your boat,
Your flowers taking root in the earth
As the making of your temples in our hearts;

Your oracle speaks in a clear voice
And we are renewed by your miracles.
May our fidelity save us;
All praises to you, Liberator, we give you thanks!

"Even at the edge of the world, Behold!
I am always in your presence!"

Hail, Hail Antinous; Hail Hail Antinous!
This is where, this is where, this is where life comes from!

Aretalogia Antinoi

An aretalogy is a Greek term for a hymn which describes the attributes and virtues of a particular deity (from Greek *arete*, "virtue/manly deed"). Some of these have survived from the ancient world, one of which is an aretalogy of Isis, which exists in Greek and was said to be copied from a stele outside the temple of Hephaistos in Memphis (i.e. the temple of Ptah),[160] and the following one is based roughly on that model. The meter and schema was adapted from a Sufi hymn. The translation is given following the text below, because it is meant to be performed primarily in Latin. It was published earlier in *The Phillupic Hymns*.[161]

Antinous sum, amator Divi Hadriani Imperatoris Romae, pontificis maximi, epoptes Eleusis, Regis Aegypti Inferioris et Superioris;

eductus Romae in litteris Latina et Graeco, et sic Novus Deus Hermes sum;

Navigator Scaphae Annorum Decies
Centena Millia sum Antinous

Filius Mantinoeiae, genii Arcadii
Liberus Bithyniae, flora Rhebas

---

[160] This can be found in Frederick Grant (ed.), *Hellenistic Religions: The Age of Syncretism* (New York and Indianapolis: The Bobbs-Merrill Company, 1953), pp. 131-133; Gail Corrington Streete, "An Isis Aretalogy from Kyme in Asia Minor, First Century B.C.E.," in Richard Valantasis (ed.), *Religions of Late Antiquity in Practice* (Princeton: Princeton University Press, 2000), pp. 369-383.
[161] P. Sufenas Virius Lupus, *The Phillupic Hymns* (Eugene: Bibliotheca Alexandrina, 2008), pp. 49-52.

Stella obscura captus in Aquila
Rejuvenator fluminis Nili

Venator Leonis Mauretaniae
Armatus cum calamo florae hasta

Rubra flora flammae aquaeque
Imago beata super piscinam

Navigator Scaphae Annorum Decies
Centena Millia sum Antinous

Synthronos cum deis Aegypto
Divinatus sum aqua Nili

Equos maximos frenaverus
Firmus in grecem canum sum

Innocens peccati Actaeonis
Spiritus qui conjugans viros cunctos

Beatus et Frugiferus sum
Invictus Iuvenis sum Antinous

Navigator Scaphae Annorum Decies
Centena Millia sum Antinous

Heros sum Propylaios
Deus Amabilis apellatus

Verba poetis datus sum
Celebratus cursibus et remis

Mysteriis exclusis aperiveram
Oraculo nominis mei responderam

Congressio deorum multi
Dominus Infernorum apellatus

Navigator Scaphae Annorum Decies
Centena Millia sum Antinous

Requiem pueris datus sum
Salvator sum morienti

Amicus Dianae Reginae sum
Gratiae Divae Sabinae dico

Cum Achilleo sto Patrocloque
Phratrias et Ecclesias ordinateram

Distributor Pacis Profundi
Liberator a vexatione

Navigator Scaphae Annorum Decies
Centena Millia sum Antinous

I am Antinous, lover of Divus Hadrianus, emperor of Rome,
pontifex maximus, epoptes of Eleusis, king of Upper and Lower
Egypt;

I was educated in Rome in letters both Greek and Latin, and
thus am the New God Hermes;

I am Antinous, the Navigator
Of the Boat of Millions of Years

I am the son of Mantinoë, of Arcadian stock;
I am the child of Bithynia, flower of the Rhebas

I am the dark star grasped in Aquila;
I am the rejuvenator of the Nile

I am the hunter of the Mauretanian lion;
I am armed with flower-stem as spear

I am the red flower of fire and water;
I am the reflection upon the pool

I am Antinous, the Navigator
Of the Boat of Millions of Years

I am enthroned with the gods of Egypt;
I am made divine by the Nile's waters

I have reined the greatest of horses;
I am strong in packs of hounds

I am innocent of Aktaion's fault;
I am the spirit which joins men together

I am Beautiful and Fruitful;
I am Antinous, Undefeated Youth

I am Antinous, the Navigator
Of the Boat of Millions of Years

I am the Hero Before-the-Gates
I am called *Deus Amabilis* ["the Lovely God"]

I have given words to the poets;
I am celebrated with races and rowing [lit. "by oars"]

I have revealed mysteries to those excluded from them;
I have given answers through the oracle of my name

100

I am the meeting-place of many gods;
I am called "Lord" in the Underworld

I am Antinous, the Navigator
Of the Boat of Millions of Years

I have given rest to children,
I am the Savior to the dying

I am the friend of Queen Diana;
I speak for the favor of Diva Sabina

I stand with Achilleus and Patroklos;
I have organized *phratriae* and *ecclesiae*

I am the giver of profound peace;
I am the Liberator from oppression

I am Antinous, the Navigator
Of the Boat of Millions of Years

Three Rhetorics

For the purposes of this piece, I am defining "rhetoric" as a "rhetorical exercise," which in the classical world was a very common type of assignment for students of the orator's art. Some of the most popular rhetorical exercises circulated widely in manuscript form, and were often used as study-pieces for students learning to write Greek or Latin, for example. It is likely that a few of the documents attributed to Hadrian and some of the other Antonines were not legitimate documents, but instead were rhetorical exercises in which someone wrote in the voice of Hadrian and based their portrayal on known aspects of his character and turns of phrase. Hadrian was an accomplished *rhetor* himself, and was friends with some of the greatest *rhetors* of the second century CE, including Favorinus of Arles, Polemo of Smyrna, Numenios, and Marcus Cornelius Fronto.

These particular rhetorics were originally written on December 1, 2006. They emerged in my own practice as not only important answers or responses to some issues I was having at the time, but also as a manner via which to discuss the three general categories that have been suggested as the "motivations," of sorts, for Antinous' death: suicide, sacrifice, and sheer accident. While I would not suggest that these are "channeled" pieces in any way, if they end up producing a positive effect in their readers that makes them feel inspired, or consoled, then I would freely defer the recognition for this from myself and my own rhetorical skills toward Antinous. They were also published previously in *The Phillupic Hymns*.[162]

The first piece is written to Lucius Marius Vitalis, a historical personage who is detailed further in a chapter below. The character addressed in the second piece, "On Sacrifice," was one created by

---

[162] P. Sufenas Virius Lupus, *The Phillupic Hymns* (Eugene: Bibliotheca Alexandrina, 2008), pp. 250-255.

Shawn Postoff on his website, *The Sacred Antinous*.[163] Indeed, Postoff's entire corpus is, in a sense, an extended series of rhetorics involving Antinous and some of the personalities connected to him, and I cannot recommend looking at them highly enough.

ON SUICIDE

Greetings to Lucius Marius Vitalis from Antinous,

I have heard it said that your state is not a happy one, and a great despair has come over you, to the point that you have considered death by your own hand to be more beneficial than continuing among the living. Sad am I to hear these words, and I wish to offer you consolation.

The causes for such feelings are manifold, and the justifications for suicide have been various in the legacies of our forbearers, from impending defeat in battle to the pain of the loss of a loved one. But the connection between cause and feeling is not one of necessity, for many have been the soldiers who chose a noble death in battle rather than in anticipation of it, or even the refuge of flight from the fray—and some might call the latter cowardice, but what is it to love one's own life at the cost of one's honor? For you and I were never meant to be soldiers, and we know too well that the life of the mind values each moment that it may further contemplate the objects of the senses, and that a hero's death in benefit of a greater cause is not what either of us shall meet.

Long has it been since you and I last witnessed the skills of the Dionysian artists in the theatre. And though the form of the

---

[163] See http://www.sacredantinous.com/ST-Epistles/000Introduction.html for further links to the entire epistolary series wherein Decentius is introduced.

drama and its content is a matter of religion, I have often wondered if there is more to this art than what can be portrayed by the mask of tragedy or comedy. Is it possible, my friend, that one can wear the mask of comedy and yet meet one's death? Is it likewise possible to wear the mask of tragedy when it is to one's own wedding which one goes? How many have we seen outside the theatre, living in the villas of Latium, who wear the mask of tragedy always, when indeed Fate has been more than kind to them? Let this never be the case for such as we, to scoff at what the gods have given in Fortune, and to weep at the boons they bestow upon us. For even as he was cut down and killed by the titans did the persistent shoots of Dionysos grow up again, and by this tenacity and the madness which does most opposite of what one might deem appropriate, did not this very god conquer the world and spread in triumph across it? (We also do well to remember that, whether it is this mask or that which we wear, there is another face beneath it; the voice through the mask may betray its identity, yet still it is hidden and unknown for those who observe it. How much more true is this for the human soul than for the spectacle of the theatre?)

But let us also never laugh and smile when indeed it is the dog's eye that is the result of the die's cast.[164] For often there is cause for sadness, which you know now more than perhaps ever before. Do not betray your sadness for a shallow smile, for your smile will make you a liar and a poor rhetoritician rather than a hero of fortitude and perseverance.

And still, your ill feelings may delude you, in their insidious logic, into thinking that in willingly facing your own death, you may be facing and overcoming the greatest fear that there is, and by conquering your fear in self-inflicted death you may become greater than your fear. However, remember this: far greater is

---

[164] The "dog's eye" was the lowest roll on the die—a one—and thus is the ancient equivalent of "snake eyes."

the ruler of an empire who can conquer his enemies not by crushing them and killing them, but instead by allowing them to live and adding their strengths to the collective of his own state. Fear, then, is best not killed and annihilated, but instead tamed and given its due rights, for then the power that it holds is no longer a threat to the peace in the state of the soul.

But these matters, I understand, will be much clearer to us once we reach Athens. Our beloved Augustus has informed me that it will be our honor to attend the Great Mysteries at Eleusis on our visit, and it is through these that we will come to an understanding of death; we will face it and triumph, and know that the fear of death will have no voice in the senate-house of the soul because of it.

May it be the love of dear friends that is the foundation and the support of you in these difficult times, and never for a moment doubt that this love is most certainly yours, for all the days we may live, as long as there is breath in these lungs. One of your name, Vitalis, must necessarily love life and thrive and prosper, rather than despise it and suffer in its squandering. I am, as ever, yours in this knowledge and friendship.

ON SACRIFICE

To M. Ulpius Decentius from Antinous,

It is with every glance toward you that my eyes afford me that I am in admiration of the virtues of the body. Apollodorus the engineer, in all of his genius in craft and design, could never create a siege engine more stout than this frame of yours, nor a weapon that can pierce the heart and draw blood from wounds more surely than these arms and hands and the other limbs which you bear. Never did the form of an object more follow its intended practical purpose than this marvelous body of yours, in its very birth a soldier and a warrior fashioned through the care of the gods.

I have heard you speak of those northern lands of your origin, the provincial isle of Britannia, which must surely border the Hyperborean lands to which Apollon goes at wintertide. Perhaps it is no wonder, then, that the peoples of that land along the *vallum* of our Imperator recognize Apollon Citharoedus in this figure you have told me they call Maponus. For what but the soothing strains of the lyre might give comfort to those longing for the sun that they see so infrequently in those frozen climes? Daily are the sacrifices to him on those distant altars, as they are in the lands from Judea to Hispania.

It is the blood of animals that is poured out on the altars for sacrifice, or the costly oils and incenses that are burned for the gods for this purpose. To sacrifice, one might say, is to take care, great expense, and difficulty on behalf of the nourishment of the gods; what is a diminishment to us mortals and a lessening of our resources is for their gain. But what does it really mean, *sacrifice*? In the Latin tongue, I have come to understand, this word means "to make holy." And what blood is it that is poured out in the entreaties to the health and success of the *Numen Augusti* and to the peace of the Empire? Whose blood but those of the soldiers, who live to serve the *Patria* and stand in its defense whenever called upon. As your body was made for the task of the warrior, then do not doubt, dear Decentius, that it is also made holy in its every movement. You stand upon a bridge between life and death at all times, the life of the Empire as well as all of its citizens and your own life, and the death of these things which can only be warded off by the death you dispense to those who mean harm. Though we who have never had to take up arms might call these matters praiseworthy, virtuous, and heroic—and by definition this certainly is the case—you might in fact find it not to be the condition with which you are

106

familiar...For what might the mouth sing in lauding the hand, when it is the hand itself which must go into the mouth of the lion?

Perhaps we who are not in the legions would do well to reflect more deeply on the status of the soldier, and for this reflection may we praise that status all the more. Who among us does not stand on that bridge between life and death? And, by the knowledge that we are so doing, who can deny that our every action should be made holy, whether it is pouring out libations to the gods or walking to the market to buy a sponge, singing a hymn of praise or snorting the smells of the city? The music of this northern "Apollo Maponus" must surely sound sweeter and more surely for those who act in this manner than for those who do not.

Let it not be the thought of our diminishment and our inconvenience that occupies us when we think on the sacrifices which the gods require. Such a one as would make their every act holy would, by no means, feel diminished in any way to give whatever it may be that the gods might require when necessary.

I look forward to the coming journey into Egypt, in which we will see the body of that great and divine hero Alexander. This, surely, was a man that understood in his body and soul what it is to make holy one's every step, whose path the gods blessed and protected, and who did not deign it wasteful to make holy the sacrifices of his fallen friends and enemies.

For now, think not on these bellicose matters, but instead on the abiding peace and tranquility which the blessings of our Augustus have bestowed upon us all. I remain your devoted friend for every step of this journey.

ON MISFORTUNES

Greetings to the Augustus, my own Hadrian, from Antinous,

It is mere moments since our parting, yet the span of ages feels like it has passed since the comfort of your visage has graced these eyes. I count the grains in the hourglass until we may see each other again.

Of late, the subject with which you have been troubled over in mind has been the status of your health. It pains me to see you in such discomfort, and yet you have not deigned it too great a task to travel across these eastern provinces despite it, when lesser men would shudder to venture down a staircase or a corridor in their own house while plagued with smaller ailments of body. You have wondered aloud to me how it is that your sturdiness in youth and the fortunes of your military campaigns under the Divine Trajan could have passed by with such little incident, and yet now infirmity seizes you in its restricting chains more and more each day, when there are men greater in years than yourself who do not suffer in these ways. Fate and Fortune are two mistresses who do not yield their secret trysts to men easily, if ever, and no oracles can reveal the truth of these matters clearly, if indeed the gods themselves know the reasons or to explain some justification for human suffering.

There is no consolation to be found in the platitudes of the Stoic philosophers, for though moderation and restraint may be worthy of esteem in the eyes of some, for those who wish to know the world as comprehensively as you do, such matters are not possible. What joy is there in a feast or in wine if they are not consumed, preferably in the company of friends?

Yet there may be something of truth in their approach. For is there a blessing hidden in this curse of ill health? Would you have had the insistent thirst for wisdom that has impelled you to seek out the Great Mysteries if the prospect of death had not forced itself into your perceptions? Has it not caused you, in fact, to appreciate your life all the more? And I recall, as we ascended Mt. Kassios and you stopped for a moment in a fit of coughing, winded from the exertion, that you told the party to continue on as planned and not stall in their onward pace, but the priest was only one step ahead of you at that point. But for the grace of ten steps, it may have been you whose soul may have been the sacrifice on the mountaintop because of Zeus' hungry thunderbolts on that day.[165] To be such a rare gift to the god is an incredible honor, but it has been the honor of the court, the Empire, and most especially myself to have had the time to spend with you since then, and may it be so for many years to come.

It is the happenstances of life in its vicissitudes which bring both lucky windfalls and unfortunate setbacks, and these we attribute to Hermes. The flights of his fancy move more swiftly than even Zeus' lightning, and what can be fortune one moment can be disaster the next. And yet, how many disdain recognition of the god for all the small messages of good news and luck and the multiple blessings of the gods that he delivers, and yet only look upon him directly as their destined guide in that final journey, not towards the east but rather towards the west into the realm of Hades? So varied and many-sided is the character of this god that any who would deny it is blind and undeserving of even his singular attention at the time of death only—though he would surely not fail to fulfill that duty to even the lowliest and most unworthy. Likewise is it with the accidents of life: for every treasure washed up on the beach that causes joy and relief from sufferings, there is a shipwreck and a loss and a drowning for some other party.

---

[165] For more on this incident, see P. Sufenas Virius Lupus, "Roman Olympians: The Cult of Zeus and Hadrian Olympios," in Melia Suez et al. (eds.), *From Cave to Sky: A Devotional Anthology for Zeus* (Shreveport: Bibliotheca Alexandrina, 2010), pp. 97-105.

But you who have traveled far, and who knows better than any in all the Empire the great power which resides in being the envoy of the message of peace across all provincial boundaries and the spans of continents, should therefore know these matters of Hermes better than any. And as you have been stalwart in your ongoing journey despite your difficulties, so too should your approach to any difficulties which may arise be as resolute and deliberate, and even joyous. If the necessity of external circumstances is your master and is allowed to dictate your inner state, then your life will surely be the stuff of tragedy rather than heroism. One is master of Fate and Fortune if one chooses to undergo its difficulties and its pleasures willingly, and the affirmation of even the deepest suffering is the material from which heroism is built. Perhaps it is not the nymphs who caused Hylas to fall and drown, but his own curiosity at the images along the surface of the water. That which is deliberate can in no way be called unfortunate, even if it is accidental.

Much of Egypt, including Hermes' own city, remains to be viewed by us in the coming weeks. How exciting to view these antiquities and the customs of this strange but wondrous land, the fountain of all knowledge of philosophy and the home of the most ancient gods! What mysteries may lie ahead to explore I can only imagine.

It will not be long until we see each other again, but I hope these few words in the meantime may be of some comfort to you, who mean more to me than my own small life. My heart, my soul, my breath, my body, and most importantly my love, are, as ever, yours, until the stars fall from the sky.

Wepwawet

In the practice of the Ekklesía Antínoou's public rituals for the past few years, I have adopted a custom that I find very amenable on a variety of levels. In order to acknowledge our debt, and the debt of Antinous' ancient cultus, to the spiritual heritage of Egypt, Greece, and Rome, we begin our rituals with prayers to three "gatekeeper" deities from these three cultures: Wepwawet, Hekate, and Ianus.[166] Further, doing this honors the multiplicity of genders in the divine world, since the first is male, the second female, and the third often (literally!) bisexual; and, it also honors the humanoid as well as animal worlds, since Wepwawet is cynocephalic, and Hekate is often portrayed as dog-, horse-, or goat-headed as well. We begin with Wepwawet, since he is Egyptian, and thus represents the oldest of the three cultures. This poem was published earlier in *The Phillupic Hymns*.[167]

Where there is no path,
he will make one.
When none may pass,
his strong arm guides.
May you go in front
to make the ways clear;
May you go in back
to shield from all harm.
May you be at my side
to place my feet
on roads of rest.

---

[166] P. Sufenas Virius Lupus, "Gatekeepers, Way-Clearers, Mediators: Wepwawet (or Anubis and Hermanubis), Hekate, and Ianus in the Practices of the Ekklesía Antínoou," in Sannion et al. (eds.), *Bearing Torches: A Devotional Anthology for Hekate* (Eugene: Bibliotheca Alexandrina, 2009), pp. 169-178.
[167] P. Sufenas Virius Lupus, *The Phillupic Hymns* (Eugene: Bibliotheca Alexandrina, 2008), p. 23.

Hekate Soteira

As mentioned in the previous chapter, Hekate is the second gatekeeper deity that we honor at the beginning of most of our public rituals, whose favor we seek in the ritual that is to follow. This poem originally only consisted of the third verse when it was published originally in *The Phillupic Hymns*,[168] but it was later expanded as it felt incomplete, and was published elsewhere.[169]

Khaire Hekate Soteira, triple-formed,
lady of lions, mistress of hounds,
favored-one of Zeus, above all
triumphant over earth, ocean,
and vaulted heaven flecked with stars.

She is glimpsed by the dark of moon
at crossroads and on-ramps alike,
no door, no gate can obstruct her path;
horse and sail are hers to influence,
whirring engine and tail-lights at night.

With bright torch and barking dog
god and titan, nymph and satyr,
daimon and *psyche*, man and hero
have no choice but to go wherever
she has directed the crowd to surge.

---

[168] P. Sufenas Virius Lupus, "Hekate's Herds," *The Phillupic Hymns* (Eugene: Bibliotheca Alexandrina, 2008), p. 102.

[169] P. Sufenas Virius Lupus, "Gatekeepers, Way-Clearers, Mediators: Wepwawet (or Anubis and Hermanubis), Hekate, and Ianus in the Practices of the Ekklesía Antínoou," in Sannion et al. (eds.), *Bearing Torches: A Devotional Anthology for Hekate* (Eugene: Bibliotheca Alexandrina, 2009), p. 81.

The three who are one, the one who is three,
knowing virgin, ferocious mother,
animal-headed, cynanthropic,
the one who is three, the three who are one,
the voice of the formless fire, *Khaire Hekate Soteira.*

Ianus

Finally, we come to Ianus, the two- (or more) headed (or, perhaps more accurately, two-faced!) patron of doorways, bridges, and ports. The series of epithets which begin each line are all attested in ancient Roman dedications to the deity.[170] This poem was also published originally in *The Phillupic Hymns*.[171]

May Ianus Patulcius open the door for me
as I open this prayer, may all doors be opened;
May Ianus Pater watch over and protect me
as he watched over Saturn in his exile;
May Ianus Bifrons keep guard before and behind me
as age is ahead of and youth is afar from me;
May Ianus Quadrifrons protect me on all sides
as ways converge in me and as paths branch out of me;
May Ianus Geminus' temple doors ever open for our aid,
and may his doors ever close for our peace;
May Ianus Clusivus close the door for me
as I close this prayer, may there be a close to all troubles.

---

[170] Lesley Adkins and Roy A. Adkins, *Dictionary of Roman Religion* (New York: Facts on File, 1996), p. 111-112.
[171] P. Sufenas Virius Lupus, *The Phillupic Hymns* (Eugene: Bibliotheca Alexandrina, 2008), p. 66.

II.
ANTINOUS THROUGHOUT THE YEAR

Tabula Feriarum

Calendar of Feasts of the Ekklesía Antínoou

One characteristic of adherents to various religions is that they keep particular days of a cyclical nature—whether the cycle concerned is within a week, a month, or a year—as special occasions on which either "historical events" in their religion's myths or in the deeds of its founders, as well as other "cosmic" or "seasonal" events, are observed. These can be as frequent as the monastic divine offices and Books of Hours of the Christian tradition, to a weekly Sabbath in the Jewish tradition, to calendrical observances of saints or gods which occur on nearly every day of the year, to various other permutations in terms of monthly or yearly celebrations, based on the lunar cycles, zodiac events, and so forth. While many religions have a universal or general calendar of such events, the records we usually have of them are from individual times and places or were the observances of particular people; thus, one church might observe the feast-days of certain saints and name them in the litanies which they use, while another might select from others; one person's Book of Hours might select certain prayers, while another may innovate or have slightly different versions; and so forth.

Thus, it should be understood initially that while this particular *Tabula* is a calendar of the Ekklesía Antínoou in the broadest sense, and the majority of the dates entered in it are ones which people throughout the Ekklesía Antínoou might observe in some manner, the interpretations, occasionally the names, and even the existence or lack thereof of some dates in the present calendar might not match the calendars of other Ekklesía Antínoou members. As there is no entirely canonical and orthodox version of the calendar, it makes sense that each one would suit the individual tastes, practices and interests of the person concerned. Some dates of particular importance tend to be shared by all, and these, along with the common interest in devotion to Antinous, is what unites us as a cultus; but (as has been emphasized repeatedly in this book!), all other matters are up to the individual to determine as best as possible for themself.

As with most religions, there are repeating feast-days or holidays (holy-days) which are observed in the Ekklesía Antínoou. Not all of them are required, but one in particular is quite important, not only for the historical cult, but for our particular incarnation and observance of it. Since this is a religion which is highly syncretistic and not exclusive in its membership, meaning that one can be a devotee, member or worshipper of any other religion, spirituality, guru, or god and still partake of what Antinous and the Ekklesía Antínoou offer, there is a lot of space for other observances. Further, private forms of daily devotion can supplement or augment the festivals below, and can be the main ritual and practical focus during the intervening times between them. Antinous is most often a god connected to the themes of regeneration and the sphere of youth in the figures to whom he was likened, and as these tend to have a seasonal aspect in most traditional religions, the pattern of festivals does tend to follow the course of the seasons and the significances assigned to each tide of the year. However, for more directly "seasonal" observances, there is nothing which would prevent one from either practicing another tradition that has such important seasonal markers, or incorporating these other practices more explicitly into what one does in relation to Antinous.

The holy days mentioned in the calendar below are ones that are recognized and practiced specifically in my own yearly cycle, and thus the present calendar is based on that of the Aedicula Antinoi.[172]

There is a twofold division in the festivals which occur in this calendar. Some events—especially the Sacred Nights of Antinous in October—are more or less "required" observances, being the most important occasion during the year, particularly Foundation Day (October 30). The next most important festival is Antinous' birthday (November 27), followed in importance by the Megala Antinoeia (April 21). Further, the Lion Hunt and Festival of the Red Lotus (August 21-22), the Equinoctical festivals of Sabina's apotheosis (March 21) and the initiation of Hadrian and Antinous at Eleusis (September 21), and

---

[172] See http://aediculaantinoi.wordpress.com/calendar/.

other events particular to the Ekklesía Antínoou and its founding Hadrianic and Antonine imperial figures, are the sort of "third tier" in importance. These various Antinous-specific observances are marked in **bold**, and the most important of these are marked in **bold and** **underline**.

The second class of festivals which are listed here commemorate certain syncretisms of Antinous, a selection of *Sancti* of the Ekklesía Antínoou, and further ancient Greek, Roman, and Egyptian holidays connected with deities and figures of the Antinoan syncretistic pantheon.[173]

The calendar below follows the usual secular year observed in the modern world, with January first and December last. The Roman custom of the ordering of the months was with March occurring first. The Egyptian custom shifted slightly from year to year, but generally the new year began in what we would reckon as the summer. Greek city-states varied from place to place in what calendars they adopted. Thus, the date of the "new year" differs widely from tradition to tradition. Some people consider Foundation Day to be the "new year" as far as Antinoan devotional outlooks are concerned; whether you do or not is up to you, though when counting years from the death of Antinous (which we sometimes do in Ekklesía Antínoou practice as _____ P.M.A., "*post mortem Antinoi*"), one should count from October 30-October 29 as the "year" concerned. Whatever your own practice happens to be in terms of your own preferences and what wider traditions you follow is what should be observed.

And thus we begin...

---

[173] Some of the holidays occurring on the Aedicula Antinoi calendar online are not listed here, which are most often specifically Celtic in nature, though they occasionally have a more "local" focus or significance as well. Those interested in these can consult the online calendar, and the corresponding entries in the blog for the dates and occasions concerned.

118

Lunar Festivals

Any **New Moon** can be an observance of the syncretism of **Antinous with Men**.[174]

Any **Full Moon** can be an observance of the syncretism of **Antinous with Endymion**.[175]

January

1 Dies Ianus: the beginning of the year, and the festival of Ianus, the god of doorways and the bringer of peace. Ianus was the first god of Rome, present even before the Saturnine Golden Age, and thus is honored before all other gods in traditional Roman practice. To paraphrase Ovid's *Fasti*,[176] may we greet each other happily on this day, may we carry out our business to set a standard of good work throughout the year, and may we refrain from disputes and anger. This is also a Roman festival in honor of Asklepios,[177] and thus is a day recognized in the Ekklesía Antínoou to honor the posited syncretism between **Asklepios and Antinous**.[178]

8 **Pan and Antinous**: This date was determined by oracular inquiry as the most appropriate for the recognition of the syncretism of Antinous and Pan.[179] In the imperial cult calendar from Doura-Europos, it is also marked as a festival to an unknown *Divae*.[180] As this

---

[174] P. Sufenas Virius Lupus, *The Syncretisms of Antinous* (Anacortes: The Red Lotus Library, 2010), pp. 70-72.

[175] Lupus, *Syncretisms*, pp. 66-69.

[176] Sir James George Frazer (ed./trans.), *Ovid's Fasti* (Cambridge: Harvard University Press, 1931), pp. 6-23.

[177] Lesley Adkins and Roy A. Adkins, *Dictionary of Roman Religion* (New York: Facts on File, 1996), p. 3 *s.v.* Aesculapius.

[178] Lupus, *Syncretisms*, pp. 9, 98, 109, 141.

[179] Lupus, *Syncretisms*, pp. 33-36; "From Arcadia with Love: Pan and the Cult of Antinous," in Diotima et al. (eds.), *Out of Arcadia: A Devotional Anthology for Pan* (Bibliotheca Alexandrina, 2011), pp. 86-93.

[180] Mary Beard, John North, & Simon Price (eds./trans.), *Religions of Rome, Volume 2: A Sourcebook* (Cambridge: Cambridge University Press, 1998), p. 72.

could be one of a variety of possibilities, including Trajan's wife Diva Plotina, or Hadrian's wife Diva Sabina, therefore the date is reckoned as the *Dies Divae*, a day to celebrate all of the deified imperial women. An ancient Egyptian calendar from Cairo states that this day is "very favorable": "It is the day of the feast of Neith, of the taking of the writing material that is in her house and the going forth of Sobek to guide her majesty."[181]

11 The Cairo Calendar for this day, the 14th in the Second Month of Proyet, says that the auspice for the day is mostly favorable, and that "It is the day of seeing the rebel and killing him by Seth at the prow of the great barque."[182] Further, this was the Roman festival of Juturna,[183] the goddess of sacred fountains, sometimes reckoned as a sister of Castor and Pollux—these twin gods marked a Roman victory in battle by making an apparition in Juturna's fountain, watering their horses.[184] Juturna was also the wife of Ianus, and thus a sacred bath on this day to cleanse ourselves of the dust of battle (whatever our own battles happen to be) is appropriate.

13 *Dies Natalis* of L. Aelius Caesar: An imperial cult calendar found in Tebtynis and dating from the late Antonine period (c. 169=176 CE) records the birthdate of a *divus* on this day,[185] and though it is thought that Hadrian did not allow his adopted successor to be deified (though in the *Historia Augusta* Hadrian was supposed to

---

[181] Bob Brier, *Ancient Egyptian Magic: Spells, Incantations, Potions, Stories, and Rituals* (New York: HarperCollins, 1980), p. 239.

[182] Brier, p. 238.

[183] Frazer, pp. 34-43; Adkins and Adkins, p. 126.

[184] T. P. Wiseman, *The Myths of Rome* (Exeter: University of Exeter Press, 2004), pp. 65-66, 87, 159; Eric M. Orlin, *Foreign Cults in Rome: Creating a Roman Empire* (Oxford: Oxford University Press, 2010), pp. 35-36; Georges Dumézil, *Archaic Roman Religion, with an Appendix on the Religion of the Etruscans*, trans. Philip Krapp, 2 volumes (Chicago and London: University of Chicago Press, 1970), Vol. 2, pp. 412-414; H. H. Scullard, *Festivals and Ceremonies of the Roman Republic* (London: Thames and Hudson, 1981), pp. 65-68.

[185] S. Eitrem and Leiv Amundsen (eds.), *Papyri Osloenses* III (Oslo: Jacob Dybwad, 1936), pp. 45-55 at 54-55.

have quipped that "I have adopted a god, not a son"),[186] it seems that custom nonetheless dictated it in the provinces under the Antonines, both in Egypt and at Doura-Europos in the imperial cult calendar discovered there.[187] Aelius Caesar was born on this day in 101 CE.

21 **Ganymede and Antinous**: As the first day of the Zodiac month of Aquarius, the capture and ascent of Ganymede by Zeus into immortality on Olympus, mirroring the story of Hadrian and Antinous, and honoring the implied syncretism between Antinous and Ganymede,[188] is acknowledged on this day. The Age of Aquarius, the latter constellation of which is Ganymede,[189] has officially begun as of February 2010; and the cultus founded by an archetypal Aquarian in many respects, the *Graeculus* Hadrian, a man of many arts and interests and a devotee of "Greek love," looks forward to sharing an important part in this age.

24 **Dies Natalis Hadriani**: Hadrian's birthday in 76 CE.[190] As Hadrian was one of the most well-known, well-traveled, and widely recognized of the Emperors throughout Roman history, his particular cultus lasted a very long time, and his likenesses are the most frequent of anyone in the ancient world apart from the first Emperor, Augustus. Therefore, marking this date, particularly due to his essential role in the life and eventual cultus of Antinous, is extremely important.

25-26 Paganalia/Sementivae: the Roman moveable festival of the Sementivae, which Ovid's *Fasti* equates with the Paganalia,[191] was held from January 24-26, thus in the context of the Ekklesía Antínoou it has

---

[186] Anthony R. Birley, *Lives of the Later Caesars: The first part of the Augustan History, with newly compiled Lives of Nerva and Trajan* (London and New York: Penguin Books, 1976), p. 91.

[187] Beard, North, and Price, p. 72; though, they do not correctly interpret this date, and misattribute it to a Severan period emperor.

[188] Lupus, *Syncretisms*, pp. .113-119.

[189] Theony Condos, *Star Myths of the Greeks and Romans: A Sourcebook* (Grand Rapids, MI: Phanes Press, 1997), pp. 29-31.

[190] Beard, North, and Price, p. 72; Eitrem and Amundsen, p. 55. See his horoscope in O. Neugebauer and H. B. Van Hoesen, *Greek Horoscopes* (Philadelphia: The American Philosophical Society, 1987), pp. 90-91.

[191] Frazer, pp. 48-53; Adkins and Adkins, pp. 172, 201.

been fixed to these two days. It was a festival of spring sowing, and for the protection and prosperity of the crops in the coming year. A pregnant cow and a spelt cake were offered to Tellus Mater, the "Earth Mother," on the first day, and to Ceres (considered equivalent to Demeter) on the second day. Garlands were hung on the plow oxen, and it seems that masks and puppets (*oscilla*) were also hung on trees in honor of the goddesses on this day.

27 **Dioskouroi (Polydeukes/Pollus) and Antinous:** This was a Roman festival commemorating the foundation of a temple to the Dioskouroi.[192] However, since Castor (Kastor) was the brother of the two more honored in Rome, and received his own temple and festival, this is the date on which Pollux/Polydeukes is honored most by name of the two brothers, in relation to the Dioskouroi's various syncretistic connections to Antinous.[193]

29 ***Stella Antinoi* and Antinous the Navigator:** The day we allocate to the first sighting of the star dedicated to Antinous, which was controversial in its own day, and was somewhat forgotten by many traditional astrological maps in the later centuries of the Western World. In the constellation of Aquila that was later named Antinous/Ganymede as a result,[194] this star first showed itself, and we still reckon the *novae* and celestial activities in this region of the heavens to be important for the Ekklesía Antínoou. The determination of this date is suggested by Chinese astrological records of the period of the second century CE as one in which a new star appeared in 131, only a few months after Antinous' death.[195] On this day, therefore, Antinous' Boat of Millions of Years sets sail for the first time in the liturgical year, heading toward his distant star on a silent course darkened in the emptiness of space. This inaugurates the third aspect of Antinous, the Navigator (or sometimes the Boatman), that which is concerned with the apophatic way, the *Via Negativa*, the unknowing which awaits and enfolds every life on earth. At the

---

[192] Frazer, pp. 52-53; Adkins and Adkins, pp. 41-42.

[193] Lupus, *Syncretisms*, pp. 87-92.

[194] Condos, pp. .33-36.

[195] J. R. Rea (ed.), *The Oxyrhynchus Papyri* 63 (London: Egypt Exploration Society, 1996), §4352, pp. 1-17 at 14.

122

revelation of the greatest mysteries, the only possible reaction is silence and awe. Like the Irish *immrama*, literally stories of "rowing around" and observation of the wonders of the world, all trust is put in the hands of divine beings, and the destination is inscrutable—truly, a "dark night of the soul"—but the journey is taken nonetheless in a spirit of hope and fidelity to all those on the Boat.

February

11 Fornacalia: this was a moveable Roman feast dedicated to the purification of grain-parching ovens (*fornax*), and could occur from anytime from the 5[196] to the 17[196] of February;[196] for Ekklesía Antínoou purposes, it has been fixed on the 11[196] of February. While we may no longer use grain-parching ovens, this is an excellent day to honor one's household deities, to clean, purify, and bless whatever ovens (toaster ovens, microwave ovens, or more traditional ovens!) one uses, as well as paying attention to the ways in which one prepares food and nourishes oneself.

13-22 Parentalia: The festival of the dead in Rome, during which no business was conducted, and going out in public was even limited, as everyone honored their ancestors in private domestic settings. Feasts were held after visits to family tombs.[197] About the 17th, the Quirinalia,[198] also known as the *stultorum feriae*, "feast of fools," little is known, except that it honored Quirinus, one of the original Capitoline Triad who had a *flamen*, and who might have originally been a Sabine war-god/agricultural god (not unlike the later Mars), to whom the deified Romulus was equated. The Feralia was the official end of the observances on the 21st,[199] followed by the Caristia on the 22nd in which good family relations with the living were established.[200] While there are various dates on which The Ekklesía Antínoou's various *Divi* and *Sancti* are celebrated, both individually and collectively, this is a date on which one should honor one's own most esteemed, personal

---

[196] Adkins and Adkins, p. 82.
[197] Adkins and Adkins, pp. 174-175.
[198] Adkins and Adkins, p. 188.
[199] Adkins and Adkins, pp. 75-76.
[200] Adkins and Adkins, p. 40.

ancestors, whether they are of one's own bloodline and genetic heritage or they are "ancestors of heart."

15 Lupercalia: The ancient, traditional Roman festival that was thought to have originated in Arcadia,[201] interpreted in Antinous' day as devoted to the promotion of fertility and in honor of Faunus (often considered equivalent to Pan), whose temple in Rome was founded on February 13.[202] which involved a youthful group of priests who performed a sacrifice of a wolf (or dog) and a goat with milk, engaged in ritual laughter, held a footrace, flogged passing women for luck, and did all of this naked! It is possible Antinous might have served in this capacity if he spent time in Rome before his journey east with Hadrian, and certainly some of the later priests devoted to him are known to have done so; one such was an *equites* named Sufenas, who was both a Lupercus and *phratriarch* of Antinous in Naples, where Antinous was honored in a confraternity together with the hero Eunostos.[203] Further, Antinous appears on coin issues from Sinope in Paphlagonia as Antinous Heros, with the *lupa* suckling Romulus and Remus on the reverse.[204] Antinous Kynegetikos, the "Master of Hounds," the hunter and loyal companion of Hadrian, with his Arcadian origins, is remembered on this day.

23 *Terminalia*: This was an annual Roman festival to Terminus, the god of boundaries and boundary stones, and to the individual *Termini* of each boundary stone that separated people's fields from one another, as well as the limits of cities. Offerings were made at these boundary stones, as well as at the shrine of Jupiter Optimus Maximus in Rome itself.[205] This is an excellent day to re-assess one's own boundaries, both physical as well as non-physical, to clearly establish or re-establish them where necessary, and to be thankful for them and their upholding, as well as committing the protection and continued

---

[201] Beard, North, and Price, pp. 119-124.

[202] Adkins and Adkins, pp. 73-74.

[203] Lupus, *Syncretisms*, pp. 81-86; see the chapter on inscriptions below for more information on Sufenas.

[204] David R. Sear, *Greek Imperial Coins and Their Values: The Local Coinages of the Roman Empire* (London: Seaby Publications Ltd., 1982), p. 122 §1320.

[205] Adkins and Adkins, pp. 221-222.

blessing of the latter to the gods.

24 *Regifugium:* Though considered an unlucky festival by the Romans because it occurred on an even-numbered day, the Regifugium was considered something like "Roman independence day,"[206] since it was held to have marked the date on which the king Tarquin was expelled from Rome, initiating the beginning of the Roman Republic.[207] It was also the date which was repeated twice during leap years, the so-called "bissextile years," because it was the sixth day (in Roman inclusive counting) before the kalends of March. On this date, consider the forces of tyranny in your own individual existence, and how they may be overthrown or expelled; and, make offerings to Libertas, and to Antinous the Liberator, for aid in your ongoing struggles for freedom and liberty, both personal and political.

25 **Adoption of Antoninus Pius:** The second adopted son of Hadrian was adopted on this date in 138 CE,[208] in the final year of Hadrian's life. Antoninus went on to become Emperor, ruling in peace until 161 CE. He granted Hadrian divine honors after his death, for which he gained his epithet, and was the first of the Antonine emperors, all of whom took their names thereafter from Antoninus as part of their imperial titles. He not only completed Hadrian's Mausoleum in Rome, which was used by emperors thereafter up to Caracalla, but he also founded the temple known as the Hadrianeum in Rome in 145 CE; a second wall was attempted in Britain north of Hadrian's Wall, but this was never as successful as his imperial father's; he was also integral in ensuring that the cultus of Antinous did not die out after Hadrian's death, and the completion of Antinoöpolis and its settlement took place especially during Antoninus' reign.

March

1 **Apotheosis of Antoninus Pius:** Together with his wife Faustina (who died in 141), the first Antonine Emperor and Hadrian's successor, both received divine honors after their deaths, and after Antoninus' death on this date in 161, a temple was dedicated to the

---

[206] Adkins and Adkins, p. 190.

[207] Frazer, pp. 106-119.

[208] Anthony R. Birley, *Hadrian: The Restless Emperor* (London and New York: Routledge, 2000), pp. 294-295.

two of them in Rome. One could do no better in honoring him than to use the words of Marcus Aurelius himself, Antoninus' successor, from the sixth book of his Meditations, in which he reminds himself to be "in all things like a pupil of Antoninus; his energy in dealing with what had to be done in accordance with reason, his equitability everywhere, his piety, the serenity of his face, his sweetness, his disregard for empty glory, and his determination to grasp his work. Also, how he allowed nothing to pass without first looking into it well and understanding it clearly; how he put up with those who found fault with him unjustly, without finding fault with them in return; how he never hurried; how he never listened to slander; what an exact critic he was of men's characters and actions, not given to reproaching, not disturbed by rumours, not suspicious, not pretending to be clever; how he was content with little, in the way of lodging, bed, clothes, food and service; how he loved work and was long-suffering. What a man he was, too, for remaining in his place until the evening, because of sparing diet not needing even to relieve nature except at the normal time. And his constancy and uniformity in his friendships, his tolerance of outspoken opposition to his views and his delight when anyone proposed something better than he did; and how he revered the gods without superstition. May your last hour find you like him, with a conscience as clear as his."[209]

5-11 Festival of the *Trophimoi* and Herodes Attikos: This is a week-long festival in honor of the *Trophimoi*—the three foster-sons—of Herodes Attikos, as well as Herodes himself and several members of his family. More information on them, as well as several texts relating to them, both historical and modern, that can be used as liturgical instruments in honoring them can be found in the later sections of this book. The festival begins on the 5th with an honoring of all three of the *Trophimoi*—Achilles, Memnon, and Polydeukion—as well as the *Treiskouroi*, the "three youths" (namely Antinous, Polydeukion, and Lucius Marius Vitalis, on whom more is written later as well). On the 6th, three children of Herodes Attikos are honored: his two daughters Elpinike and Athenais, and his son Regillus. On the 7th, Memnon, the African (and eldest) *trophimos* is honored. On the 8th, Achilles, the

---

[209] Anthony R. Birley, *Marcus Aurelius: A Biography* (London and New York: Routledge, 1993), p. 115.

youngest *trophimos* is commemorated. On the 9th, Polydeukion, the "hero of Herodes," and foremost of the *Trophimoi*, has his main festival. On the 10th, Herodes' wife Appia Annia Regilla, who was heroized after her death, is celebrated. Finally, on the 11th, Herodes Attikos himself has a feast dedicated to him. On the 11th as well, there is a syncretistic honoring of **Antinous and Echmoun**.[210] Offerings particularly beloved of this group of important heroes and *Sancti* include grapes, apples, and milk and honey, the latter of which is a traditional offering for Greek heroes.

15 Procession of Set: In the Cairo Calendar, this date reads as follows: "It is the day of the going forth of Set, son of Nut, to disturb the great ones who check him in his town of Sew. These gods recognize him and repel his followers until none remains."[211] While the general auspice of the day is "very adverse" (as is the day that follows), specific advice is not given for this day; but as the following day is also "very adverse" but no mythic precedent is given, perhaps the advice for that day which follows can be heeded on this day instead: "Do not approach in the morning. Do not wash yourself with water on this day."

17 *Liberalia*: The Roman festival of Liber Pater—another name for Bacchus/Dionysos—and his sister Libera, celebrated with sacrifices, lewd songs and masks hung on trees,[212] with the latter being a definite Dionysian feature. In this "liberated" atmosphere, it was likely that the consumption of wine was an essential aspect of the rites; and it is interesting that this day is St. Patrick's Day in the present, when the whole world celebrates the Roman Briton who converted the King of Tara in Ireland, by doing that most Irish custom: getting completely pissed.

19 *Quinquatrus*: This was a five-day festival, beginning with the Roman celebration of the *dies natalis* of Minerva on the 19th.[213] It is likely that all her temples in Rome—on the Aventine, at the eastern end

---

[210] Lupus, *Syncretisms*, pp. 140-142.
[211] Brier, p. 243.
[212] Adkins and Adkins, p. 133.
[213] Adkins and Adkins, pp. 153-154, 188.

of Nerva's Forum (indeed, Minerva was Nerva's patron goddess, and Hadrian's first legionary command in 105 CE was the I Minervia!),[214] and that of Minerva Capta at the foot of the Caelian Hill—all celebrated this day. Ovid's *Fasti* remarks at one point in his entry on this festival, "When once they have won the favor of Pallas, let girls learn to card the wool and to unload the full distaffs. She also teaches how to traverse the upright warp with the shuttle, and she drives home the loose threads with the comb."[215] While Ovid later gives several possibilities for the etymology of the epithet *Capta*, I have a novel suggestion in relation to Antinous. Athena/Minerva is famed for her transformation of her mortal rival in weaving proficiency, Arakhne, into a spider; and, a particular spider (*Pamphobeteus antinous*) is named after Antinous. Like spiders "capture" their prey in webs, and like Minerva herself eventually caught Arakhne in her own web, perhaps this will be a future festival in honor of the spider aspect of Antinous, and even the proposed "Spider Hunt," in which the metaphorical object of the activity is to face one's own fear and attempt to conquer it. Indeed, Minerva would be an ideal goddess to propitiate in such actions, in any case.

21 **Apotheosis of Sabina**: Though the relationship Hadrian had with his wife appears from all sources as less than happy, she received her due honors as Augusta with deification after her death. She died sometime in late 137, just before Hadrian's adopted son Aelius Caesar, but she was not officially deified until March of 138 CE.[216] Reliefs of the Empress show her being taken into the immortal realms, and statues of her equate her to Ceres, a Roman goddess similar to the Greek Demeter, and thus quite appropriate for thought during the beginning of Spring; Sextus Aurelius Victor says that Hadrian instituted festivals to Ceres (meaning a similar observance to the Mysteries of Eleusis) when he returned to Rome from his eastern journey.[217] As the primary female figure of the triad of the three most

---

[214] Birley, *Hadrian*, p. 50.

[215] Frazer, pp. 180-181.

[216] Birley, *Hadrian*, p. 178; Barbette Stanley Spaeth, *The Roman Goddess Ceres* (Austin: University of Texas Press, 1996), pp. 120, 178-179.

[217] Mary Taliafero Boatwright, *Hadrian and the Cities of the Roman Empire* (Princeton: Princeton University Press, 2003), p. 198.

important deified mortals in the reckoning of the Ekklesía Antínoou— Antinous, Hadrian, and Sabina—she represents the epitome of the divine feminine, the Generative Mother (though she never did have children), the Chaste Virgin (though she was very likely neither!),[218] and the Queen of the World, at this time of the Vernal Equinox, which is at the opposite end of the year as the Ekklesía Antínoou celebration of the Eleusinian Mysteries. She is specifically named on the Obelisk of Antinous, as well as in some of the district names of the city of Antinoöpolis, thus the evidence for her importance in the historical Antinous cult and its constellation with the Imperial Cult is certain. Also, by the rough laws of human physiology, this would be the day roughly corresponding to all the December wonder-child births, so their conceptions would have taken place near this time— again, motherhood and fertility and conception are emphasized. Thus, while we cannot be certain what date Sabina's apotheosis took place, nor do we know any other dates in her life with any certainty, this is the date upon which the Ekklesía Antínoou honors her, and all of the female *Sanctae*.

22-25 *Hilaria*: The three-day festival of Attis, first recorded in Rome in the time of Antoninus Pius. On the 22nd of the month, a procession of *dendrophoroi* or "tree-bearers" went to the temple of Magna Mater in Rome to commemorate her dead lover as a prelude to the actual three-day event. On the first day of the festival proper, the 23rd, the death of Attis was recognized and mourned; on the second day, the 24th, known as the *dies sanguinis* or "day of blood," it is likely that the *taurobolium* bull-sacrifice, as well as rites of self-flagellation and self-castration, were enacted by the *galli* priests; and finally on the third day, the 25th, the Hilaria proper, great rejoicing and celebration took place for the resurrection of the deity. The 25th is also the date on which the conjectural syncretism of **Attis and Antinous** is observed.

25 Hypatia of Alexandria: While the date of the birth of Hypatia is as unknown as the exact date of her death, it is known that it took place

---

[218] For further reflections on these ideas, see Erynn Rowan Laurie, "His Mother's Whole Body Heals: Gender and Ritual in the Ekklesía Antínoou," in *Women's Voices in Magic*, ed. Brandy Williams (Stafford: Megalithica, 2009), pp. 167-173.

during Lent of the year 410. As an important female historical figure, scientist, mathematician, philosopher, and "pagan martyr," Hypatia is commemorated as a *Sancta* of the Ekklesía Antínoou on this date.

April

1 Veneralia: The old festival of Venus, commemorating the day which commences her sacred month.[219] It is also a festival, for those who follow the Serpent Path in the Ekklesía Antínoou, known as the **Glykonalia** in honor of the snake god Glykon. Glykon has many similarities in common with Antinous, including the start of his cultus being in the 130s CE, his origins in Asia Minor, and his oracular status;[220] but, there is also one occasion on which an inscription in Rome, by one Aelia Ehorte, to the *Deus Amabilis*, might be equally to either Phosphoros/Lucifer (the god of the morning star), Glykon, or to Antinous![221]

4-10 Megalensia: The week-long national holiday of Magna Mater/Cybele in Rome, first established in 191 BCE with the foundation of her temple in Rome. Processions carrying the goddess' image occurred throughout the week, to the accompaniment of cymbals, until the final day, reckoned as the goddess' birthday, on which great games were held in the Circus Maximus.[222] In the practice of the Ekklesía Antínoou, particular days in the period of this festival have been given to certain figures in the story of Cybele and Attis: on the 5th, Agdistis is honored; on the 6th, Attis; on the 7th, Cybele herself; on the 8th and 9th, the many *galli* and *archigalli* who served her in the ancient world are remembered; and then on the 10th, the various goddesses of Anatolia who became known as "Magna Mater" in Rome

---

[219] Adkins and Adkins, p. 232.

[220] Martin Henig, "*Ita intellexit numine inductus tuo*: Some Personal Interpretations of Deity in Roman Religion," in Martin Henig and Anthony King (eds.), *Pagan Gods and Shrines of the Roman Empire* (Oxford: Oxford University Committee for Archaeology, 1986), pp. 159-169 at 160.

[221] Hugo Meyer, *Antinoos: Die archäologischen Denkmäler unter Einbeziehung des numismatischen und epigraphischen Materials sowie der literarischen Nachrichten, Ein Beitrag zur Kunst- und Kulturgeschichte der hadrianisch-frühantoninischen Zeit* (Munich: Wilhelm Fink, 1991), p. 165.

[222] Adkins and Adkins, pp. 150-151.

are celebrated.

5 Death of Kurt Cobain: The blond front-man and guitarist, or as he sometimes preferred, "mouth," of the archetypal grunge-band Nirvana died on this day in 1994 (whether it was suicide, or perhaps something else, remains somewhat uncertain). A native of Aberdeen, WA, the music of Nirvana was considered the founding strains of the "Seattle-Sound," which in one of his journals Kobain said "actually came from Portland, Oregon." In the best Western Washington fashion, he was immediately honored with a candlelight vigil at the Space Needle in Seattle Center (which itself was "born" on April 17, 1962)—about as close as the Northwest gets to an acknowledgement of apotheosis. He was a champion of anti-misogyny and queer rights as well, and is considered the "voice of his generation," Generation-X, in its angst-ridden anti-establishment extreme. He viewed his commercial success as the use of the tools of the "empire" towards a revolution from within; however, more than a decade after his death, it seems that his appropriation by many of the establishment people he so resented in real life is sadly ironic indeed. While he may not have appreciated it, we consider him a *Sanctus* anyway.

21 **Megala Antinoeia**: An important and major, multiply-faceted observance, of which one or all parts should be celebrated by members of the Ekklesía Antínoou according to taste and interest. A date connected to many goddesses, games, city foundations, and...bears! *Antinoeia*: The Sacred Games commemorating Antinous, taken part in by ephebes, youths of the ages between about seventeen and twenty-two. Many atheletic competitions, including footraces, wrestling and boxing, chariot races, swimming, and rowing were held; but also artistic competitions, possibly involving music and poetry (for which the Curium Citharode's hymn was probably a winner) as well as theatre (the latter in the Dionysian tradition) also took place, in the hopes of gaining the coveted *Antinoeios*, or red-lotus flower garland. These began to take place as early as 131, less than a year after Antinous' death. Hadrain founded games in many cities, including "mystical" games based most likely on re-enactments of mystery rites or episodes from mythology. <u>*Veneralia*</u>: The foundation by Hadrian of the Temple of Venus and Roma Aeterna,[223] one of his greatest building projects in Rome, made with the intent of showing that though Civitas Romae was the child of Venus (through Aeneas) and Mars (through Romulus), but that Venus was the more important of the two. The original Veneralia was on April 1, as this entire month was considered sacred to the goddess, but the celebration of the foundation of the temple shifted the focus. The great goddess of love emerged from the ocean and landed first on Cyprus, where it was said that Aphrodite would yearly renew herself by bathing in a spring to cleanse herself of the bad influences of males; as an annual purification rite, this seems an appropriate time to be renewed in the waters of early spring, wherever you might find them. _Natalis Urbis:_ Originally, April 21ˢᵗ was also the festival of the Parilia, sacred to the deity Pares, who was associated with shepherds, but it was not known whether this god was singular or dual, nor male or female. Various events took place having to do with the guardianship and maintenance of sheep and flocks, including distribution of blood from the October Horse sacrifice and the Vestal Virgin's distribution of burnt ashes of cattle from the Fordicidia—a festival on April 15 in honor of the Roman earth-goddess Tellus Mater.[224] The sheep were lead between bonfires in order to bless and protect them on the Parilia, which is reminiscent of the Irish practice on Beltaine with their cattle, and Beltaine is not far off from this holiday. This was also considered the traditional foundation day of Rome itself, in 753 BCE; but after the commissioning of Hadrian's new temple to Venus and Roma Aeterna in 121, it was re-instituted as the festival of _Natalis Urbis_ "in the 874ᵗʰ year A.U.C. (_ab urbe condita_)," and celebrated across the Empire, from Doura-Europos to Northern Britain.[225] This was also traditionally held to be the birthdate of Rome's second king, Numa Pompilius, the peaceful successor to Romulus to whom Hadrian liked comparing himself. _Venatio Ursae/Erotikon:_ Also, we commemorate on this day the Bear-Hunts of Hadrian—he had one that killed a she-bear in Mysia in 123 or 124, because of which, Hadrian commissioned the city of Hadrianoutherae, "Hadrian's Hunts," in Bithynia, and later coins from that city show

---

[223] Mary Taliaferro Boatwright, _Hadrian and the City of Rome_ (Princeton: Princeton University Press, 1987), pp. 120-128.
[224] Adkins and Adkins, p. 175; Beard, North, and Price, pp. 63, 65.
[225] Adkins and Adkins, p. 161; Beard, North, and Price, pp. 68, 73.

Antinous on one side and a bear on the other.[226] But his successful killing of a bear in the Spring of 125 near Thespiae on his Greek sojourn is of further interest.[227] A bear hunt is commemorated on a tondo of the Arch of Constantine, with a subsequent sacrifice to Diana/Artemis[228]—the Greek form of the goddess' name contains the Indo-European word for "bear"; indeed, bears are connected to many goddesses, and to various aspects of homoeroticism. Thespiae was the seat of the god Eros, and Hadrian's dedication and poem found near there, commemorating his slaying of the bear, expresses a wish to the Cyprian Aphrodite Ourania (goddess of homoerotic love) and the archer Eros (connected to homoerotic love of youths), by the flowering garden of Narcissus, to have a lover granted to him—thus this day is also called the "Erotikon." (The inscription can be read in a subsequent chapter.) Hadrian may have met Antinous by this time, but it is not certain; Marguerite Yourcenar's book certainly puts this incident in that context.[229] Further, Antinous' homeland of Bithynia was a colony founded by Arcadians, and the Arcadians trace their roots back to Arkas (whose name means "bear"), son of Kallisto, who was a beloved of Artemis, and became the constellation Ursa Major.[230] In a sense, Hadrian's re-foundation of Rome based in a dedicatory gesture to Venus, and a wish for love expressed to Aphrodite and Eros in Thespiae on the occasion of successfully hunting a bear, all point toward his eventual attainment of his own love, a descendant of the bear Arkas (which is the Latin word for an Arcadian in its form *Arcas*), the Arcadian-Bithynian Antinous, who was remembered for centuries afterwards in the form of his sacred games, which were especially celebrated in the Greek states, Bithynia, and Arcadian Mantineia. While Joseph Campbell used the following statement to make an entirely different point, it bears repeating here: AMOR, "love," spelled backwards is "ROMA"; and it would not be surprising if Hadrian realized this himself. As a further result, this is the date on which we celebrate the entry of **Antinous the Lover** into precedence throughout the majority of our ritual year. The Lover represents the Via Positiva in

---

[226] Boatwright, *Hadrian and the Cities*, pp. 184-190.

[227] Birley, *Hadrian*, pp. 184-185.

[228] Boatwright, *Hadrian and the City*, pp. 192-194, 198.

[229] Marguerite Yourcenar, *Hadrian's Memoirs*, trans. Grace Frick (New York: Farrar, Straus and Young, 1955), p. 160.

[230] Condos, pp. 197-200.

mystical practice, the praise of creation through words, celebration, and acknowledgement of divine beauty in all things. The Megala Antinoeia represents an amazing set of coincidence in correspondences and events on a day that should loom large in one's sacred calendar. If a wish for love is harbored in one's heart, today is the day to work poems, prayers, and magic to bring it about...or just pick up the phone and call the guy!

25 Serapeia: On April 25th, the calendar of Filocalus (from the mid-4th century CE) records the celebration of this festival in Rome.[231] Serapis is the highly syncretistic deity that helped to fuse Greek and Egyptian religion together during the reign of the early Ptolemies,[232] and this continued once Rome conquered Egypt as well. As a syncretistic deity, he is in many respects comparable to Antinous, and in some sense is his "grandfather" because of the super-syncretistic precedent that he set.[233] Indeed, Hadrian himself revered Serapis, and built a temple for him in Rome.[234] Further, today is the most appropriate date to honor the syncretism of **Antinous with Apis**.[235] It was also the Roman festival of the Robigalia, in which a rust-colored dog and sheep were sacrificed to propitiate Robigus and Robiga, deities who presided over grain rust and mildew, in order to prevent these blights from attacking the crops in Rome.[236]

May

1 **Venatio Apri/The Boar Hunt**: Coinciding with the Celtic quarter-day (under the Irish name) of Beltaine, this day is connected with a number of the hunter figures to whom Antinous was

---

[231] Beard, North, and Price, p. 68.

[232] John E. Stambaugh, *Sarapis Under the Early Ptolemies* (Leiden: E. J. Brill, 1972).

[233] P. Sufenas Virius Lupus, "My Travels with Serapis (and Antinous)," in Rebecca Buchanan, Jeremy J. Baer et al. (eds.), *Waters of Life: A Devotional Anthology for Isis and Serapis* (Eugene: Bibliotheca Alexandrina, 2009), pp. 191-207.

[234] Rabun Taylor, "Hadrian's Serapeum in Rome," *American Journal of Archaeology* 108.2 (April, 2004), pp. 223-266.

[235] Lupus, *Syncretisms*, pp. 137-139.

[236] Adkins and Adkins, p. 192.

syncretized, including the syncretisms of **Belenus and Antinous**,[237] and **Androklos and Antinous**.[238] Hadrian's favorite horse Borysthenes, to whom he composed a poem inscribed on the horse's gravesite, speaks a great deal about boar hunting (and is given below). The hunting *tondo* on the Arch of Constantine featuring Hadrian on a boar-hunt, possibly including Antinous,[239] could have originally taken place in 129, while the imperial party was passing through Bithynia and the rest of Asia Minor. This festival is at the opposite point of the year to the death of Antinous—indeed, this would have been the high point of his youthful vigor and skill. Unlike the later hunt of the Antinoan year, this one is concerned with success and the bringing about of plenty, of sumptuousness, and of sensuality.

7 Boukoklepteia: This modern Greek festival, innovated by Sannion, is devoted to Hermes the cattle-rustler, and the aftermath of his stealing of Apollon's cattle in terms of telling lies and making the world's first fart joke.[240] Games of chance (over which Hermes rules), storytelling, and competitive joke telling should accompany the observances on this day, as well as attempts at telling the biggest and most extravagant lies possible while remaining straight-faced.

10 **The Antinoöpolitan Lovers:** This date, noted as 15 Pachon on a painting from Antinoöpolis depicting two males who were probably lovers,[241] is the date we commemorate the historical personages who we know—either by name from inscriptions or by face from paintings such as this one—that contributed to the devotional life of the ancient cult of Antinous. Known or unknown, whether we have dates associated with them or not, they are the *Sancti* who have made our modern work

---

[237] Lupus, *Syncretisms*, pp. 25-26.

[238] Lupus, *Syncretisms*, pp. 128-131. See also Gustav Blum, "Numismatique d'Antinoos," *Journal International d''Archéologie Numismatique* 16 (1914), pp. 33-70 at 41-42, for Ephesian coins that link Antinous and Androklos.

[239] Boarwright, *Hadrian and the City*, pp. 192, 195.

[240] Norman O. Brown, *Hermes the Thief* (Great Barrington: Lindisfarne Press, 1990).

[241] Ann E. Haeckl, "Brothers or Lovers? A New Reading of the 'Tondo of the Two Brothers'," *Bulletin of the American Society of Papyrologists* 38 (2001), pp. 63-78 and Plate 6.

possible, and thus this day is the *Dies Sancti Ignoti.*

15   Mercurius et Maia: This was the date of the festival of Mercury in Rome, commemorating the foundation of his temple in 495 BCE,[242] as well as the day on which his mother Maia was celebrated, who gave her name to this month in the Roman calendar.[243] As perhaps one of the foremost of the several gods to whom Antinous was syncretized, and the patron god of Arcadia in his Greek form Hermes, this day is an important one to consider, and to celebrate **Hermes and Antinous, and Antinous as Neos Hermes.** As the ruler of the Zodiac sign of Gemini in later May, Mercury's qualities of youthfulness, communication and the ability to reconcile oppositions are good attributes to meditate upon at this time of the year.

16 Festival of Bes: Antinous' holy city of Antinoöpolis was sometimes called "Besantinoë," and it seems that a shrine of Bes existed on the spot as well. Further, the *deme* in which Hadrian was enrolled at Athens as a citizen was named Besa, which was considered to have been named after the Egyptian god.[244] Bes is an interesting and multi-faceted deity, connected with dreams and oracles (just as Antinous is), and so he is honored on this day.

19 Bendideia: The Athenians held a festival in honor of the Thracian horse goddess, Bendis, with festivals on 19 and 20 Thargelion,[245] a month which generally fell in the range of May, thus we have fixed the festival on this date. While she was syncretized to Artemis and Hekate by the Greeks, it seems very likely that in Bithynia, which was a place that considered itself Thracian in origin, that the local mother-goddess with whom Antinous would have been acquainted would have been Bendis; and because of her connections with hunting, horses, and the moon, and these are all attributes Antinous eventually shared, it is appropriate to celebrate the Thracian dimensions of late antique Greek

---

[242] Adkins and Adkins, p. 152.

[243] Adkins and Adkins, p. 139.

[244] Royston Lambert, *Beloved and God: The Story of Hadrian and Antinous* (New York: Viking, 1984), pp. 127, 138, 150, 160.

[245] Christopher Planeaux, "The Date of Bendis' Entry into Attica," *The Classical Journal* 96.2 (December 2000-January 2001), pp. 165-192.

culture on this day.

22 Canis Erigoneius: In Ovid's *Fasti*, it is reported that on this day, the XI Kal. Iun., the star of the dog of Erigone rises.[246] Erigone was the daughter of Ikarios, the first man to harvest wine in Dionysian myth, whose dog Maira found his murdered body. Maira was identified with the dog-star Sirius, which does not rise for another two months—strange. However, this is also my own birthdate, and thus this canine connection seems notable simply as a matter of personal interest to me! The date of one's own birthday, however, as being celebrated as important by members of particular religious groups has precedent in the Lanuvium collegium's practices,[247] and it is suggested that one's honoring of **the Daimon Antinous** take place on one's own birthdate. It is also the beginning of the Zodiac period of Gemini, and thus it can be a day to honor the **Dioskouroi and Antinous.**

Memorial Day Whenever this date falls in late May is a good occasion on which to honor the syncretism of **Achilleus and Antinous.**[248]

29 Ambarvalia: This was a ritual of lustration for the fields and farms that supported Rome; the corresponding lustral occasion for the city of Rome itself was the *Amburbium* (though when the latter was held is unknown). It involved processions around the fields, and sacrifices of pigs, sheep, and oxen—known as the *suovetaurilia*—as well as honoring of the deities Ceres, Bacchus, Mars, Jupiter, and Ianus.[249]

June

1 Marguerite Porete Day: In 1310, this was the day that Marguerite Porete was burned at the stake by the Paris Inquisition, a day that should live in infamy forever. Not only was she the most profound and difficult mystical theologian to have ever written in the Christian tradition, but the inquisitors who condemned her lambasted her as a

---

[246] Frazer, pp. 314-315.
[247] Beard, North, and Price, p. 294.
[248] Lupus, *Syncretisms*, pp. 57-61.
[249] Adkins and Adkins, pp. 6-7.

pseudo-mulier ("false woman") because they did not believe she could have been a "real" woman because of her education, her audacity, and her disobedience of their authority. As a result, I think she is not only a great spiritual exemplar, but also a figure of gender variance. I have celebrated this day since the year 2000 (twice that year: an initial inauguration of the feast on May 10, and then a second observance on the day proper, June 1), usually by reading her writings[250] to others (especially those of like minds who have not heard of her), and with e-mails to relevant spiritual and queer spiritual groups on her life, and often by a short ritual is also completed, either with candles or a bonfire present. Marguerite Porete was the first *Sancta* recognized in the practice of modern Antinoan devotion on Foundation Day in 2002.

11 Death of Alexander the Great: On this day in 323 BCE (approximately, between the 10th and 12th of June), Alexander the Great died, and after receiving divine honors, early in the next year he was entombed in Alexandria. One of Alexander's foremost biographers, Arrian of Nikomedia, was a friend of Hadrian and a fellow countryman of Antinous, and it not only seems likely that Alexander's various examples inspired and supported Hadrian's actions and his furtherance of the cultus of Antinous, but also that Hadrian's cultus to Antinous influenced certain details in the biography of Alexander that Arrian wrote.

12 *Rhodophoria*: A "rose festival" in honor of Aphrodite. Along with the Megala Antinoeia's various festivities, this would be an ideal time to honor the Greek form of the goddess, to thank her for all of the loves in one's life (not just the erotic or romantic ones, but also patriotism and enjoyment of one's work, etc.), and to ask for further boons in all of the areas over which she presides.

14 *Naukrateia*: The Egyptian emporium of Naukratis was the city upon which the constitution of Antinoöpolis was based.[251] The deities of the city—Zeus, Hera, Apollon, Aphrodite, and the Dioskouroi—

---

[250] Ellen J. Babinsky (trans.), *Marguerite Porete: The Mirror of Simple Souls* (New York and Mahwah: Paulist Press, 1993).

[251] Boatwright, *Hadrian and the Cities*, p. 194.

should be honored on this date, as well as the Pharaoh, Amasis, who loved Greek culture so much that he founded the city. I wrote a short story based on this festival called "Reunion."[252]

21 **Apollon and Antinous**: As this day is the Summer Solstice, when the sun is highest and the day longest, and thus it is ostensibly a "happy" time of the year, it is also a day tinged with sadness, for the sun will never be this brilliant again in the year, and thus at the high-point of the sun, Apollon strikes down by accident the beautiful flower of Hyakinthos, reminding us not only of the seasonal change, but also that even the most beautiful things, including love, only last for a short while. While the brilliant and joyous aspects of Antinous' syncretism with Apollon, as Neos Pythios and Musegetikos[253] are acknowledged, so too is it apparent that things must be enjoyed while they can be, and that one's "day in the sun" should never be taken for granted.

27 The Stonewall Riots: In 1969, a group of drag queens, butch lesbians, and other queer folks at the Stonewall Inn on Christopher Street in New York's Greenwich Village fought back against another raid by police, and several days of riots ensued. This event is hearkened as the beginning of the public gay liberation movement, and so the Ekklesía Antínoou marks it as one of importance both culturally and spiritually in the lives of modern queer people.

July

1 **Disciplina**: One of the practices of the Imperial Army that arose during Hadrian's time,[254] and very likely under his direct inspiration, was the cultus of Disciplina, or Disciplina Augusta. This date, therefore, has been innovated in the Ekklesía Antínoou to honor this most essential goddess.

4 *Dies Natalis* **of Diva Matidia Augusta**: The Imperial Cult Calendar

---

[252] P. Sufenas Virius Lupus, "Reunion," in Rebecca Buchanan et al. (eds.), *The Scribing Ibis: An Anthology of Pagan Fiction in Honor of Thoth* (Bibliotheca Alexandrina, 2011), pp. 105-116.

[253] Lupus, *Syncretisms*, pp. 23-27.

[254] Adkins and Adkins, p. 63.

from Doura-Europos designates this date as the birth of Matidia,[255] Hadrian's mother-in-law, whom he deified and for whom he composed a funeral oration which has been mostly preserved, which is given in a subsequent chapter below.

9 **First Entry of Hadrian into the City of Rome:** As Emperor, in the tradition of Julius Caesar, Hadrian was also the *pontifex maximus*, the highest religious official of the Empire, its "head priest," whether in name only or in actuality. He very likely accepted this title on his first visit to Rome on this date in 118, just under a year after the time he was officially hailed as Emperor after Trajan's death, when all the titles and ceremonies which recognized him as the living *Augustus* were conferred.[256] As a religious seeker and devotee of the mysteries, Hadrian took his title quite seriously, and his promulgation of the cults of Disciplina, his deified wife Sabina, of Antinous, and of the *Divae* Matidia, Plotina, and Domitia Paulina were all done by his powers as highest priest of the Empire.

10 **Death of Hadrian:** In 138 CE, Hadrian died, and soon after was deified by his adopted son and successor Antoninus Pius. The verse he wrote on death before it occurred is given later in this book, but it would be an appropriate reading for recitation and study on this date.

16 **Silvanus and Antinous, Antinoan Arbor Day, Hadrian's Wall Day:** Around this date in 122, Hadrian arrived in Britain, having gone there to correct various abuses and to personally oversee the transfer of a legion to the island province. The earliest documents from this visit, giving privileges to soldiers, are dated to July 17 of that year.[257] He also embarked upon one of his most grand and enduring building projects, the construction of Hadrian's Wall from nearly shore to shore across the north, from Arbeia, Pons Aelius and Segedunum (modern South Shields, Newcastle and Wallsend) to Maia (Bowness), and the *vallum* and forts which augmented it. He left inscriptions at such places as Condercum (Benwell), and probably also went hunting in the prime wilds of Britain, where boar were common. A larger-than-

---

[255] Beard. North, and Price, p. 73.
[256] Birley, *Hadrian*, pp. 93-101.
[257] Birley, *Hadrian*, pp. 127-128.

life-size statue of him, quite young-looking and virile, was turned up in the Thames, of which the damaged head and possibly one hand has been found. This activity was all before he ever would have met Antinous. Because this visit to Britain was connected to establishing the outermost northern boundary of the Empire, it has been given as a day to honor Silvanus' syncretism to Antinous, as Silvanus is connected to boundaries, and he has several further syncretisms in Britannia (e.g. Cocidius, Callirius, Vinotonus, and Pantheus). Silvanus has no "official" holidays recorded in the Roman calendar, nor did he have any temples dedicated to him; but, he was rather uniquely honored amongst the Emperors Trajan, Hadrian, and Antoninus Pius.[258] This date has been chosen, therefore, because it was the culmination of a pilgrimage I made to Hadrian's Wall in 2003, a day on which I held a ritual in the ruins of an ancient temple in Condercum (a for where Hadrian himself left an inscription), and on which there were three *novae* in the constellation of Aquila/Antinous. Because of Silvanus' other connections to hunting and to forests, Hadrian's acts to preserve the forests of Judea are also honored on this day, which should be spent (if possible) in appreciating and enjoying the outdoors, and in thanksgiving for all the things which the forest provides for human usage. Remembering as well, therefore, the destruction of Judea in the Bar Kochba Rebellion/Second Jewish War in the mid-130s, also might be desirable for some people on this date, as well as the honoring of the ancient heroes Gilgamesh and Enkidu, who came to the forests of Lebanon (which Hadrian sought to protect) on their adventures.

20 Birth of Alexander the Great: The portended birth of the divine son of Philip II of Macedon to the maenad Olympias happened on this day in 356 BCE, on the same day that the Temple of Artemis at Ephesus burned down—it was said that such was no wonder, since the goddess herself would have been at Olympias' bedside to ensure the easy birth of the future divine king! And, strangely enough, Alexander later in life enjoyed dressing as the great virgin goddess.

23 *Neptunalia*: The Roman festival of Neptune is one of the oldest

---

[258] Peter F. Dorcey, *The Cult of Silvanus: A Study in Roman Folk Religion* (Leiden: E. J. Brill, 1992).

festivals in the Roman calendar, and yet very little is known of it.[259] For our purposes, it is an excellent day to honor the syncretism of **Poseidon and Antinous.**[260]

25   Dies Caniculares: The beginning of the so-called "dog days" of Summer, the rising of the star Sirius was an important date in the calendars of the ancient world. In Egypt, the star was called Sothis and was sacred to Isis; its rising heralded the inundation of the Nile, the end of the Egyptian year, and Hermanubis was honored on this day.[261] Sirius rose in the ancient Egyptian "Sothic cycle" calendar on June 21, which is when it rose in about 3000 BCE, but as the earth has tilted slowly, this is its rising now (usually between the 25th of July and August 1). It is possible that both the Hyakinthia and the Carneia, festivals dedicated to dead flower-identified lovers of Apollon, also coincided with this day,[262] either in the ancient dates of the Sothic cycle or in its later summer manifestations from subsequent periods. Sirius was also identified as the star which Gilgamesh saw falling to earth, which was his comrade/lover Enkidu, and the lesbian lovers Agido and Hagesichora, Spartan priestesses of Artemis Orthia, were also identified poetically with Sirius. Antinous Kynegetikos, the Master of Hounds, receives our attentions on this day, along with Hermanubis, who was honored in Antinoöpolis (as evidenced by the tomb painting mentioned on May 10 above). Many traditions of canines, cynocephali, and related figures are connected to this day, but also the heroic accomplishments of Aristaios, and the festival of Adonis. Thus, the syncretisms of **Aristaios and Antinous**[263] and **Adonis and Antinous**[264] are also observed on this day. Offerings to Zeus, Herakles, and Dionysos would also not go amiss on this day.

31   River Gods and Antinous: Antinous is syncretized to the river-

---

[259] Adkins and Adkins, p. 163.

[260] Lupus, *Syncretisms*, pp. 53-56.

[261] David Gordon White, *Myths of the Dog-Man* (Chicago and London: University of Chicago Press, 1991), pp. 42-46.

[262] Michael Pettersson, *Cults of Apollo at Sparta: The Hyakinthia, the Gymnopaidiai and the Karneia* (Stockholm: Svenska Institutet i Athen, 1992).

[263] Lupus, *Syncretisms*, pp. 62-65.

[264] Lupus, *Syncretisms*, pp. 44-49.

deities Alpheios and Cydnos,[265] and this date is one on which they can be honored, as well as the life-giving necessity of one's own local rivers. Pray for their protection and preservation on this day.

August

11 **Accession of Hadrian:** In Nikomedia, capital of the Roman Province of Bithynia, Hadrian was declared Emperor by the Legions after the death of Trajan in 117.[266] Empress Plotina perhaps had a part to play in this; but nonetheless, the acceptance by the Legions was the necessary prerequisite for the subsequent success of Hadrian's imperial career. On this day in 128, he accepted the title *Pater Patriae*, one of the typical imperial titles, after refusing it for a number of years.[267]

13 *Natalis Dianae:* The birthday of Diana, as celebrated in Rome, commemorating the foundation of her temple on the Aventine Hill in the 6th century BCE,[268] and at the Lanuvium Temple of Antinous and Diana.[269] As Lanuvium is near Lake Nemi, where Diana Nemorensis was particularly revered, this is also significant. Both Diana and Silvanus (in whose likeness Antinous is portrayed in a relief sculpture from Lanuvium, which was likely on private property in the town, and not in the Temple itself) were deities revered by slaves, and slaves could be part of the collegial activities at the Lanuvium temple; this date was taken as a holiday of importance to slaves in Italy, any of whom could take refuge in Diana's temples. Thus, the importance of this date in its connection to Antinous the Liberator who frees all from bondage is one possible significance. However, it was also the festival of Vertumnus in Rome,[270] and was a festival in honor of Castor (Kastor) of the Dioskouroi as well,[271] so it can be a date on which to honor the syncretisms of **Vertumnus and Antinous** and the **Dioskouroi and Antinous** (particularly Castor). Hercules Victor's temple in Rome was

---

[265] Lupus, *Syncretisms*, pp. 132-136.
[266] Birley, *Hadrian*, pp. 77-80.
[267] Birley, *Hadrian*, pp. 189-202.
[268] Adkins and Adkins, p. 60.
[269] Beard, North, and Price, p. 294.
[270] Adkins and Adkins, p. 236.
[271] Adkins and Adkins, pp. 41-42.

also founded on this day.[272]

20 Battle of Chaeronea: The battle in 338 BCE in which King Philip II of Macedon fought and killed the entire Sacred Band of Thebes, the army of paired charioteer-chariot warrior lovers. His son Alexander the Great, only eighteen at the time, was said by Plutarch to have been the first of the Macedonians to break the battle-line of the Sacred Band. Philip's sadness at this necessity was great, and a memorial in the form of a lion statue was erected at the site, where archaeologists in the nineteenth century discovered the remains of nearly 300 men—with the number of the Sacred Band said to be 150 pairs of lovers.[273] The Order of Chaeronea, founded by George Cecil Ives (an Ekklesía Antínoou *Sanctus*), was founded in the late 1800s on the spiritual homoerotic principles of the Sacred Band and this historic battle.[274]

21-22 *Venatio Leonis*/**Lion Hunt and Festival of the Red Lotus**: The famed Lion Hunt of Antinous and Hadrian[275] is celebrated on this day at the end of Leo; and the subsequent first appearance of the Red Lotus which sprang from the lion's blood is on the following day, a miraculous sign that Antinous had been victorious and had become the Lion-Hearted One in the strength of his love and devotion. (Various ancient texts recount this event, which are given in a subsequent chapter of the present book.) However, unlike the Boar Hunt in May, this hunt is not meant to be unproblematically "successful," as Antinous was nearly killed in the process of it, had it not been for Hadrian's intervention. This is a day to ponder the spiritual virtues, often obscured, in the experience of failure and powerlessness, and also how the assistance, support, and presence of our friends and lovers can be essential to any success we might have in

---

[272] Adkins and Adkins, pp. 100-101.

[273] David Leitao, "The Legend of the Sacred Band," in Martha C. Nussbaum and Julia Shivola (eds.), *The Sleep of Reason: Erotic Experience and Sexual Ethics in Ancient Greece and Rome* (Chicago: University of Chicago Press, 2002), pp. 143-169.

[274] Randy P. Conner, David Hatfield Sparks and Mariya Sparks (eds.), *Cassells' Encyclopedia of Queer Myth, Symbol and Spirit* (London and New York: Cassell, 1997), p. 257.

[275] Birley, *Hadrian*, pp. 240-242; Lambert, pp. 118-121; Boatwright, *Hadrian and the City*, pp. 191-199.

life. On the 21st, we recognize the syncretism of **Herakles and Antinous**[276] since he was the great lion-slaying hero; and on the 22nd, we honor all of the **Flower-Heroes and Antinous**, including Hyakinthos, Hylas, Narcissus, Krokus, Ampelos, Daphne, and Kyparissos.[277]

29 Matidia named *"Augusta"* in 112 CE: On this date, Trajan named his sister Marciana, and her daughter Matidia, *Augusta*, which was usually only a title reserved for the Emperor's wife herself.[278]

September

6 Lucius Marius Vitalis: By this day in 128 CE, Antinous and Hadrian had probably arrived in Athens in preparation to receive the Eleusinian Mysteries later in the month, which prefigure the death and rejuvenation of Antinous. The imperial entourage stayed there until the early months of 129. This was the Hellenophile *"Graeculus"* Hadrian's favorite city in the empire, where he lived from 110 and over which he was *Archon* in his early career in 112, and during which time he met King Philopappus and his sister Julia Balbilla—who became friends with Sabina at that time—as well as their further relative, the young Spartan C. Julius Eurykles Herculanus, who later made an altar dedication in Mantineia to Antinous. At this point, Antinous was likely to have visited the theatre of Dionysus in which his priest later had a seat of honor, and may also have enjoyed Platonic learning and Epicurean philosophical discourses. But this time was also touched with sadness, as a youth of roughly Antinous' own age, Lucius Marius Vitalis, died at the age of seventeen years and fifty-five days (as his epitaph, translated and discussed in a further chapter below, states). Before becoming the Neos Iakkhos after his Eleusinian initiation, this death of his companion no doubt set Antinous' mind toward his own mortality. We honor Lucius Marius Vitalis, called *Sanctissimus* in his funeral inscription, as the "Prince of the *Sancti*" and one of the *Treiskouroi* in the Ekklesia Antinoou.

---

[276] Lupus, *Syncretisms*, pp. 93-96.

[277] Lupus, *Syncretisms*, pp. 120-127.

[278] Julian Bennett, *Trajan: Optimus Princeps*, Second Edition (London and New York: Routledge, 2001), p. 183.

145

18 Dies Natalis Traiani: On this date, sometime between 53 and 56 CE, the Emperor Trajan was born.[279]

19 Dies Natalis Antonini Pii: The birthday of Antoninus Pius in 86 CE. This is also the date on which we have chosen to mark the syncretism of **Eunostos and Antinous**.[280]

21 **The Eleusinian Mysteries**: As agricultural mysteries connected with the regeneration of the earth, the Autumnal Equinox and its common coincidence with the harvest season, all seem to indicate that this would be a good date to observe the initiation of Antinous (and Hadrian's second initiation) into these rituals,[281] and his "first meeting" with Persephone, which would have been in 128. The syncretism of **Antinous as Neos Iakkhos** is also marked on this occasion.

23 Celebrate Bisexuality Day: This is an annual observance. Many may not know this, but it was through bisexual theology that I got into queer theology, and most of the difficulties I saw in queer theology (which is mostly "gay theology") when I started that work still apply today, sadly, in every religion where such a thing as queer theology exists. Bisexuality is a persistent phenomenon, and one that has been around–at least from a descriptive viewpoint–for a very long time. In fact, most premodern "gay" people were actually bisexual, whether by choice or necessity. Alexander the Great certainly was; Hadrian certainly was; and, likely as not, Antinous would have been had he lived longer. (And, myth took care of it for him a century and a half after his death, as Selene was suggested to have been responsible for his apotheosis in a text from the 280s CE because she wanted him for her bridegroom!) And, the list of deities who are technically bisexual...well, forget it, because it's nearly all of them! So, it's very important to remember this, and to be as inclusive as possible in one's theological enterprises under the "queer" rubric; and, thus, it's important to give the "B" and the "T" dates of their own outside of the usual Pride and other LGBTQ events, since that often, in practice, just means "gay" (and not always even "gay/lesbian").

---

[279] Bennett, pp. 12-13; Beard, North, and Price, p.74.
[280] Lupus, *Syncretisms*, pp. 81-86.
[281] Birley, *Hadrian*, p. 215; Lambert, pp. 105-106.

146

25 Carpocrates: The gnostic father Carpocrates, whose sect's usage of alternate gospels is the reason that we now possess the Secret Gospel of Mark—the most erotic encounter of Jesus and his mystical revelations to any of his disciples[282]—was very likely to have been operating in Alexandria when the imperial party passed through. His doctrine of libertinism, and their rituals of "naked man to naked man" that were for healing and resurrection, perhaps had their influence on Hadrian and Antinous; this would have been a form of the monotheistic faiths that would have appealed to their Greek philosophical and mystical interests. Some of the patristic authors who wrote against heretics mention that Carpocrates' son Epiphanes was only seventeen when he died—yet another youthful figure to count amongst the many who died before their full flowering. For those who are gnostically inclined in the Ekklesía Antínoou, Carpocrates is revered as a *Sanctus* on this day.

October

11 **Coming Out to Ancestors Day/** *Dies Sanctorum Omnium*: While much of the United States (and some other places in the world) celebrate this day as National Coming Out Day, in the Ekklesía Antínoou we have utilized it in two further ways: as "Coming Out to Ancestors Day," and as a day to celebrate all of the *Sancti*, and particularly all of the queer *Sancti*. "Coming Out to Ancestors" is exactly what it sounds like. As polytheistic deities are not all-knowing, the same certainly applies to our ancestors, who do not automatically know everything simply because they are dead. In order to preserve good relations between our ancestors—both of blood and of heart—and ourselves, it is good to come out to them and let them know who and what we are in this life. Therefore, use this opportunity to come out to any of them who did not get the chance to know about this dimension of your life while they were still living—it can be a profound and cathartic experience. And, as our *Sancti* are our group's ancestor, one will certainly find welcome amongst them in this as well.

12 Matthew Shepard Day: An important day for anyone of the

---

[282] Will Roscoe, *Queer Spirits: A Gay Men's Myth Book* (Boston: Beacon Press, 1995), pp. 246-248.

modern out queer consciousness, when an innocuous youth was crucified for being gay. Yet another needlessly dead, beautiful youth lost to the forces of evil and hatred in this world. A day, therefore, after National Coming Out Day on the 11th, to remember how difficult it is and how disapproving of queerness this world remains, and to remember all the other martyrs to *homoeros* and gender variance whose blood has been spilled on the earth. A number of books could be read in honor of this very important *Sanctus* on this day.[283]

THE SACRED NIGHTS OF ANTINOUS: These final days in Antinous' life, and his subsequent death and deification, are some of the most important in the Ekklesía Antínoou's ritual year. In the Cairo Calendar, this stretch of days are all, almost unprecedented in the remainder of the calendar, blessed with a "Very Favorable" auspice, and the events listed in them are concerned with the setting into order of the universe and peace amongst the gods, with the reconciliation of Horus and Set.[284]

24 **Death of Osiris**: The festival of the Egyptian God (who had a mystery tradition devoted to him, which Hadrian and Antinous very likely witnessed just before the Boy's death), prefigured Antinous' equation with Osiris in his deification less than a week later. It is possible that during these circumstances, the Egyptian priest Pancrates met the couple and performed the spell bearing his name for Hadrian. In Hermopolis Magna, just to the West of the future site of Antinous' holy city, the priests of Thoth—the Egyptian Hermes—performed their rituals and imparted their secrets to the Imperial Lovers. This was the final initiation which Antinous undertook in this life. **Osiris and Antinous'** syncretism is recognized on this day. In 2002, just before the first Foundation Day of the modern period of Antinoan devotion, Harry Hay, the gay rights activist and founder of the Radical Faeries, died, which was like the "death of Osiris" for modern queer spirituality, hopefully presaging the coming birth of Horus and his own

---

[283] Scott Gibson (ed.), *Blood & Tears: Poems for Matthew Shepard* (New York: Painted Leaf Press, 1999); Judy Shepard, *The Meaning of Matthew: My Son's Murder in Laramie, and a World Transformed* (New York: Penguin/Hudson Street Press, 2009).

[284] Brier, pp. 232-234.

148

rejuvenation, of course...

25 *Panthea*: The feminine divinities, including Isis in search of her husband/brother Osiris, Aphrodite and her slain lover Adonis, Astarte and Melqart, Innana and Tammuz, or whomever else, are the theme and focus of this day. Antinous, mindful of his observations of the rites of many goddesses, turns his attention to these matters, as does Hadrian.

26 *Ophidia*: Whether through the (later) Hermetic mysteries—which aimed for the comprehension of the *Nous* (the mind of the creator and the demiurge of the universe), and thereby to achieve divinization—or not, the mystery of deification is a deep, profound, and enticing one. The pursuit of devotion to Antinous does not accomplish the traditional goal of mysticism—union with one's deity—but instead aims for the ultimate goal of these mysteries, namely to become a god oneself, as great as the *Nous*. The Serpent Path in the Ekklesía Antínoou, recognizing Glykon and Chnoubis, aims to fully explore and comprehend every aspect of potential deification, both light and dark, positive and negative, permitted and forbidden, unitary and deifying. This is a day of reversals, of the unexpected, and of the transformative, so that one is no longer simply the creation of the *Nous* and a spark from its flame, one is the fire itself, the (as it were) *anti-Nous* (a pun that only works in the Latin spelling of Antinous' name). Honor all of those things on this day which seem to be the "opposite" of what the rest of the world and its order seems to be saying is "good," "proper," and "right" for both everyday life and for fulfilling religion.

27 *Ananke Antínoou*: Fate and the devices of the Ordered Universe are not always kind to anyone, and as a living human Antinous was still under the sway of this Absolute Necessity, Unavoidable Fate, or *Ananke*, understood both as a concept, a deified abstraction, and a serpentine primordial goddess in the Orphic cosmologies. No matter what happened in the days or months before, and uncertain of his immediate future, Antinous returned to the everyday life he had known for so long, eating and drinking and taking what would be his final rest alongside his lover Hadrian. Knowing that he would be rejuvenated after his death because of his Eleusinian Mystery initiation, and that there was nothing left to fear, like all the mystery gods he had encountered, he came back like every hero does to the world he loved so much to share these gifts; and the events of the next day had yet to unfold...This is a day, therefore, to appreciate everything about everyday existence and its manifold joys.

28 <u>Death of Antinous</u>: The day that, for our purposes, was the one on which the Boy disappeared and was last seen alive. At some point, whether he fell by accident or deliberately plunged in, the waters of the Nile with their divinizing powers had their way with Antinous and swallowed his beautiful body. Knowing that life and death were inconsequential because of his future assurance of rejuvenation, it would have been very easy to become careless—this could have looked like the typical youthful attitude of invincibility, but with the crucial difference of his accomplished salvation through his mystery initiations—and all it would have taken was one momentary lapse of caution to see his mortal life extinguished on the journey up the Nile. When or how it happened is the ultimate mystery, but it is a day of great solemnity, mourning and sadness. Silent lamentation is the only way that we can respond to this greatest tragedy. Any images of Antinous one has in one's home shrine should be covered up or hidden on this day, not to be revealed again until Foundation Day. No prayers to him are to be said, but prayers on his behalf to many other gods (including Hermes Psychopompos) are very appropriate. Also, I've often avoided swimming or bathing on this day, as being around water—no matter how sacred it might be—could possibly invite trouble for those who revere a deity that drowned. I've even shaved my head in mourning on this occasion several times. Interestingly, this was a day on which games were held in Antinous' honor in Memphis in the early third century CE,[285] so following in that tradition may not be out of the question either.

29 Antinous in the Underworld: After passing the threefold jaws of Cerberus, the morbid skiff of Charon over the Styx, and the gates of Anubis which many had entered but few had left, Antinous has his reunion with Persephone in the Underworld, during which he prepared for his deification and subsequent conquest of death. On

---

[285] Marcus N. Tod, "An Ephebic Inscription from Memphis," *The Journal of Egyptian Archaeology* 37 (December 1951), pp. 86-99.

this day of the Houses of Re and Osiris, the scales of Ma'at not only find Antinous just, but his heart is perfectly balanced with Ma'at's feather. Thoth as a cynocephalus greets Antinous' rising in the East, and places Antinous' face in his own mirror, the Moon. This is an appropriate day for one of the Foundation Day ritual dramas to be performed.

30 **FOUNDATION DAY**: The most important day in the modern cultus of Antinous, commemorating the day in which Hadrian found Antinous' drowned body and wept like a woman; the day on which he founded the city of Antinoopolis at Hir-Wer/Besa where Antinous' body was discovered; the day on which Antinous was first deified by the Egyptian priests, and thus the basis of his Empire-wide cultus was founded; and the day on which all of the important foundational rituals of the Ekklesía Antínoou take place, including the recognition of new *Sancti*. An ancient calendar from Oxyrhynchus marks this festival.[286] The Cairo Calendar says that this day is "very favorable":"It is the day when Re is joyful in his beauty. His Ennead is in festivity. Everyone, every lion and every single one among the *ankhy*-reptiles, the gods, goddesses, spirits, dead, and those who came into being in the primordial age, Nun's form is in their bodies."[287] Nun is the Egyptian god representing the primordial, uncreated essence of all things before the beginning of the universe; and in the Obelisk of Antinous (on which, see the subsequent chapter in this book), the phrase that "the semen of god is truly in [Antinous'] body" reflects this same idea expressed in the Cairo Calendar. The means by which all things can be restored has, thus, been established. The one absolute **Day of Obligation** as far as the Ekklesía Antínoou is concerned.

31 *Antinous Triumphantus*: The day after his deification, the first sunrise on Antinous the God, is greeted with happiness by all the world; but the new god's battle is not over yet—he has conquered death, which many before had done, but he had yet to face the full force of the Archons of the universe, who keep all people in bondage, but over

---

[286] J. W. B. Barns, Peter Parsons, John Rea, and Eric G. Turner (eds.), *The Oxyrhynchus Papyri* Volume 31 (London: Egypt Exploration Society, 1966), §2553, pp. 72-77.

[287] Brier, p. 234.

whom he will eventually triumph as well. This date is, therefore, a momentary and promising initial victory, though there is still a great battle to be fought, nonetheless. This also happens to be the day of Samain in Irish practice, a time connected with the opening of the Otherworld to this world. Celebrate this day however you wish, preferably with great merriment, but always with care!

November

1 **Antinous the Liberator**: On this day, often a holdover of the previous day in many traditions, Antinous assumes his aspect as Antinous the Liberator, who slays the Archons of the universe over the next ninenty days. The Liberator also symbolizes the *Via Transformativa* in mystical practice, the alchemical process by which vices and difficulties are transmuted into virtue and blessing, poisons become elixirs, and the forms of all things are mutable; remember that all things are subject to change, and can be changed if we take the effort required to do so. A time to enkindle the warrior energy in oneself, the need to fight against earthly oppression and to show the less beautiful, fierce and angry, and even frightening aspects of the god and of oneself. This day breaks the favorable chain of auspices of the previous eight in the Cairo Calendar, and it is said that "it is the day of smashing into the ears of Bata in his own inaccessible temple."[288] Indeed, none of the unjust gods of this world are safe with the unleashing of the Liberator.

19-21 **Visit to the Colossoi at Memnon**: Not long after Antinous' death, the journey up the Nile continued, with Hadrian arriving in Thebes on about the 18th of November, and then three days of visiting the famous Colossoi at Memnon, where Sabina and Julia Balbilla left many inscriptions in graffiti.[289] Symbols of both royalty and immortality, the imperial party came to hear the ancient statues "sing"

---

[288] Brier, p. 234.

[289] André Bernand and Étienne Bernand (eds.), *Les Inscriptions Grecques et Latines du Colosse de Memnon* (Paris: Institut Francais d'Archéologie Orientale, 1960), pp. 80-100 §28-32; T. C. Brennan, "The Poets Julia Balbilla and Damo at the Colossus of Memnon," *Classical World* 91.4 (March/April 1998), pp. 215-234.

152

as the dawn arrived, but the first attempt by Hadrian to hear the singing yielded nothing. On subsequent days, however, he did finally experience the sound of the statues. A major disappointment to be sure, but also highly symbolic—for his recent loss of Antinous had been great, and the passing of his favorite must have brought forth the idea of his own passing from life and from the pinnacle of earthly power as the greatest ruler of his time; and yet, in the end, the beautiful sounds of ages past echoed into the present, and the emperor heard it. The first day in the cycle (the 19th) is dedicated to "disappointment"; the second to "consolation"; and the third to "jubilation." The 20th is also International Transgender Day of Remembrance, and this should be marked by all interested parties who practice queer spirituality.

20 International Transgender Day of Remembrance: As mentioned under September 23rd above, inclusively queer theology does need to take the "T" in LGBTQ very seriously, and it is unforunate that this particular day, celebrated annually, is one that focuses not upon the contributions of transsexual and transgendered people, but instead focuses upon the remembrance of all the victims of transpohobic violence. All such victims, casualties of the continued bigotry and misunderstanding that occurs even within gay and lesbian circles about trans people, are considered *Sancti/Sanctae* of the Ekklesía Antínoou, and recognition and remembrance of them on this date is extremely important.

27 ***Dies Natalis Antinoi***: Antinous' birthday, as established in the Lanuvium inscription and held as one of their feast-days,[290] as well as the cult calendar found in Oxyrhynchus (which indicates a three-day festival),[291] and it may also be referred to in a fragmentary calendar from Tebtynis that refers to a "ship-procession" around this date.[292] While his birth year is estimated at *circa* 110-112, I generally reckon it as 110 CE, so that when he died, he was nineteen—nearly twenty, when society would have begun to expect the things of childishness to be put away in favor of adulthood. One astrologer I've consulted has suggested the date of 110 (at 8:50 PM!) as probable because it would

---

[290] Beard, North, and Price, p. 294.
[291] Barns, Parsons, Rea, and Turner, p. 75 lines 4-5.
[292] Eitrem and Amundsen, p. 48.

align with certain asteroid astrological aspects that would account for some events in Antinous' life and death. One of the paradoxes of the liturgical year is that his birth and his death happen within a month of one another, and that Foundation Day and his *Dies Natalis* are always on the same day of the week, four weeks apart. The fact that the holiday commemorating the first event chronologically (Antinous' birth) comes second in the yearly cycle after the observance of his death, thus might prompt thoughts on rebirth. It is technically one full lunar cycle from the day of his death to the day of his birth, and one of his symbols was the moon, as illustrated on many coins and mentioned by Tatian the Assyrian.

29 *Epibatéria* of Hadrian in Oxyrhynchus: the celebration of a "first arrival" of a ruler into a city was an institution which Hadrian, probably more than any other emperor, caused to be created in many cities of the Empire. Downstream from Antinoöpolis, he visited this city in the latter part of his Egyptian circuit.[293] So much important Antinoian material originates from papyri found amongst the vast volumes of fragments discovered in this city, it is a day that we reckon with great thanks; the Emperor favored the city with a visit, and the city has favored us with much information about Antinous.

December

1 *Epibatéria* of Hadrian in Tebtynis: Not long after his visit to Oxyrhynchus, Hadrian visited the city of Tebtynis in Egypt.[294] A very important papyrus for the ancient cult of Antinous was also found there (which may even have been written on this occasion), and thus we commemorate the day. This is also World AIDS Day, an important one to consider in one's regular devotions as a queer spiritual practitioner.

11 *Dies Natalis* of Vesta: The city of Naukratis—from which Athenaeus hailed (on whose contributions to the ancient cultic records of Antinous, see the subsequent chapters below)—celebrated the birthday

[293] P. J. Sijpesteijn, "A New Document Concerning Hadrian's Visit to Egypt," *Historia* 18 (1969), pp. 109-118 at 114; Eitrem and Amundsen, pp. 48-49.
[294] Sijpesteijn, p. 115; Barns, Parsons, Rea, and Turner, p. 76 lines 11-13.

of the Roman goddess Vesta/the Greek Hestia on this date, as recorded on an imperial cult calendar from Tebtynis.[295] As the laws and customs of Naukratis were transferred, by Hadrian, to become some of the guiding customs of the city of Antinoöpolis (where the *deme* of Hestia was under Nerva's *phyla*), following this particular practice in relation to this most important goddess seems appropriate for the Ekklesía Antínoou.

13 Vicennalia **of Hadrian:** From the same Tebtynis calendar comes the information that this date was observed as an anniversary "on the occasion of the god Hadrian having fulfilled the second ten-years'-term of his reign" in 136.[296]

17-23 Saturnalia: The celebration of Saturn's Golden Age, usually from December 17 to 23, fluctuated in the late Republic and into the Imperial period. On these days, a public feast was held after a great Saturnine sacrifice, all business ceased, and gambling in public was allowed. Less formal clothes were worn, soft caps called *pillei* were sported, slaves were given reprieve and were even served by their masters, and each household honored a mock king for the duration of the festivities, which ended with the days known as the Sigillaria.[297] Gift-giving and candle-lighting were also aspects of the festival. During these final days of the calendrical year, a time outside of time was acknowledged, the perfection of the past Golden Age was honored. A number of further festivals are subsumed into this observance for the Ekklesía Antínoou. On the 18th is the *Eponalia*, the Roman festival in honor of the Gaulish horse goddess Epona,[298] and considering that Hadrian's favorite horse Borysthenes died in Gaul, she would have perhaps been in his mind on that occasion. On the 19th is the *Opalia*, the festival in honor of the goddess Ops, a goddess of abundance.[299] On the 21st was the *Angeronalia*, held in honor of the goddess Angerona, a goddess of secrecy,[300] as well as the dedication of one of

---

[295] Eitrem and Amundsen, pp. 50-51.
[296] Eitrem and Amundsen, pp. 52-53.
[297] Adkins and Adkins, p. 200.
[298] Adkins and Adkins, p. 69.
[299] Adkins and Adkins, p. 169.
[300] Adkins and Adkins, p. 9.

the other temples of Hercules Victor.[301] On the 22nd, the temple of the Lares Permarines was founded.[302] On December 23rd, the Larentalia was held,[303] and the Sigillaria—the final day of the Saturnalia, in which gift-giving occurred—took place.

21 *Antinous Epiphanes*: Winter Solstice is not an Antinoian holiday specifically, nor a Dionysian one, but as it is at the other end of the year from the date on which we celebrate Antinous' syncretisms to Apollon, on this date we honor his syncretisms to Dionysos, particularly as *Epiphanes*, the "god who comes." Don't give gifts, don't spend loads of money; rather, ponder the mystery of what it means to have a "child of light" arrive—or, epiphanate, if you like!—on this day, and what it also might mean to steal back the light from the Otherworld at this time of the year.

25 *Sol Invictus*: The birth of Sol Invictus was reckoned on this day in his third-century CE cultus,[304] founded during the reign of Aurelian after the disastrous reign of Elagabulus (in which Sol Invictus El Gabal was the supreme god of the empire), as a return to the more humble roots of the older cult of Sol Indigenes.[305] This can be observd in many different ways by modern polytheists.

? Death of Sabina: This event most likely happened sometime toward the end of December 137.[306] As this time of year is the darkest, and the light is beginning to be reborn, it is appropriate to think of Sabina Ceres at this stage as she awaits the return from her mourning for the loss of Libera, and to eventually put on the bright veil of Spring.

31 **Death of Aelius Caesar**: Hadrian's first adopted son, Lucius Ceionius Commodus, who became Aelius Caesar, died on this day in

---

[301] Adkins and Adkins, p. 100.
[302] Adkins and Adkins, p. 130.
[303] Adkins and Adkins, p. 130.
[304] Adkins and Adkins, pp. 209-210.
[305] Gaston H. Halsberghe, *The Cult of Sol Invictus* (Leiden: E. J. Brill, 1972).
[306] Birley, *Hadrian*, p. 294.

137, the day before he was to address the Senate on his adoption.[307] He was called the "Western favorite," and the possibility that he was a lover of Hadrian has been suggested—it was said that the only thing that recommended him was his beauty. Deification was offered to him by the Senate, but Hadrian refused it, and forbade public mourning over his death, though it seems he was honored as a *Divus* in some eastern provinces, as evidenced by the Doura-Europos Imperial Cult calendar. Why this refusal on Hadrian's part occurred is unknown, but he is an important figure nonetheless, not only to the Hadrianic/Antonine dynasties, but also as a cultist of Antinous in at least two known locations (on which, see below in a subsequent chapter). The fallen Prince of Flowers' death is the absolute end of one's Saturnalia observances (if they have not ceased before now!), and the end of our ritual year.

Antinous-Bakchos (no. 127)
St. Petersburg

---

[307] Birley, *Hadrian*, pp. 288-294.

Fasti Metri Antinoi

For a variety of reasons, calendars that give even the slightest descriptions of the significance of holidays are very difficult to remember, and unless an abbreviated version of some sort is posted and accessible for a person at all times, the wide variety of feast-days in ancient religious systems can be very difficult to recall. Therefore, like many such works, the versification of a calendar would allow it to be remembered more easily. But, by doing so, one also has access to short and easy phrases for meditation or a sung acclamation on a particular holiday, if no other ritual or observance takes place or is enacted for the individual devotee. The result can be somewhat similar to a medieval "Book of Hours," therefore.

The following metrical calendar of Antinoan holidays is a selection of a mere forty-two occasions from the *Tabula Feriarum* of the Aedicula Antinoi, with an introductory and closing verse, as well as a linking verse for the Sacred Nights (when the meter and style of the work changes). It was written in 2005-2006, in fulfillment of a devotional vow that year. It begins with the holidays of major significance in the latter part of November. Some of my own thoughts and theologies have shifted since writing this, but consider the relics of those older notions found strewn throughout this as odd and poetic (possibly!) curiosities rather than hard-and-fast, universally applicable theological premises or syncretistic equations.

The entire calendar can be "sung" in one piece, or perhaps the previous and following dates of significance can be sung in addition to the date in question at a particular ritual or observance. No matter how an individual decides to use this, I hope it proves to be more than a mere curiosity of versification.

1. Invocation

Permittere me, Caelis Musae
Ave Melpomene!
Cantare causa Mnemosyne
Io Polymnia! Io Kalliope!
Ave Omnis Musae!
Sanctarum Feriae Antinoi

Sanctarum Feriae Antinoi...

Permit me, O Heavenly Muses
(Hail Melpomene!)
to sing for the benefit of Mnemosyne
(Io Polymnia! Io Kalliope!
Hail Muses all!)
of the Sacred Feasts of Antinous

2. November 19-21—Colossoi of Memnon

Balbilla et Sabina
Poeta, Augusta
Inscripserunt in magna statua petra

Cantent pro nobis statuae

Julia Balbilla and Sabina—
Poet and Empress—
Wrote upon the great stone statues;

May the statues sing for us!

3. November 27—*Dies Natalis Antinoi*

In Bithynia Rhebas limina
Nascit Mantinoeia
Superexultate Arcadia!
Beatus carus filius
Puer Antinous
Dies clarus hic felicissimus!

Dies clarus hic felicissimus!

In Bithynia, on the shores of Rhebas,
Mantinoë gave birth—
Rejoice exceedingly, O Arcadia!
The beloved and beautiful son,
the boy Antinous—
Most joyful is this bright day!

4. November 29—Hadrian in Oxyrhynchus

Imperator Hadrianus
In Oxyrynchus
Aegypti civitas erat adventus
Verba scripta conserventur in aeternm!

The Emperor Hadrian
at Oxyrhynchus—
the city of Egypt—had arrived.

May written words be preserved forever!

5. December 21—*Antinous Epiphanes*

Surgens ortus clarae lucis
Eros, Phanes
Ex obscurite Dionysus

Antinous Epiphanes!

The rising birth of the bright light—
Eros, Phanes—
Dionysos from the darkness!
Antinous Epiphanes!

6. December 31—Death of Aelius Caesar

Adoptus Lucius Aelius
Caesar Commodus
Mortis diem tristitiam lugemus

Princeps floris succidetur!

The adopted Lucius Aelius
Commodus Caesar—
We mourn the sorrowful day of (his) death.

The flower-prince cut down!

7. January 24—*Dies Natalis Hadriani*

Natalis Imperatoris
Hadriani
In hunc diem in Roma celebramus

Dies beatus et benedictus!

The birth of the Emperor
Hadrian
In Rome on this day we celebrate.

Lovely and blessed is the day!

8. January 29—Star of Antinous/Antinous the Navigator

In noctis caelo primus
Hadrianus
Videbat stella Antinoi
Clara stella obscura
Captus in Aquila
Divina caelestis haec flamma

Dona nobis lucem obscuritati!

Ex opera eius Inferna
Ave Victor Ave
Antinoe nunc emerge!
Archon Domini subiecti
Ave Antinoe
Liberamurque in aeternum victore!

Ave Ave Victor Antinoe!

Annorum Decies Centena
Millia Scapha
Ad stellam obscuram perducta

Navigator Antinoe custodi nos!

First in the night's sky
Hadrian
Saw Antinous' star
A clear, dark star
Grasped in Aquila—
this divine heavenly fire—

Give us light for darkness!

From his toils in the Underworld—
Hail, Victorious One, Hail! —
Emerge now, O Antinous!
The Lord Archons are subjected—
Hail Antinous! —
and we are liberated eternally by (your) victory!

Hail, Hail, Antinous the Victorious!

The Boat
of Millions of Years
is guided toward the dark star.

Antinous the Navigator protect us!

9. February 15—Lupercalia

Romulus et Remus
Lupa nutritus
Pulchri pueri circumeunt certantibus

Luperce Antinoe nos benedice!

Romulus and Remus
nursed by the She-Wolf;
Beautiful youths go around racing.

Antinous Lupercus bless us!

10. February 25—Adoption of Antoninus Pius

Hadriano est traditus
Fax Augusti
Antonino factum eius ultimum

Operem Divi extende Pie!

By Hadrian was passed
the Augustan Torch
to Antoninus as his final act.

Continue the work of the Divus, O Pious One!

11. March 1—Apotheosis of Antoninus Pius

Antoninus Pius carus
Adoptivus filius
Imperatoris Hadriani
Accepit in hoc die
Dignitatem divinum
In principium hoc annus fortunet!

In principium hunc annus fortunet!...

Beloved Antoninus Pius
Adopted son
of Emperor Hadrian
received on this day
divine honors;
In this beginning, may the year prosper!

12. March 5-11—*Treískouroi* and *Trophimoi*

Herodes Atticus
Tutor filii
Amicus Augusti et sapiens
Tui Tripueri
Polliculus
Sunt inlustris herois;

Dedisceramus nunquam eis!

Herodes Attikos—
ward of children,
friend of the Emperor, and wise—
your Three Boys,
Polydeukion (especially),
were celebrated heroes;

May we never forget them!

13. March 21—Apotheosis of Sabina

Diva Vibia Sabina
Ceres Antinoi
Uxor cara Venus Hadriani
Accepit in hoc die
dignitatem divinum
Tempus Vernum ea inlucescat!

Tempus Vernum ea inlucescat!...

Diva Vibia Sabina—
Ceres of Antinous,
Beloved wife, Venus of Hadrian—
Received on this day
Divine honors;
May the Spring be brightened by her!

14. April 21—*Megala Antinoeia*

Hadrianus est venatus
Ursam magnam
Pro Erote et Aphroditeque
Hadrianus reconditus
Pro Venere Romam
Laudo pro ludis omne Antinoo!

Laudo pro ludis omne Antinoo!

Hadrian hunted
the great she-bear
for Eros and Aphrodite;
Hadrian refounded
Rome for Venus;
For all the games, praise to Antinous!

15. May 1—*Venatio Apri*

Hadrianus est venatus
Aprum Bithynium
Cum equo fidele Borysthene,
Apollonis et Adonitis
Gloriae aeternitae!
Antinous Belenus laudatur!

Antinous Belenus laudatur!...

166

Hadrian hunted
the Bithynian boar
with the loyal steed Borysthenes,
to the eternal glory
Of Apollon and Adonis.
Antinous Belenus be praised!

16. May 7—Antinoöpolitan Lovers

Duo vultus pulchre pictus
Spectant trans aetates
Triumphanti super mortem ducti Anubidi
Amatoris duo humati
Requiem inventi
Osiris Antinous Purgator!

Osiris Antinous Purgator!...

Two faces, painted beautifully,
peer across the ages,
triumphant over death, guided by Anubis;
two lovers buried
find rest.
Osiris Antinous the Justifier!

17. May 22—*Canis Erigoneius*

In hoc diem invenit corporem
Maira vinarium
Dionysus tollat stellam canem

Dionysus favet sobrios!

On this day, Maira found
the body (of) the winemaker;
Dionysos elevated the dog-star;

Dionysus favors the sober ones!

18. June 1—Marguerite Porete Day

Margarita Dei in flamma
Erat occida
Perstat alios erudire eius Anima

Gregemus eius cinerem!

The Pearl of God in flames
perished,
Her soul persists to enlighten others.

May we gather her ashes!

19. June 11—Death of Alexander

Alexander Rex victor
Hephaestionis amator
Ivit eius requiei hodie

Memoremur eum Deus Heros!

King Alexander the Victorious,
Lover of Hephaestion,
Went to his rest today

Hero, God, may we remember him!

20. June 21—Antinous and Apollon

Altitudines aestivus
Flos amoris
Et accedunt felices coetus

168

Apollo laudantur Antinousque!

At the heights of summer
(is) the flower of love,
and auspicious meetings occur.

Antinous and Apollon be praised!

21. July 9—Hadrian's Entry into Rome

Imperator intrat Romam
Erat acclamatus
Conditorem Pontificem Maximum

Disciplina Hadrini ducat nos!

The Emperor enters Rome,
he was acclaimed
Founder, Pontifex Maximus.

May Hadrianic Discipline guide us!

22. July 10—Death of Hadrian

Ignis animae Hadriani
Exstinguerebatur
Sed in mortem in deorum numerum

Trans caelos super omnes moveat!

The fire of Hadrian's soul
was extinguished,
But in death he was counted among the gods.

May he move across the heavens above all!

23. July 16—Antinous and Silvanus; Hadrian's Wall Day

In Condercum in Murum
Custodivit
Silvanus Cocidius
Saltat stella haec causa
In Aquila
Obscura stella ibi captiva!

Silvane Antinoe Defensor!

In Benwell on (Hadrian's) Wall
Silvanus Cocidius
defended.
A star dances because of this
in Aquila,
the dark star held there!

Antinous Silvanus the Protector!

24. July 20—Birth of Alexander the Great

Deae Artemis Ephesus
Templum incendens
Filius Philippi et Ammonis natus est

Alexander Rex Heros Deusque!

The Goddess Artemis at Ephesus'
temple burning,
The son of Philip and Ammon was born.

Alexander, king, hero, and god!

25. July 25—*Dies Caniculares*

Stella Sirius Flumen Nilus
Surget inundat
Dies Canes aestatis advenit

Custodi nos Canum Magister Antinous!

The Star Sirius, the River Nile,
Rises, floods;
The Dog-Days of summer arrive.

Antinous Kynegetikos/Master of Hounds protect us!

26. August 11—Accession of Hadrian in Nikomedia

Legionibus Hadrianus
Salutabatur
Imperator Romae in Nikomedia

Hadriani regnum praeclarum!

By the Legions Hadrian
was hailed
Emperor of Rome in Nikomedia.

Hadrian's reign was splendorous!

27. August 13—*Dies Natalis Dianae*

Diana Regina
Clara Luna
Venatrix, Soror Apollonis
Ortus eius libertas
Omni servo
Antinous Lanuvium te coniunget!

171

Natalis Dianae celebremus!

Diana, Queen,
the bright Moon,
Huntress, Sister of Apollon,
Your birth is freedom
for all slaves;
At Lanuvium Antinous joins you!

May we celebrate the birth of Diana!

28. August 20—Battle of Chaeronea

Exercitus amoris
Milites aurigae
In proelium oppetivit hodie

Amor ferocior quam sagittae!

An army of lovers—
Warriors, charioteers—
Today met its death in battle.

Love is more fierce than arrows!

29. August 21/22—*Venatio Leonis*/Festival of the Red Lotus

Hadrianus et Antinous
Sunt venatus
Leonem sanguis fit ruber flos!

A morte floret pulchritudo!

Hadrian and Antinous
hunted
the lion; blood becomes a red flower!

172

From death, beauty flowers!

30. September 6—Death of Lucius Marius Vitalis

Puer Lucius Vitalis
Pulcher Iuventus
Oppetivit immature in Athenae

Iuventutis flamma nunquam exstinguatur!

The boy Lucius Vitalis,
beautiful youth,
Met his untimely death in Athens.

May the fire of youth never be extinguished!

31. September 19—*Natalis Antonini Pii*

Natalis Antonini
Hodie Pii
Successor Hadriani imperii

Dona ei praemium Antinous!

The birth of Antoninus
Pius today,
the successor of Hadrian's Empire.

Antinous give him reward!

32. September 21—Eleusis

Proserpinae et Cereris
Mysteria
Apertum Hadriano et Antinoo

Mysteria tangat nullum verbum!

Demeter and Persephone's
Mystery
Revealed to Hadrian and Antinous.

No word may touch the mystery!

33. September 25—Carpocrates

Carpocrates philosophus
Doctrinae occulti
Nudo ad nudum sanans

Nos libera ex determinatione!

Carpocrates, philosopher
of secret teachings,
healing by naked man to naked man;

Free us from all limitations!

34. October 12—Matthew Shepard Day

Mattheus Shepardus
Pulcher Iuventus
In tenebras frigidumque occisus

Hic fiat nunquam fiat iterum!

Matthew Shepard—
beautiful youth—
murdered in darkness and cold;

May this never happen again!

35. Sacred Nights:

Sacrae Noctis, Sacra Nox!
Benedicta est haec Sacra Nox!

Sacred Night, Sacred Nights;
Blessed is this Sacred Night!

36. October 24—Passion of Osiris

Dies Passio Osiris
Mysteria mortis mortis

Benedicta est haec Sacra Nox!

The day of the Passion of Osiris:
The mystery of the death of death.

37. October 25—*Panthea*

Mater Sancta Magna Dea
Felicissima sunt dona!

Benedicta est haec Sacra Nox!

Holy mother, Great Goddess:
Most happy are your gifts!

38. October 26—*Ophidia*

Sancta via, anguis sanctus,
Ritu deorum ambulemus

Benedicta est haec Sacra Nox!

Holy path, holy serpent,
Let us walk like gods!

39. October 27—*Ananke Antínoou*

Gaudium et amor vitae
Fatum Antinoi mysteriae!

Benedicta est haec Sacra Nox!

The joy and love of life—
The Fate of Antinous' mystery!

40. October 28—Death of Antinous

Dies Mortis Antinoi
Velate imagines lamentari!

Benedicta est haec Sacra Nox!

The day of Antinous' death:
Cover the images and weep!

41. October 29—Antinous in the Underworld

Peregrinatio Inferna
Domino ianuas aperite!

Benedicta est haec Sacra Nox!

The pilgrimage in the underworld:
Open the doors for your master!

42. October 30—FOUNDATION DAY

Fundamentorum hic Dies
Ecclesia Antinoi laudens!

Benedicta est haec Sacra Nox!

This is Foundation Day:
The Ekklesía Antínoou is rejoicing!

43. October 31—*Antinous Triumphantus*

Trimphantus Antinous
Mors vinctus est, dei est homines!

Benedicta est haec Sacra Nox!

Antinous is triumphant;
Death is conquered, humans are gods!

44. November 1—Antinous Liberator

Incipit opus Antinoi
Liberatio homini!

Benedicta est haec Sacra Nox!

The work of Antinous begins:
The liberation of men!

45. Closing

Tota Feriae hae Anni
Gaudete Ecclesia Antinoi!

Sacrae Noctis, Sacra Nox!
Benedicta est haec Sacra Nox!

These are the sum of the year's festivals;
Rejoice, O Ekklesía of Antinous!

Sacred Night, Sacred Nights;
Blessed is this Sacred Night!

Antinous of the Moon

This hymn was written in 2011, as my own yearly contribution for the Megala Antinoeia festival on April 21st. It can be used anytime one is honoring the lunar aspects of Antinous, and in particular his syncretisms to Endymion and Men,[308] which one may choose to observe on the full and new moons respectively; or, it can serve as a "night office" to prepare for dream oracles. The verses are modular, so they can be subtracted as desired, or further ones can be added as well depending on one's own tastes.

Antinous of the Moon

His face and hair in pale white marble
ever-shines, radiant like the moon
in the day and by night
in darkness and in light

His countenance upon the firmament
between stars and crater's shadows
in the day and by night
in darkness and in light

The spider weaving between stars in the void
the one who bears children of his own
in the day and by night
in darkness and in light

Like Endymion he is silent
amidst his ever-pleasant dreams
in the day and by night
in darkness and in light

---

[308] P. Sufenas Virius Lupus, *The Syncretisms of Antinous* (Anacortes: The Red Lotus Library, 2010), pp. 66-72.

Like the king-god Men
the anchor of his cosmos
in the day and by night
in darkness and in light

Artemis is his hunting companion
and Selene his bridal-bed sharer
in the day and by night
in darkness and in light

He shares the shade of the Apis Bull
and takes the form of wine-mad Dionysos
in the day and by night
in darkness and in light

As Hermes, he slays monsters and forms words
and as Silvanus he draws boundaries with his *falx*
in the day and by night
in darkness and in light

The new Pan of Arcadia, flock-protector
the new Herakles of Pontus, Cerberus-tamer
in the day and by night
in darkness and in light

As Osiris he reigns over the Nile
and as Apollon he speaks oracles
in the day and by night
in darkness and in light

The Liberator, he comes to shatter shackles
The Navigator, his strong arm points the way
in the day and by night
in darkness and in light

180

Antinous the Lover, he arrives tonight
with soft and silent blue luminescence
in the day and by night
in darkness and in light

Hadrian was fortunate in his sorrows
for he felt your shadown upon his own flesh
in the day and by night
in darkness and in light

Now favor me this night, Antinous
and may my dream be a part of your dream
in the day and by night
in darkness and in light

Panantinous

The single instance of this combined syncretic name of the deities Pan and Antinous occurs in a papyrus fragment found in Oxyrhynchus, which tells of a ship's figurehead in the shape of "Panantinous." While Pan is syncretized to Antinous on other occasions in his ancient cultus,[309] the fact that we hear of an actual image of this syncretism is highly intriguing. What would it have looked like? Antinous with goat horns? Or would it be more like the contorniate medals that depict Antinous-Pan, simply as his familiar image, with a *pedum* as the attribute of Pan? It is impossible to know, but it is intriguing nonetheless to contemplate these possibilities.

The poem here can be used as a prayer to honor this particular syncretism, particularly on January 8th, or on other occasions. It was originally printed in the Bibliotheca Alexandrina devotional anthology for Pan.[310]

Panantinous

The ships of Arcadia
go safely across seas
storm-tossed and treacherous
with protection at their prow.

---

[309] For more information on these, see P. Sufenas Virius Lupus, "From Arcadia with Love: Pan and the Cult of Antinous," in Diotima et al. (eds.), *Out of Arcadia: A Devotional Anthology for Pan* (Bibliotheca Alexandrina, 2011), pp. 86-93. For the papyrus document from Oxyrhynchus itself, see a later chapter in the present volume.

[310] P. Sufenas Virius Lupus, "Panantinous," in *Out of Arcadia: A Devotional Anthology for Pan* (Bibliotheca Alexandrina, 2011), pp. 22-23.

The gods of Arcadia
that protect travelers
like shepherds over sheep
on rustic hillsides.

The sons of Arcadia
in Mantineia's city
who hunt like wolves
in mountainous forests.

The voices of Arcadia
that instill fear
amidst battle's roar,
that shake Hades' gates.

The dancers of Arcadia
wild on the plains
with pipes shrieking
and footsteps like rainfall.

The waters of Arcadia
that drown the careless,
that yield diverse fish
and wash the seashore.

The symbols of Arcadia,
gods and heroes alike,
sons of Hermes,
Pan and Antinous together.

Panantinous, Arcadian god,
protect this ship
and its cargo and crew
from Poseidon's waves.

Rituals for Lupercalia

We know of at least one sacred functionary of Antinous—one P. Sufenas, who was a *phratriarch* of Antinous and Eunostos in Naples—who was also a *Lupercus*. If Antinous spent time in Rome as a youth, it seems possible that he may have played this role as well, or if not, that he would at least have enjoyed the festivities on this day. As a result, this has been a ritual held in great importance in the modern Ekklesía Antínoou, and it has been performed with a largue number of participants at PantheaCon over Presidents' Day weekend in February in San Jose in 2007, 2009, and 2010, as well as privately or with many fewer participants in other years before and since.

As luck would have it, we do have a number of texts describing the practices of the Lupercalia ritual;[311] however, the exact interpretations of these remain a mystery for the most part. Comparitive work can make some suggestions, though, and one such is that it is based on some sort of initiation ritual, which could equally be one of incorporation into a youthful hunter/warrior-like class, or re-integration into society after such a period.[312]

The outlines of the ritual run as follows: two teams of *Luperci*, composed of upstanding youths of the higher ranks in society, would run a footrace, ending at the Lupercal, the cave on the Palatine Hill where Romulus and Remus were suckled by the Lupa, the she-wolf that was either sent by or identical to Mars (later interpreted as a prostitute, as *lupa* could mean equally she-wolf or prostitute). In a shrine within this cave, the priests sacrificed a goat and a dog (it is likely that the dog stood in for an earlier wolf sacrifice), and mixed the blood together and marked the foreheads of several youths with it. After this, the

---

[311] Lesley Adkins and Roy A. Adkins, *Dictionary of Roman Religion* (New York: Facts on File, 1996), p. 136; Mary Beard, John North, & Simon Price (eds./trans.), *Religions of Rome, Volume 2: A Sourcebook* (Cambridge: Cambridge University Press, 1998), pp. 119-124.

[312] Phillip A. Bernhardt-House, "Imbolc: A New Interpretation," *Cosmos: The Journal of the Traditional Cosmology Society* 18 (2002), pp. 57-76 at 64-65.

blood was wiped from their foreheads with wool saturated in milk, and there was then "ritual laughter." The sacrificed goat's skin was then divided and given to each of the various *Luperci* to wear as a loincloth, as well as made into thongs which were then used in a further run around the city's bounds, during which the *Luperci* flogged anyone they encountered on the way—it was held to be lucky and to promote fertility, and women freely offered their hands for this purpose (the flogging was probably light and mostly symbolic, and only on the hands, in later periods). Mark Anthony, as a youthful *Lupercus*, offered the crown to Julius Caesar on this occasion; and it has been suggested that the subsequent imperial cult took some of its inspiration from these events and rituals. It has also been suggested that Gerald Gardner's various suggestions in terms of the use of flogging in Wiccan ritual also originate from this ritual in particular, although there are a number of other rituals in Europe in which this activity also took place (e.g. the cultus of Artemis Orthia in Sparta).

On the day of the Lupercalia, we commemorate Antinous Magister Canum or Kynegetikos, Antinous the Master of Hounds or Hunter; and again, at the opposite end of the year, on the Rising of Sirius and the coming of the *Dies Caniculares*, he is again commemorated under this title. We also pray to him as Antinous Lupercus, honoring the many other deities and figures associated with the festival, the myths of Romulus and Remus' births, and the general season around it, alongside Antinous on this day. An adapted form of this sort of ritual is therefore suggested here.

This ritual should take place outside, preferably during the daylight, but after dark and/or indoors can also be effective. The officiating priests/functionaries can be wearing whatever they wish, but the *Luperci* to be initiated should be lightly clad, or completely without clothes if that suits them better. There should be at least three *Luperci* under ideal circumstances; if there are fewer or more, that is also permissible. Two runners or teams of runners should be nominated from the *Luperci* and a short race should be run around a set course—in effect, a sacred boundary of some kind—which the spectators can place bets on or in some other way decide to support with their cheering. (If there is only one *Lupercus*, or one is celebrating this ritual by oneself, then a race of some sort or a physical exertion of a type determined by

185

oneself should be performed.) In the modern Ekklesía Antínoou's practices, the *Luperci* can be anyone, regardless of age or gender, though when possible, we have preferred to get three *Luperci* who, between them, have the following characteristics: a woman; a queer person; a person under the age of thirty. While new *Luperci* need not be initiated each year or each time the festival is celebrated (provided that previous *Luperci* are available to fulfill the role of the racers and the floggers), it is certainly enjoyable to add further ones whenever possible.

A series of offerings should be made to the various gods along the lines suggested in the ritual text to follow. A knife with some of the dark liquid representing blood (usually wine) on it should be touched to each person's forehead by the officiant, followed by the wiping off of the red stain with wool saturated in milk. Ritual laughter follows this—and this is the part of the ritual that is foolproof, because even if one has to fake laughing, the effort to do so will probably be laughable in itself, and thus the requirement of it will be accomplished! As the dripping milk-soaked wool often gets a bit messy, the laughter often starts before it is officially supposed to, and in several occasions in the past of this ritual, the dripping milk has also been flung on the remainder of the spectators in order to further facilitate their laughter as well.

Luperci ibi ad me venite...[313]

From beyond the boundaries you have come;
from the border-fields of Rome you have come;
from further than the fields of Mars you have come.

---

[313] P. Sufenas Virius Lupus, "Lupercalia," *The Phillupic Hymns* (Eugene: Bibliotheca Alexandrina, 2008), p. 70. This line translates as "*Luperci*, come here to me."

186

The skin of one goat, the skin of many goats,[314]
the hides of the herds of Faunus—
To Ianus and Quirinus,
Mars and Venus,
Vesta and Roma,
Faunus, Silvanus, Romulus
And Antinous Lupercus.

The blood of one hound, the blood of many hounds,[315]
the rage of the wolves of Mars—
To Ianus and Quirinus,
Mars and Venus,
Vesta and Roma,
Faunus, Silvanus, Romulus
And Antinous Lupercus.

The milk of one cow, the milk of many cows,[316]
the feast of the cattle of Vesta—
To Ianus and Quirinus,
Mars and Venus,
Vesta and Roma,
Faunus, Silvanus, Romulus
And Antinous Lupercus.

By this blood, the mark of the beast,[317]
may youth and strength be forever yours.

May you have luck,
may you have blessings,
May you be productive in all things.[318]

---

[314] The flogging implement should be presented and offered at this point.

[315] Wine (or whatever substance is being used to approximate blood) should be presented and offered at this point.

[316] Milk should be presented and offered at this point.

[317] The knife should be used to mark each of the *Luperci*'s foreheads with "blood" at this point.

By this nourishing milk, the liquid of life,[319]
may you be cleansed and consecrated, *Lupercus!*

[*Ritual Laughter.*]

Depending on a variety of factors, the above can be inserted as a modular part into a larger Antinoan (or any other type of) ritual, or it can be the central event in a ritual strictly dedicated to Lupercalia and its activities. After the above, one of the *Luperci* goes around and flogs all of the spectators. Then, the race is generally run, and the winning individual *Lupercus* goes around and gives their blessing to all of those who wish to partake of it. In our own observance of these rituals, I've often had a "red" and a "white" team, each represented by the *Luperci* running against each other, who have been so signified by carrying a red fox tail or a grey coyote tail, and then they have used these to lightly flog the spectators afterwards to give them their further blessings.

If a flogging device of goat or lambskin can be obtained, it should be used in the ritual text given above on each of the *Luperci* during their initiation, and then again when the *Lupercus* goes around to the spectators. If one cannot be obtained, a leather implement would be sufficient, or even a cloth belt for those of less-enterprising tastes. Hands should be presented as consent to be flogged lightly, as this was the traditional practice in Rome; but, other parts of the body could also be presented as one feels able or is interested in doing so— however, unless one is an experienced flogger, a *Lupercus* should not attempt to flog anyone on any body part other than the hands. ***DO NOT ALLOW SOMEONE WHO IS NOT AN EXPERIENCED FLOGGER FLOG YOU ANYWHERE BUT ON THE HANDS!!!***

---

[318] Each of the *Luperci* should be flogged lightly at this point.
[319] The milk-soaked wool should be used to wipe the "blood" from the *Luperci's* foreheads at this point.

If the number of participants is relatively small, or the time which one has to complete this ritual is flexible, or the interests of the participants is of a particular aesthetic, more than just a single slap on the palms can be done for the flogging. The floggings can be administered in such a way that they are not the rather token slap on the palms, but are of a more forceful nature, if the people involved consent to the process being such. These heavier types of flogging can be a single slap, a set number of slaps, a true contest of endurance (!?!), or with an accompanying rhyme along the lines of the following, stopping at each point to see if one wishes to go further:

One for good luck, two for great;

Three for long life, four thwarts fate;

Five against poison, six against fire;

Seven is steadfast, eight doesn't tire;

Nine for better, ten's the best;

With eleven and twelve, you've passed the test.

After everyone has experienced this, the remaining libations of milk and red liquid should be disposed of or consumed by those present. A closing formula for the entire observance might run as follows:

Antinous Master of Hounds:

From time immemorial young men have gathered in groups,

Hunted and fought in each other's company, loved and died;

The youthful Romulus and his brother Remus founded Rome [current year plus 754] years ago,

The boys who had been suckled on the milk of wolves;

Hadrian, son of Rome, of the wolf-brood of Mars

Called you into his sacred company of youths.

You became his greatest hunting hound, and we are your loyal friends.

Give us celerity like the hounds on the trail,

Give us the taste of blood so that we may be fierce in each other's defense,

Give us nourishing and purifying milk,

Give us the strength to strike blows and to endure them.

Antinous Master of Hounds, let your call beckon us onwards,

And may we pursue you, Hunter and Hunted,

Until our breath stops, until our blood runs dry.

AVE VIVE ANTINOE.

Finally, one more dose of ritual laughter might not be a bad way to end!

Megala Antinoeia

The Great Festival of Antinous, Megala Antinoeia, takes place in Ekklesía Antínoou practice on April 21ˢᵗ yearly. Several different aspects of the multi-part festival are observed, and the present hymn mentions all of them. Even if one is not able to commemorate each individual part of the festival on one's own or with one's associates, offering this hymn on the day can serve as a stand-in for those parts which one is not able to perform. This hymn has been in use since 2005, and can be found in The Phillupic Hymns.[320]

Megala Antinoeia

Ave Hadriane Auguste
Romae Imperatore
Princeps Poeticae
Venatoris Maxime

Veneris Romae Templum
populo praemium
pro gaudio datum
benefactorium

Urbs Romae Nova
in amore condita
Romulum contra
filium magna lupa

---

[320] P. Sufenas Virius Lupus, The Phillupic Hymns (Eugene: Bibliotheca Alexandrina, 2008), pp. 213-214.

Venatus est ursa
in terra Mysia
in provincia Asia
et Eroti dedita

Puer aeternus
beatus Antinous
dedicatus ludus
in honorem eius

Venatrix Diana
Noctis Regina
Beata Luna
accipe sacrificia

In dies hodie
Megala Antinoeiae
Hadrianum Antinoum laudo

Hadrianum Antinoum laudo
Hadrianum Antinoum laudo
Hadrianum Antinoum laudo

"Sacred Games and Great Festival of Antinous"

Hail, Hadrian Augustus,
Emperor of Rome,
Prince of Poetry,
Greatest of Hunters!

The Temple of Venus and Roma
a gift for the people
given for the joy
of the benefactor.

193

The New City of Rome
founded on love,
contrary to Romulus
son of the great she-wolf.

A she-bear was hunted
in the land of Mysia
in the province of Asia
and dedicated to Eros.

The eternal boy,
beautiful Antinous—
games were consecrated
in his honor.

Diana the Huntress,
Queen of the Night,
Beautiful Luna,
accept our offerings!

On today's day,
of the Megala Antinoeia
I praise Hadrian and Antinous!...

Antinous Agonodikes

A novel concept to emerge in the practice of the modern Ekklesía Antínoou is that of Antinous as the judge of the artistic contest in the Sacred Games celebrated for him each year during the Megala Antinoeia on April 21st. In 2008, this was one of the five preliminary poems that "broke the floodgates," as it were, in writing *The Phillupic Hymns*, of which over 100 of the 130 poems contained in it were written in two intense periods, starting with April 21st of 2008, and going through May 1st, and then from May 15th through June 9th. It was included in *The Phillupic Hymns* as well.[321]

Antinous Agonodikes

It is fitting that you judge
the games held in your honor.
For you sweat is poured out
as a bodily libation.

Your beautiful form
never shied from showing
the shine of olive oil
on your skin at wrestling.

Your sturdy torso topped
by a broad smooth chest
pushed through waves of water
with dolphin grace.

---

321 P. Sufenas Virius Lupus, *The Phillupic Hymns* (Eugene: Bibliotheca Alexandrina, 2008), p. 217.

You rowed in rivers,
ran races of horses
as well as on foot,
hurled the discus far and true.

May athletes and artists
in their friendly competition
strive to please you
in their sacrifices,

and be blessed by you, O Antinous,
just judge of the contest.

Vox Venari

Vox Venari, "the Call to Hunt," is a poem first used in the 2005 celebration of the Megala Antinoeia to accompany a blessing on each person present, which took the physical form of using sacred oil and making the shapes of the weapons of the deities mentioned in the poem on their hands or foreheads. It was also included in *The Phillupic Hymns*.[322]

From the light of the heavens you were begotten,
From the soil of the earth you were born,
May the light of the stars watch over you,
May the strength of the rocks support you.
May the swift bow of Apollon be in your hand,
May the keen arrows of Diana fly forth from you,
May the knife of Silvanus be guided by your skill,
May the mighty club of Herakles find its mark with you.
Your senses be sharp in open eye and closed,
Your stalking be stealthful and true,
Let your strikes be swift and decisive,
Let pain never be prolonged at your hand.
Never take more than what you need,
Never take any from the unfortunate;
Give thanks in every success,
Give mercy in every encounter.
May your paths on the hunt be wide,
And may you never be lost in the woods;
Antinous, Master of Hounds and his pack
Guide and defend you, and steady your will.
Success to you, plenty, and victory,
Antinous to live in your every sinew.

---

322 P. Sufenas Virius Lupus, *The Phillupic Hymns* (Eugene: Bibliotheca Alexandrina, 2008), p. 147.

Historia Venationis Apri
Hadriani Augusti et
Antinoi Pueri Aeterni Magistris Equi

As with the other hunts of Antinous and Hadrian (apart from the lion hunt), this one is sparsely attested—in fact, only the epitome by Xyphilinus of Cassius Dio's work *Roman History* 69.10.3[2] mentions that Hadrian's hunting skills were so great that he once brought down a boar with a single blow;[323] and see Hadrian's elegy on Borysthenes (which can be found later in the present volume), which also mentions a boar hunt—but neither of these texts mentions Antinous. The hunting *tondo* on the Arch of Constantine that shows the boar hunt seems to have a figure in it that strongly resembles Antinous.[324] As a result, if the *Venatio Apri*, "Boar Hunt," was to be a major festival of the modern Ekklesía Antínoou, it needed an epic myth to accompany it. The present poem is one such offering in that regard, and it was the culmination of the first group of roughly fifty poems written in the period of late April and early May of 2008 that eventually became *The Phillupic Hymns*.[325]

Antinous is here named "master of horse" for the Emperor; his later cult had some relationship to horses in its celebrations, as outlined in an Egyptian cult calendar found in Oxyrhynchus.[326] The date of May 1, on which the feast of the *Venatio Apri* in the Ekklesía Antínoou occurs, is also the usual date for the Irish festival of Beltaine, and indeed Antinous is connected to the Continental Celtic god Belenus

---

[323] Mary Taliaferro Boatwright, *Hadrian and the City of Rome* (Princeton: Princeton University Press, 1987), pp. 194, 201.

[324] Anthony R. Birley, *Hadrian The Restless Emperor* (London and New York: Routledge, 2000), pp. 284-285.

[325] P. Sufenas Virius Lupus, *The Phillupic Hymns* (Eugene: Bibliotheca Alexandrina, 2008), pp. 141-146.

[326] J. W. B. Barns, Peter Parsons, John Rea, and Eric G. Turner (eds.), *The Oxyrhynchus Papyri* Volume 31 (London: Egypt Exploration Society, 1966), §2553, pp. 72-77.

in one inscription from Hadrian's Villa.[327]   As a result, a particular
Irish boar hunt myth is incorporated into this poem in a covert
manner, that of the death of Diarmaid Úa Duibhne as found in
Tóruigheacht Dhiarmada agus Ghráinne,[328] where the hero is wounded by
the boar of Beann Gulban and Finn mac Cumhaill refuses to give him
a drink from his hands, which would cure him.   Here, the Galatian
huntsman Demetrios is wounded, but does heal when Hadrian gives
him a drink of water. This poem was first published in *The Phillupic
Hymns*.[329]

Historia Venationis Apri Hadriani Augusti et Antinoi Pueri Aeterni Magistris Equi

Hadrian, bearer of the *Numen Augusti*,
was a veritable Zeus Olympeios,
Zeus Philios, Zeus Ktesios, but also
Zeus Kynegesios, whose spear never missed.

In the plains of Asia, not far
from Mysia of bear-slaying fame,
it pleased the Emperor to search
the wilds and wastes for a boar.

With Arrian of Nikomedia
and Polemo of Smyrna,
Hadrian took to the hoof
with faithful Antinous at his flank.

---

[327] P. Sufenas Virius Lupus, *The Syncretisms of Antinous* (Anacortes: The Red
Lotus Library, 2010), pp. 25-26.
[328] Nessa Ní Shéaghdha (ed./trans.), *Tóruigheacht Dhiarmada agus Ghráinne:
The Pursuit of Diarmaid and Gráinne*, Irish Texts Society Vol. 48 (London and
Dublin: Irish Texts Society, 1967).
[329] P. Sufenas Virius Lupus, *The Phillupic Hymns* (Eugene: Bibliotheca
Alexandrina, 2008), pp. 141-146.

A fair Galatian huntsman
called Demetrios in the Greek tongue
(but known by another name among
his people) accompanied the small cohort.

Hounds, called by Gauls *vertragi*
would be used in the pursuit,
while sturdy Molossian dogs
would harry and harangue the boar.

Hadrian had hunted boar before:
in the northern forests of Britannia,
in Pannonia with Borysthenes—
famous horse, like Bukephalos of old.

Antinous, youthful, only knew
of boar hunts in Arcadian tales—
of Herakles and the Erymanthean's
capture, creature of Apollon and Adonis.

Demetrios reassured the *eromenos*,
told him to trust in his steed
and the skill and speed in handling
of horses at which he excelled.

Small lances thrown at a distance
would wound the tusked tufted beast,
then on foot the heartier men
would engage it in the final charge.

A long spear with crossing bars
would be set firmly into the earth,
its wielder kneeling alongside,
waiting for the fateful advance.

If the aim of the spear was true
in the final moments of adjustment,
boar's head would be impaled,
its impact followed shortly by death.

If the spear point penetrated its body,
wounded, the beast would charge on,
thrashing, thrusting, likely carrying
spear and side of hunter as spoils.

Demetrios, as was the custom
of his people in heroic contest,
mentioned that the victor in valor
would have the portion of champions.

Each man among them pondered
in silence amid the hound's cries
and the chirping of birds and buzzing
of summer's insects their plans for the chase.

At last, the *vertragi* spotted, pointed
the path toward the brown-skinned boar;
the Molossians were unleashed,
and men and horses galloped at speed.

A fight amidst thorns and thickets
raged between mastiffs and beast;
at a signal from Arrian's well-bred bitch
the hounds gave chase, tiring the boar.

Hadrian dismounted, gave his horse
to Antinous to tend, while Polemo,
Arrian and Demetrios continued
their final pursuit on foot.

The hounds cornered the creature,
circling back to the hunting party
with boar leading, gashed and bleeding
but with a forceful, chthonic persistence.

Arrian of perfect Apollonian aim
launched his lance at the advance
of the boar, piercing its back
as bristles sharpened—a rough comb.

Polemo like tridentian Poseidon
sent three sharp spears in succession,
but only one struck, like the stone
of Hermes in Argus' eye, blinding the boar.

Hadrian with the hafted spear
set himself down, stout-hearted
as the wild boar advanced squealing,
foam scattering from its curled tusks.

Yards away, fire-eyed it stared;
feet away, it rutted and roared;
inches away, Hadrian realigned his grip...
the boar slid along the spear's length.

Point had impaled through the snout
of the boar, into its brain—
but, possessed of godlike fury
it did not expire immediately.

Thrashing and tearing the earth around,
boar struggled with hardened hunter;
Herculean the feat, Hadrian
turned spear-shaft, throwing the beast.

202

Spear snapped, leaving head and shaft
driven through the skull—deadly thrust—
of the boar, wild in its death throes,
righting itself, seeking a target.

Snorting and snarling, scaring the horses
Antinous tried to calm the mounts;
in unutterable and insane rage
the boar came charging equines and keeper.

Demetrios, with his spear and sword
put himself between horses and boar;
he stabbed with both weapons skillfully,
leaving them embedded in the beast's hide.

Half-blinded, bleeding rivers of red
the boar's charge found fleshy target
for sharp-tipped tusk in the thigh
of Demetrios, trampling his torso.

With a single baleful red eye
the boar did not cease his advance;
the Hadetic hog set his sights
on fair Antinous and the horses.

A second boar-spear was unreadied,
lying across the back of Hadrian's horse;
Antinous unfastened its hold and set
himself before horses, held the shaft.

As he had heard Demetrios describe
and saw from afar Hadrian's feat,
he crouched down, stoic, heroic,
waiting for the crazed creature.

The charging boar in madness attacked;
Antinous backing down the length a step,
his knees shaking—suspenseful squat—
until at last boar's breath touched him.

The eternal ephebe moved the spear
at the last second masterfully—
point pierced boar between its eyes,
the crack of its skull muffled by baying.

The boy held fast, pushed back forcefully,
the thrashing boar now pounced upon
by Molossians far ahead of the three
heroes of hunts in times passed.

The boar's legs crumpled amidst the crush
of the jaws of the pack of mastiffs;
panting, wheezing, bleeding out
the terrible beast lay on its side.

Antinous pulled out his sturdy spear
now coated in red film—beast's hot blood—
the boar sighed, squealed, spurt
a small gush of red from its wound.

Hadrian, now at the center of strife
removed the stump of his spear from snout;
the beast's heart burst inside it,
shaking, ceasing, seized with death.

Demetrios, dirty, limping, bandaged,
came to the side of the carnage.
"The kill goes to he whose spear,
extracted, causes its last breath."

Arrian and Polemo, amused and polite
wondered whether the Galatian
was merely flattering the Emperor
at the Bithynian's expense.

The Emperor offered water to the man
who was the only one wounded by the boar;
as if by Asklepios, in a week's time
Demetrios only had a nasty scar.

The choice of the boar's spoils, therefore
was given to the Zeus-like Emperor.
Tusks, tail and hide would make
a trophy most pleasing and envied.

"I give the best meat of its haunch
to my friend, Arrian, whose hound,
as all loyal and skilled lieutenants,
sustains legions and strengthens all.

The head of the boar, save for the tusks,
I give to Polemo of Smyrna,
whose perceptiveness in all things
dazzles some eyes and blinds others.

For myself, nothing more do I wish
than to feast on the meat with friends,
for what should an Emperor enjoy more
than to see his people prosper from his deeds?

The hide, the tusks, and the tail,
like Meleager for Atalanta,
I leave to my master of horse, Antinous,
matching in beauty and bravery those heroes."

Thus the division of those spoils
of hunt of boar to Bithynian
was pleasing to the goddess of Ephesus
and of Silvanus of the ferocious forest.

Apollon and Hermes, Eros,
Aphrodite Ourania and Herakles,
look kindly upon daring men,
both hunters and lovers alike!

Antinous Neos Hermes

There is every reason to assume that if there was a wider, motivating "program" to Hadrian's spread of Antinous' syncretistic cultus to other places in the Roman Empire, Hermes was a deity prevalent in his perceptions under whose syncretistic guise to do so.[330] Whether this was due to Hermes' importance in Arcadia, from whence Antinous' genetic line originated,[331] or whether it was because Antinous died near Hermopolis,[332] the Egyptian city of Thoth who in the Greek view was equivalent to Hermes, or for some other reason, cannot be said with any certainty. But, no matter the reason, the reality of this syncretism remains, and looms large, in the cultus of Antinous, from the Alexandrian coins bearing the image of Antinous as Hermes,[333] to the inscription hailing him as the *Neos Hermes* from Rome,[334] to the acrostich in Dionysius of Alexandria's poem *Periegete* which names Antinous as the "God Hermes under Hadrian."[335] The festival honoring the syncretism of Hermes and Antinous on May 15th, therefore, is important in a variety of ways to mark.

---

[330] P. Sufenas Virius Lupus, *The Syncretisms of Antinous* (Anacortes: The Red Lotus Library, 2010), pp. 14-17.

[331] P. Sufenas Virius Lupus, "From Arcadia with Love: Pan and the Cult of Antinous," in Diotima et al. (eds.), *Out of Arcadia: A Devotional Anthology for Pan* (Bibliotheca Alexandrina, 2011), pp. 86-93.

[332] Caroline Vout, *Power and Eroticism in Imperial Rome* (Cambridge: Cambridge University Press, 2007), p. 132n176; J. R. Rea (ed.), *The Oxyrhynchus Papyri* 63 (London: Egypt Exploration Society, 1996), §4352, pp. 1-17 at 10.

[333] Gustav Blum, "Numismatique d'Antinoos," *Journal International d"Archéologie Numismatique* 16 (1914), pp. 33-70 at 53-57.

[334] Hugo Meyer, *Antinoos: Die archäologischen Denkmäler unter Einbeziehung des numismatischen und epigraphischen Materials sowie der literarischen Nachrichten, Ein Beitrag zur Kunst- und Kulturgeschichte der hadrianisch-frühantoninischen Zeit* (Munich: Wilhelm Fink, 1991), pp. 169-170.

[335] Kai Broderson (ed./trans.), *Dionysios von Alexandria, Das Lied von der Welt* (Hildesheim: Georg Olms AG, 1994), pp. 74-77 lines 513-532; P. Sufenas Virius Lupus, *The Phillupic Hymns* (Eugene: Bibliotheca Alexandrina, 2008), pp. 135, 263-264.

While modern mythology and psychology often suggests a kind of dualism between the "Dionysian" and the "Apollonian" tendencies or archetypes, Karl Kerényi was correct, in my view, in suggesting that there is in fact a third, synthesizing, possibility in terms of viewing some things as "Hermetic,"[336] not in the philosophical or theurgic sense, but as concerned with the communicative and interpretive faculties, and in the reconciliation of these apparent opposites, just as Hermes himself functioned in essential manners in myths related to both Apollon and Dionysos. So, too, should Antinous function in this manner, not only because he has syncretisms with each of these three deities, but because through syncretism itself he functions in a manner that is inherently "Hermetic." Thus, the present poem is an attempt at a meditation on some of those aspects of the Hermetic character or archetype, which though not represented in the direct syncretisms or epithets applied to Antinous from a Hermes-related context in all cases, nonetheless can convey some of the experience of Antinous through these particular Hermes-based lenses nonetheless. It was first published in *The Phillupic Hymns*.[337]

Antinous Neos Hermes

Some will sing of Antinous
as "Epiphanes" or "Choreios,"
he who appears, he who dances;

some will call him "Pythios,"
the oracular inspirer,
a Belenus for youth and beauty;

---

[336] Karl Kerényi, *Hermes Guide of Souls*, trans. Murray Stein (Putnam, CT: Spring Publications, 1976).

[337] P. Sufenas Virius Lupus, *The Phillupic Hymns* (Eugene: Bibliotheca Alexandrina, 2008), pp. 228-229.

some will chant "Antinosiris"
and "Oseirantinous" daily,
the Nile's mysterious one;

but I sing not of he who moves,
or he who comes or speaks,
nor he who conquers death.

I sing of the new Argus-slayer,
the one who with deftness
destroys the all-seeing terror.

I sing of the Arcadian
who hunts and herds and steals
in and to and from the underworld.

I sing of the hero at the gate
who is not initiated
because he has already seen.

I sing of the New Hermes,
the son of the great god,
the emissary.

But no mere messenger,
the one who is exchange
and reciprocity as well.

He who stands between
seer and what is seen,
sound and listener.

He who gives and takes,
buys and sells, carries,
bridges boundaries.

He is there where visions are,
he is there where words sound,
he is there where hearts stir.

But more, he is between
image and eye, ear and music,
lover and beloved and love.

He is a god most alive
when he is used, employed
to engage the world.

To interpret, to intercede,
he is *hermeneusis*
and epistemics.

He is a son of Hermes,
rejuvenated by Thoth,
favored by Re-Harakhte.

It is no hymn I make,
no song to sweetly sing,
no rhymes to write,

for how can one convey
that who one is conveying
is how one conveys it...

Antinous Musegetikos

Musegetikos, "Leader of the Muses," is an epithet applied to both Apollon and Dionysos, though more commonly the former. It is also one of the names of the *demoi* in the *phyla* of Oseirantinoeioi in Antinoöpolis.[338] This poem, therefore, is appropriate for the honoring of Antinous on June 21st, when his syncretism to Apollon is particularly recognized. As Antinous is celebrated in the sculptor's art, as well as in a great deal of poetry from the ancient world, thinking of him in these terms is very apt. It was first published in *The Phillupic Hymns*.[339]

Antinous Musegetikos

He who was the bow-carrier,
healer and averter of evils,
far-seeing one of oracular utterance
was also the lyre-striker.

Therefore, like he who gave water
to the Castalian spring,
may you, Antinous, lead
the Muses in inspiring praises.

---

[338] Mary Taliaferro Boatwright, *Hadrian and the Cities of the Roman Empire* (Princeton: Princeton University Press, 2003), p. 194n124.

[339] P. Sufenas Virius Lupus, *The Phillupic Hymns* (Eugene: Bibliotheca Alexandrina, 2008), p. 216.

It is for you that artists
have painted fair images,
shaped stones to statues,
given words for hymns.

Hadrian, Emperor-poet,
sang with a sweet tongue
under the Muses' gifts,
as did she who was Sappho

for Sabina, Julia Balbilla;
Strato, Pancrates, Mesomedes,
Numenios, Dionysius of Pharos
all bloomed with the arts

blessed through you, O Antinous,
leader of the Muses.

Disciplina

On July 1st in the Ekklesía Antínoou, we devote attention to the goddess Disciplina; though, in order for one's practice to be effective, Disciplina's gifts and favor must be cultivated at all times—indeed, Disciplina is one of the divine beings who receives daily recognition in my own personal practice.

It was during Hadrian's reign that Disciplina was first honored,[340] and it is probably due to Hadrian's assiduous dedication to precision military maneuvers and readiness that this deified abstraction first proliferated amongst the Roman military, particularly in outlying areas like Germania, Britannia, and North Africa-all of which Hadrian visited and where he is known to have inspected the troops. There are eight total dedications to Disciplina (often as *Disciplina Augusta*) in Roman Britain, and it is known that this is the first place in which she was honored.[341] Fragments of a speech that Hadrian gave when inspecting troops in Numidia have also survived,[342] making it likely that Disciplina's introduction to the legions may have occurred on such occasions.

A coin from late in Hadrian's reign (c. 134-138 CE) shows several Roman legionaries dressed in lion skins, with the motto DISCIPLINA AUGUSTA on it.[343] I happen to have a replica of this particular coin, and on most days I carry it with me, not only to honor Hadrian but also to honor Disciplina and to cultivate the virtues associated with Disciplina on a daily basis. It is pictured on the next page.

---

[340] Lesley Adkins and Roy A. Adkins, *Dictionary of Roman Religion* (New York: Facts on File, 1996), p. 63.

[341] Guy de la Bédoyère, *Gods with Thunderbolts: Religion in Roman Britain* (Stroud: Tempus Publishing, 2002), pp. 249-250.

[342] Michael P. Speidel, *Emperor Hadrian's Speeches to the African Army–A New Text* (Mainz: Römisch-Germanischen Zentralmuseums, 2006).

[343] Rainer Pudill, *Hadrian–Münzen als Zeugnisse einer Glanzvollen Epoche Roms* (Speyer: Numismatische Gesellschaft Speyer, 2008), p. 72.

"*Disciplina*," a Latin noun, means many things: education and training, self-control and determination, knowledge in a particular field of study (or "discipline"!), and an orderly way of life. Virtues associated with her in the life of a Roman soldier included *frugalitas, severitas,* and *fidelis*: frugality (with money, energy, and actions), severity (in focus, determination, decisiveness, and not being easily dissuaded), and faithfulness (to one's unit, to the larger army, to one's commanding officers, and to Rome and the Roman people). In many respects, *devotio,* which is the entire focus of the present book, would also be equally covered by devotion to Disciplina.

Even though Disciplina's cultus originated in a military context,[344] I don't think that she should be focused solely on military matters today, or that only military personnel should be interested in cultivating her favor and enacting her virtues, I think she is here for everyone. In reflecting on Disciplina on July 1, 2011, I had some interesting thoughts arise, particularly in relation to the word "discipline" as it is understood and commonly defined in English in the modern world.

1) Discipline does not mean asceticism. For some people in some

---

[344] Though, when "Don't Ask, Don't Tell" ended on September 20, 2011, I think it was a date of triumph for Disciplina, personally!

walks of life or on particular spiritual or career paths, asceticism can be a form of discipline, but discipline in itself and attention to it does not require asceticism. Indeed, for those of an ascetic tendency, true attention to discipline might in fact point toward someone being less ascetic and more indulgent in order to maintain a healthy balance. The *frugalitas* associated with Disciplina need not mean that one can't enjoy one's money and other resources, within reason.

2) Discipline is not a synonym for "punishment." Unfortunately, in English, this is the context in which we often first learn the word "discipline." I remember I first heard it used in the third grade, on the first few days of class, when we discussed what would happen if students misbehaved, and the stages one would go through before being sent to the office or going to detention or having one's parents notified. "Discipline" can mean that, certainly, and "disciplinary actions" are things we usually associate with censure or reprimand (e.g. members of Congress and so forth...). In the BDSM/kink subcultures, the "D" in the acronym can stand for "discipline," and so it often has that meaning in an even more heightened manner for such people. But, it doesn't have to. "Discipline" also gives us the roots for the terms "disciple" and "discipleship," which is to say, *devoted studentship*, and "disciplinary" matters in academia are matters having to do with one's specialized field and the norms observed in it in terms of research, prevailing theories, and so forth. So, understanding this widespread range of semantic content in the English term gives one a more broad and accurate approach to the full range of its meanings in the original cultures in which the concept was developed.

3) An important element of any practice of discipline as a virtue is *diligence*. Diligence is a term which also comes from Latin. In Latin, *diligo, diligere* is often the verb used (particularly by Christians) to mean "to love," and it derives from the verb *lego, legere*, which means (amongst other things) "to choose." (In an interesting development, it also eventually meant "to read," because there were no spaces between words most often in Latin manuscripts, and thus one had to "choose"

215

the words out of the letters on the page.) The ideas of both doing one's activities with love, and actively choosing to do them, is a very important element of discipline, and when due diligence is applied to any matter, both love and choice should be foremost in one's mind. There is a phrase that I've heard in different contexts, sometimes positively and sometimes somewhat ambivalently, that advises one to "work out thy salvation with diligence." This is traditionally said to have been the final words of the historical Buddha, and thus somewhat flies in the face of some ideas on salvation from a Christian viewpoint; and yet, because the Christians used the word which eventually became "diligence" for us as their preferred term for "love," perhaps there really is something to its understanding in this matter, even within a specifically Christian context.

So, honoring Disciplina throughout the year is a good practice to have in assisting one's devotions to Antinous, and to Hadrian, and the many other deities and divine figures associated with the Ekklesía Antínoou. But, on July 1st, Disciplina should be particularly honored with specific rituals, offerings, meditations, or other activities. The poems below were both written for Disciplina on different occasions: the first in 2008, and it was included in *The Phillupic Hymns*,[345] while the second is from 2011 and was written on Disciplina's actual festival.

Disciplina's Tragedy

It is said that I was unknown
until the time of Hadrian of the Aelii;
but I have existed ever since
Minerva deflected Mars' advance.

Parthenogenerated virgin, never born,
but daughter all the same of Minerva,
sister of Honos, nurturer to all
who study and with devotion are dedicated.

---

[345] P. Sufenas Virius Lupus, *The Phillupic Hymns* (Eugene: Bibliotheca Alexandrina, 2008), p. 93.

Legionaries used to call me lover,
though a chaste love I had with them;
now, I am no longer remembered
even by the strictest of soldiers and officers.

None call me "goddess," instead they say
by intellect's parsing "deified abstraction,"
but even the least part of my body
is the curved line of artists' intention.

Mine has been a quiet might,
understated but undoubtedly present,
people know me when they see me
even if they do not use my name.

But now, those who most cultivate
the *kharis* of the divine realms
toss me aside like a broken altar,
a relic priceless but unperceived.

Let it be known that those who honor me
are possessed of a power unparalleled:
what Delphian Apollon called "moderation"
is my very presence, which I taught the god.

Disciplina Doctor

She is the greatest teacher,
the one who knows to instruct
the best ways to think,
not what one's thoughts should be;
how to ask questions
rather than knowing answers;
that method is medium
and diligence better than definition;
true learning is derived from consent,
and the best disciples are those who choose to be.

Antinous Silvanus

The relief sculpture of Antinous as Silvanus from Lanuvium presents him in a manner consistent in all ways with Silvanus' other depictions throughout history, with the attributes of the *falx* (curved vineyard knife) and with a small sight-hound used for hunting, with one exception: he is portrayed young and beardless.[346] Given that portraying Silvanus otherwise would therefore have lost the specific Antinoan identification, this is therefore understandable! While Antinous as Silvanus would make a good pairing with Diana as two hunter deities honored in the temple at Lanuvium, it does not appear that the relief sculpture depicting him thus was from the temple itself, but instead from a private estate, possibly belonging to one of the members of the *collegium* that built the temple. This poem was written to honor this particular syncretism of Antinous, and the wider associations of the date, on July 16, 2009 during the festival itself. I have also included three Silvanus inscriptions that I translated.

Antinous Silvanus

In Bithynia, flourishing green pines
where e'en forgotten serpent cult survives
the *falx*-bearer prunes meandering vines.

At Lanuvium, the *collegium* dines
rememb'ring, where Diana's cult derives,
Bithynia's far flourishing green pines.

---

346 Peter F. Dorcey, *The Cult of Silvanus: A Study in Roman Folk Religion* (Leiden: E. J. Brill, 1992).

Abusing Palestina's forests? Fines!
The memory of cedars tall revives...
the *falx*-bearer prunes meandering vines.

Socanica's Dalmatian silver mines
with Caesar honored hero who arrives
from Bithynia's flourishing green pines.

In Britannia, on wall's dividing lines
as tribesmen wage their wars and cattle drives
the *falx*-bearer prunes meandering vines.

Alexandria's oracle divines
the god's actions amidst worshipper's lives
like Bithynia's forests of green pines.

As undergrowth with tendrils tough entwines
the whole of forest, now the good god strives
to pour for all to share the finest wines
and feast with rich meats impaled on fork's tines
and in the evergreen and storax? Signs
as *falx*-bearing deity trains the vines
and in Bithynia yet grow the pines.

Three Silvanus Inscriptions [347]

[Axina, Gallia Narbonensis, c. 161-169 CE]

O Silvanus, with this holy ash-tree enclosure,
and these grown trees, O greatest overseer of the gardens,
to you we give thankfully these hymns
which we, through plowed fields and through the Alpine
    mountains,
even to the host of your pleasant grove;
while I govern the jurisdiction and the appointment I undergo
    for Caesar,
by your prosperous, lucky favor
may you lead me and mine back to Rome permanently
and may you give us in Italy, where you live, land we may
    cultivate by your protection;
I will soon vow a thousand great trees for this.
Titus Pomponius Victor, Augustan Procurator.

[Capestrano, Italy, c. 156 CE]

Under the camp of Capestrano,
sixteen before the Kalends of April [March 17],
the year of the consulships of Silvanus and Augurinus;

Dedicated to Holy Silvanus
by Athenius Sextus Lateranus
freedman and treasurer, for good fortune;

O Great God, O Powerful Silvanus, O Most Holy Shepherd
who watches over the Idaean Grove and directs Roman camps,
sweet docile one, a shepherd's pipe image was joined to you

---

[347] These three inscriptions are found respectively in *CIL* XII §103; IX §3375; and VIII §27764. They were translated earlier in P. Sufenas Virius Lupus, *The Phillupic Hymns* (Eugene: Bibliotheca Alexandrina, 2008), pp. 80-81.

for it was fixed near your depiction that is connected to the
stream;
it was sinking in the water, and I raised it through the moist
meadows of Ticinus
by the low eddies in bright silvery waters,
and I prevented the carrying away of the cypress root, O Silvanus;
attest this for me, O Holy One, favoring the divine commands
you return
which I vowed to you for the worth of your image and your altar.
These things, which I have done on behalf of the lords' health
and for the fruitfulness of my and my own's life praying,
and dutiful conduct; you, a propitious patron, to whom I have
come,
until I return and restore what is on these altars for you, O
Rustic One
out of my vow and deservedly, and my sayings fulfilled,
that I am he whose name was included on my altar.
Now ye, O well-done joyful deeds and material things,
administrate men and always hope for the future.
Decreed by the Decurion.

[Africa Proconsularis]

All that is sown, all that is born from the earth, now, the grasses
rise
and their sharp blades thrive which the weakened soil carried
alone.
All together are commanded and enlivened and made green
throughout the grove you make leafy,
carefully from new flowers and from trained plants truly.
Wherefore may you give to the god of our fathers which we honor—
to Silvanus—from the leaf-enclosed spring to which they call out:
the sacred grove is brought forth from the rock and into the tree branches!
We give this difficulty to you according to custom...
We give this kid to you according to the voice of the *Falx-*
Carrying Father,

We give this to you according to your custom, crowned Pine-
  Branch-Carrier:
Thus the priest recalls to me.
Sport, O Fauns, with the Dryad girls;
play and celebrate now in my shrine;
Naiads from the grove are my country-women!
Pan the Goat-Foot One is accustomed to play with the reed-
  pipe
sitting and sporting—the custom at Parnassus—
even rose-colored, foxy Bassareus Bacchus plays the flute
and the god Apollon presses his yoked chariot-horses.
The god lightens the war of enemies; yet you, Silvanus,
I stand surety for with indulgences as most beloved father of
  peace,
and ask that you consider your disciple and servant.
Wherefore may you give to the god of our fathers which we honor—
to Silvanus—from the leaf-enclosed spring to which they call out:
the sacred grove is brought forth from the rock and into the tree branches!

224

Antinous Kynegetikos

Though never applied to Antinous in any currently known historic or cultic source, the epithet *Kynegetikos,* "hunter," but more literally "leader of hounds," is entirely appropriate to what we know of him, and how he is portrayed in a few sculptural reliefs. Hadrian's friend, the Bithynian governor Arrian of Nikomedia, wrote a treatise called *Kynegetikos* during Hadrian's lifetime, possibly due to Hadrian's known interest in hunting.[348] As there are multiple "hunting festivals" observed in relation to Hadrian and Antinous in the modern Ekklesía Antínoou's ritual calendar, this poem might be a further one that would be appropriate to recite on those occasions (April 21st, the *Venatio Ursae*/Bear Hunt; May 1st, the *Venatio Apri*/Boar Hunt; and August 21st, the *Venatio Leonis*/Lion Hunt, as well as other hunts that may be adopted into common practice in the years to come). However, it could also be used to honor Antinous on the *Dies Caniculares* on July 25th, as his specific aspect as "master of hounds" would be particularly appropriate to employ on that date. It was first published in *The Phillupic Hymns.*[349]

Antinous Kynegetikos

You who are of Arcadian stock,
offspring of the Great Bear,
Kallisto, daughter of Lykaon
of wolfish aspect—

---

[348] A. A. Phillips and M. M. Willcock (eds./trans.), *Xenophon and Arrian On Hunting* (Warminster: Aris & Phillips, 1999).

[349] P. Sufenas Virius Lupus, *The Phillupic Hymns* (Eugene: Bibliotheca Alexandrina, 2008), p. 215.

You are the new Arkas,
the young bear venturing forth.
Many wish to possess your hide
as a trophy of their successful hunt.

But you are a ferocious creature,
a wolf and a stalker of prey
as swift as a Gaulish greyhound
and as dogged in the pursuit.

May not a hair of your smooth skin
succumb to the harm of the hunt,
may hare and deer, boar and lion
be scattered and broken by you.

May the lion-slaying Herakles,
far-shooting Apollon and his arrows,
fierce Ephesian maiden Artemis
and Silvanus of the bordering woods

bless you, O Antinous,
master of hounds and hunter.

Dies Natalis Dianae

This holy-day has been celebrated in modern Antinoan devotion ever since we learned of its existence in the ancient practices of the Lanuvium *collegium*'s ritual year in 2003,[350] but the present hymn for the occasion was not written until 2005. In addition to this particular local practice from Antinous' ancient cultus, there are a variety of other matters which suggest a connection between Antinous and Artemis/Diana.[351] Her festival on August 13th, therefore, has been one which I have celebrated with particular joy for a number of years, and I hope this hymn adds to that joy in your own observances of the festival. It was first published in *The Phillupic Hymns*.[352]

Natalis Dianae

Ave Diana Regina
Lanuvii Domina
virgo beatissima
lucis argenti luna

Latonae prima filia
sine dolore nata
dona omnis praemia
qui tua beata

---

[350] Mary Beard, John North, & Simon Price (eds./trans.), *Religions of Rome, Volume 2: A Sourcebook* (Cambridge: Cambridge University Press, 1998), p. 294.

[351] P. Sufenas Virius Lupus, "Artemis and the Cult of Antinous," in Thista Minai et al. (eds.), *Unbound: A Devotional Anthology for Artemis* (Eugene: Bibliotheca Alexandrina, 2009), pp. 106-112.

352 P. Sufenas Virius Lupus, *The Phillupic Hymns* (Eugene: Bibliotheca Alexandrina, 2008), pp. 87-88.

Favere omnis nobis
cum praeda venationis
ursae et leonis
et celeris leporis

Regina Nemorensis
Lanuvii Specularis
servorum liberationis
Sacra tu appellaris

Requiem Donatrix
Diva Dea Venatrix
nymphae curatrix
naturae protectorix

Antinoo communica
in multa templa
tua gratia divina
tua magna benefica

Cum Antinoo laudata
Dea Splendissima
Ave Lunae Dea Diana!

Ave Lunae Dea Diana!
Ave Lunae Dea Diana!
Ave Lunae Dea Diana!

"Diana's Birthdate"

Hail Diana the Queen
Lady of Lanuvium
most beautiful virgin
moon of silver light

First child of Leto
born without pain,
give to all the gift
which is your blessedness

Favor us all
with the spoils of the hunt—
bear and lion
and swift hare

Queen of the Sacred Grove
Mirror-like one of Lanuvium
by liberation of slaves
you are called "Holy"

Giver of rest
Divine Huntress Goddess
overseer of nymphs
protectress of nature

Share with Antinous
into many temples
by your divine grace
your great favors

Praised with Antinous
O Most Splendid goddess,
Hail, Goddess of the Moon Diana!

Ritual for the Lion Hunt
and the Festival of the Red Lotus

by Erynn Rowan Laurie

Though this particular ritual occasion has been celebrated since 2003 in the Ekklesía Antínoou, the ritual text given here was first written in 2008 by Erynn, and has been celebrated yearly since that time. As the Lion Hunt/*Venatio Leonis* and the Festival of the Red Lotus is a two-day festival, it is appropriate that the two rituals correspond to one another closely. The Lion Hunt is an occasion on which to reflect upon our failures, based upon one of the ancient poetic fragments relating to Antinous and Hadrian's lion hunt as reflected in a piece from Oxyrhynchus[353] (possibly by Pancrates) and the information on Pancrates given in Athenaeus of Naukratis' *Deipnosophistae*;[354] both of these texts are given in full in a subsequent chapter below. The failures of the first day, however, are transformed into the triumphs and beauty of the second day.

August 21: The Lion Hunt

[Offerings are prepared and nine candles—red if possible—are laid out on the altar or shrine space.]

Even the eternal gods are not perfection. Even the eternal gods may fail. Divine Antinous, when he hunted the Mauretanian lion, fell before the creature, his pride and eagerness making him careless. It was only the hand of the Divine Hadrian that saved

---

[353] Arthur S. Hunt (ed.), *The Oxyrhynchus Papyri* 8 (London: Egypt Exploration Society, 1911), §1085, pp. 73-77.
[354] Charles Burton Gulick (ed./trans.), *Athenaeus, Deipnosophistae*, Volume 7 (Cambridge: Harvard University Press, 1941), pp. 126-129, XV.677.

the Bithynian, he who is enthroned with the Gods of Egypt.

In remembrance that even the gods may fail, we acknowledge our own failures on this day. We ask the aid of the God Antinous— *Beatus, Iustus, Benevolens*—to hold us up despite our failings, to help us release these failures and forgive ourselves for our errors and our hubris. *In nomine Antinoi Aeterni:*

[After acknowledging each failure, light one of the candles at the invocation.]

When we are blinded by pride
    Antinous-Apollon, Navigator, give us sight.

When we are numbed to compassion
    Antinous-Dionysos, Lover, give us kindness.

When we are consumed by greed
    Antinous-Hermes, Liberator, free us from desire.

When we lose our path
    Antinous-Hermes, Navigator, be our compass.

When we are driven to obsession
    Antinous-Apollon, Lover, show us the truth.

When we are enslaved to habit
    Antinous-Dionysos, Liberator, break our chains.

When we fall to illusion
    Antinous-Dionysos, Navigator, clear away the mists.

When we lose heart
    Antinous-Hermes, Lover, steal our hearts back for us.

When intelligence fails us
Antinous-Apollon, Liberator, open our minds.

As these candles burn, may Antinous the Beautiful, the Just, the Benevolent, burn away our flaws and our failures. Accept our offerings and work change within us. Antinous, *Salvator, dona nobis pacem.*

August 22: Festival of the Red Lotus

[Offerings are prepared, red flowers should be on the altar, and nine candles—red if possible—are laid out.]

The ancient tales speak of those who in death became green. Adonis, Narcissus, Hyakinthos, Hylas, Daphne, and even Miach, son of Dían Cécht,[355] bloomed in their deaths. Yet the divine Antinous created his lotus from the blood of the Mauritanian lion, defying death by the hand of the Divine Hadrian.

From blood, beauty. From defeat, victory. The Divine Antinous is the lotus undying, flower without corruption, risen from the waters undefiled, risen like Osiris. In remembrance of this victory, we acknowledge our own victories. With the aid of the God Antinous—*Beatus, Iustus, Benevolens*—we give thanks for the power to transcend our failures. *In nomine Antinoi Aeterni:*

[After acknowledging each victory, light a candle at the invocation.]

As we acknowledge the best of our accomplishments

---

[355] Elizabeth Gray (ed./trans.), *Cath Maige Tuired: The Second Battle of Mag Tuired*, Irish Texts Society Volume 52 (London and Dublin: Irish Texts Society, 1983), pp. 32-33 §33-35.

232

Antinous-Apollon, Navigator, we give you thanks.
As we revel in the giving and receiving of love
Antinous-Dionysos, Lover, we give you thanks.

As we celebrate the abundance of the world
Antinous-Hermes, Liberator, we give you thanks.

As we see the way before us and set our feet to it with joy
Antinous-Hermes, Navigator, we give you thanks.

As we embrace our passions and follow them
Antinous-Apollon, Lover, we give you thanks.

As we act in devotion and maintain ourselves in fidelity
Antinous-Dionysos, Liberator, we give you thanks.

As we clarify our visions to the brightness of crystal
Antinous-Dionysos, Navigator, we give you thanks.

As we give ourselves to wisdom like a lover
Antinous-Hermes, Lover, we give you thanks.

As we cultivate steadfast courage
Antinous-Apollon, Liberator, we give you thanks.

As these candles burn so then, Antinous—Beautiful, Just, and Benevolent—may our hearts burn with your light. Accept our offerings and our gratitude for your transforming power. Antinous, *Salvator, dona nobis pacem.*

Eleusis

We have observed the initiation of Hadrian and Antinous into the Eleusinian Mysteries in 128 CE in the context of modern Antinoan devotion since 2003 on the date of September 21st annually. This particular poem came about on that particular festival in 2011, not only in relation to it, and to some recent work I had been doing on Hadrian and Antinous' relationships to Persephone and the Eleusinian Mysteries,[356] but because Antinous, Hekate, and the Agathos Daimon were the "Gods of the Month" in Neos Alexandria in September of 2011. In an effort to honor all of them, and the occasion, this poem came about.

The Eleusinian Mysteries took place in the month of Boedromion,[357] which generally fell in the period of our modern September/October; it is thus the month from whence this poem takes its name.

Boedromion

In the consulships of L. Nonius
Calpurnius Torquatus Asprenas
and Marcus Annius Libo they went—
O joyous day! O sacred night!—
to fast in cleansing all felonious
thoughts, purging from themselves the dust and dross
of all the unenlightened years they spent—
O torchbearer, bring forth the light!

---

[356] The main exponent of this work is an essay called "'I Have Seen The Maiden': Hadrian, Antinous, and the Eleusinian Mysteries," which will be released soon in the Bibliotheca Alexandrina anthology *Queen of the Sacred Way*, roughly concurrent with the completion of the present publication.

[357] Marvin W. Meyer (ed.), *The Ancient Mysteries: A Sourcebook of Sacred Texts* (Philadelphia: University of Pennsylvania Press, 1999), p. 18.

Hadrian was nearly bursting his seams,
eager to speak of what he'd seen before
when he had been initiated then—
O joyous day! O sacred night!—
but he was silent, like sleep without dreams,
long forgotten; banks of Stygian shore,
the fate of less fortunate mortal men—
O torchbearer, bring forth the light!

Antinous trod the old Sacred Way,
crossed the Cephisus River's sturdy bridge
which Hadrian built before they had met—
O joyous day! O sacred night!—
but lack of food and sleep made his stride sway,
as distant Athens' Acropolis ridge
faded from view, each foot to front he'd set—
O torchbearer, bring forth the light!

Abusive insults hurled at passersby
brought groans and smiles, occasional laughter
to the crowd of pilgrims proceeding thence—
O joyous day! O sacred night!—
like Baubo and Iambe brought tears to eye
of Demeter from merriment after
her sadness departed, returning sense—
O torchbearer, bring forth the light!

He had drunk the *kykeon*, and the cists
were carried by children not half his age,
as days-old echo of squealing pigs fades—
O joyous day! O sacred night!—
when, before his eyes, clouded with grey mists
a drama unknown on Athens' great stage
began to unfold in figures like shades—
O torchbearer, bring forth the light!

From her cave, Hekate, torches ablaze,
came bearing the news: Persephone's rape,
while Helios' indifferent eyes poured down—
O joyous day! O sacred night!—
meanwhile, Artemis' silver arrow rays
pierced Dionysos' bounty of the grape
and, in the distance, Hylas fell to drown—
O torchbearer, bring forth the light!

But Hekate, now horse-headed, saw him,
Antinous, not mere audience lout,
and called his name, summoning him to her—
O joyous day! O sacred night!—
he stood before her, naked without trim
of cloud-white *chlamys*, not a stitch about,
while deep within his soul began to stir—
O torchbearer, bring forth the light!

A serpent made of subtle matter snaked
from his solar plexus, slithering low,
then came to rest beside him on the ground—
O joyous day! O sacred night!—
but, as a marble statue's features, faked,
the subtle serpent, skin like moon a-glow,
a humanoid form—his own!—soon had found—
O torchbearer, bring forth the light!

"This is your *Agathos Daimon*; look well!
The serpent slithering from form to form,
the god in all, but each is different!
(*O joyous day! O sacred night!*)
"But do not fall under the dreadful spell
of loving his face! Am I not the storm?
By Zeus, do I bring warning sufficient?"
(*O torchbearer, bring forth the light!*)

"I am not Narcissus, I'm not deceived
into folly at my own beauty's face;
I revere this god, but know his limit!"
(*O joyous day! O sacred night!*)
Now hound-headed, Enodia received
the answer that proved Antinous' grace;
"Then bear this fire, dear boy, and don't dim it!"
(*O torchbearer, bring forth the light!*)

The snake twined 'round her feet, then expanded
across aeons of time to heroes past,
demigods enrolled in Eleusis' rites—
O joyous day! O sacred night!—
Herakles with club, who had demanded
Cerberus from Hades; and Zeus' blast
that brought Asklepios to Hades' sights—
O torchbearer, bring forth the light!

Polydeukes and Kastor, brothers two,
one ever-living, one ever-dying,
wrestler unmatched and master of horses—
O joyous day! O sacred night!—
all these came into Antinous' view,
the single stretched serpent on feet lying,
connecting their diverse lives' long courses...
O torchbearer, bring forth the light!

The "Good Spirit," slithering further still
came to the lap of another maiden,
burrowed out of sight, as Hekate cried—
O joyous day! O sacred night!—
and shone her beacons, by her divine will
on Persephone, with her womb laden
with child not-yet-born, who had not-yet-died—
O torchbearer, bring forth the light!

In that moment, Persephone gave birth
to Iakkhos, the child of Eleusis' land,
and his face resembled Antinous'—
O joyous day! O sacred night!—
child and mother sank deep into the earth,
and Hekate over all heaven spanned,
illumination stayed continuous—
O torchbearer, bring forth the light!

He came back to his senses, moments passed,
and still upon the Sacred Way he walked,
uncertain what he'd seen, or what he'd see—
O joyous day! O sacred night!
Later, they reached Eleusis' grounds at last,
and afterwards, he and Hadrian talked
of what the Hierophant did decree...
O torchbearer, bring forth the light!

Mantinoë's Prayer

According to a papyrus hymn fragment from Oxyrhynchus (which is given in a subsequent chapter below), Antinous' mother's name was Mantinoë, which recalls the Arcadian city-state that founded the colony of Bithynion-Claudiopolis in which Antinous was born. (The foundress of Mantineia was Antinoë, which is the feminine form of Antinous' name, and which was also a name sometimes given to the city of Antinoöpolis.) The Obelisk of Antinous, in a section that is sadly damaged, does mention Antinous' mother, but not by name in the extant portion. In absence of any better suggestions, the name "Mantinoë" seems very sensible to assume as correect, given Antinous' own name and his ethnic origins in Arcadia.

This prayer was written in October of 2010, not long after the first Spirit Day, held in honor of the large number of youthful male suicides due to homophobic bullying. Given that it was written in that immediate context, there is certainly some of that feeling accompanying it. This prayer presumes that Antinous' mother predeceased him, and she is therefore expressing this prayer from her afterlife as Antinous is dying. It is a prayer, perhaps, that can be used on the date of Antinous' death (October 28), or which can be performed as a dramatic monologue in a liturgical setting on Foundation Day.

Mantinoë's Prayer

Hermes Psychopompos, hear my plea!
Right now, a beautiful boy is dying.

He is slipping beneath the surface of the waters,
he is being carried away by a mighty river.
In his last breaths, he called for me,
and now I am crying out to you
who is stronger and mightier than myself.

239

He has seen the maiden Persephone
at the side of his lord and lover.

He received the favor of the Apis Bull,
the animal form that many known of Serapis
but who is the herald of the god Ptah of Memphis.
May you entreat Ptah, Hermes, to bear him up,
to swell the river to bring him to shore.

He has given food to the Petsuchos in his city,
therefore let Sobek, whether he be One or Two,
find him and leave him unharmed and whole,
and carry him safely to the black soil's banks
like Kastor and Polydeukes, ever-friends of sailors,
the heroes who carry the strength of their father Zeus
just as you, O Sobek, carry the glory of Re—
Hermes, entreat him with your words of magic.

And if your swift feet and swifter speech
does not spare him his death, then send
your brother Anubis and your colleague Thoth,
for it is in Thoth's nome that this tragedy happens,
and guide him before Osiris to be judged free of blame,
rejuvenate his soul with your holy symbols,
and deliver him into your skillful hands, O Hermes,
to convey him to the Isles of the Blessed
to drink the waters of Mnemosyne
and become a hero at Antinoë's hearth-side.

I speak these words as every mother speaks
who loves the children she bore from her own womb
as truly as the Memphite Sekhmet is fierce
and the ferocity of Set is indomitable.

I sound this prayer to you, O Hermes,
on behalf of my son, Antinous of Bithynia,
paidika of the emperor Aelius Hadrianus of Rome,
mystes of Eleusis, child of the land of Bendis,
of Arcadian stock, descendant of Lykaon
and Arkas and Parhassios and Pan and Antinoë,
son of Hermogenes, son of my own flesh,
I, Mantinoë of Bithynion-Claudiopolis.

I have crossed the Styx, and by that river
my prayers are stronger than those who are living
for I have my own form and my own breath in me.
May the gods be favorable to this, my entreaty,
and may Hermes answer as swiftly
as wordless thoughts behind dazzled eyes.

Hadrian and Antinous

This is one of the oldest, continuously used devotional texts in the modern cultus of Antinous, which I wrote as one of two liturgical dramas for the first Foundation Day in October of 2002. One of the most enjoyable parts of Foundation Day rituals for me has been to sit back, relax, and see what happens during these ritual dramas, as my tendency has been to assign parts to people who show up without having them know anything about it in advance. While one day, perhaps, we'll be able to plan these things more deliberately and have designated actors for each part (whether they recite it from memory or from a script), in the meantime it has been a way to get as many people involved in the ritual proceedings as possible, so that I am not the only person reading prayers, singing hymns, and the like as ritual leader, *sacerdos*, and *Doctor* of the Ekklesía Antínoou.

I must share one of the most moving and beautiful events in the entirety of my time in modern Antinoan devotion that has to do with this text specifically. At the 2003 Foundation Day that I held in Cork (Ireland), there was one person present who had attended the ritual the previous year, a good Irish Catholic (and straight!) friend of mine who was fully in support of my activities in polytheism, my queerness, and every other possible thing with which one might assume a straight Irish Catholic might have some difficulties. This friend was also a champion *sean nós* singer, and I assigned him Antinous' role for this piece. He improvised an Irish air and sang it in *sean nós* style, and it was one of the most beautiful and moving things I've ever heard in my life—and every time I relate this story (and even as I'm typing it!), tears start to come to my eyes. It was an incomparable moment, and one where I truly felt Antinous' presence reaching out across the centuries and the geographic distances. But, more than that, it was a moment in which I was certain that, had Antinous been Irish, *this is what he would have sounded like*. No person who has performed this ritual drama since then has ever been brave enough to venture singing it, but I hope that some others in the future (including the readers of this text!) may do so one day.

This liturgical drama can be performed on Foundation Day itself, or on October 29th, as it reflects Antinous' death (still unknown to Hadrian) but also the infinite possibilities inherent in his future godhead. The text of this liturgical drama was also given in *The Phillupic Hymns*.[358]

Hadrian and Antinous

[Hadrian]

Where is he? I seek but do not find,
I call his name, but only hear the splashing river.

[Antinous *Respondit*:]

I am the lantern, I am the light
I am the darkness, I am the night
I am the cup, I am the water
I am the blood, I am the slaughter

I am the breather, I am the breath
I am the living and dying and death
I am the rose and the fish in the pool
I am the clay and the dust and the fool

I am beauty, destruction and strife
I am the poet whose words are his wife
I am the dancer, I am the spirit
I am the voice for those who can hear it

---

358 P. Sufenas Virius Lupus, *The Phillupic Hymns* (Eugene: Bibliotheca Alexandrina, 2008), pp. 230-231.

I am the longing the lover holds
I am the bird wings which wind enfolds
I am the tree and every green leaf
I am the pain and feeling of grief

I am the bones and the flesh and the fire
I am the peace for those who are tired
I am the labyrinth and the way through it
I am *ekstasis* and wine that leads to it

I am the boat and the tide and the ebb
I am the net and the spider's web
I am the boar who dwells in the fog
I am the star with the head of a dog

I am the cock, the ram, and the flower
I am the moon at the midnight hour
I am the sword, I am the spear
I am the shield against all fear

I am the skin and the penis and hand
I am the power to understand
I am the blindness with eyes to see
I am the guard, the gate and the key.

Foundation Day: Prologue

As with everything in the Ekklesía Antínoou and with modern Antinoan devotion, the way in which individual devotees of Antinous will observe and celebrate Foundation Day will vary, depending on whether it is a private devotion or a public ritual, a celebration with invited guests who aren't involved with Antinous or only with co-practitioners, and from year to year, place to place, person to person, and many other possible factors besides. The following framing proclamation is one I've used every year since 2002, which seems to accomplish what is necessary on the occasion, giving those familiar with the story of Antinous and Hadrian a few moments to reflect upon it, and giving those who are not familiar with it enough of an idea about it to be able to derive more meaning from the observances which follow.

As is true of a great deal of the texts, activities, and suggestions in this book, ritual procedures are modular, and can be slotted in or removed quite easily depending on one's own needs, interests, and intentions. Therefore, any number of things could follow this in one's observances, including the recitation of many of the sacred texts found in this book, invocation of the Obelisk of Antinous, singing of hymns, performance of liturgical dramas, offerings of incense and other things, blessing, sharing, and consumption of various foods or drinks, songs and dances, labyrinth walks, meditations, recognition and honoring of various *Sancti*, as well as the honoring of other deities, are all very valid potential possibilities. Use your own imagination, and consult the other participants and your own community of associates to determine what will work the best for you in a given year and in your particular context during that year.

On this day, October 30th, two before the Kalends of November, Hathyr 3, in the year 130 of the current era, 18__ years ago,

245

during the fourteenth year[359] of the reign of Aelius Traianus Hadrianus Caesar, in the consulship of Q. Fabius Catullinus and M. Flavius Aper, in the Two-Hundred and Twenty-Seventh Olympiad, Eight-Hundred and Eighty-Five years after the foundation of Rome, in Egypt on the River Nile near Hermopolis, at a bend in the river called Hir-Wer, a great tragedy occurred, a great mystery was revealed, and a great tradition began. We come together tonight to remember those events, to re-enact those mysteries, to rebuild that tradition, and to let the name of Antinous be heard once again. This is Foundation Day: the day Antinous' two-days-dead-and-drowned body was *found*, the day Hadrian *founded* the city of Antinoöpolis in his honor, the day Antinous was called a hero and a god for the first time, the day many of his temples were opened and his games were enacted, and the day that we begin to re-establish and re-create tradition in our own times and for our own times.[360]

We confront death with fear and sadness in our hearts, but unshakeable knowledge that peace, light, and the fire of love are unconquered and unquenchable.

Blessings to all who hear these words,
Blessings to all who see these images,
Blessings to all who have drawn near to this fire,
Blessings to all who contemplate these mysteries,
Blessings to all who love and are loved,
Blessings to all who keep the name of their ideals alive,
and Blessings to all who remember the name of Antinous.

AVE VIVE ANTINOE!

---

[359] Using the inclusive counting which the Romans employed throughout their history.

[360] As of the writing of this book, we are less than a decade into this endeavor. However, I expect that this wording will hold for a long time in my own practices, since every Foundation Day is the celebration of the re-foundation of the tradition and the cultus of Antinous.

246

We pour out water, the source of all life, and drink deeply, knowing that without it we cannot live. We recall its power to drown, to cleanse, to renew, and its many forms, but especially in the blood of our bodies.

[Pour a glass of water and share it with everyone present.]

We light the flame and draw near to it, the same fire that burns within the earth and in the heart of every star, the brightness that is life and the warmth which is spirit, remembering all it symbolizes, both dangers and splendors.

[Light a candle and pass it around to everyone present.]

Foundation

This, along with "Hadrian and Antinous," is also one of the earliest ritual texts to have been continuously used in modern Antinoan devotion, originating in the Foundation Day 2002 festival that inaugurated the Ekklesía Antínoou. This liturgical drama should be performed on Foundation Day itself. The text of this liturgical drama was also given in *The Phillupic Hymns*.[361]

Hadrian and Antinous

[Chorus]
Hadrian like Alexander who united the world,
Hadrian like Herakles the lion-slayer,
Hadrian like Zeus at the head of Olympus,
lost his Hephaistion, his Hylas, his Ganymede,
the hunter, the cupbearer, the drowned boy.

[Hadrian]
Antinous! The word like breath ripped from my lungs!
Antinous! The name which was honey on my lips, lost!
Antinous! Face bright as sun, gentle as moon!
Grief and pain are all I know until I die!
The Nile which took him is not equal to my tears!

[Persephone]
Fear not, you who know the mysteries of renewal;
Fear not, for a sacrifice has been received;
Fear not, for Persephone is a friend to you.
Your beloved has wedded death and stolen back
the heart of the light from beneath this world.

---

[361] P. Sufenas Virius Lupus, *The Phillupic Hymns* (Eugene: Bibliotheca Alexandrina, 2008), p. 232.

[Chorus]
We will rejoice with every tear shed,
We will rejoice every time his name is spoken,
We will rejoice in the beauty which is inescapable;
All the world has been redeemed without blood,
an unknowable fire burns and lights the way.

His body is found, let it be preserved in our minds,
His body is found, let his name be remembered and praised,
His body is found, let it become incarnate again
in the flesh of those who have tasted his sweetness
and in this world that becomes his image.

AVE VIVE ANTINOE.

Bakkhoí Antínoou: Tragedoeia

At the 2011 PantheaCon, rather than do a more traditional ritual, the Ekklesía Antínoou presented a three-part sacred drama in which the first act was a tragedy, the second a comedy, and the third a satyr-play, all themed around Antinous and his history and mythology.[362] The obvious choice for the subject of the tragedy was Antinous' death, and that particular piece was so effective and evocative that it has been decided to keep it as a set-piece, and to vary the comedies and satyr-plays depending on the occasion and the likely audiences involved in the future.

So, if you are feeling more ambitious and want to put on a larger production than those given in the previous two chapters as a ritual drama for Foundation Day, or indeed for any occasion involving Antinous, the below is a possible script for such an event.

BAKKHOÍ ANTÍNOOU: TRAGEDOEIA

DRAMATIS PERSONAE

Pancrates, An Egyptian Priest
Hadrian, A Roman Emperor
Antinous, A Deified Mortal
Sabina, A Roman Empress
Julia Balbilla, A Greek Poetess
Chorus [the audience/spectators]

---

[362] The other two parts of this drama performed on that occasion can be found at http://aediculaantinoi.wordpress.com/2011/03/04/bakkhoi-antinoou-act-ii-comedeia/ and http://aediculaantinoi.wordpress.com/2011/03/04/bakkhoi-antinoou-act-iii-satyreia/.

[Prelude: the stage is set with ANTINOUS under a sheet, dead, attended by Pancrates.]³⁶³

[Enter HADRIAN.]

HADRIAN: Any news of the boy, Pancrates? Has any word come?

PANCRATES: No, your divine majesty.

HADRIAN: Has anyone seen him?

PANCRATES: No, your divine majesty.

HADRIAN: No, no...If I may confide in you, Pancrates, I am worried about him.

PANCRATES: I assure your divine majesty that your divine majesty need not fear.

HADRIAN: Yes, yes...It isn't as if young men his age don't have their own minds, and he has been on his own before. I shouldn't worry so much, I suppose.

PANCRATES: Whatever your divine majesty may worry does nothing to change circumstances. If he were here, he would still be here; if he were not, he would still be absent.

---

363 In our production of this play in 2011, Pancrates began by singing *Ave Ave Antinoe*, which can be found in an earlier chapter of the present book; however, a variety of other possibilities can serve to transition from a wider ritual into the ritual drama, or indeed the rest of the drama's action can simply begin with no prelude whatsoever.

HADRIAN: Cryptic, but true, Pancrates. Now, what is this?

[Pause.]

PANCRATES: A...new god.

HADRIAN: A new god? You mean a new statue of a god?

PANCRATES: No, your divine majesty, a new god, once mortal but now of the divine race, an Osiris.

HADRIAN: Ah, yes! You Egyptians have far thinner boundaries in that regard, don't you?

PANCRATES: It is as your divine majesty says.

HADRIAN: Well, how did this one become a god, then?

PANCRATES: By drowning in the most holy and sacred Nile, your divine majesty.

HADRIAN: Ah! Of course! Just like in Herodotus!

PANCRATES: And as it has been for thousands upon thousands of years, your divine majesty.

HADRIAN: Those crocodile tracks along the bank...did they feast on this body?

PANCRATES: Not at all, your divine majesty. It seems the sons of Sobek came from the depths and carried the body, whole and undefiled, to lie on the shore.

252

HADRIAN: The immortal gods are astonishing! What a blessed individual this must be!

PANCRATES: It is as your divine majesty says.

HADRIAN: That temple of those two brothers, Petesi and Paher—they drowned as well, didn't they?

PANCRATES: The Osiris-Petesi and the Osiris-Paher were similarly blessed by Hapi and Re, your divine majesty.

HADRIAN: And that girl, Isidora?

PANCRATES: The Osiris-Isidora is in the lap of Isis now, your divine majesty. [364]

HADRIAN: So this one, too, will be an Osiris?

PANCRATES: He is an Osiris already, your divine majesty. The rites of mummification and of opening the mouth have not been performed, but they will be soon.

HADRIAN: What luck! May I participate in these rites?

[Pause.]

PANCRATES: Your divine majesty is Re and Horus upon the earth; it will be as your divine majesty says.

HADRIAN: Good! So, does this new Osiris have a name?

---

[364] On Petesi, Paher, and Isidora, see Jack Lindsay, *Men and Gods on the Roman Nile* (New York: Barnes and Noble, 1968), p. 304.

[Pause.]

PANCRATES: He does, your divine majesty.

HADRIAN: So he was known locally, was he?

PANCRATES: And further afield, your divine majesty.

HADRIAN: What was his name, then?

[Pause.]

PANCRATES: He is Osiris-Antinous.

[Pause.]

HADRIAN: Ha! Such a common name, "Antinous"! Everyone who has read Homer knows it, and despite his ignominy, Greeks from Egypt to Britannia bear the name!

PANCRATES: It is as your divine majesty says.

HADRIAN: So, is he from Hermopolis Magna, then?

PANCRATES: No, your divine majesty.

HADRIAN: Perhaps a Memphite, then?

PANCRATES: No, your divine majesty.

HADRIAN: An Alexandrian, or even a Cretan?

PANCRATES: No, your divine majesty.

HADRIAN: Maybe he is from Attica or Boeitia, then?

PANCRATES: No, your divine majesty.

HADRIAN: Where, then?

[Pause.]

PANCRATES: From Bithynia, of Arcadian descent, your divine majesty.

[Pause. HADRIAN becomes more agitated.]

HADRIAN: Yes, Bithynia! That new slave we acquired in Alexandria as a translator was a Bithynian, right? Yes, he was...and I distinctly recall my wife Sabina mentioning he was an accomplished kitharode...wasn't his name Antinous?

PANCRATES: I have no knowledge of this, your divine majesty.

[Pause, as HADRIAN paces, getting more worried.]

HADRIAN: And you said no word of the boy, didn't you?

PANCRATES: No word has come, your divine majesty.

HADRIAN: And none have seen him?

PANCRATES: None who are living, your divine majesty.

[Pause.]

HADRIAN: Hmm! Ha, ha, ha!...Well, what a relief, then! And what a coincidence! A new god, with the name of my favorite! He'll be amused to know this, I'm certain! Ha, ha, ha! So, what of my wife and her "Sappho"?

PANCRATES: Her divine majesty and the Greek poetess are celebrating the rites of Osiris, your divine majesty. Her divine majesty is due to return at any moment.

HADRIAN: Well, how fortunate and auspicious for the new god! The great Osiris is celebrated at the same time this new Osiris has arisen!

PANCRATES: It is as your divine majesty says.

HADRIAN: So tell me, Pancrates, may I see him?

[Pause.]

PANCRATES: None but the prophet-priests of Egypt are permitted to see or touch the new Osiris, your divine majesty. It is custom.

HADRIAN: You Egyptians and your thousand customs!

PANCRATES: It is as your divine majesty says.

HADRIAN: But you forget—I am Pontifex Maximus. There is no greater priest than I in all of the Roman Imperium.

PANCRATES: It...it is...

HADRIAN: And I am Pharaoh over the Two Lands, Pancrates.

PANCRATES: It is...it is...

HADRIAN: If it is my wish, I can do as I please...

PANCRATES: *ABLANATHANALBA...*

HADRIAN: And I wish to see this new god...

PANCRATES: *ABLANATHANALBA...*

HADRIAN: Right now!

PANCRATES: *IA, IA, IAO, IAO, IAOAI...* [PANCRATES rises.] Very well, your divine majesty. Please stand here, and I will reveal the new Osiris.

HADRIAN: Splendid! Now, what shall I do?

PANCRATES: Stand as you are, gather your wits about you, and do not give in to worry...

[PANCRATES unveils ANTINOUS' head. Hadrian is initially in stunned silence, then collapses to his knees, audibly inhaling several times, gradually louder each time, clutching his chest, until he begins to sob, gradually increasing in volume and intensity as PANCRATES recites.]

PANCRATES: *A request for salvation, which is expressed by Osiris-*

Antinous, whose heart exceedingly rejoices, since he recognized his shape after revival, and he has seen his father, Re-Harakhte. His heart spoke—

HADRIAN: NOOOOOOOOOOOOOOOOOOOOOOOOO!!!

PANCRATES: *His heart spoke—*

HADRIAN: NOOOOOOOOOOOOOOOOOOOOOOOOO!!!

PANCRATES: *His heart spoke—*

HADRIAN: NOOOOOOOOOOOOOOOOOOOOOOOOO!!!
Oh, why, cruel gods? Why? NOOOOOOOOOO!!!

PANCRATES: *His heart spoke—*

HADRIAN: You bastard! You stinking Egyptian scum! You poison-mouthed   double-dealing   shit-slinging   charlatan!
NOOOOOOOO!!!

PANCRATES: It is as your divine majesty says.

HADRIAN: Enough! Do not call me "divine majesty" again, you sniveling piece of garbage!

PANCRATES: Very...very well.

HADRIAN: You lied! Why would you lie like that?

PANCRATES: I have not lied. None had seen nor heard from the boy, no word had come regarding him.

258

HADRIAN: But this IS HIM!

PANCRATES: The young man majesty called Antinous has not been seen since the holy river's waters closed above him as he sank. What came to the shore was not the boy, it was a god—he is a god.

HADRIAN: You two-tongued viper!

PANCRATES: Goddess Ma'at before and behind me, not a word that I have said is untrue!

HADRIAN: LIAR!

PANCRATES: Stay your tongue, majesty, lest you blaspheme the gods of the Two Lands.

HADRIAN: You threaten me?

PANCRATES: Majesty threatens himself.

[Pause. HADRIAN quietly sobs for a moment in his reflection.]

HADRIAN: You're right...you're right! But...he's gone!

PANCRATES: The boy you knew is gone, yes. All of Egypt will weep with you at this. But the god remains, and all the world will rejoice at that.

[HADRIAN continues weeping quietly. Enter SABINA and JULIA BALBILLA, singing with sistrums.]

SABINA AND JULIA: *Red barley and grape on the vine*
Green waters of the rising Nile
Red barley and grape on the vine
Green waters of the rising Nile

Osiris lives, Osiris returns
What is true will never die
Osiris lives, Osiris returns
What is true will never die[365]

[Repeat this again, with the CHORUS joining in.]

SABINA, JULIA, and CHORUS:
Red barley and grape on the vine
Green waters of the rising Nile
Red barley and grape on the vine
Green waters of the rising Nile

Osiris lives, Osiris returns
What is true will never die
Osiris lives, Osiris returns
What is true will never die

JULIA: Oh, what fun!

SABINA: These Egyptians know how to celebrate a god's death!

PANCRATES: Your divine majesty, welcome. Seshat's handmaiden, welcome.

---

[365] This song can be found on Sharon Knight and T. Thorn Coyle's album *Songs for the Waning Year.*

SABINA: Dear gods, what happened?

PANCRATES: It is as your divine majesty says: Egypt celebrates a new god, come about through the drowning of a boy.

JULIA: Antinous? NO!

SABINA: Oh immortal gods, no!

[JULIA and SABINA go to touch his body, but PANCRATES gets in their way.]

PANCRATES: Your divine majesty must not touch the Osiris-Antinous.

JULIA: We'll wash off the miasma afterwards!

PANCRATES: It is not defilement for you to touch him, it is defilement for him to be touched by that which is not Osiris.

JULIA: What are you saying?

PANCRATES: He is a god already by Hapi and Re-Harakhte. He is too holy even for his divine majesty to touch.

[SABINA comes forward while JULIA and PANCRATES seem to continue talking and HADRIAN still sits and weeps to give a soliloquy.]

SABINA: Gods, what will we do now? It's been more than ten years since my mother died, and still Hadrian weeps for her away from prying eyes, all the while cold to me, his own wife. He has never disrespected me, and I know he never will, even if it is only out of the honor he holds for my mother more than his own regard for me. But this! This could kill him. I can see he's already crushed by this in a way that he will never recover from, no matter what I or anyone else may do. And Antinous...gods, what a tragedy! Truth be told, I loved him, too—but more like a son, and all the more because he made Hadrian happy in a way I never could. It is the pinnacle of desolation to know one will never be as pleasing to one's husband as another, be it mother or favorite; and yet, Antinous made us all amicable. This year together with them has been like none other before it, full of joy and blessings, such that I have even found my own joy with Julia Balbilla and the other women—and my husband wished me well in it! All because of Antinous...and now he is gone. My own tears will fall behind closed doors for him—but meanwhile, I must be the strength that gets Hadrian through. He is a good man and a good Emperor, but without Antinous, he will falter. I am the Augusta, and in the forge of this trial I will be the tempered ore that upholds the Empire where my husband falls. I've never liked the Stoics, but if I must wear their mask to save Hadrian, then a Stoic I shall be. [To HADRIAN.] I weep with you, dear husband, but you must get up.

HADRIAN: But he is gone!

SABINA: Didn't you hear what the Egyptian said? Antinous is a god now. He'll always be with you—with us.

HADRIAN: But...noooo!

[JULIA starts to talk to herself, counting syllables on her fingers silently.]

PANCRATES: Majesty, you must compose yourself. The Osiris-
262

Antinous must be embalmed without tears or cries.

HADRIAN: Embalmed? You mean mummified!

PANCRATES: Yes, majesty.

SABINA: But he's not Egyptian!

PANCRATES: It is custom, majesties.

HADRIAN: And I am custom itself! He will not be mummified!

PANCRATES: Majesty is still troubled, but he will come to his senses...

HADRIAN: No! I will not allow it! Am I not Pharaoh of the Two Lands?

SABINA: You're right, husband. A pyre befitting the greatest of the heroes of Greece, then.

HADRIAN: He will be like Achilleus, like Herakles who slew the lion...

PANCRATES: It will be as you say, majesty.

SABINA: He will be like Hermes, his Arcadian father, and like Dionysos.

PANCRATES: It will be as your divine majesty says.

JULIA: Aha! I have it!

263

SABINA: What?

JULIA: A hymn for Antinous!

PANCRATES: You will sing the praises of the Osiris-Antinous already?

JULIA: I'll leave that to you, Egyptian; I will only sing of Antinous himself.

HADRIAN: Let me touch him! Let me hold him!

PANCRATES: You must not, majesty!

SABINA: Do as the Egyptian advises, husband. He is powerful and knows the ways of the gods.

HADRIAN: Then let me at least take this shroud that covered him!

[Pause.]

PANCRATES: It will be as you say, majesty.

[PANCRATES takes the shroud off ANTINOUS' body and hands it to HADRIAN.]

SABINA: Cherish it always, husband—the first clothes of a god!

HADRIAN: Yes...a god...my god...

SABINA: Julia, your hymn?

JULIA: *Red lotus and starlight divine*
Black soils on the banks of the Nile[366]

JULIA and SABINA: *Red lotus and starlight divine*
Black soils on the banks of the Nile

JULIA, SABINA, and PANCRATES:
Antinous lives, Antinous returns
This is where life comes from!
Antinous lives, Antinous returns
This is where life comes from!

ALL, with CHORUS: *Red lotus and starlight divine*
Black soils on the banks of the Nile
Red lotus and starlight divine
Black soils on the banks of the Nile

Antinous lives, Antinous returns
This is where life comes from!
Antinous lives, Antinous returns
This is where life comes from!

[SABINA leads HADRIAN out, with JULIA following them closely, and PANCRATES leaving last.]

---

[366] This should be sung to the same tune as "Osiris Lives" earlier.

Opening of the Pantheon

The Ekklesía Antínoou is not an exclusivist religious group or practice. It becomes apparent quite quickly when the original Antinoan devotional sources are consulted that other deities are not only acknowledged, but are often recognized as superior to Antinous and the Emperors. The relative ranking of Antinous in your own beliefs is up to you to decide; but the rituals of the Ekklesía Antínoou, as I have conducted them, always have space to honor many goddesses, gods, heroes, ancestors, land spirits, and other holy and divine powers as deemed appropriate by the participants. As a result, the following short rubrics are used to open and close the section of a ritual called the Pantheon, which is named after one of Hadrian's most well-known and enduring architectural creations,[367] which also likely reflected his religious beliefs and approach~namely, that there was room for all gods to be worshipped as one saw fit.

It is assumed that this will take place at Foundation Day, thus the references to the eighth month (i.e. October); it can be adapted for usage at other times of the year easily. Because there is a line on the Obelisk of Antinous suggesting that all of the gods and goddesses honored him, Foundation Day itself becomes a kind of "god-party" in honor of Antinous, as well as honoring the other assembled gods.

With a dome like the vault of the heavens,
In a circle of union and equality,
In eight spaces in this eighth month,
Sixteen columns to support its opening,
Hadrian who made bridges and walls
Fashioned a temple for all the gods.

---

[367] Mary Taliaferro Boatwright, *Hadrian and the City of Rome* (Princeton: Princeton University Press, 1987), pp. 42-50.

May all gods and heroes, spirits and powers,
now find welcome here in this place.

[Closing of the Pantheon]

In the Underworld, the Otherworld, the Realms Beyond,
for seventy-two and eighteen days,
behold, Antinous the Liberator slays in turn
each of the restraining Archons
who imprison and bind us by their laws in this world.
Our freedom is accomplished.

All gods, all powers, all spirits in this place
may now depart in peace with our thanks.

[This is often followed by the decommissioning of the City of
Antinoöpolis created by the Invocation of the Obelisk, on which
see the later chapters in the present book.]

Dies Natalis Antinoi

In Ekklesia Antínoou practice thus far, this particular holiday on November 27th—arguably, the second-most important of the year—has been observed in a far more laid-back and informal fashion. It is certainly a time to gather, to have a feast, and if possible to have a bath and enjoy one's time with one's friends, as was the custom of the Lanuvium *collegium* dedicated to Antinous and Diana. However, formal ritual with specific texts to recite has rarely been the option we have gone with in our history.

After my own purificatory bath (if possible, using the Inundation ritual), I usually have a Mediterranean dinner of some sort, during which all food consumed is first offered to Antinous. If I've had this feast in my own residence, I've often paraded in my principal image of Antinous and seated him at the table for this purpose. I also often sing the hymn *Ave Ave Antinoe* at some point after the formal dinner is completed. And, in "American Latin" tradition, I've also usually sung the following song:

Felix natalis tibi,
Felix natalis tibi,
Felix natalis Antinoo,
Felix natalis tibi!
Et multique!

This translates to "Happy birthday to you, happy birthday to you, happy birthday Antinous, happy birthday to you! And many more!"

This has been a holiday, therefore, of community fellowship as much as it has been communing with the deity and celebrating him. If something more formal for this is desired, please use your own imagination and particular aesthetics to innovate something suitable for yourself and your co-practitioners and celebrants on the occasion!

Antinous Epiphanes

On December 21st, which is on or around the Winter Solstice,[368] the Dionysian aspects and syncretisms of Antinous are celebrated, in particular his epithet *Epiphanes*, "the god who comes," which is attested on an inscription from the city of Antinoöpolis itself. Given the "spirit of the season" in the wider culture, the following songs for the day are to tunes you may otherwise recognize, and the two different tunes can be performed back-to-back directly without any separation quite easily.

After these, a hymn to Sol Invictus is given as well.

Khaire, Khaire Epiphanes[369]
The god who shows his beautiful face
He brings our cares to close on this night
And with his wines he fires the light
Khaire, Khaire Epiphanes
And now be welcome in this place!

Veni, Veni Antinoe
And come with joy beside you on the way!
In waters cold from depths of dark
May you now rise in fire and spark!
Ave, Ave Antinoe!
You light our year beginning on this day!

---

[368] It is only with the advent of modern science's advanced instruments that the "exact time" of the solstices and equinoxes—which are often up to two days in difference between the 21st dates previously assigned to them in the calendar—can be known. For simplicity's sake, the 21st is always the date that certain festivals (including the present one) are held.

[369] These first two verses should be sung to the tune of "O Come O Come Emmanuael"; the third verse to the tune of "God Rest Ye, Merry Gentlemen."

With Dionysos on this night
and all throughout the year
Antinous and Hadrian
come banishing all fear
And with Sol Invictus' light
they dry each mortal's tear
Haec est unde vita venit!
Vita venit!
Haec est unde vita venit!

Gaudete Invictus Natus

Gaudete, gaudete Invictus natus[370]
nobis matre ex Nocte, gaudete!

Sol et Luna praesident
super firmamento
Duo nunquam resident
manent permanento

Gaudete, gaudete Invictus natus
nobis matre ex Nocte, gaudete!

Deus Sol Invictus est
Imperator caeli
Sustentatus terrae est
similiter Nili

Gaudete, gaudete Invictus natus
nobis matre ex Nocte, gaudete!

---

[370] This should be sung to the tune "*Gaudete*," a medieval Latin Christmas carol. Various versions of it are available on YouTube and a number of recordings.

270

Lux fietur caritas
Lux caelorum Solis
Te agemus gratias
multis benedictis

Gaudete, gaudete Invictus natus
nobis matre ex Nocte, gaudete!

Rejoice and delight! The Unconquered One is born
from our mother, Nox [Night]—rejoice!

Sol and Luna preside
over the firmament;
The two, never subsiding
remain with permanence.

Rejoice and delight! The Unconquered One is born
from our mother, Nox [Night]—rejoice!

The Unconquered Sun God is
Emperor of the sky,
He is the sustenance of the earth
like the Nile.

Rejoice and delight! The Unconquered One is born
from our mother, Nox [Night]—rejoice!

Light becomes love—
the light of the heavens of Sol;
We give you thanks
for (your) many blessings.

Rejoice and delight! The Unconquered One is born
from our mother, Nox [Night]—rejoice!

271

III.
THE *DIVI* AND THE *SANCTI*

Honoring the _Divi_ and the _Sancti_

Amongst its many other descriptors, the Ekklesía Antínoou is a polytheist organization. Though our primary devotion to Antinous is always our foremost concern, Antinous does not exist isolated from other deities (as mentioned in a previous chapter), or other divine figures of various types. On the Obelisk of Antinous, other gods—including Re-Harakhte, Thoth, and Hapi—are listed along with Osiris-Antinous; but, the Emperor Hadrian and Empress Sabina are also mentioned. It has been suggested by Caroline Vout that the devotion to Antinous which flourished in the mid-second and into the third centuries CE was not only a phenomenon in itself, but that it served as a "friendlier," more attractive, and more approachable version of the Roman Imperial Cult,[371] since Antinous' story was inextricable from that of the Emperor Hadrian. This is an important matter to consider in our modern engagement with this particular cultus.

However, the idea of divine rulers is one that does not sit particularly well with many modern people. No one can imagine that either George W. Bush or Barack Obama were or are in any sense "deigned by the gods," or that they are in some way incarnate carriers of a numinous essence. However, in other parts of the world, ideas like this still persist—Japan's Emperor is still held in divine awe, just as all his predecessors were, due to his lineage from and ancestry with Amaterasu-Omikami, the _kami_ of the sun. In cultures where the ruler is considered divine or sacred, it is generally because the individuals in question function as an important intermediary between their people and the gods. The justice of the ruler tends to be beneficial for the people, while the ruler's injustice and unfitness for the position lead to ruin and disaster. (Based on this, anyone who lived through the two Bush Jr. administrations might long for the days when unjust rulers were dealt with severely!)

The Roman Emperors also had the title of _Pontifex Maximus_, which

---

[371] Caroline Vout, _Power and Eroticism in Imperial Rome_ (Cambridge: Cambridge University Press, 2007), pp. 113-121.

they all considered their own in the tradition of Julius Caesar, the first proto-emperor, since he also held this title. It literally means "greatest bridge-builder," and while the original pontiffs in Rome were in charge of the sacred duty of bridge-building (since the Tiber was not only a sacred river, but a god); but more metaphorically, the *pontifex* acted as a bridge between the gods and the people. It is in this capacity, as highest religious official of the Roman state, that Hadrian allowed the deification of Antinous to be generalized throughout the Empire. Deification used to be the exclusive province of the Senate, and it was in every case before and after Antinous (including Hadrian's own deification, which almost didn't occur). If it is possible for a human functionary to make a god of another human, then it is because of the power and authority vested in positions like the *Pontifex Maximus*, who was the Emperor (and could only be the Emperor) during the periods in which we are dealing.

While imperial cult calendars do exist from the third century CE, and list a large number of deified emperors and their other family members, there are a number of them that we focus on within the Ekklesía Antínoou (although one may choose to honor others if they so wish). The two most important of these are Divus Hadrianus Augustus and Diva Sabina Augusta, the Emperor and Empress at the time of Antinous' death (apart from the fact that Antinous was Hadrian's lover!). Divus Aelius Caesar was Hadrian's first adopted successor, but he died before he was able to assume the principate; and while official deification on the part of Hadrian is not recorded directly, Aelius Caesar does appear in cult calendars from elsewhere in the Empire. Hadrian's two deified predecessors—Divus Traianus Augustus (Trajan) and Divus Nerva Augustus—appear in Hadrian's imperial titulature, and thus should likewise be honored. Hadrian's further successors that he either adopted or appointed to eventually be in the imperial lineage—Divus Antoninus Pius Augustus, Divus Lucius Verus (the son of Aelius Caesar) and Divus Marcur Aurelius—are also to be honored for their contributions and continuation of Hadrian's work. And, other members of the imperial family of Hadrian and Trajan who were deified—Diva Plotina Augusta (Trajan's wife and a good friend of Hadrian), Diva Matidia Augusta (Sabina's mother and Hadrian's mother-in-law, whom he loved greatly), and Diva Marciana (Trajan's sister, the mother of Matidia)—are likewise important to consider. There are others as well, but these are the most important.

However, one cannot research the story of Antinous and Hadrian without encountering a vast assortment of personages who in various ways added color and character, and also often made great contributions to literature, philosophy, and history generally, or the story and eventual cultus of Antinous in particular. These include Julia Balbilla, the "friend" (and possible lover) of the Empress Sabina, who was a poet and was referred to as the "Sappho of Hadrian's court";[372] Pancrates/Pachrates, the Egyptian priest, magician, and poet who wrote an epic poem about Hadrian and Antinous' lion-hunt;[373] Polemo of Smyrna, a provincial governor and Sophist who wrote a treatise on physiognomy, and who patronized coins of Antinous in his province;[374] Arrian of Nikomedia, an important writer on topics like hunting and the most complete biography of Alexander the Great, who made allusions to Antinous in some of his writings;[375] and Favorinus of Arles, a Gaulish Sophist and orator who was also a eunuch.[376] This present list is not exhaustive, as there are many such people in the immediate circle of Hadrian and Antinous who are worthy of remembrance and celebration. As a result, we have decided to honor these figures as *Sancti*, or "blessed." (Males are *Sanctus*, genitive or plural *Sancti*; females are *Sancta*, genitive or plural *Sanctae*; gender-variant individuals could be designated by the Latin neuter version, *Sanctum*, genitive *Sancti*, plural *Sancta*; collectives of mixed gender are

---

[372] Anthony R. Birley, *Hadrian: The Restless Emperor* (London and New York: Routledge, 2000), pp. 240-251; Patricia Rosenmeyer, "Greek Inscriptions in Roman Egypt: Julia Balbilla's Sapphic Voice," *Classical Antiquity* 27.2 (2008), pp. 334-358.

[373] Birley, *Hadrian*, pp. 240-252; Matthew W. Dickie, *Magic and Magicians in the Greco-Roman World* (London and New York: Routledge, 2003), pp. 205, 212-215; Daniel Ogden, *In Search of the Sorcerer's Apprentice: The Traditional Tales of Lucian's Lover of Lies* (Swansea: The Classical Press of Wales, 2007), pp. 231-270.

[374] Birley, *Hadrian*, pp. 164-174; Maud W. Gleason, *Making Men: Sophists and Self-Presentation in Ancient Rome* (Princeton: Princeton University Press, 1994), pp. 21-54.

[375] Royston Lambert, *Beloved and God: The Story of Hadrian and Antinous* (New York: Viking, 1984), p. 137.

[376] Birley, *Hadrian*, pp. 193-195; Gleason, pp. 3-20.

always *Sancti*.)

But, the presence of blessedness in one's work and example did not end with the Roman Imperial Period. There have been countless individuals over the centuries who have done wonderful and important things, not only for Antinous in terms of their scholarship or devotion, but also for the wider purposes of queer spirituality, acceptance, and contribution to society. As a queer group, the Ekklesía Antínoou considers these individuals important to recognize and remember, and thus they are equally worthy of being called *Sancti*.

People in the modern world get the wrong idea when they hear the word "*Sancti*" and think it is exactly the same as "saint." They think that it is an entirely Christian concept, that it is inextricably tied to that particular form of religion's way of looking at the world and reckoning who is in heaven and who is not, particularly with Orthodox Christianities and Roman Catholicism. In the Catholic church, Pope John Paul II canonized more saints than all of his predecessors combined,[377] and to deny that there is political motivation in the canonization of all saints, for all times, is to be quite ignorant of the truth of the matter. Since he and his successor Benedict XVI (formerly Joseph Cardinal Ratzinger) have been more openly aggressive toward queer people than any of their predecessors, we obviously should not only take everything they have done with a grain of salt, but also openly oppose this moral and religious hegemony on every front on any occasion that presents itself.

For us in the Ekklesía Antínoou, sanctification is a very different thing. None of these figures are actually worshipped or venerated as spiritual powers, unlike the practice of intercessory prayer to saints for particular purposes in Catholicism. Those who are observant see in that practice a distorted but nonetheless correct perception of the absorption of many pagan deities or powers of particular forces and concepts into the Christian milieu—and in certain cases, this is even more transparent (e.g. St. Christopher, who was adapted from Anubis,

---

[377] And, as an aside, recall that the Roman Catholics have appropriated the title of *Pontifex Maximus* and consider it the exclusive province of their Pope, thus giving him the authority to officially recognize saints.

right down to being dog-headed in his earliest *vitae*!).[378] Neither do we pronounce about these people's abidance in a blessed afterlife or "chosen flock" of "saved" individuals. These are people without whom we cannot imagine the Ekklesía Antínoou and what we know now being in existence; they are people who we admire for their style of life or the arts they practiced. They are like the "spiders" of Antinous, those who have weaved a web so subtle and intricate that has enthralled us and brought us to be where we are today.

The Greek idea of *heros* ("hero") is somewhat similar, but also the Latin idea of those who were *sanctus*, holy or sanctified, because of what they did. The idea of "martyrs," which in Greek means "witnesses," means not that someone gave their life for something greater than themselves or died on behalf of others, but that they "witnessed" to a particular devotion in their spirituality, or that divine powers witnessed to that same devotion. In Latin, the word for witness is *testis*, which is the same as the word for the male gonads, so that word is used in all of its good senses here! In Syriac, the word for saints is *athletikos*, so that saints are thought of as spiritual athletes and achievers who through perseverance and discipline and practice attain spiritual goals. In Irish, saints are called *naomh*, which means "beautiful," but also implies "heavenly," so that saints are people who are beautiful and heavenly, in whatever sense that is understood--spiritually, physically, or both, as in the case of Antinous and the idea of *kalokagathia*, beauty of body reflecting beauty of spirit. So, many of these ideas come into play with the *Sancti* who are in the roll of the Ekklesía Antínoou. They are teachers and exemplars to be admired, they are achievers, they are witnesses, they had balls (not to be sexist, as there are loads of women who are ballsy!), they are beautiful.

But, most fundamentally, the *Sancti* are people who are to remain in "sainted memory." By including a person among the *Sancti*, we are committing ourselves to remembering them for as long as we are in existence because of their contributions in making our lives—spiritually, in general, or in terms of our visibility and public acceptance as queer people—better and more productive, meaningful, and enjoyable for us

---

[378] David Gordon White, *Myths of the Dog-Man* (Chicago and London: University of Chicago Press, 1991), pp. 22-46.

who are living right now. They are our collective divine and honored ancestors in the Ekklesía Antínoou, who represent the best parts of our tradition's history in the past, and who remain as actively inspiring exemplars for our present and future activities as well.

A future publication may detail in full who all of the current *Sancti* of the Ekklesía Antínoou are,[379] some of the reasons why they are considered such, and what dates on which it is appropriate to celebrate them. A number of them whose veneration is more important, who come from the immediate circle of Hadrian and Antinous, are detailed in the pages to come in the present book, and several have also been mentioned on the *Tabula Feriarum* and in the *Fasti Metri Antinoi*.

Apart from reading extant texts that are specific to particular *Divi* or *Sancti*, or making ones of your own, what can be done for honoring them ritually on their specific *dies sancti*? Several things have developed in general practice within the Ekklesía Antínoou, as well as with my own devotional habits.

First, where it is possible to do so, get an image of the person in question, and build a shrine for them.

Second, if a particular *Sanctus/a/um* is a poet, musician, or artist of some sort, then read their poems, play their music, study their writings, admire their paintings, and do all of this actively in the presence of your shrine for them.

Third, make offerings to them. The general offering for the dead was water, so offer them a portion of cool water to parch their dry throats. (I would suggest not drinking this water after it is offered, but instead give it to one's "offering plant" or dispose of it in some responsible, utilitarian manner—which is not to put it down the drain!) For those who are heroes, milk and honey would be traditional. For some of the *Divi*, you might develop particular foods, incenses, and other types of offering that could be given.

---

[379] The current list can be found at
http://aediculaantinoi.wordpress.com/tabula-sanctorum-of-the-ekklesia-antinoou/

278

Fourth, express your appreciation for them and their work—but try not to restrict this just to the date on which you are holding an explicit observance for them. Dates to honor them may be their birthdate (if it is known) and their death-date (if it is known), or any dates on which something important happened in their life.

Some practices that I have adopted include the use of an Egyptian *ushabti* (a small humanoid figure often included in tombs, which was thought to do the work of the deceased in the afterlife), not only to relieve them of any of their pains in the afterlife, but also to be a representation of the continuation of their work here on earth with those of us who are still living and who remember their names and carry on their examples.

There are also lines from one of the Hadrian hymns, given below, which I've generalized to usage in any ritual for the *Sancti*. The lines are:

Ignis corporis infirmat,
Ignis sed animae perstat.

"The fire of the body diminishes,
But the fire of the soul persists!"

There is a video of the tune available on YouTube.[380] It is in the key of C. The first line of the tune can simply be done over and over again, or the first and second lines can be alternated, or (if you have multiple singers) they can both be done at the same time for some interesting harmonies!

Individual rituals and observances that are more appropriate to particular *Sancti* and *Divi* will be detailed in the future book, and can certainly be generated and innovated in one's own practices however one sees fit.

---

[380] http://www.youtube.com/watch?v=CsUhi7CLtow (Please excuse the bad sound quality, and my not-always-perfect voice!)

There are two mini-groups of *Sancti* that are also important to recognize within the context of the Ekklesía Antínoou: the *Treískouroi* and the *Trophimoi*.

The *Treískouroi* are a group of three individuals—Antinous, Lucius Marius Vitalis, and Vibullius Polydeukion—that were all youthful in their deaths, and who merited particular recognitions afterwards. Of course, readers are now abundantly familiar with Antinous, the god and hero, at this stage of the present book! Lucius Marius Vitalis (as mentioned on the entries for September 6 in the calendars given earlier) was a young man apprenticed at Hadrian's court, learning the arts, who very likely knew Antinous before his death. In Lucius' funeral inscription (given below), he is called *Sanctissimus*, "most blessed," and thus we consider him the "prince of the *Sancti*," and one of the foremost individuals in their membership. Vibullius Polydeukion was one of the *Trophimoi* of Herodes Attikos (on which, more in a moment), who after death was considered a hero in several locations. Herodes Attikos was a friend of Hadrian, and had several shrines to Antinous in his various places of residence, and very clearly based his heroic cultus for Polydeukion on that of Antinous, such that there are now more surviving images of Polydeukion than there are of Herodes himself—and, indeed, more than any other non-imperial or governing Greek individual for the entirety of ancient history! These three youths, untimely dead, represent three types of post-mortality: sanctification, heroization, and deification. They are intimately involved in the evolving form of Antinoan practical magic/mysticism known as the Serpent Path, which will be detailed in future publications.

The *Trophimoi* refers to the three foster-sons of Herodes Attikos: Polydeukion, Memnon, and Achilles. A festival for these, as well as for other members of Herodes' family, including his wife, two daughters, and one son (though he did have other children), is held in the early part of March, as detailed in the calendars given earlier. Though present in various manners for several years of Ekklesía Antínoou practice (at least since 2006), they have been particularly present and active in 2010 through the time of publication of this book, and will no doubt continue to be so. It is hoped that the *Trophimoi* will be active in working toward helping to foster the participation of particular groups of people—especially younger people, as well as more traditional families—in their own engagement with Antinoan spirituality and the Ekklesía Antínoou in particular. More information is given about them in the chapters to follow.

The Ekklesía Antínoou is not an authoritarian group with a centralized administration or a strongly institutional methodology; everything we do is at the individual participant's discretion. As a result, even though there is a centralized list of *Sancti* that is available for anyone to use and consult as they like, in the future the task of commemorating and recognizing *Sancti* is likewise at the disposal and preference of anyone who is interested. No one must honor all—or even any—of the *Sancti*, and everyone is free to honor further *Sancti* that they have found inspirational or influential themselves. In accordance with this approach, the ritual below is given as a suggestion of how to initially induct a particular *Sanctus/a/um* into this body of collective ancestors. This was previously performed once a year on Foundation Day from 2002 through 2007; a second performance of the ritual was enacted in 2008 to induct a large groupu of *Sanctae* on the occasion of the Apotheosis of Sabina, and on a few further occasions between then and 2011. As of April 21, 2011, the practice of inducting *Sancti* has been generalized to be available to all who wish to do so. It is given in both Latin and English below; the practice previously has been to read it through in English once, and then to read it in Latin while doing the ritual actions. A bell, water, and a candle are needed for this ritual.

Sanctification Ritual

We. the gathered faithful of Antinous, in collaboration and with one voice, do declare [what follows]:

We call out the name(s) of _____, ending the silence of forgetfulness and the darkness of oblivion, and add this/these name(s) to the litany of the Blessed Ones forever.

We gather your ashes, unearth your bones, search for your

remains, and reunite your shattered images, and like a phoenix from the flames of birth and death, we elevate you to the stars and into the company of the Celestial Boat of Antinous for all the ages.

We take up the wisdom of your words, the virtues of your actions, and the true example of your earthly works, and we divide these out to be shared by all the faithful who remain in this life, to be drunk like clear and pure water to revivify and nourish.

We scatter upon the winds the renown of your deeds and the fullness of your knowledge, Venerable _____, that it may be spread to every corner of the world, the farthest shores and the highest points, so that it might encircle all like the *ouroboros* who swallows its own tail.

Blessed _____,
By your light, we redeem you from all slander;
By your darkness, we accept you in every part;
By your love, we embrace you as a Blessed One;
By your truest nature, we acknowledge you as holy.

By your teachings, may we be elevated;
By your life, may you be celebrated;
By your death, may you be deified.

[In your own words, ...[381]]

Holy _____,
May your light illuminate the universe, give color to the flowers, and shine like a strand in the grand web of Antinous' glory.

---

[381] If possible, a quotation from the person being sanctified at this point should be read. Note that there is no corresponding part to this in the Latin version which follows.

282

Sanctus/a/um _____,
Be blessed, be praised, be glorified!
AVE VIVE ANTINOE!

✳ ✳ ✳ ✳ ✳[382]

Ekklesía Antínoou, collaboratione et in una voce, declaramus:

Nominem/nominees[383] _____ ✳ *invocamus, finimus silentiam et tenebras oblivionis, et addemus nominem/nominees pulchrem/pulchres hoc/haec ad Tabulum Sanctorum in aeterna.*

Cineres te/vos gregamus, osses te/vos effodemus, relictos te/vos quaeremus, et imagines fractos te/vos conjungemus iterum, et similis phoenici ex flammis mortis ortusque, extollemus te/vos ad stellam et ad societatem Scaphae Caelestiae Antinoi in saecula saeculorum. [light candle]

Sapientiam verborum tui/vestry suscipimus, virtutes actionis tui/vestry, et exemplum veritatem operis saeculis tui/vestry, dividemusque haec/hae partiri ab omnis fidelitatibus quibus durant in hac vita, bibitus esse similis aquae clarae sanctitatique recreari et alere. [pour out/drink water]

Famam facti tui/vestry et plenum scientiae tui/vestry in ventis dispergemus, _____ *Venerabile/a/um/Venerabili/ae/a*[384] ✳, *tam*

---

[382] Each "✳" in the Latin rubrics to follow indicates where a bell should be rung.

[383] In what follows, the singular form of a word is always given first, followed by the plural, so that the ritual can be done for a singular individual or for several at the same time at the preference of those performing it.

[384] On vocatives like this (and the ones to follow), the singular and plural forms (respectively) are given in the masculine gender first, followed by the feminine ending (thus *Venerabila*) and the neuter; if it is a group of individuals who are of mixed gender, but one who should be masculine is among them, Latin grammar dictates that the masculine form of the plural is used. Handle this however you might wish, though! If a group of individuals is being

283

extendeatur ad omnibus angulos mundi, litores ultimos et locos altissimos, tam circumdet totum similis ouroboro cui devorant caudam sui.

Benedicite/a/um/Benedicti/ae/a _____ *,
Luce te/vos, redimus te/vos ab calumniis omnibus; *
Tenebra te/vos, accipemus te/vos in omnibus partibus; *
Amore te/vos, amplexamur te/vos sanctus/a/um/sancti/ae/a; *
Natura veritatissima te/vos, agnoscemus te sacrus/a/um/sacri/ae/a; *

Doctrina/is te/vos, extolleamur; *
Vita/is te/vos, celebrere; *
Mortie/ibus te/vos, faciare in deorum numerum. *

Sacre/a/um/Sacri/ae/a _____ *,
Illuminet lux tui/vestry universam, coloret flora, et splendeat similis filo in tela magna Antinoi gloriae.

Sancte/a/um/Sancti/ae/a _____ *,
Benedicare/amini *, laudare/amini *, glorificare/amini *!

AVE VIVE ANTINOE! HAEC EST UNDE VITA VENIT!

---

named, simply referring to them collectively as *Sancti, Sanctae,* or *Sancta* (etc.) at these points would also be appropriate, rather than naming each one in the blanks.

Hadrian and Plotina

Diva Pompeia Plotina Claudia Phoebe Piso was born sometime during the reign of Nero (54-68 CE)–not unlike her imperial successor and great-niece Sabina, we do not know the exact date of her birth, nor her death. However, if we were to venture a guess and suggest that she was younger than Trajan by about ten years (as that was often the case in Roman marriages, at least minimally), she may have been born in c. 63 CE. She was married to Trajan before his accession as emperor in 98 as the adopted successor to Nerva, and their marriage was a happy one. However, it was a childless marriage, which necessitated the adoption of Hadrian as imperial successor. When Trajan died during a campaign on August 9, 117 CE, it was Plotina who, in the end, seems to have either negotiated Hadrian's adoption from Trajan on his deathbed, or (in some interpretations) conspired to forge statements that would have Hadrian be the adopted successor. Though Hadrian's marriage to the granddaughter of the deified sister of Trajan, Marciana, certainly would have favorably placed Hadrian for succession, nonetheless it was this last-minute situation which determined Hadrian as the ultimate successor.

Some have also suggested throughout history that Hadrian was having an affair with Plotina, and that it was through this means that he secured his imperial succession. That would be a very strange situation indeed, if what some others have suggested about Trajan and Hadrian were true–namely, that Hadrian was once a youthful lover (however briefly) to Trajan, despite being his cousin.[385] But, as ever, the public, whether ancient or modern, academic or not, is eager for a sex scandal and a tabloid story.

---

[385] Caroline Vout, *Power and Eroticism in Imperial Rome* (Cambridge: Cambridge University Press, 2007), p. 63.

What is certain is that Hadrian clearly honored and esteemed her greatly, and that the two of them enjoyed discussing philosophy. Correspondence survives between them in which they debate the succession of the School of Epicurus in Athens, which is given below.[386] A notice by Hadrian that he would like to have dinner with her on the occasion of his birthday also survives, likely from 120 or 121 CE–much of it echoes the praises he gives to Matidia in her funeral oration, found below in a subsequent section.

Plotina died in c. 121-122, and Hadrian had her deified, as well as having her honored alongside Trajan in a temple in Rome afterwards, and founding a temple for her in her birthplace of Nemausus (modern Nimes, France). Plotina was reluctant to receive the title of Augusta from her husband, which he had been urging since 100, but she at last relented in 105, and thereafter appears on imperial coinage. She was honored with a *deme* named after her in the city of Antinoöpolis, in the *phyla* named for Matidia.[387] We celebrate her on January 8th, the *Dies Divae*, because an unknown *Diva* is recorded on this date on the calendar from Doura-Europos.[388]

Letter of Plotina to her Adopted Son, Hadrian

...in the consulship of Marcus Annius Verus for the second time and Gnaeus Arrius Augur [121 CE].
From Plotina Augusta.
How great my enthusiasm is toward the school of Epicurus, you know very well, my lord. Prompt assistance from you must be

---

[386] Robert K. Sherk (ed./trans.), *Translated Documents of Greece & Rome 6: The Roman Empire: Augustus to Hadrian* (Cambridge: Cambridge University Press, 1988), p. 184.

[387] Mary Taliaferro Boatwright, *Hadrian and the Cities of the Roman Empire* (Princeton: Princeton University Press, 2003), p. 194n124.

[388] Mary Beard, John North, & Simon Price (eds./trans.), *Religions of Rome, Volume 2: A Sourcebook* (Cambridge: Cambridge University Press, 1998), p. 72.

given to its succession, for, because it is only permitted Roman citizens to be successors to head the school, the opportunity of choosing one is reduced to narrow limits. Therefore, I ask in the name of Popillius Theotimus, who is presently the successor [head of the school] at Athens, that he be permitted by you to write his testament in Greek about the part of his testamentary decisions which pertain to the regulation of the succession and that he be empowered to name as successor to himself a person of non-Roman status, if such a person's qualifications convince him; and I ask that what you grant to Theotimus, the future successors to head the school of Epicurus thereafter may also enjoy the same legal rights. All the more do I ask because it has been the practice, as often as an error has been made by a testator about the election of a successor, that by common consent a substitution is made by the students of the same school of the person who will be the best successor, and that will be done more easily, if he is chosen from a greater number of candidates.

The Temples of Antinous by Aelius Caesar

Aelius Caesar was born Lucius Ceionius Commodus Verus, and was the first adopted heir of Hadrian. Many have suggested that Aelius Caesar was an unsuitable candidate for the principate in a variety of ways, including his narcissism, and it was also suggested that he was an *eromenos* of Hadrian as well, just as Antinous was—the "Western Favorite" where Antinous had been the "eastern." It has been suggested in a number of pieces of fiction that Aelius Caesar and Antinous may have had some resentment or rivalry for one another—but more on this in a moment. This may or may not be the case, and either way, it doesn't make much of a difference to our purposes here; that he was the legally adopted and recognized heir of Hadrian, and was a holder of the "tribunician power" of the Emperors is the essential matter. He was born on January 13, 101 CE, and died on December 31, 137 CE.

However, it seems that—in at least two instances—Aelius Caesar can also be said to have been a devotee of Antinous, which (at least in my mind) puts the suggestion that they were rivals to serious question. The remains of two temples with inscriptions have been discovered that seem to indicate Aelius Caesar founded them while he was the designated imperial heir, thus putting their dates to c. 136-137 CE. One was in Socanica, in Dalmatia (modern Croatia), which was a temple he founded together with Hadrian,[389] while the other was a small temple near Carnuntum, in Pannonia (modern Austria).[390]

I learned about the latter by complete and utter happenstance (with the help of Mary Taliaferro Boatwright, for which I'm most grateful) while looking for information on the former. Royston Lambert mentioned

---

[389] S. Dusanic, "The Antinous Inscription at Socanica and the Metalla Municipii Dardanorum," *Ziva Antika* 21 (1971), pp. 241-261.

[390] Zsolt Mräv, "Kaiserliche Bautätigkeit zur zeit Hadrians in den Städten Pannoniens," *Acta Antiqua Hungaricae* 43 (2003), pp. 125-137.

the Socanica temple,[391] which was discovered in the early 1970s, but never gave any references to it in his notes (though the Croatian title of the article is given in his bibliography). After years of searching, and being told by co-religionists and scholars that it must be a mistake, I finally found the necessary reference in the Ph.D. dissertation of Caroline Vout, upon which her later excellent book was based.[392] My persistence paid off, and this temple has held a great connection to Antinous for me in a variety of ways.

While other ways of honoring Divus Aelius Caesar might be imagined, both on the date of his birth (January 13) and his death (December 31), reading these texts and uniting one's own devotion to Antinous with his is certainly not inappropriate. Both of these texts were translated by me earlier in *The Phillupic Hymns*.[393]

The Temples of Antinous by Aelius Caesar

[Socanica]

This temple is dedicated to Antinous the Hero,
by command of the Emperor Caesar Trajan Hadrian Augustus
and his son Lucius Aelius Caesar Augustus,
the colonists of the Dardanian silver mines,
by the administration of the Imperial Procurator Telesphoros,
freely made this.

---

[391] Royston Lambert, *Beloved and God: The Story of Hadrian and Antinous* (New York: Viking, 1984), pp. 178, 185-186, 191.

[392] Caroline Vout, *Power and Eroticism in Imperial Rome* (Cambridge: Cambridge University Press, 2007), p. 123n36.

[393] P. Sufenas Virius Lupus, *The Phillupic Hymns* (Eugene: Bibliotheca Alexandrina, 2008), p. 185.

[Carnuntum]

Imperator Lucius Aelius Caesar
son of Trajan Hadrian Augustus,
of tribunician power, consul,
twice proconsul, *quindecemvir*,
made this temple sacred to Antinous.

Dies Julii Hadriani

This hymn was originally written in July of 2004 by myself and the former oracle of Antinous, Aristotimos, who was also the first recipient of the Antinoan Mysteries earlier that year. It was meant to be used on the "Days of July of Hadrian," which is to say July 9th (his first entry into Rome) and 10th (his death), hence the title; but it can be used for any date honoring Divus Hadrianus, including his birthdate on January 24th, or any of the festivals in which he first entered cities in Egypt (Oxyrhynchus on November 29th, Tebtynis on December 1) or on his *Vicennalia* celebration (December 13th), or, indeed, at any point at which one wishes to honor him. It was first published in *The Phillupic Hymns*.[394]

Dies Julii Hadriani

Ave Musae Cantate
demissorum Plutone
filio Cybele
amplectrice in morte

Clementisque Iovis
cujus immortalitatis
honorem donat eis
virtutis populis

Honora Hadrianum
Imperatorem Romanorum
Traiani filium
amatorem Antinoum

---

[394] P. Sufenas Virius Lupus, *The Phillupic Hymns* (Eugene: Bibliotheca Alexandrina, 2008), p. 185.

Permitte ad caela
similiter aquila
in divorum mensa
ascendere ingenia

Animula vagula blandula
quo nunc abibis in loca
pallidula rigida nudula
conservabit eum Memoria

Graeculi virtutibus
liberalitas disciplina munus
beneficio hujus
te iterum honorabimus

Ignis corporis infirmat
Ignis sed animae perstat
Ave Dive Hadriane Graecule.

Ave Dive Hadriane Graecule
Ave Dive Hadriane Graecule
Ave Dive Hadriane Graecule

In profundis tui tristitiae, nunquam oblivisci ut aliquando non solum
leones venatus sumus sed etiam illos letavimus.

"The Days of July of Hadrian"

Hail! Sing, O Muses,
of the reapings of Pluto,
son of Cybele—
embracer in death—

292

and of Merciful Jove
who bestows the honor
of immortality to them—
the people of worthiness—:

Honor Hadrian,
Emperor of the Romans,
son of Trajan,
lover of Antinous;

Allow his intelligences
to ascend
like an eagle
into the table of the divinized.

Little wandering charming soul,
where will you now abide?
In pale, stark, bleak places?
Memory will preserve him.

By the virtues of the Greekling—
liberality, discipline, beneficence—
for the benefit of this,
we will honor you again.

The fire of the body diminishes,
but the fire of the soul persists.
Hail Divus Hadrianus the Greekling...

In the depths of your sadness, never forget that once we not only
hunted lions, but slew them.

Herodes Attikos, His Family, Polydeukion, and the *Trophimoi*

Lucius Vibullius Hipparchos Tiberius Claudius Attikos Herodes, or more simply Herodes, was a rich man who is known for many public benefactions in Athens (including the Odeon/Theatre). He was born between 101 and 103 CE at Marathon, and died at the age of 76 sometime in the late 170s. He eventually went to Rome, was acquainted with Hadrian and became the tutor of the young Marcus Aurelius and Lucius Verus from 141-146. He was considered a Sophist (acquainted with both Favorinus of Arles and Polemo of Smyrna), as well as an *exegete* (an authority on religious matters), and he held many priesthoods, as well as civic posts—he was the quaestor of Hadrian in 129, tribune in 131, praetor in 133, Corrector of the Free Cities of Asia in 134/135, and *consul ordinarius* of Rome in 143. In the 170s, he came into some difficulty with the Athenians, who thought he was seeking to be a tyrant over them; the matter was eventually settled by Marcus Aurelius. In writings about him, he comes across as an excellent and encouraging teacher, but also as very sad and given to extreme displays of grief, and considering his life and family this is not surprising.

He was married just before his consulship to Appia Annia Regilla (who died in 160 and was heroized by Herodes),[395] and they had six children, only one of whom survived Herodes (an unnamed son, Elpinike, Athenais, Regillus, another child, and the survivor Attikos Bradua). He also adopted three boys, the *Trophimoi* ("foster-sons"), who he raised as his own. Their names were Achilles, Memnon and Polydeukion, and all three of them died before Herodes. Sometimes in the 160s, he

---

[395] Sarah B. Pomeroy, *The Murder of Regilla: A Case of Domestic Violence in Antiquity* (Cambridge and London: Harvard University Press, 2007), contains a great deal of useful information, though I cannot agree with Pomeroy's over-reading of the situation, and her accusations of Herodes' responsibility for Regilla's murder, nor her reading of the pederasty of Herodes with Polydeukion, who was a close kinsman of his.

adopted a further son, who was also a close kinsman to both himself and Polydeukion, named Lucius Claudius Herodes; this took place so that his surviving son Attikos Bradua would not inherit his fortune, and it likely happened after the death of the three *Trophimoi*. However, it was Polydeukion (connected to Herodes' maternal kin somehow and of high social standing in his own right) who received divine honors after his death, had games instituted in his honor, and was considered a Hero in certain locales in Greece (though some statues of him have been found in Italy). The date of his death is uncertain; it could have been as early as the late 140s, but a date closer to 160 seems likely, as he was roughly the same age as Attikos Bradua (born c. 145), this would have occurred after Regilla's death, and Polydeukion's depictions show hm to be roughly the age of fifteen. It seems possible that the three *Trophimoi* were among the "alphabet boys" that Herodes recruited in order to teach his son Attikos Bradua (who had some sort of learning disability) how to read: Herodes figured that if Attikos could learn the names of all of his friends, each one of which had a name beginning with one of the Greek alphabet's letters, he would therefore know the alphabet.

The parallel of Polydeukion's death with Antinous and Hadrian's situation was quite obvious, and it has been suggested that Herodes and Polydeukion may have had a romantic relationship in the same way that Hadrian and Antinous did, but it is not by any means as certain as some have suggested. Most of the inscriptions Herodes made for Polydeukion portray him in a filial rather than amorous role—as a son rather than a lover, and very likely perhaps the son Herodes wished he'd had instead of Attikos Bradua. Several statue depictions of Polydeukion have survived, at least 25 of which are ancient, which is more than any other private individual in the entirety of Greek history. Some of these statues have a heroic quality, perhaps linking Polydeukion to his namesake, Polydeukes of the Dioskouroi.[396] There are several unidentified Egyptianizing statues associated with

---

[396] I have written a little on this connection in P. Sufenas Virius Lupus, *The Syncretisms of Antinous* (Anacortes: The Red Lotus Library, 2010), pp. 90-92; more will be written on this in the upcoming Bibliotheca Alexandrina volume dedicated to the Dioskouroi.

Herodes' benefactions which might be portrayals of Polydeukion as an Egyptian god in the same way Antinous was syncretized to Osiris.

Herodes was mocked for his honoring of the *Trophimoi* and his wife, and curse inscriptions (a practice which was particularly popular in Phrygia) thus accompany some of his monuments, with further sections to some of them added over time. Philostratus informs us that many of Herodes' statues of the *Trophimoi* were in various stages of hunting; the connection of hunting to ideas of triumph over death and immortality, is something familiar from Hadrian's hunting *tondi* which depict Antinous. Heroized and deified beautiful dying youths in the Antonine Age were fortunate to have Antinous as a predecessor.

Much of the information above is found in Jennifer Tobin's excellent study of Herodes Attikos,[397] as well as a short article by Elaine Gazda on the head of Polydeukion now in Ann Arbor, Michigan.[398] I had the good fortune to be working for a short time in Michigan during early 2010, and was able to visit the statue head of Polydeukion (the only one not located in a museum or private collection in Europe) and to do cultus to Polydeukion before it, which inaugurated the first festival of the *Trophimoi* that takes place in March in the Ekklesía Antínoou.

In addition to the inscriptions given below, several excerpts from the works of Lukian of Samosata, Philostratus, and Aulus Gellius are also given in relation to Herodes Attikos' cultus of Polydeukion and the *Trophimoi*.

From Lukian of Samosata, *Demonax*

When Herodes, the superlative, was mourning the premature death of Polydeuces and wanted a chariot regularly made ready and horses put to it just as if the boy were going for a drive, and

---

[397] Jennifer Tobin, *Herodes Attikos and the City of Athens: Patronage and Conflict under the Antonines* (Amsterdam: J. C. Gieben, 1997).
[398] Elaine K. Gazda, "A Portrait of Polydeukion," *The University of Michigan Museum of Art and Archaeology Bulletin* 3.1 (1980), pp. 1-13.

dinner regularly served for him, Demonax went to him and said: "I am bringing you a message from Polydeuces." Herodes was pleased and thought that Demonax, like everyone else, was falling in with his humour, so he said: "Well, what does Polydeuces want, Demonax?" "He finds fault with you," said he, "for not going to join him at once!"[399]

Touching Herodes he [Demonax] remarked that Plato was right in saying that we have more than one soul, for a man with only one could not feast Regilla and Polydeuces as if they were still alive and say what he did in his lectures.[400]

From Aulus Gellius, *Attic Nights*

I once heard Herodes Atticus, the ex-consul, holding forth at Athens in the Greek language, in which he far surpassed almost all the men of our time in distinction, fluency, and elegance of diction. He was speaking at the time against the *apátheia*, or "lack of feeling" of the Stoics, in consequence of having been assailed by one of that sect, who alleged that he did not endure the grief which he felt at the death of a beloved boy with sufficient wisdom and fortitude. The sense of the discourse, so far as I remember, was as follows: that no man, who felt and thought normally, could be wholly exempt and free from those emotions of the mind, which he called *páthe*, caused by sorrow, desire, fear, anger and pleasure; and even if he could so resist them as to be free from them altogether, he would not be better off, since his mind would grow weak and sluggish, being deprived of the support of certain emotions, as of a highly necessary stimulus. For he declared that those feelings and impulses of the mind, though they become faults when excessive, are connected

---

[399] A. M. Harmon (ed./trans.), *Lucian, Volume I* (Cambridge: Harvard University Press, 1913), §24, pp. 156-159.
[400] Harmon, §35, pp. 160-161.

and involved in certain powers and activities of the intellect; and therefore, if we should in our ignorance eradicate them altogether, there would be danger lest we lose also the good and useful qualities of the mind which are connected with them. Therefore he thought that they ought to be regulated, and pruned skillfully and carefully, so that those only should be removed which are unsuitable and unnatural, lest in fact that should happen which once (according to the story) befell an ignorant and rude Thracian in cultivating a field which he had bought. "When a man of Thrace," said he, "from a remote and barbarous land, and unskilled in agriculture, had moved into a more civilized country, in order to lead a less wild life, he bought a farm planted with olives and vines. Knowing nothing at all about the care of vines or trees, he chanced to see a neighbor cutting down the thorns which had sprung up high and wide, pruning his ash-trees almost to their tops, pulling up the suckers of his vines which had spread over the earth from the main roots, and cutting off the tall straight shoots on his fruit and olive trees. He drew near and asked why the other was making such havoc of his wood and leaves. The neighbor answered; 'In order to make the field clean and neat and the trees and vines more productive.' The Thracian left his neighbor with thanks, rejoicing that he had gained some knowledge of farming. Then he took his sickle and axe; and thereupon in his pitiful ignorance the fellow cuts down all his vines and olives, lopping off the richest branches of the trees and the most fruitful shoots of the vines, and, with the idea of clearing up his place, he pulls up all the shrubs and shoots fit for bearing fruits and crops, along with the brambles and thorns, having learnt assurance at a ruinous price and acquired boldness in error through faulty imitation. Thus it is," said Herodes, "that those disciples of insensibility, wishing to be thought calm, courageous and steadfast because of showing neither desire nor grief, neither wrath nor joy, root out

298

all the more vigorous emotions of the mind, and grow old in the torpor of a sluggish and, as it were, nerveless life."[401]

From Philostratus, *Lives of the Sophists*

A charge of murder was also brought against Herodes, and it was made up in this way. His wife Regilla, it was said, was in the eighth month of her pregnancy, and Herodes ordered his freedman Alcimedon to beat her for some slight fault, and the woman died in premature childbirth from a blow in the belly. On these grounds, as though true, Regilla's brother Bradua brought a suit against him for murder. He was a very illustrious man of consular rank, and the outward sign of his high birth, a crescent-shaped ivory buckle, was attached to his sandal. And when Braduas appeared before the Roman tribunal he brought no convincing proof of the charge that he was making, but delivered a long panegyric on himself dealing with his own family. Whereupon Herodes jested at his expense and said: "You have your pedigree on your toe-joints." And when his accuser boasted too of his benefactions to one of the cities of Italy, Herodes said with great dignity: "I too could have recited many such actions of my own in whatever part of the earth I were now being tried." Two things helped him in his defence. First that he had given orders for no such severe measures against Regilla; secondly, his extraordinary grief at her death. Even this was regarded as a pretence and made a charge against him, but nevertheless the truth prevailed. For he never would have dedicated to her memory so fine a theatre nor would he have postponed for her sake the casting of lots for his second consulship, if he had not been innocent of the charge; nor again would he have made an offering of her apparel at the temple of

---

[401] John C. Rolfe (trans.), *The Attic Nights of Aulus Gellius* (Cambridge: Harvard University Press, 1927), Vol. 3, pp. 392-397 19.12.

Eleusis, if he had been polluted by a murder when he brought it, for this was more likely to turn the goddesses into avengers of the murder than to win their pardon. He also altered the appearance of his house in her honour by making the paintings and decorations of the rooms black by means of hangings, dyes, and Lesbian marble, which is a gloomy and dark marble. And they say that Lucius, a wise man, tried to give Herodes advice about this, and since he could not persuade him to alter it, he turned him into ridicule. And this incident must not be omitted from my narrative, since it is held worthy of mention by learned writers. For this Lucius ranked among men renowned for learning, and since he had been trained in philosophy by Musonius of Tyre, his repartees were apt to hit the mark, and he practiced a wit well suited to the occasion. Now, as he was very intimate with Herodes, he was with him when he was most deeply afflicted by his grief, and used to give him good advice to the following effect: "Herodes, in every matter that that which is enough is limited by the golden mean, and I have often heard Musonius argue on this theme, and have often discoursed on it myself; and, moreover, I used to hear you also, at Olympia, commending the golden mean to the Greeks, and at that time you would even exhort rivers to keep their course in mid channel between their banks. But what has now become of all this advice? For you have lost your self-control, and are acting in a way that we must needs deplore, since you risk your great reputation." He said more to the same effect. But since he could not convince him, he went away in anger. And he saw some slaves at a well that was in the house, washing radishes, and asked them for whose dinner they were intended. They replied that they were preparing them for Herodes. At this Lucius remarked: "Herodes insults Regilla by eating white radishes in a black house." This speech was reported indoors to Herodes, and when he heard it he removed the signs of mourning from his house, for fear he should become the laughing-stock of wise men.

...Thus, then, his grief for Regilla was quenched, while his grief for his daughter Panathenais was mitigated by the Athenians, who buried her in the city, and decreed that the day on which she died should be taken out of the year. But when his other daughter, whom he called Elpinike, died also, he lay on the floor, beating the earth and crying aloud: "O my daughter, what offerings shall I consecrate to thee? What shall I bury with thee?" Then Sextus the philosopher who chanced to be present said: "No small gift will you give your daughter if you control your grief for her." He mourned his daughters with this excessive grief because he was offended with his son Atticus. He had been misrepresented to him as foolish, bad at his letters, and of a dull memory. At any rate, when he could not master his alphabet, the idea occurred to Herodes to bring him up with twenty-four boys of the same age named after the letters of the alphabet, so that he would be obliged to learn his letters at the same time as the names of the boys. He saw too that he was a drunkard and given to senseless amours, and hence in his lifetime he used to utter a prophecy over his own house, adapting a famous verse as follows: "One fool methinks is still left in the wide house," and when he died he handed over to him his mother's estate, but transferred his own patrimony to other heirs. The Athenians, however, thought this inhuman, and they did not take into consideration his foster-sons Achilles, Polydeukes, and Memnon, and that he mourned them as though they had been his own children, since they were highly honourable youths, noble-minded and fond of study, a credit to their upbringing in his house. Accordingly, he put up statues of them hunting, having hunted, and about to hunt, some in his shrubberies, others in the fields, others by springs or in the shade of plane trees, not hidden away, but inscribed with execrations on any one who should pull down or move them. Nor would he have exalted them thus, had he not known them to be worthy of his praises. And when the Quintilii during their proconsulship of Greece censured him for putting up the statues of these youths on the grounds that they were an extravagance, he retorted, "What business is it of yours if I amuse myself with my poor marbles?"[402]

Inscription by Polydeukion

[Marathon]

Polydeukion to Dionysos, for the sake of piety.[403]

Inscriptions for Polydeukion

[Delphi, Roman Agora]

The Delphians for Vibullius Polydeukion because of his decency. The hero of Herodes.[404]

[Delphi]

Tiberius Claudius Attikos Herodes the Athenian, by decree of the Amphictyonic league, dedicated the statue of Vibullius Polydeukion, his own *trophimos.*[405]

[Kato Souli, headless herm]

Polydeukion, whom Herodes loved as if he were a son. Herodes set it up here where they used to hunt.[406]

---

[402] Wilmer Cave Wright (ed./trans.), *Philostratus, Lives of Sophists; Eunapius, Lives of Philosophers* (Cambridge: Harvard University Press, 1921), 2.555-559, pp. 158-167.
[403] Tobin, p. 276.
[404] Tobin, p. 100.
[405] Tobin, p. 100.

302

Before the gods and heroes: Whoever you are who hold the land, on no account move any of these things. And as for the images and honors of these statues, whoever either pulls them down or moves them, may the earth not bear fruit for him, nor the sea be navigable, and may he and his race die miserably. But, whoever keeps watch on this place and continues giving the customary honor and exaltation, may there be many favors to him himself and his children. But neither maltreat or knock over or break up or demolish anything of this shape and image. But if anyone does this, this curse be on them.

But leave the *epithémata* of the images and *hypostémata* undamaged and unharmed, and the bases as they were made.

And in addition to the first clause and first clauses, whoever either orders another or governs the intentions or influences the intentions concerning moving or destroying anything of these, this curse on them.[407]

[Kephisia, statue bases]

The hero Polydeukion. When Vibullius Polydeukes was *agonothetes*, during the archonship of Dionysios. The *rhabdophoroi*:   Ploution, Euporos,
          Philoserapis, Protagoras,
          Onesimos, Theophilos,
          Kosmos, Menodoros,
          Metrobios, Chryseros,
          Aristokrates, Athenaios,
          Leukios, Philetas,
          Kasianos, Helix,

---

[406] Tobin, p. 131.
[407] Tobin, p. 115.

Eisidotos, Epaphrodeitos,
Leochares, Kallineikos.[408]

Vibullia Alkia dedicated this statue of the hero Polydeukion, dearest to her son and herself, to Poseidon.[409]

[Kephisia, headless herms]

The hero Polydeukion. Lucius Octavius Restitutus of Marathon set it up at his own expense.[410]

The Hero Polydeukion. Once I used to walk with you at this crossroad. [The same curse as that at Kata Souli above, follows this.][411]

[Kephisia, altar]

Asiatikos Lanptreus, to the hero Polydeukion.[412]

[Rhamnous]

By decree of the Boule of the Areopagus and the Boule of the 500 and the people of Athens, Herodes, who raised him like a son, set up the statue of Vibullius Polydeukion, Roman Knight, to Nemesis, to whom he used to sacrifice with him, the kindly and ever-remembered *trophimos*.[413]

---

[408] Tobin, p. 230. It is possible that the Vibullius Polydeukes here named as *agonothetes* may have been Polydeukion's father, or at least a close kinsman of his. This inscription indicates that sacred games of a private nature were once held in honor of Polydeukion.
[409] Tobin, p. 216.
[410] Tobin, p. 218.
[411] Tobin, p. 122.
[412] Tobin, p. 235.
[413] Tobin, p. 279.

[Varnava, headless herm]

Polydeukion the hero, watcher of the baths.[414]

[Vrana, statue base]

The hero Vibullius Polydeukion, Vibullia Alkia the mother of Herodes set this up.[415]

[Markopoulou, headless herm]

Polydeukion the hero, for [the protection of] these baths and their sweetening, Herodes dedicated this.[416]

Inscriptions for Memnon

[Beh, headless herm, with curse inscription similar to the one above following it]

Memnon Topádein ("little topaz"), beloved of Artemis.

[Skorpio River, near Marathon]

Memnon Topádein.[417]

---

[414] Tobin, p. 101n131.
[415] Tobin, p. 250.
[416] Tobin, pp. 280-281. The translation here is my own, and very provisional.
[417] Tobin, p. 97.

Inscriptions for Achilles

[Oinoe: headless herm, accompanied by a curse similar to the one above following it]

Achilles.[418]

[Varnava: headless herm]

Herodes to Achilles. So that I may see you in this vale also, I and any other (who passes). And to the former, you call to mind the memory of this great friendship which was ours. I consecrate you to watchful Hermes the protector of shepherds.[419]

Inscriptions to all the *Trophimoi*

[unknown findspot]

And here where we used to eat together and pour libations together. [Followed by a curse similar to the ones above.][420]

[unknown findspot; relief sculpture showing a youth with a horse in front of a tree, with the full curse inscription given above.][421]

---

[418] Tobin, p. 96.
[419] Tobin, pp. 277-278.
[420] Tobin, p. 142.
[421] Tobin, pp. 118-119.

Elpinike

[Akraiphia in Boeitia: Sanctuary of Apollon Ptoos]

Annia Atilia Regilla Elpinike Agrippina, daughter of Tiberius Claudius Herodes and Regilla. The people dedicated it.[422]

[Delphi: exedra]

By decree of the city of Delphi. Annia Claudia Regilla Agrippina Elpinike Appia Polla, daughter of Herodes and Regilla. Her father set it up.[423]

[Olympia: base from nymphaeum]

Appia Annia Atilia Regilla Elpinike Agrippina Atria Polla, daughter of Herodes and Regilla. The city of the Elians dedicated it.[424]

[Eleusis]
Appia Annia Atilia Regilla Agrippina Elpinike Atria Polla, daughter of Herodes and Regilla...[425]

[Kephisia]

Appia Annia Atilia Regilla Agrippina Elpinike Atria Polla, wife of Lucius Vibullius Hipparchos, daughter of Tiberius Claudius Attikos Herodes of Marathon, consul, and of Annia Appia Regilla, the daughter of Appius, consul.
The sun and the earth and the heavens and all the days witness

---

[422] Tobin, p. 84.
[423] *Ibid.*
[424] *Ibid.*
[425] Tobin, p. 201.

how the bitter pain bites me because of my daughter, on whose account the cicadas sitting in the trees and the wells pouring water, weep...
You, Regilla...[426]

Athenais

[Athens]

Domitianos set up the statue of Athenais, daughter of his teacher Herodes.[427]

[Athens: Asklepieion]

By decree of the council of the Areopagos, Flavius Macer set up a statue of Marcia Athenais, daughter of his friend and teacher Claudius Herodes. When Eudemos son of Hermeios of Gargettos was *zakoros* and Evangellos son of Demetrius of Gargettos was assistant *zakoros*.[428]

[Delphi: exedra]

By decree of the city of Delphi, Marcia Alkia Athenais Gavidia Latiaria, daughter of Herodes and Regilla. Her father set it up.[429]

[Olympia: nymphaeum]

Marcia Claudia Alkia Athenais Gavidia Lateria, daughter of Herodes and Regilla. The city of the Elians set it up.[430]

---

[426] Tobin, p. 235.
[427] Tobin, p. 86.
[428] Tobin, pp. 86-87.
[429] Tobin, p. 87.
[430] *Ibid.*
308

Regillus

[Delphi: exedra]

By decree of the city of Delphi, For Lucius Vibullius Regillus Claudius Herodes, son of Herodes and Regilla. His father set it up.[431]

[Olympia: nymphaeum]

Lucius Claudius Vibullius Regillus Herodes, son of of Herodes and Regilla. The city of the Elians set it up.[432]

Herodes' Unnamed Three Children

[Kephisia]

Herodes, set in the depths of the earth this his lock of hair,
Having dampened the tips of the hair with his tears,
When for less than the cycle of a year
He had neither grown his hair nor reared you, dear son,
For he cut this lock in the third month.
May it be a true token to you three children's souls
That you will someday receive among the coffins the body of
    your father.[433]

Lucius Claudius Herodes

[Kephisia]

Lucius Vibullius Claudius Herodes, the natural son of Rufus, adopted son of Herodes.[434]

---

[431] Tobin, p. 89.
[432] *Ibid.*
[433] Tobin, p. 225.
[434] Tobin, p. 217.

Inscriptions to Appia Annia Regilla

[Delphi: Temple of Apollon]

Appia Regilla, wife of the benefactor Claudius Herodes, for her family, her decency and her good repute, all her traditional excellent traits and on account of her goodness, decency and kindness. The Boule and the people of Delphi dedicate to Apollon Pythios.[435]

[from Regilla's estate on the Via Appia, Italy; cenotaph inscription by the poet Marcellus Sidetes]

Come her to this shrine surrounding the seated statue
of Regilla, women of the Tiber, bringing sacred offerings.
She was descended from the prosperous line of Aeneas, the
    renowned blood of
Anchises and Idaean Aphrodite.
She married into a family at Marathon.
The heavenly goddesses honor her, both the New Deo[436] and the
    Old.
To them the sacred image of the well-girt wife is consecrated.
She, however, has been allocated a place among the heroines
in the islands of the blessed, where Kronos is king.
This she has received as her reward for her noble mind.
Thus Zeus had pity on the grieving spouse
lying in the middle of his widower's bed in harsh old age,
since from his blameless house
the black Harpy Fate-Spinners carried off half of his many
    children.
Two young children are still left,

---

[435] Tobin, p. 79.
[436] Empress Faustina the Elder, as syncretized to Demeter.

innocent of harm, still completely unaware
that a pitiless fate seized their mother
before she had reached the years when old women spin.
To him, grieving without respite, Zeus
and the emperor, who is like Zeus in nature and intelligence, has
given
consolation. Zeus ordered that Herodes' fertile wife be brought
to the Ocean stream on the Elysian breezes of Zephyr.
Caesar Antoninus Pius granted his son Attikos Bradua the
privilege of wearing on his feet the sandals decorated with
stars
which they say Hermes too wore
when he lead Aeneas from the war against the Achaians
through the dark night; around his feet was set,
shining as a protecting savior, the half globe of the moon.
The descendants of Aeneas once stitched this on the sandal
to be an honor for the noble Ausonians.
Not begrudged to him, a descendant of Kekrops,
is this old gift of Tyrrhenian men on his ankle
if truly born of Hermes and Herse was
Keryx, ancestor of Herodes, descended from Theseus.
Therefore he is honored and gives his name to the year.
He is included at the lordly Senate in the front row of seats.
In Greece there is no family or reputation more royal than
Herodes'. They call him the voice of Athens.
But Regilla of the beautiful ankles was descended from Aeneas
and was of the race of Ganymede, for she is of the Dardanian
race from Tros,
the son of Erichthonios. As for you, dear friend, please go and
make sacrifices
and burn them. But it is necessary that the one who sacrifices be
not unwilling.
It is good for the pious to also care about heroes.
For Regilla is neither mortal, nor divine.
Therefore she has neither sacred temple nor tomb,
neither honors for mortals, nor honors like those for the divine.

In a deme of Athens is a tomb for her like a temple,
but her soul attends the scepter of Rhadamanthys.
This image of her so gratifying to Faustina has been erected
in the area of the Triopeion, where there were formerly broad
fields,
rows of cultivated vines, and acres of olive trees.
Nor would the goddess, queen of women [Faustina], disdain her,
who was a priestess for Faustina's sacrifices and an attendant in
Regilla's youth.
The archeress with the beautiful throne[437] did not disdain
Iphigeneia
nor did fierce-eyed Athena disdain Herse.
The grain-giving mother of powerful Caesar,[438]
who rules over the heroines of the past, will not despise her
as she goes to the chorus of earlier semi-divine women,
and with her Alkmene, whose lot is to rule over Elysian choruses
of women,
and the blessed daughter of Kadmos.[439]
Powerful ruler of Athens, born of Triton,[440]
and you who see the deeds of mortals from your lookout at
Rhamnous,[441]
next-door neighbors of hundred-gated Rome,
goddesses, honor also this fruitful estate
of Deo of the Triopeion, a place friendly to strangers.
So long may the Triopeion goddesses be honored among
immortals,
surely as when you came to Rhamnous and to Athens of the
broad streets
leaving the homes of your loud thundering father.
So surely make this vineyard flourish rich in grapes throughout,
taking care of the crop of grain and vines with clusters of fruit

---

[437] Artemis.
[438] Domitia Lucilla.
[439] Semele.
[440] Athena.
[441] Nemesis.

312

and tresses of grasses in the soft meadows.
For you Herodes sanctified the land
and built a rounded wall encircling it
not to be moved or violated, for the benefit of future
generations.[442]

[near Kephisia: temple ruins]

Appia Annia Regilla, wife of Herodes, the light of the house
[followed by curse inscription similar to those above][443]

[Athens: Temple of Tyche]

Appia Atelia Regilla, wife of the *archiereus* Herodes, first priestess
of the Tyche of the City, according to the sanction of the
powerful Areopagos. Those working in Piraeus, Balerios
Agathopodas of the *deme* of Melite and his colleagues...[444]

[Eleusis]

Appia Annia Regilla Atilia Caucidia Tertulla, daughter of Appius
the high priest and consul, wife of Herodes of Marathon, consul
and exegete. Her husband dedicated it.[445]

---

[442] Sarah B. Pomeroy, *The Murder of Regilla: A Case of Domestic Violence in
Antiquity* (Cambridge and London: Harvard University Press, 2007), pp. 170-
174.
[443] Tobin, p. 126.
[444] Tobin, p. 176.
[445] Tobin, p. 207.

[Marathon: Herodes' estate]

The Gate of Eternal Harmony. The place you enter is Regilla's.[446]

Ah, happy is he who has built a new city, calling it by name
    Regilla's; his life is one of joy.
But my life is one of grief at what this estate has become for me
    without my beloved wife, and my home is half complete.
For in truth, the gods, when they mixed the cup of life for
    mortals, poured out joys and griefs side by side.[447]

Inscriptions for and by Herodes Attikos

[Via Appia: Herodes' estate]

The columns record gifts to Demeter and Kore and the
Chthonic Deities, and no one is allowed to carry anything from
the Triopeion, which is at the third milestone of the Via Appia,
in the estate of Herodes; no good to you moving things. Enodia
as witness.[448]

[Athens: Theatre of Dionysos]

By decree of the city and the people, Claudius Herodes put this
up, on account of his friendship, for Flavius Dorotheos, having
served as *strategos* and *agonothete* of the greater Eleusinian
Mysteries.[449]

---

[446] Tobin, p. 243.
[447] Tobin, p. 248.
[448] Tobin, p. 152.
[449] Tobin, p. 199.

314

[Eleusis]

To Good Fortune!
Upon the victory of the most revered emperors Marcus Aurelius and Lucius Verus, Sebastoi, Armenikoi and Parthikoi Megistoi, during the archonship of Sextus of Phaleron, the *cosmete* of the ephebes Lucius Herrenius Cornelius and Attikos Azerieos recorded those becoming ephebes under him, those who first wore white, on account of the most munificent donation of the excellent high priest Tiberius Claudius Herodes of Marathon. The president asked: to whom does it seem good that the ephebes wear white on the day on which the band marches to Eleusis, and to whom does it not seem good? No one rose in objection. Herodes said: "O ephebes, with me around you will never lack white chlamydes."[450]

Herodes had Asklepios represented as a Mystes of Deo. Showing kindness and warding off sickness.[451]

[Beh, near Marathon]

Blessed were you, O Marathon, just now, and an object of care to men more than before, as you looked upon the glorious Alkaides, who returned from the Sarmatian nomads at the outermost edge of the world, whither he had followed the warlike, far-traveled emperor of the Ausonians. Him Bacchus Eiraphiotes, the ivy-bearing son of Zeus, himself conducted to his famous fatherland, his own priest. Behind came the two life-giving goddesses in escort, Athena, protectress of the city, met them as they were approaching the sacred Rheitoi, which are two Chalcidic rivers, and Thria, where the sea and stream join at the shore. She was leading the people, all the citizens gathered together, first the priests with the unbound, flowing hair, in full

---

[450] Tobin, p. 203.
[451] Tobin, p. 202.

regalia, and all resplendent, and behind them the priestesses, who had wisely loving Aphrodite with them; next to them the glorious boys' class busy with a song, a lusty choir for Olympian Zeus; behind them the young students of manhood, sons of the Athenians, ephebes gleaming in bronze, youths whom he himself, when they were still mourning Theseus' forgetfulness of the father Aegeus, separated from the black raiment of atonement and clothed in shining garb at his own expense, the gift of costumes fastened with amber clasps over the shoulder; behind them the select council of the Kekropians, standing out in precedence, marched all together, the higher corporation, named for Ares, while the other, of lesser rank, followed behind it. They all arrayed themselves in newly washed, white cloaks. Close to them strode forward all the rest of the people, denizens and strangers and even slaves. No watchman was left in the halls, no boy, no fair-skinned maiden but all were gathered to receive Herodes...as when a mother embraces her child...from afar...[452]

[Marathon: Herodes' estate]

The Gate of Eternal Harmony. The place you enter is Herodes'.[453]

[Markopoulo]

Herodes Attikos of Marathon rebuilt the temple and dedicated the statue to Athena.[454]

---

[452] Tobin, pp. 273-274.
[453] Tobin, p. 243.
[454] Tobin, p. 281.

Herodes Attikos and Polydeukion

This poem was written in 2008, and was published earlier in *The Phillupic Hymns.*[455]

Herodes Attikos and Polydeukion

Of all my sons and daughters
and three foster children
who died before the Fates saw them
as adults healthy and whole,
there is one I miss the most.

Polydeukion is his name,
hero in bath, grove, and shrine,
hero to me no less than god,
an Antinous for his virtue,
an Antinous in his beauty.

And yet, how unfortunate he,
for even Antinous had his time
to shine briefly on the earth,
to stand against lions
and prevail over them.

In Egypt with the gods
was Antinous enthroned;
therefore, in Greece where heroes
once lived, loved, and died,
let Polydeukion be crowned.

---

[455] P. Sufenas Virius Lupus, *The Phillupic Hymns* (Eugene: Bibliotheca Alexandrina, 2008), pp. 193-194.

Memnon and Achilleus
were as dear to me,
and may their names not die,
but Polydeukion more—
may the gods pour them wine!

I am old and ignored,
a rich benefactor of Athens,
but they sneer at me
in public for my sadness;
so it is for wisdom's lovers.

I weep for the lost potential,
for what these boys could have been—
and for those who will come after,
which Helios will lament likewise
for kissing them with his rays too briefly.

I care not for my own name
so long as their names live on;
Memnon, Achilleus, Polydeukion—
may rivers of Elysium quench their thirsts,
may the Aegean long sing their dirge!

The *Trophimoi* Praise the *Trophimoi*

In 2011, the Ekklesía Antínoou celebrated the first festival of the Trophimoi and the other members of Herodes Attikos' family. The dates were chosen based on three factors: 1) they were six months off the festival for Lucius Marius Vitalis in early September, which had been a long-established date in modern Antinoan practice; 2) this was the timeframe during 2010 in which I not only first learned that a statue-head of Polydeukion was in the museum in Michigan near where I was living at the time, but it was also the first time that I visited it; and 3) an oracular reading with the *Trophimoi* and other *Sancti* of the Ekklesía Antínoou confirmed that the date on which to celebrate Polydeukion in particular was to be March 9th. The week-long festival, with dates for each of the *Trophimoi*, Herodes Attikos, Appia Annia Regilla, and their other children, was therefore devised.

In addition to the poem just given, which was used in the festival, further poems were written (some of which are not given in this book), and three of the most interesting were the series which follows, "The *Trophimoi* Praise the *Trophimoi*." In each poem, the speaker (indicated by the title) praises his two brothers, and some of their individual characters emerge in the process. Memnon writes a villanelle, in a heroic style, using Homeric spellings for his brothers' names; Achilles writes free verse with acrostichs spelling out his brothers' names; and, not to be outdone, Polydeukion writes in a villanelle format with acrostichs spelling out his brothers' names.

The *Trophimoi* Praise the *Trophimoi*

I. Memnon

Young Achilleus' praises now I sing;
the boys and brothers, pleasure to my sight;
good Polydeukes' virtues 'ever-ring.

320

His sword-arm reached not far, but still would ding
the breastplate of each enemy he'd fight—
young Achilleus' praises now I sing.

When offerings to Dionysos bring
to bathe the world in salvific light—
good Polydeukes' virtues 'ever-ring.

His sling-stones, like a hail from Hades, fling
a show'r of damage, vigorous in might—
young Achilleus' praises now I sing.

No object of mind or physical thing
was out of grasp for his hand or sense bright—
good Polydeukes' virtues 'ever-ring.

Their loss is sadness to Marathon's king,
father Herod, and my own bitter plight—
young Achilleus' praises now I sing
while Polydeukes' virtues 'ever-ring.

II. Achilles

Memnon my brother
Ethiopian in origin
Multiple in talents
None more stalwart
Outstanding in letters
Never without excellence.

Polydeukion my friend
Opposed to frivolity
Likes to contemplate
Years of wisdom
Dreaming of greatness
Excited at esteem
Uninterested in quarrels
Kind to everyone
Indomitable on horseback
On philosophy inscrutable
Not without humor!

III. Polydeukion

My *Topádein*, a Nubian moon-child—
Each of my brothers' qualities I praise—
My little hero, rambunctious and wild.

No shepherd in the field would be more mild
Or just beneath the bright sun's saving rays—
No, my little Topaz, the moon-shade child!

At play, his sense of fairness undefiled,
Climbed past the stamina of gods for days—
Heroic one, rambunctious and wild.

In virtue, Antinous' deeds compiled;
Lady of Rome, Regilla's greatness stays;
Like Herakles, calmness Herod exiled...
Excellent Topaz, Nubian moon-child,
Stay well, remember brothers who were wild.

Laudatio Sabinae

March 21st, the date we observe as the Apotheosis of Diva Sabina Augusta, is honestly one of my most favorite holidays of the year in the Ekklesía Antínoou; considering, however, how much of a "rough" start it had in my own case, that's quite a wonder. We established the date in late 2003, and then the first occasion on which we could observe it was in March of 2004; but, a few days before that, I went into the hospital, and had hoped to be released by the 21st, but was not. I ended up having to make do with very little to observe the holy day on that occasion. The following year, this hymn was written, and I have used it ever since. The first "proper" celebration of the festival, in my case, involved two of my friends and myself observing it in my tiny front room in Ireland in 2005; one of my friends happened to be Sharynne MacLeod NicMhacha, lead singer of the band The Moors, who very kindly lent her voice to several of the hymns, as well as performing an *a capella* solo of The Moors' song *"Dea Noctu Imperatrix"* which would have knocked me off my feet if I had been standing! The date has been one on which the accomplishments of women, and women's roles in the cultus of Antinous, the lives of Hadrian and his associates, and various goddesses have been highlighted above all. In 2008, the enrollment of many *Sanctae* also took place on this day.

This hymn was originally published in *The Phillupic Hymns*.[456]

Laudatio Sabinae

Ave Diva Sabina
uxor Hadriani beata
Iuno Ceres et Venus Dea
Imperatrix Augusta

---

[456] P. Sufenas Virius Lupus, *The Phillupic Hymns* (Eugene: Bibliotheca Alexandrina, 2008), pp. 222-223.

Filia Matidiae
Hadriani deditae
eo superexultate
filia divae

Sororis Filia Traiani
Imperatoris Maximi
ordinata nuptiali
esse uxorem Hadriani

Mater Imperii
lux Tiburis Latii
villa Hadriani
nos ignorationem erudi

Urbis Romae Regina
Dui Aegypti Domina
bovis et frumenta
tibi amplificanda

Amica Antinoi
amantis Hadriani
multi benedicti
omni amatori donate

Laudationis tibi
resonent clarissimi
Ave Diva Sabina Augusta!

Ave Diva Sabina Augusta!
Ave Diva Sabina Augusta!
Ave Diva Sabina Augusta!

Pax Cererem nutrit, Pacis alumna Ceres, AVE.

"Sabina's Praises"

Hail, Divine Sabina,
fair wife of Hadrian;
Juno, Ceres, and Venus, Goddess,
Empress, Augusta.

Daughter of Matidia—
devoted-one of Hadrian
much praised by him—
daughter of the divine one.

Niece of Trajan—
Greatest Emperor—
arranged for marriage
to be wife of Hadrian.

Mother of the Empire,
Light of Tibur of Latium,
the villa of Hadrian,
enlighten our ignorance!

Queen of the City of Rome,
Lady of the Two Egypts,
the cattle and grains
will be increased for you.

Friend of Antinous—
lover of Hadrian—
may many blessings
be given to all lovers.

May the brightest praises
resound to you,
Hail Divine Empress Sabina!...

326

Peace is nourished by Ceres, Ceres is the daughter of Peace,[457]
HAIL.

[457] Barbette Stanley Spaeth, *The Roman Goddess Ceres* (Austin: University of
Texas Press, 1996), p 150, gives this line from Ovid's *Fasti*, in her discussion
of Ceres' connection to Pax, and the importance of an abundant grain crop to
the maintenance of peace in the Empire; the line itself is found in Sir James
George Frazer (ed./trans.), *Ovid's Fasti* (Cambridge: Harvard University Press,
1931), pp. 52-53 line 1.704.

Sabinian Petition

On the dates in which Diva Sabina is honored—particularly March 21st—the following litany would be appropriate to offer. It can also be used on other dates when the *Divae* or particular goddesses are honored in one's practice of Antinoan devotion. It is based on the "Antinoan Petition," given in a previous chapter, but it is entirely in Latin, with the appropriate Latinate forms of the various figures' names.

In nomine Divae Sabinae, Imperatricis et Augustae,[458]
Ave Vive Diva Sabina!

Sabina cum[459] *Cerere,*[460] **DONA NOBIS PACEM**
Sabina cum Iunone,[461] **DONA NOBIS PACEM**
Sabina cum Venere,[462] **DONA NOBIS PACEM**
Sabina cum Proserpina et Libera,[463] **DONA NOBIS PACEM**

---

[458] "In the name of the Divine Sabina, Empress and Augusta."

[459] "Sabina, with..."

[460] Ceres (Greek Demeter). Sabina is portrayed as Ceres on coins and statues, and is honored as the "New Demeter" in Eleusis; Barbette Stanley Spaeth, *The Roman Goddess Ceres* (Austin: University of Texas Press, 1996), pp. 120, 178-179; Anthony R. Birley, *Hadrian The Restless Emperor* (London and New York: Routledge, 2000), p. 178.

[461] Juno (Greek Hera). On certain altars in Greece, Sabina is honored as the New Hera; Anna S. Benjamin, "The Altars of Hadrian in Athens and Hadrian's Panhellenic Program," *Hesperia* 32.1 (January-March 1963), pp. 57-86 at 77 §139.

[462] Venus (Greek Aphrodite); Sabina is depicted as Venus in a statue from Ostia; Fred S. Kleiner, *A Hsitory of Roman Art, Enhanced Edition* (Belmont: Wadsworth Publishing, 2010), p. 173.

[463] Proserpina is the Latin rendering of Persephone; Libera is the daughter of Ceres and the sister (and/or consort) of Liber, and thus likewise equivalent to the Greek Persephone.

328

Sabina cum Magna Matre et Cybele et Agdistis,[464] *DONA NOBIS PACEM*

Sabina cum Roma Domina et Vesta,[465] *DONA NOBIS PACEM*

Sabina cum Diana,[466] *DONA NOBIS PACEM*

Sabina cum Minerva,[467] *DONA NOBIS PACEM*

Sabina cum Disciplina et Abundantia et Pace,[468] *DONA NOBIS PACEM*

Sabina cum Victoria et Fortuna,[469] *DONA NOBIS PACEM*

Sabina cum Iside,[470] *DONA NOBIS PACEM*

Sabina cum Lupa et Rhea Silvia,[471] *DONA NOBIS PACEM*

Sabina cum Iulia Balbilla et Sapphone,[472] *DONA NOBIS PACEM*

Sabina cum Matidia et Plotina et Marciana,[473] *DONA NOBIS PACEM*

---

[464] Magna Mater is the name via which Cybele (and the various other goddesses of Asia Minor to whom she was syncretized) was known in Latin; Agdistis was either the progenitor of Cybele, or an associate of hers, or was the androgyne precursor of her.

[465] The Lady Roma, goddess of the city personified, as well as of the wider Roman Empire. Vesta is the equivalent of the Greek Hestia.

[466] Diana is the Latin equivalent of the Greek Artemis.

[467] Minerva is the equivalent of the Greek Athena.

[468] Disciplina, Abundantia and Pax are the Roman deified abstractions representing discipline, abundance, and peace. Greek equivalents for Abundantia and Pax would be Euthenia and Eirene respectively; Disciplina has no precise singular cognate, as the cultus emerged during Hadrian's reign, but both Sophrosyne and Arete would have a large amount of overlap with her in many respects.

[469] Victoria is equivalent to the Greek Nike; Fortune is equivalent to the Greek Tyche.

[470] This is the ablative form of the Latin rendering of the Egyptian goddess commonly known as Isis.

[471] The Lupa is the she-wolf who suckled Romulus and Remus; Rhea Silvia was their mother, who had been a Vestal Virgin.

[472] Julia Balbilla was a Greek poetess at Hadrian's court who was a close friend (and possible lover) of the Empress, about whom more is written in chapters below. Sappho is the famous poetess of Lesbos, who was widely honored in the Graeco-Roman world.

[473] The three *Divae* here are Sabina's mother, great aunt, and grandmother respectively.

Sabina cum Faustina,[474] ***DONA NOBIS PACEM***
Sabina cum Antinoëia et Mantinoëia,[475] ***DONA NOBIS PACEM***
Sabina cum Omnibus Deis, Heroibus, Divis, et Sanctis,[476] ***DONA NOBIS PACEM***

---

[474] There were two Empress Faustinas: the wife of Antoninus Pius (who is the one referred to here), and the wife of Marcus Aurelius.

[475] Antinoë was the foundress of Mantineia, the Arcadian city-state from which Antinous' ancestry emerged; Mantinoë was the name of Antinous' mother, as recorded in a papyrus fragment to be dealt with. further in a chapter below.

[476] "with all the goddesses, heroines, *Divae,* and *Sanctae.*"

The Birth of Matidia

It is one of the supreme ironies of history that, due to accidents of survival, we know more definite dates in the life of Diva Matidia Augusta, the mother-in-law of Hadrian, than we do in the life of Trajan's wife, Diva Plotina, or of Hadrian's wife Diva Sabina. We do not know the exact date of Matidia's death (though it was in the year 119 CE), but we know her birthdate, which was July 4th 68 CE, and we know that she was given the title of *Augusta* on August 29th in 112 CE. Hadrian's relationship with his mother-in-law was especially close and cordial, which seems like it should be counter-intuitive. Some have suggested that Hadrian may have even had amorous feelings toward her, as she was closer to his age, and would have been a more suitable match for him than Matidia's daughter Sabina. Whatever the truth of the matter is, Hadrian honored and esteemed her greatly, and she was the first of many *Augustae* to be deified in his principate. This hymn was written for our observance of her birthdate in 2009.

The Birth of Matidia

On the fourth day before the *Nones* of July,
praise and supplication to the great lady,
Diva Salonia Matidia Augusta—
daughter of Diva Ulpia Marciana Augusta,
mother of Diva Vibia Sabina Augusta,
linchpin of the principates of the Antonines.

Your birthdate is known, and your elevation
into the company of the *Numen Augustorum*,
but your death-date has eluded us.
Your son-in-law, Divus Hadrianus Augustus,
the man most devoted to his mother-in-law,
spoke your funeral oration with grave sadness.

331

Your birth would coincide many years after
with the liberty of a new republic
founded under Pax and the goddess Columbia,
and like the goddess Pietas, to whom you were equated,
the Daughters and Sons of Libertas with fidelity
will remember the birth of their independence on this day.

We can never equal the praises of Hadrian for you,
nor the filial piety of Sabina and Mindia Matidia,
but we can offer the libation of wine
and the sweet fragrance of incense in supplication;
and millions, with barley's beer and bright fires in the night sky
will salute you unknowing, and keep your death-day far from
      memory!

Laudatio Matidiae

With Matidia, we are also very fortunate to have an inscription recording her funeral oration, which was given by Hadrian himself, and found near his villa at Tibur (modern Tivoli). This is my own provisional translation of the fragmentary inscription.[477]

Laudatio Matidiae

[three fragmentary lines]...most beloved mother-in-law...and to her the safety of my Sabina...would have done to my mother...after having obtained my principate and indeed successively, thoroughly unto that ultimate weakness which brought her death, companions and comrades...venerable that her daughter by accompanying no one...she was not seen.

...my mother-in-law [goes] to death, for whom it was able to do...to/for a woman will bear a burden wholly not...she would have summarily approved.

...singly concerning her virtues to which all...if thus I would have been living to presupposing in confusion...I would wish also to say so much which I may be able to require...either to her deserving praises or to my pain...she is the image of greatest sadness, the best mother-in-law beginning to falter...even whether they cry out mournfully shouting together...passing.

...of my soul is alleviated and it, which you know beautifully concerning deaths...if rather that the sign would have been spoken in order that new...she lived I marry the dearest, after it

---

[477] E. Mary Smallwood (ed.), *Documents Illustrating the Principates of Nerva Trajan and Hadrian* (Cambridge: Cambridge University Press, 1966), p. 56.

the lengthiest widowhood in an exceptional prime of life and the purest height of excellent beauty, most obedient to my mother, the very most tender mother, blood-relation most devoted, all-gratifying, unpleasant to none, gloomy to none. Moreover, as far as I am concerned...after such great modesty, how nothing at any time she would have asked from me which...and more she would not have asked for, what she asked I would have wished among my...of more will and the longest desired prayer of such kind...she saw. My fortune wished to rejoice that to benefit...granddaughter by blood of my deified father, by adoption in place of my cousin I arrange...daughter of Augusta and goddess, uncle...honor on behalf of deserving respectability...you considered worthy I request...[three fragmentary lines]

Funeral Inscription of Lucius Marius Vitalis

An historical personage who has received little attention—scholarly or otherwise—outside of the Ekklesía Antínoou is Lucius Marius Vitalis, a young man who died while at Hadrian's court under imperial tutelage. He is mentioned in an article focusing on the likely members of Hadrian's entourage when he went to the Eastern Empire in 128 CE,[478] and Royston Lambert also gives a brief account of him with a translation of the inscription below.[479] Shawn Postoff's website The Sacred Antinous has also featured Vitalis as a major character.[480]

Because of his importance as "Prince of the *Sancti*" and one of the *Treískouroi*, I sought out the original Latin of the inscription myself to make my own translation.[481] When I consulted the volume of *Corpus Inscriptionum Latinarum* containing the inscription, I noted that the editors suggested the Latin inscription could be understood as iambic trimeter for large parts of it; I have given the full Latin below as well, therefore. In making my own translation, which I decided to do as if it were a poem, I used anapest trimeter rather than iambic trimeter, as Lucius Marius Vitalis' name itself is anapest trimeter, and would make a suitable opening line. I had to embellish slightly to make the meter work throughout, but I liked the pattern created by the last words of each line which resulted from doing so.

---

[478] Richard H. Chowen, "Traveling Companions of Hadrian," *The Classical Journal* 50.3 (December 1954), pp. 122-124.

[479] Royston Lambert, *Beloved and God: The Story of Hadrian and Antinous* (New York: Viking, 1984), pp. 101-102.

[480] http://www.sacredantinous.com/.

[481] *Corpus Inscriptionum Latinarum* VI (2), §8991. My apologies that my reference on this matter is not more complete at present.

L MARIVS L F
VITALIS
VIXI ANN XVII D LV
CONSVMMATVS LITTER
PARENTES SVASI ARTEFIC
DISCEREM DISCESSI AB
VRBE IN PRAETORIO
HADRIANI AVG CAESAR
VBI DVM STVDEREM FATA
INVIDERVNT MIHI RAPTVM
QVE AB ARTE TRADIDERVNT
HOC LOCO
MARIA MALCHIS MATER
INFELICISSIMA FILIO SANCTISSIMO

Lucius Marius Vitalis,
I, Son to Lucius, lived for years
seventeen and for days fifty-five.
Perfected in ways literate, I
persuaded my parents to allow
me to learn the craft of artifice.
With Caesar Hadrian Augustus
I departed from the city, Rome,
companion in the suite of Caesar's
imperial entourage. The Fates,
becoming jealous, snatched me away
from art while I was studying thus,
to this place.

Maria Malchis, his
most infelicitious mother, wrote
and did this for her holiest son.

336

Dies Lucii Marii Vitalis

The following hymn was written in 2010 for the occasion of Lucius Marius Vitalis' festival on September 6th.

Dies Lucii Marii Vitalis

Lucius filius Lucii
Princeps ecclesiae sancti
Sanctissimus mortui beati
Consummatus literati

Primus initiati
Mysteriae Antinoi
Coviator Hadriani
Peritus arteficii

Cereris fortunatus
Liberaque amplexus
Matris eius defletissimus
Mariae Malchis filius

Musae Nonae flerete
Atrox Fata tremeque
Antinoe eum protege
et custody Hadriane

Data Lucie Sancte nobis
sapientiam subtilitatis
sub consilio Thothis
et tutela Sethis

Gaudete pro filio Mariae
et triumpho Memoriae
Ave Lucie Marie Vitalis

Ave Lucie Marie Vitalis
Ave Lucie Marie Vitalis
Ave Lucie Marie Vitalis

Vitae Tripuerorum nunquam e memoria excideatur.

<u>"Lucius Marius Vitalis' Day"</u>

Lucius, son of Lucius,
Foremost of the Ekklesía's *Sancti*,
Most blessed of the holy dead,
Most learned in letters;

First of the initiates
of the Mysteries of Antinous,
Fellow traveler of Hadrian,
Skilled one of art;

Favored one of Ceres
and embraced by Libera;
most mourned of his mother
the son of Maria Malchis.

Weep, O Nine Muses
and shudder, cruel Fate!
Protect him, Antinous,
and look after him, Hadrian!

Give us, O Sanctus Lucius
the wisdom of subtlety
under the guidance of Thoth
and the protection of Set.

338

Rejoice for Maria's son
and the triumph of Memory!
Hail Lucius Marius Vitalis!...

May the lives of the *Treiskouroi* never be forgotten!

Hadrian Praises Trajan

Marcus Ulpius Traianus, better known as Trajan in English, was Hadrian's imperial predecessor, the man who was responsible for his education and promotion through the ranks of the military and the Roman administration, and ultimately his adopted father. He was born on September 18th, between 53 and 56 CE, and is recorded as being celebrated in the Doura-Europos calendar like many of the other deified emperors.[482] Trajan and Hadrian shared a great deal in common, and of course Trajan's deification was carried out dutifully by Hadrian after his death and Hadrian's subsequent adoption.

It therefore seems appropriate to honor Hadrian's imperial father, Divus Traianus, with words that Hadrian himself wrote on another occasion for him, namely a poem inscribed at the temple of Mt. Kassios in Syria[483] before one of their Parthian expeditions.[484]

Trajan, Aeneas' son, dedicated this image to Kasian Zeus,
     the lord of men to the lord of immortals,
a pair of much-decorated cups and from an aurochs
     a horn adorned with all-shining gold,
set aside from previous booty, when tireless
     he destroyed the proud Getae with his spear:

---

[482] Mary Beard, John North, & Simon Price (eds./trans.), *Religions of Rome, Volume 2: A Sourcebook* (Cambridge: Cambridge University Press, 1998), p. 74.

[483] Mt. Kassios has further significance to Hadrian later in his life; see P. Sufenas Virius Lupus, "Roman Olympians: The Cult of Zeus and Hadrian Olympios," in Melia Suez et al. (eds.), *From Cave to Sky: A Devotional Anthology for Zeus* (Shreveport: Bibliotheca Alexandrina, 2010), pp. 97-105 at 100-101.

[484] Ewen L. Bowie, "Hadrian and Greek Poetry," in Erik Nis Ostenfeld, Karin Blomqvist and Lisa Nevett (eds.), *Greek Romans and Roman Greeks: Studies in Cultural Interaction* (Aarhus: Aarhus University Press, 2000), pp.172-197 at 180.

but do you promise him, dark-clouded one, this
strife too to accomplish gloriously against the
Achaemenids,
so that as you gaze on them your heart may be doubly warmed
by a pair, the Getae's spoils, and the Arascids'.

Inscriptions on the Colossus of Memnon by Julia Balbilla and Sabina

Not long after Antinous' death, on November 19th-21st of the year 130 CE, Hadrian's Imperial Party continued their journey up the Nile, and came to one of the most famous antiquities in Egypt of the time. Hadrian's visit actually galvanized tourism to the site in the following decades. There are two colossoi at the site, both about 65 feet tall, and they were originally erected in about 1400 BCE to honor the Pharaoh Amenophis (also known as Amenhotep III). However, the Greeks of the area began to equate the statue with Memnon, the Ethiopian ally of the Trojans, who was son of the goddess of the dawn, Eos, by Tithonos, and was slain by Achilleus. An earthquake in about 26 BCE caused the upper part of the so-called Memnon statue to topple, and soon after a high-pitched noise began to emanate from the statue-base, especially in the early morning, probably from moisture expansion amidst the cracks in the statue due to the heat of the desert. This was first reported by Strabo in about 24 BCE. Pausanias compares the sound to a *kithara* or lyre string which has been broken. Thus, the statue became famous for its "singing," and to hear it sing was considered a somewhat religious experience by the Greeks.

Initially, after Antinous' death, on the first day of their visit, Hadrian did not hear the sound—an ill omen indeed—but on the following days he did. Four members of the Imperial Party recorded their visit on the statue; a small group of priests were set up there to do this, and the inscriptions were probably done by a professional engraver for a price, as none of them are true "graffiti," but all are well-wrought and deep-cut inscriptions. The only surviving poetry of Julia Balbilla, a friend of Sabina's, the "Sappho of Hadrian's court," is on this statue in four separate poems from the three days.[485] Julia's poetry is not particularly

---

[485] André Bernand and Étienne Bernand (eds.), *Les Inscriptions Grecques et Latines du Colosse de Memnon* (Paris: Institut Francais d'Archéologie Orientale, 1960), pp. 80–100 §28-32; T. C. Brennan, "The Poets Julia Balbilla and

good, however she did write in the archaized Aeolian dialect of Sappho,[486] and was apparently quite well-read and intelligent, and learned in astrology, occult matters, and perhaps herbalism and poisons (as her grandfather before her was reputed to be). Further, she was related to all of the major dynasties of the Middle East (Commagene and Seleucid), her grandfather was prefect of Egypt under Nero, her brother was King Philopappus of Athens, a friend of Hadrian, one of her cousins was another friend of Hadrian, C. Julius Eurycles Herculanus, who set up a memorial to Antinous in Mantineia, and she was also related to Herodes Attikos.

A further fragmentary inscription in short, possibly poetic lines, seems to begin with Sabina,[487] but is unfortunately incomplete. Three other members of Hadrian's court also wrote inscriptions on the colossoi; Damo, the other woman, was probably Claudia Damo Synamate, an Athenian landowner and poet, probable further companion of Sabina. These women—and indeed all four women who wrote inscriptons on the colossoi of Memnon in all of its years—each had their inscriptions on the left leg of the statue, significantly the first place on the statue illuminated by the rays of the sun at dawn. The question of whether Sabina's friends were "Sapphic" in more than the poetic sense is one which has drawn some attention and speculation in the last few decades: if Hadrian had his Antinous, why not Sabina her Julia? While the facts of this matter are uncertain, Julia Balbilla's praise of the Empress is certainly something of which to take note. Thus, this entire incident is important for how close it actually comes to giving first-hand accounts both of the life of women in Hadrian's immediate court, and for how close it gets to the divine Sabina and her own life.

When observing this occasion (as noted in the calendar above), the 19th is an occasion of "disappointment," for which the first of the inscriptions below can be read; this particular one was translated by me

Damo at the Colossus of Memnon," *Classical World* 91.4 (March/April 1998), pp. 215-234.
[486] Patricia Rosenmeyer, "Greek Inscriptions in Roman Egypt: Julia Balbilla's Sapphic Voice," *Classical Antiquity* 27.2 (2008), pp. 334-358.
[487] Bernand and Bernand, pp. 99-100 §32.

previously in *The Phillupic Hymns*.[488]   The second day, the 20th of November, is themed "consolation," and the second and third inscriptions below can be read on that occasion; these were translated by Ewen Bowie, with additions on the third one by myself.[489]   The third day, "jubilation," on November 21st, can be observed by reading the fourth inscription of Julia Balbilla, which was translated by Mary R. Lefkowitz and Maureen B. Fant.[490] The first three were all written on November 20th, but as the first refers to events on the day before, it seems appropriate for that occasion. The inscriptions by the Empress Sabina and by the poetess Claudia Damo Synamate can be read on any of these days; Damo's poem was translated by T. C. Brennan.[491] Unfortunately, only my contribution to the texts below is translated as if it is a poem.

[November 20th, 130 CE]

The first day we did not hear Memnon.
Yesterday Memnon received the spouse
in silence so that the fair Sabina might come back again,
for the lovely form of the Queen delights you.
But if the sound had come,
a growing divine cry of fright,
the king might not have grown angry against you:
with your audacity, you were overly cautious
a long while with the Emperor and his lawful wife.
Likewise Memnon, you feared the power of the great Hadrian,
yourself pronouncing an unexpected cry that was heard, not
without joy.

[488] P. Sufenas Virius Lupus, *The Phillupic Hymns* (Eugene: Bibliotheca Alexandrina, 2008), p. 53.
[489] Ewen L. Bowie, "Greek Poetry in the Antonine Age," in D. A. Russell (ed.), *Antonine Literature* (Oxford: Oxford University Press, 1990), pp. 53-90 at 64-65.
[490] Mary R. Lefkowitz and Maureen B. Fant, *Women's Life in Greece & Rome* (Baltimore: The Johns Hopkins University Press, 1992), p. 10 §26.
[491] Brennan, p. 228.

[November 20th, 130 CE]

By Julia Balbilla, when Hadrian Augustus heard Memnon: I had been told that Memnon the Egyptian, warmed by the ray of the sun, spoke from his Theban stone. And when he saw Hadrian, king of all, before the rays of the sun, he greeted him as best he could. But when Titan, driving through the sky with his white horses, held the second measure of the hours in shadow, Memnon again uttered a sharp-toned cry as of bronze being struck: in greeting he also uttered a third call. Then the lord Hadrian himself also offered ample greetings to Memnon and on the monument left for posterity verses marking all that he had seen and all he had heard. And it was made clear to all that the gods loved him.

When I was staying near Memnon, in the company of Sabina Augusta: Memnon, son of Dawn and of renowned Tithonus, sitting before the Theban city of Zeus, or Amenoth, Egyptian king, as the priests who know the ancient tales relate, hail! and may you be keen to welcome by your cry the august wife too of the lord Hadrian. Your tongue and ears were cut by a barbarian, the godless Cambyses; hence by his wretched death he paid the penalty, smitten by the same sword with which in his heedlessness he slew the divine Apis. But I do not judge that this statue of yours could perish, and I perceive within me that your soul shall be immortal. For pious were my parents and grandparents, Balbillus the wise and Antiochus the king, Balbillus the parent of my royal mother, and Antiochus the king, father of my father. From their line do I too draw my noble blood, and these are the writings of Balbilla the pious.

[November 21st, 130 CE]

I, Balbilla, when the rock spoke, heard the voice of the divine Memnon or Phamenoth. I came here with the lovely Empress Sabina. The course of the sun was in its first hour, in the fifteenth year of Hadrian's reign, on the twenty-fourth day of the month Hathor. I wrote this on the twenty-fifth day of the month Hathor.

[c. November 20th-21st, 130 CE]

Sabina Augusta, wife of the Emperor Caesar Hadrian, in the course of the first hour, having heard Memnon twice...

[c. November 19th-21st, 130 CE]

Hail, son of Dawn, for favorably you spoke to me, Memnon, for the sake of the Muses, to whom I am dear~Damo, lover of song. Showing favor/bringing aid, my *barbitos* shall ever sing your power, O holy one.

IV.
HISTORICAL AND CULTIC
DOCUMENTS

Hadrian's Thespiae Inscription

As mentioned in the calendar above on April 21ˢᵗ, we know that Hadrian had many bear hunts. His successful killing of a bear in the Spring of 125 near Thespiae on his Greek sojourn is of further interest,[492] however, because in my own view it gives us a glimpse into the possible start of his relationship with Antinous, and ultimately with the cultus of Antinous.

Hadrian may have met Antinous by this time, but it is not certain; Marguerite Yourcenar's book certainly puts this incident in that context.[493] But, no matter what, Hadrian's wish for a youthful lover, as expressed in this inscription, ended up coming true in the years to come, and Antinous was quite literally the answer to his prayer on this occasion, granted by the grace of Aphrodite and Eros themselves.

I have not translated the final word in the inscription, as given below, because of its particular valences in ancient Greek. The word *kharis* is often translated "grace" in Christian contexts. In ancient polytheism, it meant the reciprocal relationship between deities and their worshippers. However, in the homoerotic context of ancient Greek love and its vocabulary, it meant the consent of a youthful *eromenos* to an elder *erastes*, the "favor" which they granted to them in accepting their love.

This text was translated previously in *The Phillupic Hymns*.[494] An alternate translation is available from Ewen L. Bowie.[495]

---

[492] Anthony R. Birley, *Hadrian The Restless Emperor* (London and New York: Routledge, 2000), pp. 184-185.

[493] Marguerite Yourcenar, *Hadrian's Memoirs*, trans. Grace Frick (New York: Farrar, Straus and Young, 1955), p. 160.

[494] P. Sufenas Virius Lupus, *The Phillupic Hymns* (Eugene: Bibliotheca Alexandrina, 2008), p. 212.

[495] Ewen L. Bowie, "Hadrian and Greek Poetry," in Erik Nis Ostenfeld, Karin Blomqvist and Lisa Nevett (eds.), *Greek Romans and Roman Greeks: Studies in*

Hadrian's Thespiae Inscription

To Eros the Archer Son of the Sweet-Tongued Cyprian
Aphrodite,
dwelling at Heliconian Thespiae
beside Narcissus' flowering garden:
I say be gracious, grant acceptance
of the best parts of this bear from Hadrian,
the very one killed by a blow from horseback.
Thou, of Thy own accord, in return for this, may *kharis* soberly
be breathed on him by Aphrodite Urania.

Cultural Interaction (Aarhus: Aarhus University Press, 2000), pp. 172-197 at
180-181.

Obelisk of Antinous

This is probably the most important text as far as our knowledge of the ancient cultus of Antinous goes. It was written on four sides of an Obelisk by someone with a rather incomplete knowledge of hieroglyphics, probably roughly translated from a Latin or Greek original. It is quite likely that Hadrian himself had a hand in the words on this monument. The Obelisk itself has a varied history, possibly originating in Egypt but most probably it was located in Italy; the latest excavations at the Antinoeion at Hadrian's Villa seem to indicate it used to be at the center of the small Antinoeion temple complex located there.[496] Its inscription describes its location as at or near Antinous' tomb (rather than a cenotaph), which seems to have been at Hadrian's Villa. The inscription further gives details of the offices of his cult, as well as linking his worship to the imperial cult, particularly Hadrian and Sabina (who were still alive when the text was originally written). Antinous is here syncretized completely to Osiris. The Obelisk is now located in Rome and stands on the Pincio Hill.

This translation is based on the German edition by Grimm, Kessler, and Meyer,[497] and the newer French edition by Jean-Claude Grenier.[498] There are other translations and discussions of the Obelisk available.[499] An earlier version of this—originally compiled in 2003 and edited on occasion—was published in *The Phillupic Hymns*,[500] but the current

---

[496] Zaccaria Mari and Sergio Sgalambro, "The Antinoeion of Hadrian's Villa: Interpretation and Architectural Reconstruction," *American Journal of Archaeology* 111 (2007), pp. 83-104.

[497] Alfred Grimm, Dieter Kessler, and Hugo Meyer (eds.), *Der Obelisk des Antinoos* (Munich: Wilhelm Fink, 1994).

[498] Jean-Claude Grenier, *L'Osiris Antinoos* (Montpellier: Cahiers de l'Égypte Nilotique et Méditerranéennes, 2008).

[499] Lorentz H. S. Dietrichson, *Antinoos: Eine Kunstarchäologische Untersuchung* (Christiania: H. Aschehoug & Co., 1884), pp. 321-327; Mary Taliaferro Boatwright, *Hadrian and the City of Rome* (Princeton: Princeton University Press, 1987), pp. 239-260. There are others as well.

[500] P. Sufenas Virius Lupus, *The Phillupic Hymns* (Eugene: Bibliotheca Alexandrina, 2008), pp. 19-22.

version below represents the most complete and comprehensive edition for devotional usage yet produced.

Obelisk of Antinous

[*East Face*]

Words spoken by the Son of Re, the Crowned Hadrian Caesar, may he live forever!: "Take your child to you that your heart loves."
Words spoken by Re-Harakhte: "I give you the power...forever."

A request for salvation, which is expressed by Osiris–Antinous, whose heart exceedingly rejoices, since he recognized his shape after revival, and he has seen his father Re–Harakhte.
His heart spoke:

"O Re–Harakhte, highest of the gods,
who hears the calling of gods and men,
the transfigured and the dead;
hear also the call of Hadrian, who approaches you!
Give Hadrian reward for this, who has done this for me—
Antinous, your beloved son—

the king of Upper and Lower Egypt,
who established a cult practice
in the temple sanctuaries for all men,
with which the gods are pleased;
who is loved by Hapi and all the gods,
the Lord of Crowns, Hadrianus Caesar,
who may live, be whole and healthy,
who may live eternally, like Re,

with a prospering and newly-risen age!
He is the Lord of Welfare, the ruler of all countries,
the Distinguished Noble Augustus.
The nobles of Egypt bow to him,
and the Nine Arches are united under his soles
as with the Pharaohs, the rulers of both Upper and Lower Egypt.
They come to being under his word every day.
His might goes as far as the borders
of the whole area of this country
in its four world-regions.

The bulls and their cows mingle lustily
and multiply their offspring for Hadrian,
to please his heart and that of his great and beloved queen,
the queenly ruler of both Upper and Lower Egypt
and their cities, Sabina Sebaste Augusta,
may she live, be whole and healthy,
and may she live eternally.

Hapi, father of the gods, make the acres fertile for them
and arrange the inundation for them in its time
to overflow the two countries, Upper and Lower Egypt!"

[*West Face*]

Words spoken by Antinous-Osiris:...
Words spoken by Twice-Great Thoth, Lord of Khemenou: "I am
certain your heart will live every day."

The God, Osiris–Antinous the Justified,
has become a youth, with perfect countenance
and festively-decorated eyes,
...strength, whose heart is glad
like the heart of a strong-armed hero,
after he received the order of the gods
at the time of his death.

On Antinous will be repeated every ritual
of the hours of Osiris together
with each of his ceremonies in secret.
His teachings will be spread to the whole country,
helpful in the instruction and effective in the expression.[501]
Nothing comparable has been done
for the earlier ancestors until today;

And the same goes for his altars,
his temples and his titles while he breathes the air of life
and his reputation comes to being in the hearts of mankind.

Lord of Hermopolis, Lord of the Words of Gods, Thoth!
Rejuvenate Antinous' *Ba* like all things at their time,
in the night and by day, at all times, and every second.
The love for Antinous is in the hearts of his followers
and the awe of him with all...
and his praise with all his subjects when they worship him.

He takes his seat in the Hall of the Just,
the transfigured and the clarified and the splendid,
who are in the entourage of Osiris in the Realm of the Dead,
while the Lord of Eternity gives him justification.
They let his words endure on the Earth,
because their hearts are pleased by him.

---

[501] Grenier's new translation, p. 16, suggests that there is a direct reference to Antinous' mummification here, and that the entire world was put into the distress of debate over the issue of Antinous' death. Until I receive more definite confirmation of these lines, I am inclined to stick with the earlier version.

He goes anywhere he pleases.
The doorkeepers of the underworld,
they say to him, "Praise to you!"
They loose their door-bolts and open their gates
before him from millions of millions of years every day.
His lifespan, never will it wither.

[*North Face*]

Words spoken by Osiris-Antinous: "...to make any oracle."
Words spoken by Ammon, Master of the Power to Issue Oracles:
"I give you the power to make any oracle."

The God, Osiris-Antinous the Justified, is there;
an arena was prepared in his place in Egypt,
Antinoöpolis, which is named after him,
for the strong athletes who are in this country
and for the rowers and the runners of the whole country,
and for all people, who belong to the place
of the holy scriptures, where Thoth is.

And they are bestowed with honor-prizes
and garlands upon their heads,
while they are rewarded with many good things.
One sacrifices on his altars daily,
after offering the sacrifice of the gods each day.
He is praised by the men of the arts of Thoth
according to his glory.

He goes out of his places to numerous temples
in the whole country, and he hears
the pleas of he who calls upon him;
he heals the diseases of the needy ones
by sending a dream.
Once he has accomplished his works among the living,
he takes on every shape of his heart,

because the semen of god is truly in his body...
his Mother's whole body heals.
He was raised at his birthplace by...

[*South Face*]

Words spoken by Osiris-Antinous the Justified: "Come to the
Master of Life..."

The god, who is there, he rests in this place,
which is in the middle of the border-fields
of the Lord of Welfare, the Princeps of Rome.
He is known as a god in the godly places of Egypt.
Temple sanctuaries are erected for him,
and he is worshipped as a god by the prophets and priests
of Upper and Lower Egypt,
as well as by the inhabitants of Egypt.

A city was named after him.
The troops of Greece, the cult members,
that belong to Upper and Lower Egypt,
the offspring of Horus and the children of Set,
who are in the cities of Egypt,
they come out of their towns and villages
and are given cultivated land,
to make their lives good beyond all measures.

A temple sanctuary of this god is therein,
who is called Osiris-Antinous the Justified,
built from good white stone,
surrounded by statues of the gods and the sphinxes,
as well as numerous pillars,
as they were made by the ancestors before,
and as they were made by the Greeks as well.

All gods and goddesses will give him the air of life,
so that he breathes rejuvenated!

Invoking and Devoking
the Obelisk of Antinous

In a number of the more important rituals during the year—particularly on Foundation Day—a regular practice of the Ekklesía Antínoou has been to invoke the Obelisk of Antinous toward the beginning of the ritual (often after the initial prayers to Wepwawet, Hekate, and Ianus, and after the procession and installation of Antinous' principal image and the presentation of food and incense offerings). As the Obelisk has four sides, it makes sense to invoke each side while facing the appropriate direction. This might appear to be similar to Wiccan and other modern pagan practices of calling the quarters, and indeed that influence cannot be dismissed; however, the significance of doing so in an Antinoan context is rather different, and the manner via which it is done is also quite in contrast to the Wiccan practice. It is abundantly clear, however, that this usage of the Obelisk of Antinous' inscription is entirely novel, and was never envisioned as even the faintest possibility for people in the ancient cultus of Antinous, including the very limited number of people who had access to the Obelisk at all, much less could read or understand the hieroglyphic inscription upon it.

Hadrian is famous for, amongst other things, his many architectural projects throughout the Roman Empire. He built bridges called *Pons Aelius* ("Hadrian's Bridge") in both Rome and in the Romano-British city that eventually became known as Newcastle-upon-Tyne;[502] but he also built walls, whether they were the mostly wooden palisades along the German frontier, or the island-spanning structure known in

---

[502] Indeed, the title *Pontifex Maximus*, which all Roman Emperors held in the tradition of Julius Caesar's holding of that position, literally means "greatest bridge builder." Whether actual bridge-building was a part of the priestly role of the pontiffs at any point is disputed, but the bridge-building aspect of the sacred function of the pontiffs in relation to the people and the gods is certainly more to the fore in most understandings of this and other priestly roles; Hadrian, perhaps more than most Emperors, literally and figuratively lived up to the title.

Roman times as the *vallum*, but now known as "Hadrian's Wall" in northern England. I am always reminded of the line from *Hedwig and the Angry Inch* when discussing this aspect of Hadrian: "Ain't much of a difference / between a bridge and a wall...." When the Obelisk of Antinous is invoked, I like to think of it as functioning simultaneously as both a bridge and a wall. Each side of it is a bridge to a particular aspect of Antinous, his cultus, and his history, and a particular bridge is created to the realms of the gods by doing so. But, each side is also like a wall that is built for the virtual temple of Antinous in which the rituals honoring him are taking place, on which the inscriptions of our modern devotions are recorded, and which symbolically re-builds the walls of the city of Antinoöpolis.

While the natural inclination of many people would be to choose a direction to start with—often East—and then read each side subsequently in clockwise (or, more rarely, counterclockwise) order, the sequence in which the sides of the Obelisk of Antinous are given above is because that is the order in which the inscription ends up making the most sense. Indeed, that order—East to West, North to South—is found in many Egyptian contexts, including tomb inscriptions[503] and in Graeco-Egyptian magical papyri.[504] This reflects the idea that the first priority is the direction of the sun as it travels from sunrise in the East to sunset in the West, and then the direction of the Nile running from its mouth in the North to its mysterious source in the South. As a result, if one turns in a clockwise direction as one invokes the East Face, then the West Face, and then turns clockwise again for the North Face, then one should turn counter-clockwise for the South Face, and continue again turning counter-clockwise back to the East, so that one in effect makes a 270 degree circle in one direction, and then 270 degrees in the reverse direction. From the ending position facing East again, a final "capstone" is invoked for the Obelisk of Antinous in Ekklesía Antínoou practice, which is given below.

---

[503] Theodor Abt and Erik Hornung, *Knowledge for the Afterlife: The Egyptian Amduat–A Quest for Immortality* (Zurich: Living Human Heritage Publications, 2003).

[504] Hans Dieter Betz (ed./trans.), *The Greek Magical Papyri in Translation, Including the Demotic Spells*, Second Edition (Chicago and London: The University of Chicago Press, 1996), pp. 145 VII, lines 9-11.

Further, while the ritual leader reads out each face of the Obelisk of Antinous (or, preferably, chants it in a monotone), all of the other ritual participants should face the appropriate directions and make hand gestures appropriate to each side (as detailed in the chapter on Ritual Acclamations and Hand Gestures above). For the East Face, one should have one's palms upright, praising a celestial aspect of Antinous; for the West Face, one should have one's palms lowered for a chthonic aspect of Antinous; for the North Face, one's palms should again be lowered; and for the South Face, one's palms should return to an upright, celestial orientation. For the final capstone of the Obelisk, one should adopt whatever hand gesture or posture one feels suggests "centering"; I've found the "Osiris position" of having one's hands crossed over one's chest to be an appropriate gesture for this activity, but whatever you might feel is most effective should be the tactic adopted in your own practices.

Further still, while the ritual leader chants each face of the Obelisk of Antinous, the other participants in the ritual, in addition to making the appropriate hand gestures, and imagining each side of the Obelisk of Antinous raising up as a wall and opening out as a bridge, should also chant the vowels of Antinous' name in a particular order, and simply hold out the sound of the vowel for the duration of the chanted recitation of each side. (For more details on this practice, see the "Sound" section of the Antinoan Feast of the Senses chapter above.) For the East Face, one should chant "A"; for the West Face, one should chant "I"; for the North Face, one should chant "O"; for the South Face, one should chant "E"; and finally, for the "capstone," one should chant "U." In terms of vowel quality, "A" is the deepest vowel, while "I" is the highest, so in the initial two sides of the Obelisk, one is going from the deepest vowel while praising the celestial Antinous to the highest vowel while one is praising the chthonic Antinous. For the North to South sweep of the Obelisk's invocation, one is chanting the second-deepest vowel "O" while praising the chthonic Antinous, to the second-highest vowel "E" while praising the celestial Antinous. And, finally, when one is centering with the Obelisk's capstone, one is chanting the medial vowel "U."

The entire effect of this practice should be to literally go from the highest to the lowest reaches of the universe and aspects of Antinous, and the lowest to the highest aspects of Antinous and reaches of the universe, in order to locate oneself and to center oneself within the vast span of Antinous, the gods associated with him, and the wider cosmos.

Pretty clever usage of a memorial inscription, eh?

The capstone of the Obelisk of Antinous, which was originally written in 2003, is not usually chanted in the way that the four faces are, but instead is recited or proclaimed by the ritual leader while the other ritual participants and attendees make the gestures to center themselves and chant the vowel "U." The capstone recitation runs as follows:

The Obelisk, like a stone phallus from the earth-god Geb penetrating the sky-goddess Nut,
the rock of Gaia reaching toward the space of Ouranos,
like a needle piercing the barriers between heavens and earth,
this world and the others,
is a visible sign that we have entered a new space,
a separate space,
a sacred space.

Across the barriers of centuries,
A city rises from the ruins of time.

The four faces of the Obelisk like four walls raised at each of the four directions,
the boundary-markers for the foundation of the new city,
the spiritual state of New Antinoöpolis,
and we each are its citizens,
free to come and go,
able to have commerce with deities,
to dwell with spirit,
to cultivate the godliness which is our birthright,
and to own a share of this place in which all people of good will and faith are peers.

We are surrounded by holy splendor:
Every brick a sacred stone, every paving slab an altar,
every building a temple, every angle a holy icon,
every breath a hymn of praise in the mouth of every person,
each one a priest and prophet,
every hour a holy day,
and where even the sewers are sacred fountains.
Salve Sacre Popule: Welcome to you, O Holy People!

When one's rituals are completed, if one has invoked the Obelisk of Antinous then one should also "devoke" or dismiss/dispell it as well. This practice follows the same general procedure as its invocation, only in reverse, and the chanting and vowel sounding is much shorter, as only a small section of each side of the Obelisk is recited again as a sort of benediction from and for Antinous.

Initially, one should face East, and while the ritual participants chant the vowel "A" and make their centering gesture, the ritual leader should proclaim:

Our time here, for now, has come to its end.

Turning clockwise to the South, the participants should gesture toward the celestial Antinous and chant "I" while the ritual leader chants:

**All gods and goddesses will give him the air of life,
so that he breathes rejuvenated!**

Turning clockwise to the North, the participants should gesture toward the chthonic Antinous and chant "O" while the ritual leader chants:

**The semen of god is truly in his body...
his Mother's whole body heals.**

Turning counter-clockwise to the West, the participants should gesture toward the chthonic Antinous and chant "E" while the ritual leader chants:

The doorkeepers of the underworld,
they say to him, "Praise to you!"
They loose their door-bolts and open their gates
before him.

Finally, turning counter-clockwise to the East, the participants should gesture toward the celestial Antinous and chant "U" while the ritual leader chants:

A request for salvation, which is expressed by Osiris–Antinous, whose heart exceedingly rejoices, since he recognized his shape after revival, and he has seen his father Re–Harakhte.

At this stage, the devocation of the Obelisk of Antinous is complete.

The Citharoedic Hymn of Curium

This hymn survives in a severely fragmentary form—the beginning and end, and good bits of the middle, are garbled or no longer existent. It appears that this hymn was made by the so-called Curium Citharode, probably for the occasion of an Antinoeion contest as the "artistic" portion of it taking place on the island of Cyprus at the southern city of Curium/Kurion. It was found inscribed in the doorway of the temple of Apollon. Lambert paints a beautiful picture of the hymn's performance, "At the theatre in Curion the festival was begun under the open sky by the citharode-priest, clad in gold and purple and plucking his gilded and ivory-inlaid lyre."[505] However, it is known that other hymns to Antinous existed, and this one may have been inspired by or indeed might incorporate parts of those other hymns. In particular, Hadrian's freedman Mesomedes of Crete wrote such a hymn, according to the *Suda Lexicon*, as well as other writings. Other hymns of Mesomedes survive with musical notation,[506] and it is known that he continued in the Museion in Alexandria after Hadrian's death, where the *Historia Augusta* reports that during Antoninus Pius' reign, his state salary was reduced.[507]

The existence of such hymnody and the circumstances under which it was composed adds an important dimension to our picture of the cult of Antinous, as well as giving us interesting details and further myths to which he was connected. The priest/speaker of the hymn himself identifies his ability to sing such a song to the influence of Apollon, the "Fair-Haired, Lyre-Striking One"; an altar to Hylas is mentioned, which would be the altar in the sanctuary at this location of Apollon

---

[505] Royston Lambert, *Beloved and God: The Story of Hadrian and Antinous* (New York: Viking, 1984), p. 187.

[506] Ewen L. Bowie, "Greek Poetry in the Antonine Age," in D. A. Russell (ed.), *Antonine Literature* (Oxford: Oxford University Press, 1990), pp. 53-90 at 84-90.

[507] Anthony R. Birley, *Lives of the Later Caesars: The first part of the Augustan History, with newly compiled Lives of Nerva and Trajan* (London and New York: Penguin Books, 1976), p. 102.

Hylates, but the name also connects Antinous with the dead and heroized youthful lover of Herakles who also became a flower; Phoroneus was the first ancestor of the Argives, and Perseus obviously was a hero of Argive origin. The "gold-winged mother" in the end probably refers to Aphrodite, a goddess especially associated with Cyprus, and thus identifies Antinous as Eros; and the Adonis ascription in the first line places Antinous firmly in the realm of dying-and-rising deities and divinized mortals with power over the forces of the underworld. The text for the translation of this hymn was found in an article by Wolfgang Dieter Lebek,[508] and this translation was published earlier in *The Phillupic Hymns*.[509]

The Citharoedic Hymn of Curium

For Good Fortune...
...priests
And the *propraetor* of Cyprus, to Antinous...
...that I be given grace under
This very cithara to which I have been accustomed.
O Muse, take this painful message:
We lament Adonis under the earth,
Whom we formerly called Antinous.
Tell me of divine songs, give me harmonious melodies!
For it is only for you that the Fair-Haired, Lyre-Striking One
Has brought me up to be a singer;
For you the barbita I shake, for you the cithara I let boom
At the sacred altar of Hylas.
For you I have established a choir of dancers...
I now call upon the Phoroneian race, that blood of Perseus,
That has saved the town situated highest.
By your command I sing, accompanied by the cithara;

[508] Wolfgang Dieter Lebek, "Ein Hymnus auf Antinoos," *Zeitschrift für Papyrologie und Epigraphik* 12 (1973), pp. 101-137 at 102-103, 113.
[509] P. Sufenas Virius Lupus, *The Phillupic Hymns* (Eugene: Bibliotheca Alexandrina, 2008), p. 227.

Dark violet curly-haired, beautiful-haired lord, blessed one, Bithynian,
Youth with a face full of grace,
Offspring of the Gold-Winged Mother...

The Tebtynis Papyrus

This papyrus is an anthology, the longest section of which is dedicated to parallels of Antinous with various mythic figures, especially ones who are commemorated by vegetation of some sort, and among these many who were homoerotically-involved with the gods, and two in particular—Hylas and Narcissus—who drowned; only one of the mentioned figures is female.

The remainder of the papyrus contains some interesting materials, some or all of which may in their own ways be further allusions to Antinous. The brief account of the phoenix, which of course was connected to Hadrian's accession, as well as a symbol of renewal and resurrection, may have been readily in mind since Heliopolis was the reputed home of the mystical bird, and had been recently visited by the imperial party when Antinous died.[510] Herakles' attempted initiation into the Eleusinian Mysteries was after his twelfth labor, the capture of Cerberus, but he was not able to be initiated on that occasion because he had committed a murder;[511] perhaps this refers in some tangential way to Hadrian and Antinous' own Eleusinian experiences,[512] or if we take Hadrian as Herakles and Antinous as the dead-and-drowned Hylas, then some sort of consolation for the emperor who remained in life, looking for comfort in the aftermath of his lover's death in attempting to prepare for death himself. This part of the papyrus is very similar to a "mystery ritual" fragment found on a piece of papyrus in Antinoöpolis itself.[513]

While it is uncertain whether a part or a whole of this papyrus was

---

[510] Anthony R. Birley, *Hadrian: The Restless Emperor* (London and New York: Routledge, 2000), p. 245.

[511] Carl Kerényi, *Eleusis: Archetypal Image of Mother and Daughter*, trans. Ralph Manheim (Princeton: Princeton University Press, 1967), pp. 83-84.

[512] Royston Lambert, *Beloved and God: The Story of Hadrian and Antinous* (New York: Viking, 1984), p. 44, 105-106; Birley, *Hadrian*, pp. 175-177, 215.

[513] C. H. Roberts (ed.), *The Antinoöpolis Papyri* Volume 1 (London: Egypt Exploration Society, 1950), pp. 39-40.

366

written by Numenios of Herakleia Pontica or not, it is known that the rhetoritician who was in Hadrian's circle wrote a list of parallels with Antinous not long after the boy's death, called in the *Suda Lexicon* a "prose Consolation" for Antinous, and this seems a likely candidate for being that composition.[514] Hadrian was in Tebtynis during the month after Antinous' death as he traveled up the Nile,[515] so if the ascription to Numenios is true, this could likely be the earliest writing preserved about Antinous.

The poem "Ganymede of Ida," written by Mark André Raffalovich in 1886,[516] compares Ganymede to many "vegetative" homoerotic figures, including Adonis whose blood became an anemone, Hyakinthos, Narcissus, Hylas, and Antinous, "the Darling of the Nile." This strain of thinking, comparing beautiful young homoerotic figures to flowers, which recurs so often in Greek myth and which continues to enthrall modern people, makes sense, as flowers are beautiful when in their bloom but the seasons change and they wither and die; the message in this type of metaphor is obvious enough, though overly pessimistic.

Whatever about the other passages in this short papyrus fragment's relevance to Antinous and his religion, the full text is translated and presented here; some parts are fragmentary because of damage to the papyrus, and it ends quite abruptly; but luckily, the Antinous section is fully intact. The text is found in Achille Vogliano's *Papiri della R. Universita di Milano*, Vol. 1,[517] and this translation was previously published in *The Phillupic Hymns*.[518]

---

[514] Birley, *Hadrian*, p. 252.

[515] P. J. Sijpesteijn, "A New Document Concerning Hadrian's Visit to Egypt," *Historia* 18 (1969), pp. 109-118 at 115; J. W. B. Barns, Peter Parsons, John Rea, and Eric G. Turner (eds.), *The Oxyrhynchus Papyri* Volume 31 (London: Egypt Exploration Society, 1966), §2553, pp. 72-77 at 76 lines 11-13.

[516] Mark André Raffalovich, *In Fancy Dress* (London: Walter Scott, 1886), p. 95.

[517] Achille Vogliano, *Papiri della R. Universita di Milano*, Vol. 1 (Milan: Ulrico Hoepli, 1937), pp. 175–183 at 176–179.

[518] P. Sufenas Virius Lupus, *The Phillupic Hymns* (Eugene: Bibliotheca Alexandrina, 2008), p. 227.

The Tebtynis Papyrus

Concerning the Holy Phoenix in Egypt:

While I have seen the form of the phoenix, that of Egypt, so far as in pictures, the bird itself I did not see, except...flocks of flying phoenixes were everywhere, just like those of geese or cranes or long-necked swans. On a certain festival in Egypt, it is sung:
"O phoenix, may you be revealed,
O more sweet-voiced than Phoebus
and more tuneful than the nightingale
and more musical than the swan...
in shape and bearing...
and not unseasonably may you be revealed."

Words of Herakles upon Being Barred from Being Initiated into the Eleusinian Rites:

"I have been initiated long ago.
Close off Eleusis
and the holy fire, torch-bearer,
and be grudging of holy night.
I have been initiated
into mysteries by far more true...
I have beheld the fire, whence...
and I have seen the Kore."

That One should not Expel a Man:

The Athenians banished Theseus and after wandering forever Theseus died on Skyros, and Solon after his laws left Athens, fleeing a city which he himself made more just. And also the Dorians, when they revolted, killed their own king, Kresphontes, son of Herakles; and the Babylonians revolted against Darius, and the Assyrians betrayed Sardanopalis, and many times the Macedonians threatened Alexander. But if mob rule seems to you to be a reverend thing, we will again commend the Athenians because they drove out Aristeides, and bound Miltiades, and fined Pericles. They drove out the Just, bound the Victor, and fined the Olympian.

In regards to the Antinoeios Flower:

Neither the Athenian narcissus, nor the Lakedaemonian hyacinth, nor the crocus was from the beginning a flower; and neither child Hylas in Thrace, nor the cypress tree in Crete, nor the daphne was from the beginning a plant. But Krokus was a Sicilian lad, child Hylas was a beautiful Thracian, and Kyparissos was a beautiful boy. Daphne was a young virgin maiden, daughter of the river, Narcissus was a beautiful Boetian boy, and Hyakinthos was a young Spartan man in the bloom of his youth. Herakles had Hylas, and Dionysos took him. Krokus joined Dionysos in his Bacchic revels. Nymphs seized Narcissus, and Apollon took Hyakinthos and Daphne. Nymphs killed Krokus, nymphs carried away Hylas, Kyparissos threw himself down from rocks and the earth received Daphne when she was fleeing. Narcissus in his arrogance loving himself like another killed himself. Only one flower, the flower of Antinous, is sweeter than all by far, not pale like the narcissus, pained by his taking; and not pale like the hyacinth, imitating the color of a corpse. Someone will gather garlands of lamented names, and will lament more the youth of the dying men.

With regards to the Cynic Agathocles:

Diogenes wore this cloak while speaking, Socrates wore this cloak while philosophizing, Solon wore this cloak while setting down laws, Demosthenes wore this cloak while orating...

Pancrates' Poem on the Lion Hunt

The one definite event, apart from his death, which seems to be indicated in all of our sources on the life of Antinous was a lion-hunt upon which he and Hadrian engaged during their stay in Alexandria in the year (possibly during late summer) of 130 before traveling up the Nile. A lion hunt is one of the subjects of the various Hadrianic hunting *tondi* on the Arch of Constantine,[519] and a figure that some identify as Antinous seems to be in the *tondo*, whether he is in the background (as some have suggested) or an older version of him stands at the lion's head.[520] The Egyptian priest Pancrates, or Pachrates, met the Emperor sometime during this period, and gave him a spell that is in *PGM IV*, the text known as the "Great Magical Papyrus of Paris."[521] He is also known to have written a poem called *Bocchoreis*, which is briefly quoted in Athenaeus on the instrument known as a *kondy*, a magical globe "from which magical wonders and profitable signs sent by the gods appear on the earth."[522] However, after Antinous' death (or perhaps even before it), Pancrates also composed an epic poem on the lion hunt, which pleased Hadrian to such an extent that he gave him a state stipend at the Museion in Alexandria.[523]

A figure called "Pancrates," who may be equivalent to or based upon the poet/priest/magician Pancrates/Pachrates who knew Hadrian, appears in Lukian of Samosata's *Philopseudes*, in an incident which is

---

[519] Mary Taliaferro Boatwright, *Hadrian and the City of Rome* (Princeton: Princeton University Press, 1987), pp. 190-200.

[520] Royston Lambert, *Beloved and God: The Story of Hadrian and Antinous* (New York: Viking, 1984), pp. 118-120; Anthony R. Birley, *Hadrian: The Restless Emperor* (London and New York: Routledge, 2000), pp. 241-242.

[521] Hans Dieter Betz (ed./trans.), *The Greek Magical Papyri in Translation, Including the Demotic Spells*, Second Edition (Chicago and London: The University of Chicago Press, 1996), pp. 82-86 (IV.2441-2621).

[522] Birley, *Hadrian*, pp. 244-245.

[523] Ewen L. Bowie, "Greek Poetry in the Antonine Age," in D. A. Russell (ed.), *Antonine Literature* (Oxford: Oxford University Press, 1990), pp. 53-90 at 81-83.

370

the first literate version of the tale known as the "sorcerer's apprentice."[524] Lukian of Samosata (c. 125-180) was a rhetoritician and satirist. There are several further allusions to Antinous and Hadrian in Lukian's other works, usually through a critique of deified mortals like Ganymede, in *The Parliament of the Gods*[525] and *Dialogues of the Gods: Zeus and Hera*[526] and *Dialogues of the Gods: Zeus and Ganymede*.[527]

Fragments of his poem were initially only known from Athenaeus' *Deipnosophistae*, but then a fragment was discovered on a piece of papyrus from Oxyrhynchus. A further possible fragment has been discovered elsewhere, which mentions Antinous and Hadrian, horses, and trumpets, but is otherwise too fragmentary to parse.[528] The miracle of the red lotus originates from this poem; that theme was one taken up with great verve by many other of the ancient Antinoian poets, as will be seen in further chapters below. The fragments from Athenaeus and from the Oxyrhynchus find are given here.

Oxyrhynchus Fragment[529]

...swifter than the steed of Adrastus, that once saved its master easily, when he was fleeing through the press of battle. On such a horse Antinous awaited the manslaying lion; in his left hand he held the bridle-rein, in his right a spear tipped with adamant.

---

[524] Daniel Ogden, *In Search of the Sorcerer's Apprentice: The Traditional Tales of Lucian's Lover of Lies* (Swansea: The Classical Press of Wales, 2007), pp. 231-270.

[525] A. M. Harmon (ed./trans.), *Lucian, Volume V* (Cambridge: Harvard University Press, 1936), pp. 426-433.

[526] M. D. MacLeod (ed./ trans.), *Lucian, Volume VII* (Cambridge: Harvard University Press, 1961), pp. 268-275.

[527] MacLeod, pp. 280-291.

[528] Ernst Heitsch, *Die Griechischen Dichterfragmente der Römischen Kaiserzeit*, Volume 1 (Göttingen: Vandenhoeck & Ruprecht, 1963), p. 52.

[529] Arthur S. Hunt (ed.), *The Oxyrhynchus Papyri* 8 (London: Egypt Exploration Society, 1911), §1085, pp. 73-77. See the alternate translation in D. L. Page (ed./trans.), *Select Papyri in Five Volumes, III: Literary Papyri, Poetry* (Cambridge: Harvard University Press, 1962), pp. 516-519.

Hadrian was first to shoot forth his bronze spear; he wounded, but slew it not, for it was his intent to miss the animal, wishing to test to the full how straight the other aimed—he, lovely Antinous, son of the slayer of Argus [Hermes]. Stricken, the beast was yet more aroused; with his paws he tore the rough ground in anger; forth rose a cloud of dust, and dimmed the sunlight. He raged like a wave of the surging sea, when the West Wind [Zephyros] is awakened after the wind from Strymon [Boreas, the North Wind]. Lightly upon both he leapt, and scourged his haunches and sides with his tail, with his own dark whip...His eyes flashed dreadful fire beneath the brows; he sent forth a shower of foam from his ravening jaws to the ground, while his fangs gnashed within. From his massive head and shaggy neck the mane rose and quivered; from his other limbs it fell bushy as trees; on his back it was...like whetted spear points. In such guise he went against the glorious god Antinous, like Typhoeus of old against Zeus the Giant-Killer....

...having seen flying fast...on his horse, Antinous...he broke the base of the neck and the muscles of the neck and split for all...he fell straight to earth...the god, killer of beasts...[530]

Athenaeus, *Deipnosophistae*[531]

Speaking of Alexandria, I know that in that fair city there is a wreath called Antinoeios made from the lotus bearing that name there. This grows in marshes in the summer season; there are two colours, one resembling the rose; it is from this that the

---

[530] This further fragment of the Oxyrhynchus text is translated into French by Jean-Claude Grenier, *L'Osiris Antinoos* (Montpellier: Cahiers de l'Égypte Nilotique et Méditerranéennes, 2008), p. 49, from which I have rendered it into English here.
[531] Charles Burton Gulick (ed./trans.), *Athenaeus, Deipnosophistae*, Volume 7 (Cambridge: Harvard University Press, 1941), pp. 126-129, XV.677.

wreath properly called Antinoeios is twined; the other is called lotus, and its colour is blue. Pancrates, a poet of those regions whom we knew, showed the Emperor Hadrian when he visited Alexandria the rosy lotus as a great wonder, alleging that it was the one which should be called Antinoeios, since it sprang, so he said, from the earth when it received the blood of the Mauritanian lion which Hadrian had killed when hunting in the part of Libya near Alexandria; it was a huge creature that for a long time had ravaged the whole of Libya, of which this lion had made many places uninhabitable. Hadrian, therefore, pleased at the originality and novelty of his thought, granted him the favour of maintenance in the temple of the Muses. The comic poet Cratinus, also, calls the lotus a wreath plant in *Odysseis*, since all leafy plants are spoken of as wreath plants by the Athenians. So Pancrates in his poem says, not without elegance: "The thyme with its woolly tufts, the white lily, the purple hyacinth, the flowers of blue celandine, yes, and the rose which unfolds to the zephyrs of spring; but not before, surely, has the earth brought to bloom the flower named for Antinous."

Oxyrhynchus Poem on Antinous

This poem, found in the 1990s in the ever-expanding corpus of the Oxyrhynchus Papyri, seems to date from the reign of Diocletian, c. 285 CE; Diocletian's accession is placed at November 20, 284, and was known in Egypt by at least March 7, 285, or possibly as early as February 10. It is possible that the whole composition, of which the beginning is about Antinous and later praises the new Emperor, was written for a poetic competition associated with the Capitoline Games. The themes dealt with here are familiar ones in terms of the corpus of ancient texts on Antinous, but we get the further details here of what Tatian alone amongst the Christian critics speaks of, i.e. the face of Antinous appearing in the moon, and thus shedding possible light on his connection at Lanuvium with Diana and also the *tondo* of the bear hunt, here appearing as Selene/the Moon.[532] It is possible that Hadrian's sister, Domitia Paulina, was deified and portrayed in some places as Selene.[533] In the notes to this papyrus fragment, it is mentioned that a "guest star," which could either have been a comet or a nova, was seen about January 29, 131 and recorded in China; the process of some mortal or hero becoming a star is called "catasterism." A small island near the city of Antinoöpolis, which was created by a canal in the city, is also referred to here. The poem is given in a prose translation here.[534]

In portions of the text too fragmentary to translate (the beginning), it seems that Antinous is given the parentage, whether mythical or not, of one Mantinoë and Hermes; he is called the son of Hermes in

---

[532] I have discussed some of this in P. Sufenas Virius Lupus, "Artemis and the Cult of Antinous," in Thista Minai et al. (eds.), *Unbound: A Devotional Anthology for Artemis* (Eugene: Bibliotheca Alexandrina, 2009), pp. 106-112.

[533] Günter Grimm, "Paulina und Antinous. Zur Vergöttlichung der Hadriansschwester in Ägypten," in Christoph Börker and Michael Donderer (eds.), *Das antike Rom und der Osten: Festschrift für Klaus Parlasca zum 65. Geburtstag* (Erlangen: Universitätsbund Erlangen-Nürnberg, 1990), pp. 33-44.

[534] J. R. Rea (ed.), *The Oxyrhynchus Papyri* 63 (London: Egypt Exploration Society, 1996), §4352, pp. 1-17.

374

Pancrates' epic, and the female foundress of Mantineia, Antinoë (essentially the feminine form of Antinous),[535] seems to have been a possible model for the name of his mother here—other names in the time after Antinous' death seemed to be formed in a fashion which included his name as an element, examples being Philantinous, Hermantinous, Ammonantinous, Besantinous, Dionysantinous, Heraklantinous, Panantinous, and Oseirantinous. Further, the fragments also seem to point toward some sort of sacrifice to Herakles—of which the lion hunt *tondi* also record—the misty morning and hunting attire of the hunting party, fearlessness, and the horses of Antinous and Hadrian, but all of these are somewhat uncertain, and suggested based on the existence of these things as documented elsewhere in the material relating to Antinous and Hadrian.

A further third/fourth century fragmentary Encomium for Antinous and Hermes has been found, and it seems to mention Hermes and Antinous,[536] and, speaking of the latter's youth, says that Apollon was invited to celebrate, and that either Antinous was born and "reached the fine flower of youth" or perhaps "Antinous is born, like a flower in the spring." The latter is favored because of his later onomastic floral memorial. A further elegiac text of the second century commemorates many famous loves between gods and male mortals,[537] referring to Apollon and Hyakinthos, Dionysos and "the Indian" (perhaps Ampelos, Hymenaeus, or Staphylos, but also possibly one of Dionysus' other loves, which include Achilleus, Adonis, Hermaphroditos, and Prosymnos), and Herakles and Hylas, in which a suggested restoration would include Antinous, in terms of references to "fire and foam," possibly meaning the fire of love drowned in water. I hope to be able to translate fragments from these eventually.

---

[535] I have discussed some of this in P. Sufenas Virius Lupus, "From Arcadia with Love: Pan and the Cult of Antinous," in Diotima et al. (eds.), *Out of Arcadia: A Devotional Anthology for Pan* (Bibliotheca Alexandrina, 2011), pp. 86-93.

[536] A. K. Bowman, H. M. Cockle, W. Cockle, R. A. Coles, P. J. Parsons, *et al.* (eds.), *The Oxyrhynchus Papyri* 50 (London: Egypt Exploration Society, 1983), §3537, pp. 59-66.

[537] R. A. Coles, H. Maehler, and P. J. Parsons (eds.), *The Oxyrhynchus Papyri* 54 (London: Egypt Exploration Society, 1987), §3723, pp. 58-64.

...She rejoiced to find the ransom for the life of Antinous, memorial of his hunt, palm of his victory,...

I revere, Narcissus, your shadowy reflection; I shed a tear for Hyakinthos, who grasped the cruel discus; I pity your hunting of the wild beast, Adonis. Yet the meadow of Antinous and his lovely new flower envy not pool, not fatal discus, not boar. The nymphs began to crown their tresses with the flower named after Antinous, which to this day preserves the mighty spear of the hunter. Into the Nile he hurried for purification of the blood of the lion, but the Moon [Selene] upon more brilliant hopes bade him shine as a star-like bridegroom and garlanding the new light with a circle she took him for her husband. A city was the gift of Hadrian, an island that of the Nile; the one lies rich in vines beside its sweet neighbor, the other welcoming the chosen flower of Achaea, has been crowned for her harbors as champion of the plain.

Capitoline Zeus took pity at last on the human race and gave the lordship of all the earth and all the sea to godlike king Diocletian. He extinguished the memory of former griefs for any still suffering in grim bonds in a lightless place. Now a father sees his child, a wife her husband, a brother his brother released, as if coming into the light of the sun a second time from Hades. Gladly Diogenes, savior of cities, received the favor of the good king and swiftly dispatched to the cities the joyful forgetfulness of griefs. The whole land takes delight in its joy as at the light of a golden age, and the iron, drawn back from the slaughter of men, lies bloodlessly in the scabbard. You too have rejoiced to announce the royal gift to all, governor of the Seven Nomes, and the Nile has praised your mildness earlier still, when you governed the towns of Nilotic Thebes with care and righteousness.

Now, blessed scepter-bearer of the chorus clad in cloaks, I pray to you to help me. Since at night and at the dawn you yourself were the watcher over our labors, garland me with the leaves of your Olympian olive.

The Lanuvium Inscription

This is an interesting document because it gives the constitution of a *collegium*, one which was specifically a burial club dedicated to Antinous and Diana, for which the two deities shared a temple at Lanuvium, which is close to the shrine of Lake Nemi, "Diana's Mirror," where Diana Nemorensis had her shrine. This particular location and the practices said to have taken place there were a major inspiration for Sir James George Frazer's speculations on the yearly divine dying-and-rising king in his book *The Golden Bough*. This text is interesting, indicating the dates of various feasts important to the members of the club, two of which are important for the Ekklesía Antínoou: Antinous' birth on November 27 (confirmed by the Cult Calendar found in Oxyrhynchus) and Diana's birthday on August 13, which was also observed in Rome and at the shrine of Lake Nemi. It also shows that this club did not allow any of its members who committed suicide their special attention or benefits, which some have taken as a sign that Antinous' death was not a suicide, but an accident. Basic ritual rubrics, use of incense and wine and oil, and baths, are also all indicated by this text in their devotions to Antinous and Diana.[538]

In the consulships of Lucius Ceionius Commodus and Sextus Vettulenus Civica Pompeianus five days before the Ides of June [June 9, 136 CE].

At Lanuvium in the temple of Antinous, in which Lucius Caesennius Rufus, patron of the town, had ordered that a meeting be called through Lucius Pompeius...us, *quinquennalis* [principal officers serving five-year terms] of the worshippers of Diana and Antinous, he promised that he would give them from his liberality the interest on

---

[538] Mary Beard, John North, & Simon Price (eds./trans.), *Religions of Rome, Volume 2: A Sourcebook* (Cambridge: Cambridge University Press, 1998), pp. 292-294.

16,000 *sestertii*, namely 400 *sestertii* on the birthday of Diana, the Ides of August [August 13], and 400 *sestertii* on the birthday of Antinous, five days before Kalends of December [November 27]; and he instructed the by-laws passed by them to be inscribed on the inner side of the porch of the temple of Antinous as recorded below.

In the consulships of Marcus Antonius Hiberus and Publius Mummius Sisenna [133 CE], Kalends of January [January 1], the Benevolent Society of Diana...and Antinous was constituted, Lucius Caesennius Rufus son of Lucius, of the Quirine tribe, being for the third time sole magistrate and also patron.

Clause from the Decree of the Senate of the Roman People

The following are permitted to assemble, convene and maintain a society; those who wish to make monthly contributions for funerals may assemble in such a society, but they may not assemble in the name of such a society except once a month for the sake of making contributions to provide burial for the dead.

May this be propitious, happy and salutary to the Emperor Caesar Trajan Hadrian Augustus and to the entire Augustan house, to us, to ours, and to our society, and may we have made proper and careful arrangements for providing decent funerals for the dead! Therefore we must all agree to contribute faithfully, so that we may be able to continue in existence a long time. You who wish to enter this society as a new member, first read the by-laws carefully before doing so, so as not to find cause for complaint later or bequeath a lawsuit to your heir.

By-laws of the Society

It was voted unanimously that whoever wishes to enter this society shall pay an entry fee of 100 *sestertii* and an amphora of good wine, and shall pay monthly dues of five *asses* [1.25 *sestertii*]. It was also voted that if anyone has not paid his dues for six consecutive months and the common lot of mankind befalls him, his claim to burial shall not be considered, even if he has made provision for it in his will. It was also voted that upon the decease of a paid-up member of our body there will be due to him from the fund 300 *sestertii*, from which sum will be

378

deducted a funeral fee of 50 *sestertii* to be distributed at the pyre; the obsequies, furthermore, will be performed on foot.

It was also voted that if a member dies more than 20 miles away from town and notification is made, three people chosen from our body will be required to go there to arrange for his funeral; they will be required to render an account in good faith to the membership, and if they are found guilty of any fraud they shall pay a quadruple fine; they will be given money for the funeral costs, and in addition a return trip allowance of 20 *sestertii* each. But if a member dies further than 20 miles from town and notification is unable to be made, then his funeral costs, less emoluments and funeral fee, may be claimed, in accordance with the by-laws of the society, by the man who buries him, if he so attests by an affidavit signed with the seals of seven Roman citizens, and the matter is approved, and he gives security against anyone's claiming any further sum. Let no malice aforethought attend! And let no patron or patroness master or mistress, or creditor have any right against this society unless he has been named heir in a will. If a member dies intestate, the details of his burial will be decided by the *quinquennalis* and the membership.

It was also voted that if a slave member of this society dies, and his master or mistress unreasonably refuses to relinquish his body for burial, and he has not left written instructions, a token funeral ceremony will be held.

It was also voted that if any member takes his own life for any reason whatever, his claim to burial by the society shall not be considered.

It was also voted that if any slave member of this society is liberated, he is required to donate an amphora of good wine.

It was also voted that if any president, in the year when it is his turn in the membership list to provide dinner, fails to comply and does not do so, he shall pay thirty *sestertii* to the fund; the man next on the list shall be required to give it, and the offender shall be required to reciprocate when it is the latter's turn.

Diary of dinners: 8 days before the Ides of March [March 8], birthday of Caesennius...his father; 5 days before Kalends of December, birthday of Antinous; Ides of August, birthday of Diana and of the society; 13 days before Kalends of September [August 20], birthday of Caesennius Silvanus, his brother; Day before Nones [of September? September 12?], birthday of Cornelia Procula, his mother; 19 days before Kalends of January [December 14], birthday of Caesennius Rufus, patron of the town.

Presidents of the dinners in the order of the membership list, appointed four at a time in turn, shall be required to provide an amphora of good wine each, and for as many members as the society has, bread to the value of two *asses* [0.5 *sestertii*], sardines to the number of four, the setting, and warm water with service.

It was also voted that any member who becomes *quinquennalis* in this society shall be exempt from such obligations for the term when he is *quinquennalis*, and that he shall receive a double share in all distributions. It was also voted that the secretary and the messenger shall be exempt from such obligations and shall receive a share and a half in every distribution.

It was also voted that any member who has performed the function of *quinquennalis* honestly shall receive a share and a half of everything as a mark of honour, so that subsequent *quinquennales* will also hope for the same by properly discharging their duties.

It was also voted that if any member wishes to lodge any complaint or discuss any business, he is to do so at a business meeting, so that we may banquet in peace and good cheer on festal days.

It was also voted that any member who moves from one place to another so as to cause a disturbance shall be fined four *sestertii*. Any member, moreover, who speaks abusively of another or causes an uproar shall be fined twelve *sestertii*. Any member who uses any abusive or insolent language to a *quinquennalis* at a banquet shall be fined twenty *sestertii*.

It was also voted that on the festal days of his terms of office each *quinquennalis* is to conduct worship with incense and wine and is to perform his other functions clothed in white, and that on the birthdays of Diana and Antinous he is to provide oil for the society in the public bath before they banquet.

Arrian of Nikomedia's
Periplus Ponti Euxini

Lucius Flavius Arrianus was a contemporary of Hadrian, born in Nikomedia, the capital of Bithynia, in circa 86-88 CE, who served on the Danube frontier and also possibly in Gaul and Numidia, and was appointed to the suffect consulship in 129 or 130. He circumnavigated the Black Sea in the early 130s and wrote a tactical manual on the Alans in 136-137. He was governor of Cappadocia in 137, but retired before Hadrian's death in 138. In later life, he became an Athenian citizen and held the archonship of the city, was a member of the council in the early 170s, and was dead by the end of that decade. He was sometimes known as a latter-day Xenophon, and also wrote a text on hunting called *Kynegetikos* ("master of hounds"), which certainly would have been a work that was of interest to Hadrian. Arrian's biography of Alexander remains the standard work on the great Macedonian.

The *Periplus Ponti Euxini*, written soon after his expedition around the Black Sea, contains a reference to Achilleus which alludes to the recent death of Antinous, especially in the final lines of the excerpt, in which the term *paidika* ("favorite," or even "boyfriend"), is particularly poignant, as the Byzantine *Suda* lexicon defines this terms with especial reference to Antinous. In Arrian's later *Anabasis*, the several references to Achilleus and Patroklos, as well as Alexander's mourning for Hephaistion, could be further allusions to the cult of Antinous and the events of Hadrian's life.[539] The text used for this translation was in

---

[539] Caroline Vout, *Power and Eroticism in Imperial Rome* (Cambridge: Cambridge University Press, 2007), pp. 117-118, argues that the denial of divine status to Hephaistion by the oracle at Siwa might be a critique of Hadrian's support of the cultus of the divine Antinous. Certainly, the death of Hephaistion and Alexander's grieving over it would certainly have suggested parallels to anyone who witnessed Hadrian's reaction, and no doubt Arrian's account of the incident in Alexander's life was given greater poignance due to the events of Antinous' death and deification.

Alain Silberman's French edition,[540] and this translation was previously published in *The Phillupic Hymns*.[541]

21. Just across from this mouth, upon sailing the sea straight with the Aparkian wind [North wind, after Aparktias, another name for Boreas], an island lies, which some call the island of Achilleus, some the Drome of Achilleus, and yet others call Leuke ["white"], because of its color. It is said that Thetis dedicated this island to her son, and that Achilleus inhabits it. And there is a temple of Achilleus on it, and a statue of ancient craftsmanship. The island is deserted of men, but it is grazed by a small number of goats. And they say that whoever comes to the island offers these up to Achilleus. And many other votive offerings are laid up in the temple, offering-bowls and rings and stones of the most valuable sort; all of these things being thanks-offerings to Achilleus. And there are also some for Patroklos. For indeed they honor Patroklos together with Achilleus, whoever wishes to please Achilleus. And many birds stay on the island, cormorants and gulls and sea-crows, innumerable in their multitude. These birds serve the temple of Achilleus. Each day, at earliest dawn, they fly down to the sea; then, after having bathed their wings, they fly back from the sea to the temple, and they sprinkle the temple. And as soon as it is ready, then they thoroughly clean the floor with their wings.

22. And they say these things also: of those who have approached the island, those who purposefully sail to it to bring sacrificial victims in their ships, and sacrifice some of these, but let the others go for Achilleus. But there are some men, on the other hand, who have been utterly forced to approach by foul

[540] Alain Silberman, *Arrien Périple du Pont-Euxin* (Paris: Les Belles Lettres, 1995), pp. 18-20.
[541] P. Sufenas Virius Lupus, *The Phillupic Hymns* (Eugene: Bibliotheca Alexandrina, 2008), pp. 195-196.

weather, and these men ask the god himself for a sacrificial victim, consulting with him concerning the sacrifice, asking if it is preferable for them to sacrifice whatever victim that they have, in their judgement, selected for its virtue with regards to pasturage, at the same time setting down an offering whose value seems sufficient to them. If the oracle declines—for there are oracles in the temple—they increase their offering. If he still declines, they increase it again. When he has agreed, they know that the offering is sufficient. Then the victim comes up to that place of its own accord, and no longer runs away. And indeed, in this way a good deal of money is given up to the hero, as offerings for sacrificial victims.

23. And Achilleus, in a vision, is revealed to those who approach the island, and also to those who are simply sailing, whenever they are not far from it, and he shows where it is better to approach the island and where to set anchor. And in a waking vision, they say, Achilleus is revealed to them atop a mast or upon the top of a yard, exactly like the Dioskouroi; in this way only is Achilleus lesser than the Dioskouroi, that the Dioskouroi reveal themselves in their own shape to sailors everywhere, and having been revealed are saviors, but he only reveals himself to those already approaching the island. And they say also that Patroklos has been seen by them in a vision. These things I have written concerning the island of Achilleus, a report from those who have either approached it themselves or have learned it from others. And it seems to me that it is not unbelievable. For I myself believe that indeed if any man or other is a hero, it is Achilleus, when I judge him by his nobility and by his beauty, by the force of his soul, by his youthful abandonment of the life of men, by Homer's poem about him, by his amorous and faithful disposition, and because he desired to die for his beloved young companions.

Dionysius of Alexandria's *Periegete*

Dionysius of Alexandria was a poet at the Museion during the reign of Hadrian, who wrote this long geographical poetic text, very likely to please the widely-traveled Emperor and to appeal to his interests, sometime between 131 and 138 CE.[542] The first section here translated (lines 513-537) contains, in the original Greek, one of two acrostics in the poem, spelling "*Theos Hermes epi Hadrianou* (To the God Hermes under Hadrian)," which is to say, an allusion to Antinous as Hermes, on lines 513-532. The second section (lines 788-798) has the river-name Rhebas repeated three times at the beginnings of lines 794-796, drawing attention to it; this was an obscure stream, but as it happened to run through Antinous' birthplace of Bithynion-Claudiopolis, this is taken as a further allusion to Antinous, especially in the superlative beauty attributed to the stream. The text used for this translation was in Kai Broderson's German edition,[543] and this translation was previously published in *The Phillupic Hymns*.[544]

...But admirably deep is the course of the Aegean Sea,
which on either side includes countless islands,
thither to the narrow waters of the Athamantidian Helles;
there lies Sestos and opposite the port Abydos.
Those belonging to Europe, you ship them through on the left-
    hand side
and those belonging to Asia, on the right-hand side;

---

[542] Anthony R. Birley, *Hadrian: The Restless Emperor* (London and New York: Routledge, 2000), pp. 252-253; Ewen L. Bowie, "Greek Poetry in the Antonine Age," in D. A. Russell (ed.), *Antonine Literature* (Oxford: Oxford University Press, 1990), pp. 53-90 at 70-81.

[543] Kai Broderson (ed./trans.), *Dionysios von Alexandria, Das Lied von der Welt* (Hildesheim: Georg Olms AG, 1994), pp. 74-77, 94-95.

[544] P. Sufenas Virius Lupus, *The Phillupic Hymns* (Eugene: Bibliotheca Alexandrina, 2008), p. 135.

stretched out far towards the Boreas, to the star-sign of the Bear.
Alongside Europe, Makris lies stretched out, island of the
      Abantians,
Skyros, which rises steeply; and Peparethos, windblown,
from there also Lemnos shows itself, the stony island of
      Hephaistos
and the ancient Thasos, which Demeter has richly blessed.
Imbros then, and Samos, the Thracian one, seat of the
      Korybantes.
Those lying closest to Asia are those
which encircle Delos, hence called "Kyklades."
All these offer repentance to Apollon in a choral dance
when sweet spring begins again, where in the mountains,
far away from men, the clear-sounding nightingale is nesting.
Thereupon, all through the floods, the Sporadic Islands are
      glittering to you;
as if through the cloudless air you saw the stars,
the might of Boreas has dispersed the wet clouds.
Then the Ionic Isles, next to the settlement of Kaunos,
thereafter Samos the Lovely, seat of Pelasgian Hera,
Chios, at the foot of the sun-climbing Pelinnaion.
From there, the mountains of the Aeolic Isles reveal themselves
      to you.
Lesbos with magnificent plains and the lovely island of
      Tenedos...

[• TO THE GOD HERMES UNDER HADRIAN •]

...And on holy ground the Mariandinians, among whom
the big brassy-voiced dog[545] of infernal Kronos[546]—
once drawn from the deep by valiant Herakles
as it is told—expels from its jaws stinking froth;
this the earth receives and disaster comes forth to mankind.

---

[545] That is, Cerberus.
[546] That is, Hades.

Close to these borders the Bithynians dwell on fertile soil;
the Rhebas River sends its sweet current,
the Rhebas which has chosen its course at the mouth of the
Pontus,
the Rhebas whose waters extend as the most beautiful on earth.
So many people have built upon the Pontos;
those that I've mentioned first are the tribes of the Scythian
peoples...

The Antinoöpolitan Lovers

There was a major discovery I made in my research on the cultus of Antinous in late April, 2005, while on a trip to Britain. I was in London, studying at the British Library, as well as trawling the bookshops of Soho, looking in my usual manner for insights and leads here and there. The entire discovery was heralded by a (literal!) flash of lightning and roll of thunder over East London, where I was staying, on Wednesday, April 27, 2005, after I finished my typical weekly devotions that I was observing during that time period.

To put this matter in context, one must understand the situation in which we were working at the time. It had seemed to many people with whom I was working on modern Antinoan devotion that there was very little material upon which to base our practices, and yet, oftentimes the nature of the material was not fully appreciated for what it was. We are very fortunate in this particular cultus to have so much specific information, in the form of dates, texts, historical documentation, archaeological remains, and inscriptions about the activities of our ancient forbearers from the foundation of the practice in late 130 CE through several centuries. To name only a few, we know of Hadrian and Aelius Caesar's foundation of the temple in Socanica; we have the allusive references to Antinous and his cult in Arrian's *Periplus Ponti Euxini* and Dionysius of Alexandria's *Periegete*; we have a poem written for the accession of Diocletian in the late third century in praise of Antinous and delineating his story, and a prose papyrus fragment from Tebtynis, perhaps dating to a time right around the foundation of the cultus, speaking of Antinous' flower and other mythic flower-figures. We even have the names of some sacred functionaries of the cultus, like P. Sufenas in Naples, T. Flavius Aristotimos in Delphi, and Nikias in Rome, as well as the names of individual devotees, like Epitynchanus and Doxa in Mantineia—the parents who commemorated their dead son Isochrysus with an Antinoian dedication[547]—and the heterosexual potential lovers

---

[547] Many of the preceding examples are dealt with in the chapters to follow.

388

Sarapammon and Ptolemais from the spell found in Antinoöpolis. Several of these were not included, nor even mentioned, in Royston Lambert's book *Beloved and God*, because they were discovered subsequently, or were simply not noted by him in his otherwise quite thorough writings; and yet, many people involved in modern Antinoan devotion thought that anything not mentioned by Lambert was not worth pursuing or considering seriously.

On the date of May 10—known as *15 Pachon* in Hellenized Egypt in the first few decades following the death of Antinous—in 2005, I first introduced modern devotees of Antinous to two such individuals involved in the ancient cultus of Antinous, who had only recently come to notice. Their likely particular form of relationship is extremely important for what it reveals about the ancient cultus and its relations to what we have been doing in our modern revival of Antinoan worship from its very beginnings in 2002.

There are many fine mummy portraits on Hellenized Egyptian mummies of the Roman period, and especially from the second century CE. Several such mummies with portraits were found in or near the ruins of the city of Antinoöpolis itself, and the particular one that I am dealing with here is unusual because it had no accompanying bodies, but might have decorated the "family feasting space" in a mausoleum. It is an elliptical wooden panel painted with two male figures, which was published in a book on mummy portraits (which had a whole chapter on Antinoöpolis) in 1966,[548] but evaded Lambert's notice. It has traditionally been called the "Tondo of the Two Brothers," but a more recent study by Anne E. Haeckl,[549] and quoted in Marilyn B. Skinner's work (where I first learned of it),[550] suggests that the two figures depicted are not brothers, but rather traditional Graeco-Egyptian lovers, *eromenos* and *erastes*. The

---

[548] Klaus Parlasca, *Mumienporträts und verwandte Denkmäler* (Wiesbaden: Franz Steiner, 1966), pp. 70-71, Tafel 19.
[549] Ann E. Haeckl, "Brothers or Lovers? A New Reading of the 'Tondo of the Two Brothers'," *Bulletin of the American Society of Papyrologists* 38 (2001), pp. 63-78 and Plate 6.
[550] Marilyn B. Skinner, *Sexuality in Greek and Roman Culture* (Malden and Oxford: Blackwell Publishing, 2005), p. 271.

information contained in the remainder of this chapter is taken from Haeckl's important study.

The two men stand facing the viewer, the one on the left of lighter complexion, younger, dressed rather more elaborately, and standing slightly in front[551] of the one on the right, who is darker and older, with more facial hair. The two men bear some resemblance to each other, but are quite clearly not brothers or necessarily related. Their

---

[551] The look of the character of Davus in the 2009 film *Agora*, which concerned the (rather freely re-interpreted) life of Hypatia of Alexandria, was based on this figure.

spatial arrangement, with the younger man on the left and slightly in front of the older, is traditional in Roman husband-wife burial reliefs, with the younger man in the place of the wife. Additionally, in much Greek and Roman portraiture of this period, youth is often signified by lighter skin and age by darker skin, and likewise the feminine is light while the masculine is dark. The youth in the depiction, moreover, does not appear to have much facial hair—only small indications of it—whereas the older man certainly does (though he is not excessively old). The youth's dress, with a decorative clasp, is also more typical of the feminine partner, and his red and white garments are the classical colors of ephebic attire (with white, black, and red or purplish-red all signifying this—all colors which we have in our own practice associated with the great ephebe god himself, Antinous). And perhaps most interesting or enticing—and thus the most surprising in terms of Lambert's lack of inclusion of this example—is that each of the figures has a depiction of a Graeco-Egyptian deity looming over one shoulder: the older man has Hermanubis (the syncretized Hermes Psychopompos-Anubis), while the young ephebe has what was initially thought to be perhaps Harpocrates, but since has been agreed to be none other than Oseirantinous—Osiris-Antinous, the patron god of Antinoöpolis. As both gods have underworld/afterlife associations, they would be appropriate for a funerary art depiction; but they also might signify which deme each of the men came from in Antinoöpolis. Either significance is equally possible and valid, and are not mutually exclusive for our purposes. The small inscription on the tondo does not give either of the men's names, but rather the date *15 Pachon*, May 10,[552] in association with the ephebe. What this date indicates is unknown—perhaps the death of the ephebe (even suggested by Haeckl as having taken place by drowning), perhaps the death of both men, but in any case the only temporal contextual clue given by the depiction. The relief dates to sometime in the 130s or 140s CE—very soon indeed after the foundation of Antinoöpolis and the death of Antinous and Hadrian, or perhaps even before Hadrian's death.

---

[552] As noted in the calendar earlier in this book, this is the date on which we not only celebrate these men, but also the date on which we recognize all of our *Sancti* whose exact dates of birth or death are not known, which includes the majority of the attested individuals from the ancient cultus of Antinous.

So, apart from general interest, why is this exciting, or at all useful for our purposes? In my view, for a number of reasons. First, it at last gives us some faces of what Antinoöpolitans looked like, and what they dressed like; and more importantly, specifically Antinoöpolitans who were dedicated to or connected to Antinous' devotion in a direct way. Second, it is one of the only painting/drawing depictions of (Osiris-) Antinous in existence. Third, it shows that in the Graeco-Roman-Egyptian culture of Antinoöpolis, that the traditional *erastes/eromenos* relationships existed amongst the non-imperial population, even in the second century. Fourth, it shows that there were specifically homoerotically-inclined, dedicated worshippers of Antinous in the cult in its early stages. This last point is perhaps the most important in terms of confirming what has been our suspicion and our contention all along in the Ekklesía Antínoou,[553] namely that while the appeal of Antinous' cult was to many people, both women and men, Greeks, Romans, and Egyptians, artists and miners, priests and citizens, that there were specifically-homoerotically-inclined people who dedicated themselves to Antinous in life and in death, whether by chance, local expediency (given their origin in Antinoöpolis), or specifically because of Antinous' own history as the youthful lover of *Divus Hadrianus*.

We do not know their names, we do not know anything about the specifics of their lives or their deaths, but we know that the date of *15 Pachons* was one of significance to them, the day in which they most likely entrusted one or both of their number to the care of Antinous the God.

---

[553] And which has been suggested, without very much definite evidence, by various queer-positive spiritual writers, including Randy P. Conner, David Hatfield Sparks and Mariya Sparks (eds.), *Cassells' Encyclopedia of Queer Myth, Symbol and Spirit* (London and New York: Cassell, 1997), p. 62.

The Love Spell of Antinoöpolis

A most curious piece of evidence for a particular theological understanding of Antinous emerges from a Graeco-Egyptian love spell, found in the vicinity of Antinoöpolis, and most likely dating from the third or fourth centuries CE. With the inscription was found a figurine of a woman, bound and pierced with pins. The entire spell closely matches the formula and instructions found in a Graeco-Egyptian magical papyrus,[554] though the expected male figure to accompany it did not seem to be part of the assemblage. Most curious, however, is that Antinous is invoked in the spell, not as a god or even as a hero, but as a *daimon*.[555] It has been debated whether or not the "Antinous" referred to therein is really the hero/god Antinous who was the lover of Hadrian, or whether it may have been just some random other young prematurely-dead male named Antinous,[556] but many scholars have decided that it must indeed be Antinous.[557]

Various translations of the text are available,[558] but the one given here is from John G. Gager.[559]

---

[554] Hans Dieter Betz (ed./trans.), *The Greek Magical Papyri in Translation, Including the Demotic Spells*, Second Edition (Chicago and London: The University of Chicago Press, 1996), IV.296-466, pp. 44-47. *PGM* IV also contains the spell that Pancrates/Pachrates gave to Hadrian (2441-2621), pp. 82-86.

[555] For a lengthy discussion of this, see P. Sufenas Virius Lupus, *The Syncretisms of Antinous* (Anacortes: The Red Lotus Library, 2010), pp. 101-107.

[556] For example, Christopher A. Faraone, *Ancient Greek Love Magic* (Cambridge and London: Harvard University Press, 1999), p. 42 note 3.

[557] Daniel Ogden, *Greek and Roman Necromancy* (Princeton: Princeton University Press, 2001), pp. 153-154; Ogden, *Night's Black Agents: Witches, Wizards and the Dead in the Ancient World* (New York and London: Hambledon Continuum, 2008), p. 116.

[558] Mary Beard, John North, & Simon Price (eds./trans.), *Religions of Rome, Volume 2: A Sourcebook* (Cambridge: Cambridge University Press, 1998), pp. 266-267; Daniel Ogden (ed.), *Magic, Witchcraft, and Ghosts in the Greek and*

I entrust this binding spell to you, gods of the underworld, Pluton and Kore Persephone Ereschigal[560] and Adonis and BARBARITHA and Hermes of the underworld and Thooth PHOKENSEPSEU EREKTATHOU MISONKTAIK and to mighty Anoubis PSERIPHTHA who holds the keys to the gates of Hades, to infernal gods, to men and women who have died untimely deaths, to youths and maidens, from year to year, month to month, day to day, hour to hour, night to night. I conjure all spirits in this place to stand as assistants to this spirit, Antinous. And arouse yourself for me and go to every place and into every quarter and to every house and bind Ptolemais, to whom Aias gave birth, the daughter of Horigenes, in order that she may not be had in a promiscuous way, let her not be had anally, nor let her do anything for pleasure with another man, just with me alone, Sarapammon, to whom Area gave birth, and do not let her drink or eat, that she not show any affection, nor go out, nor find sleep without me, Sarapammon, to whom Area gave birth. I conjure you, spirit of the dead man, Antinous, by the name that causes fear and trembling, the name at whose sound the earth opens, the name at whose terrifying sound the spirits are terrified, the name at whose sound rivers and rocks burst asunder. I conjure you, spirit of the dead man, Antinous, by BARBARATHAM CHELOUMBRA BAROUCH ADONAI and by ABRASAX and by IAO PAKEPTOTH PAKEBRAOTH SABARBAPHAEI and by MARMARAOUOTH and by MARMARACHTHA MAMAZAGAR. Do not fail, spirit of the

Roman Worlds: A Sourcebook (Oxford and New York: Oxford University Press, 2002), pp. 250-251.

[559] John G. Gager, *Curse Tablets and Binding Spells from the Ancient World* (Oxford and New York: Oxford University Press, 1992), pp. 97-100.

[560] On this particular set of syncretisms, see P. Sufenas Virius Lupus, "Ereshkigal in the Graeco-Egyptian Magical Tradition," in Tess Dawson (ed.), *Anointed: A Devotional Anthology for the Deities of the Near and Middle East* (Asheville, NC: Bibliotheca Alexandrina, 2011), pp. 213-224.

dead man, Antinous, but arouse yourself for me and go to every place, into every quarter, into every house and draw to me Ptolemais, to whom Aias gave birth, and do not allow her to accept for pleasure the attempt of any man, just that of me, Sarapammon. Drag her by the hair and her heart until she no longer stands aloof from me, Sarapammon, to whom Area gave birth, the daughter of Horigenes, obedient for all the time of my life, filled with love for me, desiring me, speaking to me the things she has on her mind. If you accomplish this for me, I will set you free.

The *Phylai* of Antinoöpolis

[The information in this section is taken from the works of Anthony Birley, Mary Taliaferro Boatwright, H. I. Bell, and Hugo Meyer, as well as some of my own research.][561]

Antinoöpolis appears in literature soon after its foundation, in the *Geographia* of Claudius Ptolemy in roughly the year 135; it also appears merely geographically, without any reference to its foundation or to Antinous' cult, in the *Itinerarium Antonini Augusti*, and the Christian writings of Stephanos Byzantinos, Hierokles Grammatikos, Photios, and the *Notitia Episcopatuum*. At a bend in the river called Hir-Wer was the site in which Antinous' body was found; this name *Hir-Wer* might mean in Egyptian "Horus the Great" or "Horus is Pleased."[562] It was on the east bank of the Nile, opposite Hermopolis Magna, and was also called Antinoë, Antenon, Adrianopolis, Besantinoë, Besantinopolis, and in Arabic documents it is called Antina; it is now called Sheikh-'Ibada, the latter of which means "the pious Sheik," named after an Arab chieftain who was martyred on the site upon his conversion to Christianity. It was built on the ancient ruins of the city of Besa, sacred to the god Bes, or at Nefrusi, a cult-site of Hathor.[563] The Greeks who

---

[561] Anthony R. Birley, *Hadrian: The Restless Emperor* (London and New York: Routledge, 2000), pp. 254-255; Mary Taliaferro Boatwright, *Hadrian and the Cities of the Roman Empire* (Princeton: Princeton University Press, 2003), p. 194n124; F. G. Kenyon and H. I. Bell (eds.), *Greek Papyri in the British Museum: Catalogue, With Texts*, Volume 3 (London: British Museum, 1907), pp. 154-167; Hugo Meyer, *Antinoos: Die archäologischen Denkmäler unter Einbeziehung des numismatischen und epigraphischen Materials sowie der literarischen Nachrichten, Ein Beitrag zur Kunst- und Kulturgeschichte der hadrianisch-frühantoninischen Zeit* (Munich: Wilhelm Fink, 1991), p. 216. As Meyer and Birley's synopses do not agree entirely with Boatwright's, with the latter putting Musegetikos in the Hadrianoi rather than the Oseirantinoi *phyla*, but Boatwright's study is the most current, I have opted to assume that her reading on that point is correct.

[562] However, don't quote me on it, as my Egyptian is not very good!

[563] Royston Lambert, *Beloved and God: The Story of Hadrian and Antinous* (New York: Viking, 1984), pp. 198-208.

colonized it were given the right of *conubium*, the right to marry Egyptian women without forfeiting their Greek privileges. Under Diocletian in 286 CE, it became the capital of the entire nome of Thebais, and in the reign of Valens (364-378 CE) it became a bishopric with one Orthodox bishop and one Monophysite bishop. Many statues were found there when it was visited in the 18th and 19th centuries during the Napoleonic expeditions, as well as two streets with double colonnades, a triumphal arch, a theatre, several temples, a circus, and a hippodrome.

Antinoopolis was divided into ten *phylai*; each *phyla* was divided into five *demoi*. The names of the known *demoi* are given below with their meanings.

The Ten *Phylai* of Antinoopolis:

Hadrianioi
Athenais
Ailieus
Matidioi
Neruanioi
Oseirantinoeioi
Paulinioi
Sabinioi
Sebastioi
Traianioi

Hadrianioi: Zenios, Olympios, Kapitolieus, Sosikosmios. This *phyla* is obviously named after Hadrian. The first three *demoi* names refer in some way to aspects or cult sites of Zeus/Jupiter. The remaining *deme* of Sosikosmios means "ruler of the universe" and makes him the universal savior and benefactor/provider.

Athenais: Artemisios, Eleusinios, Erichthonios, Marathonios, Salaminios. This *phyla* is named after Athens, and the *demoi* names are significant to that city and its culture. Artemis is obvious, with a connection to Artemis of Brauron no doubt implied in her placement within this *phyla*. Eleusis and Marathon are both near Athens, and Marathonios and Salaminios both have significant histories within the period of the Persian Wars. Erichthonios was a son of Hephaistos, engendered when the smith-god desired Athena, ejaculated on her leg, and the goddess wiped his semen away with wool and threw it to the ground, from which came Erichthonios, who became an early king of Athens.

Ailieus: Apideus, Dionysieus, Polieus. Aelius is the birth-family name of Hadrian, which was then given to his first adopted son, Lucius Ceionus Commodus, who became Aelius Caesar. The *deme* named after Dionysos is obvious; Dionysian worship flourished in Rome under Hadrian, and he portrayed himself as the *Neos Dionysos*, "New Dionysos" on occasion. Apideus seems to commemorate the incidents early in Hadrian's reign of the replacement of the Apis Bull in Egypt. Polieus is an epithet of Zeus, again in self-reference to Hadrian's comparison to the chief Olympian god.

Matidioi: Demetrieus, Thesmophorios, Kalliteknios, Markianios, Plotinios. This *phyla* is named for Matidia, the mother-in-law of Hadrian, his wife Sabina's mother, with whom he had a very close relationship. One *deme* is named for Plotina, Matidia's aunt and the empress of Hadrian's predecessor Trajan, with whom he also had a close (some suggested adulterous) relationship; and Matidia's own mother Marciana, who was declared a *Diva* by Hadrian. The first two titles refer to Demeter and the Eleusinian Mysteries. Kalliteknios means "breeder/mother of beautiful children," thus referring to Sabina and a possible identification with Kore/Persephone.

Neruanioi: Genearchios, Eirenieus, Hestieus, Propatorios. Nerva, the emperor previous to Trajan, is the person for whom this *phyla* is named. Two *demoi* are "fatherly" titles, meaning "father of the family" and "grandfather," plus references to Hestia/Vesta and the goddess of Peace, Eirene.

398

Oseirantinoeioi: Bithynieus, Hermaieus, Kleitorios, Parrhasios, Musegetikos. This is the *phyla* named for the principal god of Antinoöpolis, the person after whom the city was founded: Antinous in his form as Osiris-Antinous. Bithynieus comes from his home province of Bithynia, and his native city of Bithynion-Claudiopolis. Hermaieus takes its name from Hermes, one of the principal gods of Arcadia, the home territory of the Greek colony which Antinous' family was associated with, and a relationship which Hadrian tried to play up in the aftermath of his death. Musegetikos means "leader of the muses," which is sometimes given as an epithet of Apollon, but also occasionally Dionysos—and in any case, both deities had syncretistic connections to Antinous. Kleitorios and Parrhasios are named for heroes of Arcadia, Parrhasios and Kleitor, respectively the father and grandson of Arkas (the eponymous hero who gave his name to the region of Arcadia), both of whom were city founders, and the latter of whom died childless. As both are descendants of Lykaon (Kleitor is also sometimes said to have been one of that ruler's fifty sons), the first lycanthrope/werewolf, and are connected with the Arkas/werebear myth as well, this is a further interesting point. Parrhasios' myth is especially interesting, related by Plutarch as being quite similar to the twin birth and suckling by a she-wolf of Romulus and Remus, a further lycanthropic connection.

Paulinioi: Isidios, Megaleisios, Homognios, Philadelphios. This *phyla* is named for Domitia Paulina, Hadrian's sister (also the name of his mother), and the *demoi* are all "sisterly" titles. Isidios refers to Isis; Megaleisios refers to the Megalensia, the Roman festival to Cybele/Magna Mater, and thus is an allusion to that goddess. Homognios shows her common family tie to Hadrian, and Philadelphios commemorates his love toward her. This *phyla*'s attribution to Hadrian's sister might have been a compensation for what Cassius Dio relates in relation to her death, to wit, that Hadrian did not properly mourn her on that occasion, and perhaps felt guilty about it later.

Sabinioi: Harmonieus, Gamelieus, Heraieus, Trophonieus, Phytalieus. The Empress Sabina gives her name to this *phyla*. The quality of harmony is evoked by the first, or perhaps is a reference to Harmonia

399

wife of the Theban King Kadmos, who both lived into old age and in the Elysian Fields were granted eternal youth. Gamelieus means "good marriage"; the third means "like Hera," to whom Sabina was connected in an imperial cult inscription at Thasos, and as Hera/Juno she would be the natural counterpart to Hadrian's Zeus/Jupiter; the fourth means "nurterer," but was also the name of a hero with an oracle at Boeotian Lebadea, though it may also have a connection to the Eleusinian Trophonios.[564] The fifth has something to do with roots, perhaps referring to good breeding, but along with Harmonieus, Gamelius and Trophonieus could refer to Eleusis and therefore Sabina's identification with Kore/Persephone; this fifth deme might have been called Matalieus or Matralieus, which would be a reference to the goddess Ceres Matralis, and Sabina was syncretized to Ceres as well.

Sebastioi: Apollonieus, Asklepios, Dioskurios, Heraklios, Kaisarios. Four of the demoi in this *phyla*, which is the typical Greek word for "Augustus" and connected with imperial titles and the imperial cult, are the names of gods, Apollon (the patron god of Julius Caesar and Augustus), Asklepios, the Dioskouroi (Kastor and Polydeukes/Castor and Pollux, better known in an astrological context as the Gemini constellation's twins), and Herakles; the fifth is the title of Caesar. Also noteworthy is that Asklepios, the Dioskouroi, and Herakles were all gods who were born of mortals and achieved apotheosis, and were initiated into the Eleusinian Mysteries before their deaths, which might hint at Hadrian's own thinking in this regard, both for himself and for Antinous.

---

[564] However, the first seems more likely, in light of the evidence of Flavius Philostratus' *Life of Apollonius of Tyana*, Book VIII.19-20, which says that Apollonius obtained a book describing the ideal way of life (which was in line with Pythagorean philosophy) after an inquiry at Trophonios' oracle, which Hadrian then preserved in a palace at Antium along with letters by Apollonius: F. C. Conybeare (ed./trans.), *The Life of Apollonius of Tyana* (Cambridge: Harvard University Press, 1912), Volume 2, pp. 378-383. For more on the oracle, see Frederick Grant (ed.), *Hellenistic Religions: The Age of Syncretism* (New York and Indianapolis: The Bobbs-Merrill Company, 1953), pp. 39-41, which is an excerpt from Plutarch on the Lebadean oracle.

Traianioi: Ktesios, Nikephorios, Stratios. The final *phyla* is named for the Emperor Trajan. The *demoi* bear titles meaning "builder," "victorious," and "of the army." The first is also an epithet of Zeus.

Several further documents giving information about the inhabitants of Antinoöpolis, particularly in the early decades of its existence, are given below.

Citizen Enrollment, May 5, 133 CE[565]

Among the Greek men who within the regulated period handed in memorials to the Senate and afterwards presented their children: Heraclides also called Valerius son of Maron, an Antinoite, a settler from the Arsinoite nome, one of the Greek men, aged 57 years, for two sons Lysimachus also called Didymus, seven years old, Philosarapis, one year old. Aelurius, an Antinoite, a settler from the Arsinoite nome, one of the Greek men; Suchus son of Ptolemaeus son of Tryphon, an Antinoite, a settler from the Arsinoite nome, one of the Greek men; Heron son of Ptolemaeus son of Tryphon, an Antinoite, a settler from the Arsinoite nome, one of the Greek men. Year 17 of Imperator Caesar Traianus Hadrianus Augustus, month of Metagitnion which is *Pachon, the 10th*. Prytanis: Castor son of Ammonius. Signed by me, Arius son of Hermias.

Colonists in the New City, c. 135 CE[566]

Petronius Mamertinus to Horion, strategos of the Thinite Nome, greetings. A copy of the letter written to me by Demetrios..., one of those chosen by lot for the city of Antinous from the city of

---

[565] H. I. Bell, "Antinoopolis: A Hadrianic Foundation in Egypt," *The Journal of Roman Studies* 30 (1940), pp. 133-147 at 138.

[566] Robert K. Sherk (ed./trans.), *Translated Documents of Greece & Rome 6: The Roman Empire: Augustus to Hadrian* (Cambridge: Cambridge University Press, 1988), p. 193 §153.

Ptolemais, I have attached to this letter of mine, wishing you to see to it that the people there and the others who have been sent to colonize the city of Antinous shall live without being insulted or molested in your nome. Year 19 of the god Hadrian, *Pharmouthis 19.*

Road Dedication, 137 CE[567]

Imperator Caesar, son of god Traianus Parthicus, grandson of god Nerva, Traianus Hadrianus Augustus, *pontifex maximus*, holding the tribunician power for the twenty-first time, *imperator* for the second time, father of his country [*pater patriae*], opened up the new Hadrianic Road from Berenike to Antinoöpolis through safe and level countryside by the Red Sea. With wells that are always full and with resting places and with garrisons he provided it from place to place. Year 21, *Pharmenoth 1.*

Notification to Nomarch, February 9, 151 CE[568]

Petronius Mamertinus, former prefect, made known to us the benefits granted to us by Divus Hadrianus, the founder of our city, by which he directed that the children of the Antinoites who are registered by us, their parents, within thirty days of their birth should be maintained from the proceeds of funds granted by him for this purpose and for other revenues. I therefore register the son born to me, Heraclides alias Valerius, twenty days old, by my wife Ninnarous daughter of Orsenuphis, an Antinoite, the fee for whose birth-certificate I paid through the most excellent Senate, furnishing three guarantors of the marriage and the parentage, Lysanias son of Didymus, of the Matidian tribe and Plotinian deme, and Ptolemaeus son of Heraclides, of the Oseirantinoan tribe and Kleitorian deme; and I swear by the Fortune of Imperator Caesar Titus Aelius

---

[567] Sherk, p. 200 §157.
[568] Bell, p. 143.

402

Hadrianus Antoninus Augustus Pius and the most great god Osirantinous that the foregoing particulars are true, or may I be subject to the consequences of this oath.

Citizen Enrollment, February 24, 151 CE[569]

Lysimachus also called Didymus son of Heraclides, of the Matidian tribe and Kalliteknian deme, 25 years old, for his son Heraclides also called Valerius, twenty days old on the 15th of Thargelion which is Mecheir in the present 14th year of Antoninus Caesar the lord. Guarantors: Lysanias son of Didymus, of the Matidian tribe and Plotinian deme, Didymus son of Didymus, of the Matidian tribe and Kalliteknian deme, Ptolemaeus son of Heraclides, of the Oseirantinoan tribe and Kleitorian deme. Fourteenth year Imperator Caesar Titus Aelius Hadrianus Antoninus Augustus Pius, month of Thargelion which is Mecheir, the 30th. Prytanis: Messius Iunianus. Signed by me, Heraclides son of Heraclides.

Record of a Sale of Acadia Trees, c. 225 CE[570]

Aurelius Ptollion son of Ptollion, of Oxyrhynchus, tutor of the children of Apollonius, also called Didymus, son of Onesas, who are minors, and the mother of the minors, who gives her concurrence, Aurelia Eudaemonis daughter of Antinous also called Hermes, of Antinoöpolis, acting without a guardian in accordance with Roman custom by the right of her children, to the Aurelii Serenus son of Aurelius Ammonius, formerly exegetes of Oxyrhynchus, and Serenus son of Serenus, and Theonas styled as having Taarmiusis as his mother, and Soterichus son of Didymus, of the said city, greeting. We

---

[569] Bell, p. 138.

[570] Bernard P. Grenfell and Arthur S. Hunt (eds.), *The Oxyrhynchus Papyri* 6 (London: Egypt Exploration Society, 1908), §909, pp. 257-259.

acknowledge that we have sold to you four in equal shares the fourteen acacia-trees in good condition growing upon the embankment of the newly-planted vineyard belonging to the minors, at the price agreed upon between us of 1200 drachmae of silver, which sum was devoted to the purchase of wheat paid for the dues upon the aforesaid vineyard in the reign of the deified Commodus, on condition that you shall perform the complete uprooting and removal of the aforesaid acacia-trees at your own expense whenever you choose, but of necessity not later than Mesore of the present 4th year, and after the pulling up and removal of the acacia-trees the place shall be set in order in equal shares, half by us and the other half by you the buyers, as hereby agreed, and in answer to the formal question we have given our consent. This sale, of which there are two copies, is valid. The 4th year of the Emperor Caesar Marcus Aurelius Severus Alexander Pius Felix Augustus, *Tybi* 15. Signature of Aurelius Ptollion.

Notification of a Victory, January 15, 272[571]

The magistrates and the council of the most glorious city of the Antinoites...to the magistrates and council of the city of the Oxyrhynchites, their most dear friends, greeting.

...that Aurelius Stephanus son of Achilleus in games held at our city on behalf of the victory and eternal permanence of our lords Aurelian Augustus and Vaballathus Athenodorus the most glorious king Imperator general of the Romans, the second occurrence of four-yearly sacred iselastic musical dramatic athletic equestrian Antinoan...Philadelphian games known as the most glorious Capitolia, after striving nobly and conspicuously has won the contest of the Dacian chariot and has proclaimed publicly your city. We therefore make report to you, dear

---

[571] R. A. Coles and M. W. Haslam (eds.), *The Oxyrhynchus Papyri* 47 (London: Egypt Exploration Society, 1980), §3367, pp. 139-140.

friends, that you may know and may furnish him with all the rewards due to the crown according to the orders proclaimed.

We pray for your health, dear friends.

Year two of Imperator Caesar Lucius Domitius Aurelianus Pius Felix Augustus and year five of Julius Aurelius Septimius Vaballathus Athenodorus the most glorious king consul Imperator general of the Romans, *Tybi 19.*

...were read out in the theatre...

Petition of a Victor, c. 275-276 CE[572]

To Aurelius...alias Hier..., administering the business of the strategus of the Oxyrhynchite nome, from Marcus Aurelius Sarapion son of Patermuthius, from the glorious and most glorious city of the Oxyrhynchites, victor in Capitoline games. Since I have gained a share in life's glory by winning the contest for two-horse chariots in the sacred, iselastic, world-wide, Philadelphian, Antinoan,..., Capitoline games auspiciously celebrated in the most glorious city of the Antinoites for the victory and everlasting might of our lord Imperator Tacitus Augustus, and, after receiving the responses customarily accompanying the crown, I made a triumphal entry here, and as a result have gained exemption from taxes and liturgies altogether, according to the ordinances governing games, I was impelled to submit this petition, requesting that by the agency of one of your assistants (the copy of this document) be communicated...

[572] J. R. Rea (ed.), *The Oxyrhynchus Papyri* 43 (London: Egypt Exploration Society, 1975), §3116, pp. 66-68.

Excerpts from the *Suda*

A number of Christian writers, from the second century CE onwards, wrote disparagingly of Antinous. These included Justin Martyr (c. 110-165), *Apologia Prima* 29; Hegesippos (c. 110-180), *Hypomnemata* (known via Eusebius of Caesarea's *Ecclesiastical History* 4.8.1-3); Tatian the Assyrian (died after 172), *Pros Hellenas* 10; Theophilus of Antioch (fl. C. 169-180), *Ad Autolycum* 3.8; Athenagoras the Athenian (fl. 177), *Presebia* 30; Tertullian of Carthage (c. 160-215), *Apologeticus* 13, *Ad Nationes* 2.10, *De Corona* 13, *Contra Marcionem* 1.18; Clement of Alexandria (died 215), *Protrepticus* 4; Origen of Alexandria (c. 185-254), *Contra Celsum* 3.36-38, 5.63, 8.9; Eusebius of Caesarea (c. 260-341), *Praeparatio Evangelica* 2.6, *Chronicorum* 2.226[th] and 231st Olympiads; Athanasius of Alexandria (296-373), *Contra Gentes* 1.9.4; *Chronicon Paschale* (c. 354) 2nd year of 225th Olympiad (which wrongly gives Antinous' death as 122 CE, but correctly names October 30th as the foundation of Antinoöpolis); Epiphanios of Salamis (c. 315-403), *Ancoratus* 109, *Expositio Fidei Catholicae et Apostolicae Ecclesiae* 12; Prudentius (c. 348-405), *Contra Orationem Symmachi* 1 lines 271-277; Jerome (c. 340-420), *De Viris Illustribus* 22, *Contra Jovinianum* 2.7, *Commentariorum in Isaiam Prophetam* 1.2.35, *Hieronymi Interpretatio Chronicae Eusebii Pamphili* 227th and 230th Olympiads; John Chrysostom (c. 347-407), *Homily 26 on II Corinthians* (12:1); Socrates Scholasticus (c. 379-450), *Historia Ecclesiae* 3.23; Theodoretos of Antioch (c. 393-460), *Graecarum Affectionum Curatio* Sermon 8; the pseudo-*Sibylline Oracles* (c. 2nd c. BCE-5th c. CE) 8; and Nikephoros Kallistos (c. 1256-1335), *Ecclesiasticae Historiae* 3.26, 10.36. Some of these references are highly derivative of earlier sources, while others introduce novel information found nowhere else in surviving records. In the latter category, Clement of Alexandria's report on the "sacred nights" of Antinous and the lascivious excesses associated with them, and his pupil Origen's discussion of the demon-inspired oracles of Antinous and the pagan-critical voice of Celsus against Antinous as being equal to his critiques of Jesus, are important sources for the survival and thriving of the cultus of Antinous into the third century in Egypt, though we know from other sources that it continued much longer than that, and was still an issue of concern in the early fifth century.[573] There are some surprising missing names in this litany, like Augustine of Hippo, who would probably have savaged Antinous as equally as he did most other late antique pagan cults and deities in his *De Civitate Dei*, and yet Antinous is absent from it, and from the bishop of Hippo's voluminous other writings.

It used to be thought that the *Suidas*, or, more properly, the *Suda*, was the author of this famous dictionary—which is actually more like an encyclopedia in terms of the depth of information given on many entries—but it has since been discovered that the name "Suda" derives from the Latin for "fortress" or "stronghold." The compiler of it was definitely Christian, but was extremely well read in the classical literatures, and for this reason the *Suda* is indispensable, because a huge number of the sources from which it draws are no longer available to us. It does give an excellent flavor, though, of what a medieval Byzantine scholar may have had at his disposal in terms of Greek sources that are now lost. The compilation of the *Suda* dates from the late 10th century CE, although there are a number of later interpolations. It was originally written in Greek, although Latin translations have been made.

The entries given here—on Hadrian, Numenios, Mesomedes, and the word *paidika*, all relate to Antinous in some manner, and indeed are the only sources for our knowledge that Mesomedes and Numenios wrote for Antinous. The following excerpts were provisionally translated by me from a parallel Latin-Greek version of the text dating from 1705, to which I had access in my university's library while I lived in Cork, Ireland.

---

[573] Though a sixth-century Christian poet and jurist in Egypt, Dioscorus of Aphrodito, wrote approvingly of both Hadrian and Antinous, since his career took place in Antinoöpolis; see Leslie S. B. MacCoull, *Dioscorus of Aphrodito: His Work and His World* (Berkeley, Los Angeles, and Oxford: University of California Press, 1989).

Hadrian

...This man was pleasant to meet and some favor graced him, as he used the languages of both the Latins and the Greeks most excellently; furthermore he was regarded as a great marvel for the gentleness of his ways, and as someone who had been zealous in the amassing of public funds. This man was by nature such a man that he was envious not only towards the living but towards those who were dead; at any rate he undermined Homer and instead of him introduced Antimachus, whose name many had never heard of before. They found fault with these deeds of his as well as with his strictness and his curiosity and his meddlesomeness; but he ameliorated and compensated for these things with other cares and forethought and munificence and cleverness; and in addition to this he began no war and stopped those that were already on, and deprived no one of money unjustly, and he bestowed a lot of money on many men, both public officials and private citizens. He was extremely superstitious and made use of various oracles and incantations. His boyfriend/favorite [Gk. *paidiká*, Lat. *deliciis*] was a certain Antinous; he founded and colonized a city and named it for him. And he even saw [or perhaps "invented"] a certain star of Antinous.

Mesomedes

Mesomedes of Crete, lyric poet, who lived in the time of Hadrian—his freedman, actually one of his greatest friends. He wrote an encomium of Antinous, whom Hadrian had as his boyfriend, and many other lyrics. Antoninus refurbished the tomb of Sulla, and Mesomedes, who composed the lyrics of songs, to which a certain one had been circulated to the music of the cithara, made the cenotaph; indeed to that one, whose cruelty was imitated.

Numenios

Numenios the rhetor/orator. He wrote *On the Figures of Diction*; introductions [Gk. *hypothéseis*, Lat. *argumentata*] to Thucydides and Demosthenes; a collection of *chreiai* [maxims]; [and a] Consolation to Hadrian for the death of Antinous.

Paidiká

This name is said so far concerning the feminine ones, who are men, who are kept as boyfriends/favorites; loved ones. And indeed concerning the men who were so called, many examples are demonstrated....And Cratinus in *The Hours*, Bacchus having advanced seductively from abroad lovingly, said concerning it: Blessed are you because of your boyfriends....*Paidikòn* in truth is said also for *paidariódes*, i.e. puerile or boyish, even fittingly to boys. However the greater part [of its usages] are said in relation to lasciviousness and foul affections. We offer [as an example] Antinous kept as a boyfriend by Hadrian himself. However, he had died before Hadrian, so this one commanded statues everywhere to honor him. At last, in truth, you have seen, some star in heaven was seen by him, which he said was to be Antinous: and a sacrificial offering will be made to have been seen in heaven, in order that it may be contemplated.

409

Hadrian's Elegy for Borysthenes

This is a poetic inscription from Apta, Gallia Narbonensis, from c. late 122 CE, written by Hadrian in honor of his dead horse. In this, he somewhat followed Alexander the Great, whose famous horse Bukephalos was commemorated in the name of a city founded in his honor where he died. As it mentions boar hunting specifically, it might be an appropriate text to recite on the *Venatio Apri* festival on May 1st. The text from which this translation was made can be found in E. Mary Smallwood's collection,[574] and this translation was previously published in *The Phillupic Hymns*.[575]

Borysthenes the Alan
Swift Horse of Caesar,
over plain and marshes
and the Etruscan mounds, hills and thickets
he was accustomed to move swiftly
against Pannonian boars—
not any of them pursued,
boar with white tusk,
would dare to wound—
even the worst, spit
from his mouth, scattered its tail,
as was usual to happen;
but renewed youth,
uninjured limbs...
killed him on a day,
he is at this site in the field.

---

[574] E. Mary Smallwood, *Documents Illustrating the Principates of Nerva, Trajan and Hadrian* (Cambridge: Cambridge University Press, 1966), p. 192 §520.

[575] P. Sufenas Virius Lupus, *The Phillupic Hymns* (Eugene: Bibliotheca Alexandrina, 2008), p. 238. For an alternate translation, see Ewen L. Bowie, "Hadrian and Greek Poetry," in Erik Nis Ostenfeld, Karin Blomqvist and Lisa Nevett (eds.), *Greek Romans and Roman Greeks: Studies in Cultural Interaction* (Aarhus: Aarhus University Press, 2000), pp. 172-197 at 182.

Animula Vagula Blandula

Many different translations of Hadrian's sepulchral epigram have been given over the years, and a great deal of speculation has also accompanied it. Did it indicate a perhaps Epicurean strain in his thought, that there was no hope in the afterlife? It seems a strange statement for one's memorial when one considers that he was a senior initiate of the Eleusinian Mysteries, and a dedicated follower of the cultus of Antinous.

I give the Latin from the _Historia Augusta_ first below,[576] followed by several different translations of it.

Animula vagula blandula
hospes comesque corporis,
quae nunc abibis in loca
pallidula rigida nudula?
nec ut soles dabis iocos!

O blithe little soul, thou, flitting away,
Guest and comrade of this my clay,
Whither now goest thou, to what place
Bare and ghastly and without grace?
Nor, as thy wont was, joke and play?[577]

Warming, wand'ring little sprite
Body's guest and company,
Whither now take you your flight,
Cold and comfortless and white,
Leaving all your jollity?[578]

---

[576] David Magie (trans.), _The Scriptores Historiae Augustae_, Volume 1 (Cambridge: Harvard University Press, 1922), p. 78.
[577] Magie, p. 79.
[578] Stewart Perowne, _Hadrian_ (New York: Barnes & Noble, 1996), p. 180.

Little spirit, gentle and wandering,
companion and guest of the body,
in what place will you now abide,
pale, stark, and bare,
unable as you used, to play?[579]

Little charmer, wanderer, little sprite,
Body's companion and guest,
To what places now will you take flight,
Forbidding and empty and dim as night?
And you won't make your wonted jest![580]

Little soul, little wanderer, little charmer,
body's guest and companion,
to what places will you set out for now?
To darkling, cold and gloomy ones—
and you won't make your usual jokes.[581]

Little wandering soul,
Guest and companion of my body,
Where are you going to now?
Away, into bare, bleak places,
Never again to share a joke.[582]

Poor little, lost little, sweet little soul,
My body's companion and friend,
Where are you going to now, little soul,
Pale little, stiff little, bare little soul,
Now that the jokes have to end?[583]

---

[579] Royston Lambert, *Beloved and God: The Story of Hadrian and Antinous* (New York: Viking, 1984), p. 175.

[580] Anthony R. Birley, *Lives of the Later Caesars: The first part of the Augustan History, with newly compiled Lives of Nerva and Trajan* (London and New York: Penguin Books, 1976), p. 85.

[581] Anthony R. Birley, *Hadrian: The Restless Emperor* (London and New York: Routledge, 2000), p. 301.

[582] Elizabeth Speller, *Following Hadrian: A Second-century Journey through the Roman Empire* (London: Review/Headline Book Publishing, 2002), p. 262.

412

Little soul, you charming little wanderer,
my body's guest and partner,
where are you off to now? Somewhere
without color, savage and bare;
you'll crack no more of your jokes once you're there.[584]

Little soul, roamer and charmer,
My body's comrade and its sometime guest,
What dominion now must be your goal,
Pale and stiff and naked?
Unable now, like us, to jest.[585]

---

[583] Trans. Margaret Hodgson in Danny Danziger and Nicholas Purcell, *Hadrian's Empire: When Rome Ruled the World* (London: Hodder & Stoughton, 2005), p. 285.

[584] Anthony Everitt, *Hadrian and the Triumph of Rome* (New York: Random House, 2009), p. 319.

[585] George Gardiner, *The Hadrian Enigma: A Forbidden History* (GMP Editions, 2010), p. 420. This one is perhaps the most interesting of all, as it occurs in Gardiner's fiction just after the official funeral of Antinous, spoken by Hadrian to Antinous and expressing his concern over him.

Historical Sources on Antinous

It may seem strange to be giving the following texts after so many others that may appear to be less relevant or important for understanding of Antinous, but the decision on my part to do so is quite deliberate. Firstly, many of the texts which have been given previously lend themselves to ritual usage, whereas these ones do not— they are usually bland and relatively uninspiring prose as opposed to poetry. But, each one is also problematic in its own way. Even though these are called "historical sources" for the most part, we cannot trust them as entirely factual history. Conjecture and bias abounds in most of them, and none (except Pausanias) were written by people who knew or saw Hadrian or Antinous; several were, in fact, written centuries later. Several of them are critical of the imperial institution generally, and thus seize upon any topic that is scandalous or which may serve to discredit an individual Emperor or the entire office of Emperor. And, several were also written in the post-Christian period for a Christian (and imperial) audience, and thus an agenda against both polytheism and homoeroticism is most certainly present. Many of these texts were the "muckraker" press of their day, the late antique equivalents of the tabloids. One can almost see "IMPERIAL GAY LOVE AFFAIR EXPOSED! EMPEROR CRIES LIKE A GIRL!" as modern headlines leading off these accounts as they were written.

Pausanias lived from the reign of Hadrian to the reign of Marcus Aurelius, and wrote his *Periegesis*, usually known as the *Description of Greece* in English, probably during Marcus' principate. It was an unpopular work, and was not quoted a single time until the 6th c. CE by a Byzantine writer, and remained unpopular throughout the medieval period. Though mistrusted by some archaeologists and historians in the 19th century, Pausanias' accounts of particular Greek cities and sites have been proven accurate in further excavations.

Lucius Cassius Dio Cocceianus, better known to the English-speaking world as Cassius Dio (or sometimes Dio Cassius), lived from c. 155 CE to after 229 CE. He wrote a work called *Historia Romana* in eighty books, but some only survive fragmentarily, and the last 20 only survive in an epitome by the 11th century Byzantine Christian John Xyphilinus. Unfortunately, the material on Hadrian and Antinous is in the last twenty books, and thus it cannot be taken as entirely reliable, despite being closer in time to the events described than any of the sources to follow.

Though the work of Emperor Flavius Claudius Julianus, better known as "Julian the Apostate," is given here, it is not history proper; however, given that it does portray a view of the past emperors from the viewpoint of an emperor and one who was attempting to restore polytheism, it is an important negative source to take into account. Julian became *Caesar* on November 6, 355, *Augustus* in February of 360, and was the sole *Augustus* from November 3, 361 to his death on June 26, 363. A philosopher who was greatly interested in Platonism, the sample of Julian's work given here is satirical in the tradition of Lukian of Samosata, only in a much more grave sense. While it is important to honor Julian for what he attempted to do for the restoration of polytheism, the Ekklesía Antínoou does not honor him as a *Divus* or a *Sanctus* because of the critiques of Antinous and Hadrian expressed in the excerpt below.

Sextus Aurelius Victor lived from about 320 to 390 CE, and he may have been the same person as the *consul* of 369 and prefect of Rome in 389. He wrote his work, *De Caesaribus*, for the Emperor Julian in 361, and it reflects the critical attitude toward Antinous and Hadrian that Julian's own work exhibits.

Ammianus Marcellinus lived from c. 325/330 to sometime after 391 CE. He was a Greek and a former soldier, who was pagan but had great tolerance for Christians. His *Res Gestae/Rerum Gestarum* was written in thirty-one (or possibly thirty-six) books, but the first thirteen are lost. In these, he would have treated Hadrian's reign, so all that is left are the minor mentions of Antinoöpolis in the later books found below.

The *Historia Augusta* is a collection of writings that purports to be from the principates of Diocletian and Constantine in the late third and early fourth centuries CE, but there are so many linguistic anachronisms and references to later historical events in it that many scholars now consider it to have been written in the late fourth century. The various books of it purport to be by about eight different authors, but even this is now doubted. There are many exaggerations and inaccuracies in it, including the use of and quotation from documents that are demonstrably false or erroneous, as the second passage given below demonstrates. It is a purported letter of Hadrian, transmitted by Phlegon of Tralles, a freedman of Hadrian who wrote several works that do survive[586] (though what does survive does not mention Antinous, unfortunately, but may in some way reflect Hadrian's tastes in other passages and subjects treated).[587] The date of the consulship of Servianus, to whom the letter is addressed, is wrong if Hadrian was writing from Egypt in 130, as his consulship was in 134. Further, Aelius Caesar was not adopted until 136, and there was no "patriarch" of the Jewish people until after the Second Jewish War/Bar Kochba Rebellion in 132-135 CE. Thus, it cannot be trusted as straight-forward history, unless it had been heavily interpolated; it is most likely a rhetorical exercise, but given that it occurs in an ostensibly historical text, its role in shaping the view of Hadrian and Antinous cannot be entirely dismissed.

Pausanias, *Description of Greece*

Antinous too was deified by them [the Mantineians]. He was a great favorite of the Emperor Hadrian. I never saw him in the flesh, but I have seen images and pictures of him. He has honors in other places also, and on the Nile is an Egyptian city named after Antinous. He has won worship in Mantineia for the following reason. Antinous was by birth from Bithynium beyond the river Sangarius, and the Bithynians are by descent Arcadians of Mantineia. For this reason the Emperor established his worship in Mantineia also; mystic rites are celebrated in his

---

[586] William Hansen (trans.), *Phlegon of Tralles' Book of Marvels* (Exeter: Exeter University Press, 1996).

[587] P. Sufenas Virius Lupus, "An Obstetrician's Nightmare: Zeus and Male Birth," in Melia Suez et al. (eds.), *From Cave to Sky: A Devotional Anthology for Zeus* (Shreveport: Bibliotheca Alexandrina, 2010), pp. 42-55 at 43.

honor each year, and games every four years. There is a building in the gymnasium of Mantineia containing statues of Antinous, and remarkable for the stones with which it is adorned, and especially so for its pictures. Most of them are portraits of Antinous, who is made to look just like Dionysos.[588]

There are roads leading from Mantineia into the rest of Arcadia, and I will go on to describe the mot noteworthy objects on each of them. On the left of the highway leading to Tegea there is, beside the walls of Mantineia, a place where horses race, and not far from it is a race-course, where they celebrate the games in honor of Antinous.[589]

Cassius Dio, *Roman History*

In Egypt also [Hadrian] rebuilt the city named henceforth for Antinous. Antinous was from Bithynium, a city of Bithynia, which we also call Claudiopolis; he had been a favorite of the emperor and had died in Egypt, either by falling into the Nile, as Hadrian writes, or, as the truth is, by being offered in sacrifice. For Hadrian, as I have stated, was always very curious and employed divinations and incantations of all kinds. Accordingly, he honored Antinous, either because of his love for him or because the youth had voluntarily undertaken to die (it being necessary that a life should be surrendered freely for the accomplishment of the ends Hadrian had in view), by building a city on the spot where he had suffered this fate and naming it after him; and he also set up statues, or rather sacred images of him, practically all over the world. Finally, he declared that he had seen a star which he took to be that of Antinous, and gladly lent an ear to the fictitious tales woven by his associates to the

---

[588] W. H. S. Jones (ed./trans.), *Pausanias, Description of Greece*, Volume 3 (Cambridge: Harvard University Press, 1933), pp. 388-391 8.9.7-8.
[589] Jones, pp. 390-91 8.10.1.

effect that the star had really come into being from the spirit of Antinous and had then appeared for the first time. On this account, then, he became the object of some ridicule, and also because at the death of his sister Paulina he had not immediately paid her any honor.[590]

Julian, *The Caesars*

Next entered an old man [Nerva], beautiful to behold; for even old age can be radiantly beautiful. Very mild were his manners, most just his dealings. In Silenus he inspired such awe that he fell silent. "What!" said Hermes, "have you nothing to say to us about this man?" "Yes, by Zeus," he replied, "I blame you gods for your unfairness in allowing that bloodthirsty monster [Domitian] to rule for fifteen years, while you granted this man scarce one whole year." "Nay," said Zeus, "do not blame us. For I will bring in many virtuous princes to succeed him." Accordingly, Trajan entered forthwith, carrying on his shoulders the trophies of his wars with the Getae and the Parthians. Silenus, when he saw him, said in a whisper which he meant to be heard, "Now is the time for Zeus our master to look out, if he wants to keep Ganymede for himself."

Next entered an austere-looking man [Hadrian] with a long beard, an adept in all the arts, but especially music, one who was always gazing at the heavens and prying into hidden things. Silenus when he saw him said, "What think ye of this sophist? Can he be looking here for Antinous? One of you should tell him that the youth is not here, and make him cease from his madness and folly." Thereupon entered a man of temperate character [Antoninus Pius], I do not say in love affairs but in affairs of state. When Silenus caught sight of him he exclaimed,

---

[590] Earnest Cary (ed./trans.), *Dio's Roman History, Volume VIII* (Cambridge: Harvard University Press, 1925), pp. 444-447 69.11.2-4.

418

"Bah! Such fussing about trifles! This old man seems to me the sort of person who would split cummin seed." Next entered the pair of brothers, Verus [Marcus Aurelius] and Lucius [Verus]. Silenus scowled horribly because he could not jeer or scoff at them, especially not at Verus; but he would not ignore his errors of judgement in the case of his son [Commodus] and his wife [Faustina], in that he mourned the latter beyond what was becoming, especially considering that she was not even a virtuous woman; and he failed to see that his son was ruining the empire as well as himself, and that though Verus had an excellent son-in-law who would have administered the state better, and besides would have managed the youth better than he could manage himself. But though he refused to ignore these errors he reverenced the exalted virtue of Verus. His son however he considered not worth even ridicule and so let him pass. Indeed he fell to earth of his own accord because he could not keep on his feet or accompany the heroes.[591]

Sextus Aurelius Victor, *De Caesaribus*

And so Aelius Hadrian, who was more suited for declamation and civil pursuits, established peace in the east and returned to Rome. There, in the fashion of the Greeks or Pompilius Numa, he began to give attention to religious ceremonies, laws, schools and teachers to such an extent, in fact, that he even established a school of liberal arts, called the Athenaeum, and celebrated at Rome in the Athenian manner the rites of Ceres and Libera [Demeter and Persephone] which are called the Eleusinian Mysteries. Then, as is normal in peaceful circumstances, he retired somewhat negligently to his country retreat at Tivoli, leaving the city to Lucius Aelius Caesar. He himself, as is the custom with the fortunate rich, built palaces and devoted himself

---

[591] Wilmer Cave Wright (ed./trans.), *The Works of the Emperor Julian, Volume II* (Cambridge: Harvard University Press, 1913), pp. 356-359.

to dinner parties, statuary and paintings, and finally took sufficient pains to procure every luxury and plaything. From this sprang the malicious rumours that he had debauched young men and that he burned with passion for the scandalous attentions of Antinous and that for no other reason he had founded a city named after him or had erected statues to the youth. Some, to be sure, maintain that these were acts of piety and religious scruple because when Hadrian wanted to prolong his life and magicians had demanded a volunteer in his place, they report that although everyone else refused, Antinous offered himself and for this reason the honors mentioned above were accorded him. We shall leave the matter unresolved, although with someone of a self-indulgent nature we are suspicious of a relationship between men far apart in age.[592]

Ammianus Marcellinus, *Rerum Gestarum*

There is a town called Abydum, situated in the remotest part of the Thebais; here the oracle of a god called in that place Besa in days of old [i.e. Antinoöpolis] revealed the future and was wont to be honored in the ancient ceremonials of the adjacent regions.[593]

Now Thebais has these among cities that are especially famous: Hermopolis, Coptos and Antinoü, which Hadrian founded in honor of his favorite Antinous; for hundred-gated Thebes everyone knows.[594]

---

[592] H. W. Bird (trans.), *Sextus Aurelius Victor, De Caesaribus* (Liverpool: Liverpool University Press, 1994), pp. 16-17 14.
[593] John C. Rolfe (ed./trans.), *Ammianus Marcellinus, History, Volume I* (Cambridge: Harvard University Press, 1950), pp. 534-535 19.12.3.
[594] John C. Rolfe (ed./trans.), *Ammianus Marcellinus, History, Volume II* (Cambridge: Harvard University Press, 1940), pp.296-297 22.16.2.

Historia Augusta: Hadrian (attributed to Aelius Spartianus)

During a journey on the Nile he [Hadrian] lost Antinous, his favorite, and for this youth he wept like a woman. Concerning this incident there are varying rumors; for some claim that he had devoted himself to death for Hadrian, and others--what both his beauty and Hadrian's sensuality suggest. But however this may be, the Greeks deified him at Hadrian's request, and declared that oracles were given through his agency, but these, it is commonly asserted, were composed by Hadrian himself.[595]

Historia Augusta: Quadrigae Tyrannorum—Firmus, Saturninus, Proculus et Bonosus (attributed to Fliavius Vopiscus of Syracuse)

But, lest any Egyptian be angry with me, thinking that what I have set forth in writing is solely my own, I will cite one of Hadrian's letters, taken from the works of his freedman Phlegon, which fully reveals the character of the Egyptians.

"From Hadrian Augustus to Servianus the consul, greeting. The land of Egypt, the praises of which you have been recounting to me, my dear Servianus, I have found to be wholly light-minded, unstable, and blown about by every breath of rumor. There those who worship Serapis are, in fact, Christians, and those who call themselves bishops of Christ are, in fact, devotees of Serapis. There is no chief of the Jewish synagogue, no Samaritan, no Christian presbyter, who is not an astrologer, a soothsayer, or an anointer. Even the Patriarch himself, when he comes to Egypt, is forced by some to worship Serapis, by others to worship Christ. They are a folk most seditious, most deceitful, most given to

---

[595] David Magie (ed./trans.), *The Scriptores Historiae Augustae*, 3 Volumes (Cambridge: Harvard University Press, 1921-1932), Volume I, pp. 44-45 14.5-7.

injury; but their city is prosperous, rich, and fruitful, and in it no one is idle. Some are blowers of glass, others makers of paper, all are at least weavers of linen or seem to belong to one craft or another; the lame have their occupations, the eunuchs have theirs, the blind have theirs, and not even those whose hands are crippled are idle. Their only god is money, and this the Christians, the Jews, and, in fact, all nations adore. And would that this city had a better character, for indeed it is worthy by reason of its richness and by reason of its size to hold the chief place in the whole of Egypt. I granted it every favor, I restored to it all its ancient rights and bestowed on it new ones besides, so that the people gave thanks to me while I was present among them. Then, no sooner had I departed thence than they said many things against my son Verus, and what they said about Antinous I believe you have learned. I can only wish for them that they may live on their own chickens, which they breed in a fashion I am ashamed to describe [i.e. by incubating the eggs in dung-heaps]. I am sending you over some cups, changing color and variegated, presented to me by the priest of a temple and now dedicated particularly to you and my sister. I should like you to use them at banquets on feast-days. Take good care, however, that our dear Africanus does not use them too freely."[596]

Inscriptions and Other Papyri Fragments

There are a variety of inscriptions, and other scraps of papyri, that give us interesting and useful bits of information on Antinous, from a variety of contexts and time periods. We cannot often date inscriptions precisely unless they give information about consuls, emperors, and other such temporal markers; and likewise, if papyri do not give some indication of such things, it is difficult to say when they were composed in many cases.

This section is by no means complete nor comprehensive, and does not contain every attested inscription or papyrus fragment known at present that mentions Antinous. The examples given here are generally illustrative and useful for a devotional context in some manner. Many of the pieces given here are referred to in various manners in the previous chapters of this book as contributing to our understanding of particular syncretisms of Antinous, or of drawing out certain relationships that have been further elaborated upon in modern practice. The (generally shorter) inscriptions are given first, followed by the (often longer) papyri. Many of these inscriptions have not appeared in English translations before, so they are necessarily tentative and provisional as given here.

Herakleia Pontica[597]

We confess to know our fellow willingly, Marcius Xenocrates; [this statue was] raised due to the seriousness of his morals and the decency of his behavior, it increases the reputation of our city and does him honor, he also embellishes our quality and provides not only the holiness of these sacred games that earned him fame, but also by his eagerness to show his benevolence is a man who is loved especially by each member of our corporation,

---

[597] *L'Annee Epigraphique* 1991, pp. 398-400 §1461.

never shirking under any circumstances to lead with enthusiasm all matters concerning the association and has already, by his foresight, successfully resolved in our interest issues that were outside of the community and were not unimportant—therefore, receiving so many benefits, we thought we could just as well give in response simply a small token of our appreciation (for the consecration of statues and portraits), that we found his statue to be the most expensive, admitting our gratefulness and even sharing our joy at having such a fellow man. For all this, it pleased our holy Hadrianic-Antinoan association, around our city, on the large *thymele*[598] and for the *Neocore* who is in Rome, to honor him by a decree and the erection of statues and portraits...

The statue was erected in the consulship of Quintus Catullinus Fabius and Marcus Flavius Aper[599] and under *basileus* Herakleides son of Herakleitos.

Tibur, Hadrian's Villa[600]

Antinous and Belenus are equal in age and beauty, thus why would Antinous not also be worshipped like Belenus appropriately? Quintus the Sicilian [made this].

---

[598] The orchestra platform in a Greek theatre in which there was a small altar to Dionysos.

[599] 130 CE. Thus, this association of Hadrian and Antinous formed within two months of Antinous' death!

[600] Hugo Meyer, *Antinoos: Die archäologischen Denkmäler unter Einbeziehung des numismatischen und epigraphischen Materials sowie der literarischen Nachrichten, Ein Beitrag zur Kunst- und Kulturgeschichte der hadrianisch-frühantoninischen Zeit* (Munich: Wilhelm Fink, 1991), pp. 164-165.

Rome, Porta San Sebastiano[601]

To Publius Sufenas son of Publius the Palmyrian, *Equites*,
Roman Decurial of Clerks and Curule Aediles,
Lupercus, Priest of Laurentis Lavinates,
Phratriarch of Antinous and Eunostos in Naples,
Member of the Council's Board of Governors;
the citizens of Alba Longa and Bovillae
on account of his worthy service,
set this up in this place by decree of the council.[602]

Rome[603]

We, the Adriatic assembly, standing in awe of the beautiful Antinous, raise you, the new god Hermes [Neos Hermes]; Nikias dedicates this, whom you, O Blessed One, made your priest, and who has been serving as a presbyter throughout his life.

Rome[604]

Sacred to the Beautiful God [DEO AMABILI]; Aelia Ehorte made this.[605]

---

[601] L. H. S. Dietrichson, *Antinoos: Eine Kunstarchäologische Untersuchung* (Christiana: H. Aschehoug & Co., 1884), p. 326 §4. This was also translated as the epigraph of the poem *"Testamentum Sufenatis"* in P. Sufenas Virius Lupus, *The Phillupic Hymns* (Eugene: Bibliotheca Alexandrina, 2008), p. 71.

[602] The identity of this particular person is somewhat uncertain; he is possibly related to or identical with P. Sufenas Verus, governor of Lycia–Pamphylia in 129 and consul in 132. Laurentes Lavinates was a priestly sodality of the old Latin community of Lavinium, and as a *lupercus* and also *phratriarch* of Antinous and Eunostos in Naples, this Sufenas was quite involved in many aspects of public religious functionality.

[603] Meyer, pp. 169-170.

[604] Meyer, p. 165.

[605] This could either be Antinous, Phosphoros/Lucifer (the morning star), or Glykon.

425

Rome[606]

To Antinous, Enthroned with the Gods of Egypt. M. Oulpios [Marcus Ulpius] Apollonios, Prophet.[607]

Antinoöpolis; now in Cairo[608]

To Antinous Epiphanes. Pheidos Akulas [Julius Fidus Aquila], Commander [*epistrategos*] of the Thebaïd.

Bithynion-Claudiopolis[609]

To the New[610] God Antinous, in thanks, from Sosthénes.

Alexandria[611]

The City of the Alexandrians and Hermopolis the Great and the Council of New Greek Antinoians, and the Greeks living in the Delta of Egypt, and those living under the law of the Thebaïs, honored Poplios Ailios [Popilius Aelius?] Aristeides Theodoros for his manly virtues and for his words.

Alexandria[612]

Isidoros Didymos son of Didymos, priest of Antinous.

---

[606] Meyer, pp. 172-173.

[607] This inscription is in Greek, and a *prophétes* in Greek signified an Egyptian-style priest.

[608] Meyer, p. 167.

[609] Arthur Darby Nock, "Deification and Julian," *The Journal of Roman Studies* 47 (1957), pp. 115-123 at 120 and n40.

[610] Or possibly "young."

[611] Dietrichson, pp. 327-328 §6.

[612] Dietrichson, p. 329 §12.

Athens, Theatre of Dionysos[613]

For the priest of Antinous Choreios, from the Dionysian artists.

Corinth[614]

Hostilios Markellos, the priest of Antinous.

Delphi[615]

Antinous the Hero Before-the-Gate [*Propylaios*], set up by the Amphictyones.

Mantineia[616]

Eurykles Herculanus built this *stoa* with the seats for the city of Mantineia, and for our fellow countryman, the god Antinous, by his heirs.

Mantineia[617]

Doxa's son, Isochrysus, whom the god Antinous himself loved dearly as one enthroned with the immortals, Epitynchanus, his father, made in the form of a bronze image there and erected a statue of his son by the decree of his fatherland.

---

[613] Meyer, p. 165.
[614] Dietrichson, pp. 329 §11.
[615] Meyer, pp. 170-171.
[616] Meyer, pp. 166-167.
[617] Caroline Vout, *Power and Eroticism in Imperial Rome* (Cambridge: Cambridge University Press, 2007), p. 123n137.

Mylai[618]

My father has set me, Antinous, up [in the form of a statue] because of my beauty; as a result of this, my mother has given me an everlasting memorial.

Leptis Magna[619]

Antinous the Fruitful God, set up by the citizens of Leptis Magna.

Oxyrhynchus Papyrus: Instructions to *Decaproti*[620]

...Aurelius Alexander (?), ex-*hypomnematographos*, *strategos* of the Oxyrhynchite nome, to the Aurelii Alexander and Stratonicus and associates, *decaptroti* of parts of the lower toparchy, his dearest colleagues, greetings.

In accordance with the written instructions given by my lord the most perfect *rationalis* Valerius Euethius, have loaded onto the public boat whose emblem is Panantinous, of 2,500 *artabas* capacity, under the command of Honoratianus, shipper, one thousand...hundred and...-ty six *artabas* of purest wheat, free from all badness, by the public measure, according to the prescribed measurement...(and for)...per cent...(total) 1900 *artabas*.

---

[618] Meyer, p. 125. While Meyer concludes that this may be the Arcadian villa of Antinous' parents, Vout, p. 131n160, argues that this need not be the case.

[619] Meyer, pp. 165-166.

[620] J. E. G. Whitehorne, "§3980: Instructions to Decaproti," in E. W. Handley, H. G. Ioannidou, P. J. Parsons, & J. E. G. Whitehorne (eds.), *The Oxyrhynchus Papyri* 59 (London: Egypt Exploration Society, 1992), pp. 99-101.

Edict of Hadrian on the Inundation of the Nile[621]

Imperator Caesar Trajan Hadrian Augustus, son of divine Traian Parthicus, grandson of divine Nerva, *pontifex maximus*, [holder of the] tribunician power for the twentieth time, imperator for the second time, thrice consul, *Pater Patriae* [father of the country], proclaims:

Even though in the previous years the Nile achieved not only its full rise but the greater rise which was almost unprecedented and, as it reached all the country, was itself the cause that the land brought forth its very plentiful and splendid crops, nevertheless, having learned that the rise of the Nile fell short or failed completely this time as it did last year, I realized that it was necessary to make some considerate adjustment for the farmers, although I expect--be it said with permission of the god--that in the oncoming years, even if now some dearth has occurred, the Nile itself and the earth will compensate, on account of the alternating nature of things in that changes occur, yesterday from a good flood and a plentiful crop to want, tomorrow from want to abundance. With Good Fortune: I decree that this year's tribute in cash shall be distributed for those from the Thebaid, who are the most likely to have suffered from the dearth, into five annual installments, for those from the Heptanomia into four, for those from Lower Egypt into three, with the understanding that those who wish may pay every six months, although the term remains of five years for those from the Thebaid, four years for those from the Heptanomia, and three years for those from Lower Egypt.

Published at Alexandria, Year twenty [136 CE], *Payni* 6.

---

[621] James Henry Oliver, *Greek Constitutions of Early Roman Emperors from Inscriptions and Papyri* (Philadelphia: American Philosophical Society, 1989), §88, p. 224.

Oxyrhynchus Papyrus: Petition to the *Epistrategos* after the Excessive Inundation of the Nile, 132 CE[622]

To Julius Varianus, *epistrategos* of the Heptanomis and Arsinoite nome, from Dionysia daughter of Chaeremon, her mother being Hermione daughter of Chaeremon, inhabitants of the metropolis of the Oxyrhynchite nome. A dispute arose between me and one Sarapion son of Mnesitheus, who with regard to a vineyard and some corn-land which I bought from his father as long ago as the 11th year of Hadrianus Caesar the lord, having paid to his father himself and to a creditor of his the price agreed upon and having received the regular official contract of the sale, declared that I held this land on mortgage. Claudius Quintianus who was then *epistrategos* heard the case and referred it to his highness the praefect. Thereupon I attended at the praefect's court, and when my opponent paid no attention and failed to appear I presented his highness the praefect with a petition, of which I have appended a copy, narrating in full the state of the affair; and he sent me on to you, my lord, to have the case tried. Since my opponent even now is absent and the time for sowing is imminent and the repair of what has been swept away by the river requires my presence, I beg you, if it please you, to permit me to sail back and have the case decided by you on the spot, that I may obtain redress. Farewell. The copy of the petition which I presented to his highness the praefect is as follows:~

To his highness the praefect Titus Flavius Titianus from Dionysia daughter of Chaeremon, her mother being Hermione, inhabitants of Oxyrhynchus. A certain Sarapion son of Mnesitheus, of the said city, charged my mother Hermione before Claudius Quintianus, late epistrategus of the Heptanomis, with poisoning, and at the same time invented a claim with regard to certain property of which he said he was defrauded, but

---

[622] Bernard P. Grenfell and Arthur S. Hunt (eds.), *The Oxyrhynchus Papyri* 3 (London: Egypt Exploration Society, 1903), §486, pp. 180-183.

which I, Dionysia, bought in accordance with official contracts, having paid the price of it to his father when he was alive and to creditors of his said father who held the land in question on mortgage; and he asserted that it had been registered in security. The *epistrategos* referred the whole case to your beneficence, and it happened that my mother died before the trial, while I thereupon in consequence of the letter of the *epistrategos* ordering me and Sarapion to sail down to Alexandria presented myself here, but Sarapion has paid no attention to the instruction to sail down. Since therefore news has reached me while staying here that all my property has been lost through the excessive rise of the most sacred Nile, both buildings, lands, and dykes, I entreat you, my lord praefect, in the continued absence of my opponent, to permit me to sail back in order that I may obtain justice there and that I may not in addition to the loss of my property also perish of hunger, that I may obtain redress. Farewell.

The 16th year of Hadrianus Caesar, Phaophi 12. Endorsed. If this is true, petition the *epistrategos*, delivering to him a copy of this.

Oxyrhynchus Papyrus: Cult Calendar[623]

Hathyr 3 (30th of October): Death and Deification of Antinous~ "On the...of Zeus [Panhellenios Eleutherios, i.e. Hadrian] and consecration of Antinous...to the house of Brittanicus [a reference to Commodus?]...and to the shrine of Fortune and to the Serapeum..."

Choiak 4 (27th of November): Birthday of Antinous~"On the

---

[623] J. W. B. Barns, Peter Parsons, John Rea, and Eric G. Turner (eds.), *The Oxyrhynchus Papyri* Volume 31 (London: Egypt Exploration Society, 1966), §2553, pp. 72-77. A third-person singular verb is always used in these entries, thus we can assume that "The priest" is the subject referred to always; it is also possible that it indicates a Roman bureaucratic official taking his seat for legal affairs as well as religious ritual obligations, but this is uncertain.

birthday of Antinous he sacrifices horse-rites...three days, whenever they are posted..."

(between 30th of November and 15th of December): Victories of Deified Marcus Aurelius; Festival held because of a banquet; day on which the Deified Hadrian entered the city [of Oxyrhynchus?]~"on behalf of the victories of the deified Aurelius Antoninus...and sits in the Lageum...and booths of spectacles whenever...contest celebrated as a result of a bequest...he offers incense in the Serapeum and sits in the Lageum...On the day on which the deified Hadrian...the city...gymnasiarchs enter the Sebasteum and sacrifices and the...and goes in procession and sacrifices and sits in the Lageum, horse-rites."

Choiak 19 (15th of December): Birthday of the deified Lucius Verus~"On the birthday of the deified Verus enters the Sebasteum and sacrifices and...on the steps of the processional way and into the Serapeum and..."

[Final fragments may indicate Tybi 4 (30th of December), the birthday of Titus, Tybi 29 (24th of January), the birthday of Hadrian, and the existence of two temples, a Herakleion and an Apolloneion.]

432

Altercatio Hadriani Augusti et Epicteti Philosophi

Hadrian was famed for his interactions with a number of philosophers (including some rabbis, which have been recorded in the Talmud) and his promiscuous interest in the subject, and this particular text is one of the earliest which attributes a philosophical dialogue to him. Later ones include *Secundus the Silent Philosopher*,[624] which is very directly based upon the present text. This one dates from the latter part of the second century CE.

The text upon which my translation is based is found in Daly and Suchier's 1939 edition,[625] and the present translation was published earlier in *The Phillupic Hymns*.[626]

The Cross-Examination of the Emperor Hadrian and the Philosopher Epictetus.

H: What will we have, if you were unbound from your girding, or if you were to denude me? Consider the body, which even you are able to instruct.

E: It is an epistle.

H: What is an epistle?

E: A quiet announcement.

H: What is a picture?

---

[624] Ben Edwin Perry (ed./trans.), *Secundus the Silent Philosopher: The Greek Life of Secundus, Critically Edited and Restored So Far As Possible, Together with Translations of the Greek and Oriental Versions, the Latin and Oriental Texts, and a Study of the Tradition* (Ithaca: Cornell University Press, 1964).

[625] Lloyd William Daly and Walther Suchier, *Altercatio Hadriani Augusti et Epicteti Philosophi* (Urbana, IL: The University of Illinois Press, 1939).

[626] P. Sufenas Virius Lupus, *The Phillupic Hymns* (Eugene: Bibliotheca Alexandrina, 2008), pp. 233-237.

E: A true deception.

H: What is this you have taught?

E: We see indeed a painted apple, flowers, animals, gold, silver, and yet they are not true.

H: What is gold?

E: The purchase of death.

H: What is silver?

E: The place of envy.

H: What is iron?

E: The implement of all arts.

H: What is a sword?

E: The ruler of fortresses.

H: What is a gladiator?

E: A murderer without guilt.

H: Who are they who depart sanity?

E: They who are concerned with strange business.

H: By what consideration is a man not made tired?

E: By the making of profit.

H: What is a friend?

E: Harmony.

H: What is the longest thing?

E: Anticipation.

H: What is anticipation?

E: Sleep for being vigilant, expecting dangerous events.

F: What is that which man is not able to see?

E: Another heart.

H: By what thing do men err?

E: Cupidity.

H: What is liberty?

E: Innocence.

H: What leads and is wretched to the community?

E: Birth and death.

H: What is the best, and indeed, the worst?

E: A word.

H: What is that which is pleasing to some and displeasing to others?

434

E: Life.

H: What is the best life?

E: The shortest one.

H: What thing is most certain?

E: Death.

H: What is death?

E: Perpetual security.

H: What is death?

E: The fearing of many, if the wise man lives, inimical to life, the spirit of the living, the dread of parents, the spoils of freedom, the cause of testaments, the conversation after destruction, the end of woefulness, the forgetfulness after memory, the leading torch, the load of burial, the inscription of a monument; death is the end of all evil.

H: Why are the dead crowned?

E: As a testament for the crossing over of life itself.

H: Why are the dead's thumbs tied together?

E: So that he may not know that he is twain after death.

H: What is the corpse-bearer?

E: The one whom many avoid but none escape.

H: What is a funeral pyre?

E: Contentment of believers, the repayment of debts.

H: What is a trumpet?

E: A battle incitement, the army-camp signifier, an exhortation of the arena, the signal for the opening of the theatre, the funeral lament.

H: What is a monument?

E: Branded stones, the spectacle of leisurely passers-by.

H: What is a poor man?

E: Namely he whom all behold in a barren pit and yet they leave him in that place.

H: What is a man?

E: Similar to a bath: the first room is the tepidarium, the warm bath, in which infants are born thoroughly anointed; the second room, the sudatorium, the sweat-room, is boyhood; the third room is the assa, the dry-room, the preference of youth; the fourth room, the frigidarium, the cold bath, is appropriate to old age, in which sense comes to all.

H: What is a man?

E: Similar to a fruit: Fruits that hang on trees, thus even are our bodies: when ripe they fall, or else they become embittered.

H: What is a man?

E: As a lamp placed in the wind.

H: What is a man?

E: A stranger of a place, the image of law, a tale of calamity, a slave of death, the delay of life; that with which Fortune would frequently make its own game.

H: What is fortune?

E: Namely the matron of nobility impinging upon servants themselves.

H: What is fortune?

E: Without justice, the closest turning-point, the fall of the good of another; at which's coming, brilliance is shown, at which's recession, shadow is made.

H: Indeed, how many are they with fortune?

E: Three: one who is blind, who impinges where he pleases; and another who is insane, who concedes, I summon to be removed; the third is deaf, who does not favorably hear the entreaties of mercy.

H: What are the gods?

E: A constellation of eyes, the spirits of understanding; if you fear, they are fearful; if you are temperate, they are sanctified.

H: What is the sun?

E: The splendor of the spheres; which takes away and places the day; through which it is given to us to know the course of the hours.

H: What is the moon?

E: The handmaid of days, the eye of night, the torch of darkness.

H: What is heaven?

E: The summit of boundlessness.

H: What is heaven?

E: The atmosphere of the world.

H: What are stars?

E: The destiny of humans.

H: What are the stars?

E: The omens of navigators.

H: What is the earth?

E: The granary of Ceres.

H: What is the earth?

E: The cellar of life.

H: What is the sea?

E: The way of doubt.

H: What is a boat?

E: A wandering house.

H: What is a boat?

E: A guest-house where it pleases.

H: What is a boat?

E: The spirit of Neptune, the archive of a year's course.

H: What is a sailor?

E: A lover of the open sea, forsaker of firmness, a despiser of life and death, from which he is a client.

H: What is sleep?

E: An image of death.

H: What is night?

E: Rest for working, the profit of weariness.

H: What is a pillow?

E: The wish of sleeplessness.

H: Why is Venus depicted nude?

E: Nude Venus painted, Lovers are shown nude; for whom nudity pleases, it is proper to dismiss nudity.

H: Why is Venus married to Vulcan?

E: To show love by the heat of fire.

H: Why is Venus a squinter?

E: Because love is crooked.

H: What is love?

E: The annoyance of heart's leisure, shamefulness in boys, reddening in virgins, fury in women, ardor in youth, laughter in age, it is worthlessness in the mocking of fault.

H: What is a god?

E: That which maintains all things.

H: What is a sacrifice?

E: A lessening.

H: What is without fellowship?

E: Kingship.

H: What is a king?

E: A piece of the gods.

H: What is Caesar?

E: The head of light for the people.

H: What is a senator?

E: A splendid ornament of a city of citizens.

H: What is a soldier?

E: The wall of authority, defender of the fatherland, a glorious servant, an indicator of power.

H: What is Rome?

E: The fount of authority of the sphere of earth, mother of nations, possessor of things, the common-dwelling of the Romans, consecration of eternal peace.

H: What is Victory?

E: Discordance of war, love of peace.

H: What is peace?

E: Generosity of calm.

H: What is the forum?

E: The temple of liberty, the arena of disputes.

H: What are friends?

E: They are the site of support.

H: What is a friend?

E: As similar to a citrus fruit: blessed on the outside, for in its heart is concealed bitterness and malice.

H: What is a parasite?

E: Those who are baited with crumbs like fish.

V.
OTHER TEXTS AND RITUAL PROCEDURES

The Child Armed and the Son of Evil

Ninety days after the death of Antinous, it is reckoned by the Ekklesía Antínoou that in the Underworld, a process was occurring with Antinous, in which he fought and slew in turn each of a number of ruling *archons* (in the Gnostic sense) of the world, thus winning for all humans—like other savior deities who harrowed the Otherworld, like Dionysos, Orpheus, and even Jesus—their rightful freedom and ultimate salvation from oblivion in further death or harm after their bodily death. The occasion of this accomplishment is celebrated as a holiday in the Ekklesía Antínoou on January 29, when Antinous is victorious as Liberator, and then gives way to his aspect as Navigator, guiding souls both in the afterlife and in the material world. It would be appropriate to recite or sing the following piece, from the *Coptic Manichean Songbook*[627] (a text which was found in the Egyptian city of Medinet Madi, where a major temple to Isis-Renenutet was located, and was a center of both native Egyptian and Hellenic religion) on that occasion.

The Child Armed and the Son of Evil

The child got through his months
until he could walk.

The little one among the tall stepped in.
He took up arms. He armed his waist.

C. R. C. Allberry (trans.) and Willis Barnstone (ed.), "*The Coptic Manichean Songbook*: The Child Armed and the Son of Evil," in Willis Barnstone and Marvin Meyer (eds.), *The Gnostic Bible: Gnostic Texts of Mystical Wisdom from the Ancient and Medieval Worlds—Pagan, Jewish, Christian, Mandaean, Manichean, Islamic, and Cathar* (Boston and London: Shambhala, 2003), p. 620.

He leapt and raced into the abyss.
He leapt and got to their center to battle them.

He humiliated the son of evil
and his seven companions and twelve slaves.

He wrecked their camp and cast it down.
He put out their roaring fire.

He bound the miserable myrmidons there,
who plotted to make war.

He grabbed their armor hanging there, readied
for war, destroyed their readied traps.

He ripped up their outspread nets.
He released the fish to go out to sea.

He let the birds fly up into space.
He let the sheep into their folds.

He seized the evil one's wealth. He went off
with it and took it up to the land of rest.

So he saved what the living took.
They will come back to what is theirs.

In Praise of the *Puer Aeternus*

Among the many titles which could be applied to Antinous—and, indeed, which I have applied to him in certain texts I've composed that are given above—is *puer aeternus*, "eternal youth." This term was originally applied to Iakkhos by Ovid in his *Metamorphoses*, but it could also be applied to Eros and Dionysos, all of whom are deities with whom Antinous was syncretized. However, it also is used as a psychological term for a certain type of negative, "Peter Pan" personality, which never desires to grow up, take responsibility, or really live in the world. This need not be the case, of course, but nonetheless, that is some of the baggage of the term in the modern world.

In Marie-Louise Von Franz's book *The Problem of the Puer Aeternus*, she gives excerpts from a text that she translated, by Bruno Goetz, called *The Kingdom Without Space* (the second edition of which was published in 1925; it is unknown when the first was published), which features a *puer aeternus*-type character called Fo. It begins with two poems that, in Von Franz's summary, could very easily be applied in praise of Antinous as *puer aeternus*. I have also given a prose excerpt from the text which could also easily apply to him.

When all we knew, destroyed, in ruins lay,
Encircled in death's mighty folds of darkness,
Our burning spirits strove
After the dream which led us on.

Far from our home and our maternal land,
On undetermined waves our ship drives on.
Laughing boldly we had ventured forth
As Vikings, searching undiscovered shores.

442

And if by night and horror overtaken, thou sing'st
Us songs of other homes,
Then phantoms vanish into gentle mist,

The world dissolves in dance and rhythm,
The stars disperse a fortune long delayed,
And radiant shines the kingdom without space.[628]

When the dark cloud
Withdrew not from the sky
And from all the world
The sun was hid,

Out of the depths
A new light neared,
And in our sleep we knew
That thou wert there.

O the suns that come
From the depths of thine eyes,
And from thy lips
The flowing streams of love.

Across the waves of an ethereal sea
The splendor of thy limbs
Entices us
To flaming courage.

Eternal youth,
Encircled by the music of the stars,
Giver of comfort,
Sparkling, free, and beautiful.

---

[628] Marie-Louise Von Franz, *The Problem of the Puer Aeternus* (Toronto: Inner City Books, 2000), p. 177.

Men and women
Dance in thy glory,
Driving into death
For sight of thee.

Forever into light
Thy white form calls
Wave after wave,
And never do we age.[629]

The circles are closing. Everything is fulfilled. My shadow has freed your shadow. The enemy is destroyed. Where on the wide earth are you? Beyond the great seas which divide us I hear your voice. Day and night, night and day, you wander over the plains and climb the high mountains. Golden ships with red sails carry you across the sea. Swarms of birds surround your head. Over wild roads you come nearer and nearer. In time it will be morning, and you will appear before me naked and glowing, stars in your hair, and your cool lips will kiss my beating heart. The earth will no longer be dumb. Your words will call all to life, your breath come from everybody, your love blossom from every heart. The cross will be raised. The newly risen will shed their blood into the veins of the world and will transform from one form into another. The new play begins. Grapes darken and await you. See, how we rest, breathing in happiness. Everything is still. Come to us in the foliage of night in naked conflagration, young flame, singing flame, Master and Child.[630]

---

[629] Von Franz, pp. 177-178.
[630] Von Franz, p. 273.

444

Completing a Ritual

So, you've prayed your guts out; you've made food, water, and incense offerings; you've had an entire feast for the gods; you've purified yourself by immersion in water; you've sung some songs and performed some dances; you've even invoked and devoked the Obelisk of Antinous.

Well, now what?

As there are multiple preludes and preliminary rites for many of my more formal rituals for Antinous, it only seems appropriate to have several that can follow and bring the events to a more appropriate closing. There are two procedures that I have often done, either together or separately depending on the context, the occasion, and who the other participants happen to be. The first is often done on Foundation Day, but can be changed slightly, omitting specific references to that particular holy day. It is a sort of meditation on the possibility of human deification and apotheosis, and draws upon a particular statement of Cicero.[631]

Cicero in his *Laws* once stated:

"Now the law which prescribes the worship of those of the human race who have been deified, such as Hercules and the rest, makes it clear that while the souls of all men are immortal, those of good and brave men are divine. It is a good thing also that Intellect, Loyalty, Virtue and Good Faith should be deified by the stroke of a pen, and in Rome temples have been dedicated by the State to all of these qualities, the purpose being that those who possess them (and all good men do) should believe that the gods themselves are established in their own souls."

---

[631] Found in Stewart Perowne, *Roman Mythology* (London and New York: Paul Hamlyn, 1969), p. 83.

Thus the hero, the god, the once-human Antinous, the Good God of Undefeated Youth, the Beautiful Boy of Bithynia, is not but the herald and the exemplar that all these good things are within each one of us.

If you look upon him and see beauty, *it is because you are beautiful;*
If you look upon him and see a god, *it is because you are a god yourself.*

This day of Foundation—of the beginning of a cult practice, of the creation of a new city, of the discovery of Antinous' body—is nothing if his rituals are not remembered daily, if his city is not re-established in every person's heart, and if one has not found one's own body to be the body of divinity.

For those who understand these mysteries, fear and doubt like clear water off a boat's keel wash away without harm.

Vel in limine mundi, Ecce! Ego semper sum coram te!

Even at the edge of the world, behold! I am in your presence!

Foundation Day has been completed; for another year, this vow has been willingly and deservedly fulfilled.

At this point, the second procedure can begin. Especially at Foundation Day, but also at other major public rituals, I have often ended by taking a small stone, and have written the letters *V S L M* on it. This is an abbreviation that often occurs on Roman altars and other votive inscriptions, which stands for *VOTVM SOLVIT LIBENS MERITO,* "Willingly and deservedly fulfilled the vow." I say the full phrase four times, inscribing each of the four letters singly as I say the phrase, with a further phrase in between each letter, as follows:

VOTVM SOLVIT LIBENS MERITO,
Ave Vive Antinoe;
VOTVM SOLVIT LIBENS MERITO,
Dona Nobis Pacem;
VOTVM SOLVIT LIBENS MERITO,
Gratias Agemus;[632]
VOTVM SOLVIT LIBENS MERITO.

If the other activities at the end of the ritual do not serve to "ground" one's energy and efforts, then encapsulating the ritual by this short recapitulation of the main actions of it—praise of Antinous, asking for peace, and giving thanks—should serve to do so, particularly since a rock, an indisputable symbol of the earth element and thus of "earthing" or "grounding," is used in order to bring it about.

What does one do with the *V S L M* stone afterwards? This varies from person to person and occasion to occasion.

The first time I did a ritual for Antinous was on Foundation Day in 2002, and at the time (and for the next two Foundation Days in 2003 and 2004), I lived in Ireland. I was looking all over for a stone on the ground, in a planter, or somewhere in one of the lawns or green areas at my college, but could not find anything larger than a very small pebble, as the student center at the college had recently been renovated and it had a huge expanse of glass for its entire front wall, thus I suspect that any potential projectiles that could damage the property were removed. After gathering all else that was necessary for the ritual, I was musing to a friend of mine that all that was now needed was a stone, and I was wondering where one could be found. I described what the desired stone would look like: it would have one or more somewhat flat sides, and be about three or four inches in length, and if it were somewhat brick-like, that would be very suitable. Suddenly, something caught my eye above a bus shelter, and when I went over to examine what it was, I found on the top of the bus shelter a small part

---

[632] This means "thank you" in Latin (literally "we do thanks"); the first person plural form is *Agemus*, the first person singular is *Ago*; the appropriate inflection of the verb should accompany whether one is doing the particular ritual with others or by oneself.

of a brick that was the perfect size for a stone for the *V S L M* part of the ritual! I had literally described an ideal, and with close observation, found it for the taking less than five yards from where I was standing at the time.

However, in keeping with the Celtic tradition of depositing votive objects into bodies of water, for the period of 2002-2004 I immediately deposited the stones into the local river after the Foundation Day rituals were completed, usually processing down to the river in silence with the other ritual attendees, and then letting out joyous cries afterwards before "going for a pint."

In the years since then, I have kept the stone for a year, and on the following year, at the very beginning of the Foundation Day ritual, I have dropped the stone into a bowl of water. I ask all of the ritual attendees to bring a stone and do likewise, putting all of their worries and troubles of the past year into their stone, and dropping it into the purifying and transformative waters of the Nile, just as Antinous' body fell into the Nile and was transformed thereby into a divinity. As we re-found the cultus of Antinous each year on that date, the cultus of the past year no longer exists, and the cultus of the year to follow emerges from the actions done in the ritual itself, not from the stone and the vows of the previous year.

When I have performed other rituals, I have often given the *V S L M* stone to one of the participants or co-ritualists afterwards. Some of them have begun making *V S L M* stones of their own, and are building small cairns or herms of them in their garden or other ritual spaces. What one chooses to do with the stone should be a matter for one's own decision, as with nearly everything that takes place in the context of Antinoan devotion. If Antinous or the other gods, heroes, *Divi, Sancti*, ancestors, land spirits, and any other spiritual beings do not make a particular preference known to you, use your own best judgment.

Of course, at the end of a ritual there are a number of other practical concerns to look after. If you're in a shared space, or have rented a semi-public facility, you'll have to have your attentions directed toward cleaning up after yourself, and making sure that you leave the space "better than you found it."

If you happen to be doing a ritual or devotional practice in your own space, develop a protocol for when to remove food offerings from your shrine or altar area and how to dispose of them—whether that means burning them, burying them, depositing them in water, or consuming them yourself. If you lit candles, which are literally an "offering of light" to Antinous and the other deities and spiritual beings concerned, do not leave them unattended if you decide to let them burn out (as I often do when I use tea lights, which don't usually burn for more than a few hours), and then clear them away as necessary, or simply extinguish longer-burning candles and store them for later use.

If you follow an Egyptian protocol for your deity images, you might want to cover them up after your ritual, or return them to their *naos* until the following day (or the next ritual, depending on how often you perform your devotions). While it isn't always possible to keep the entire room, or even the immediate area around, one's home shrine completely clean and tidy, one should certainly do everything possible not to leave one's actual shrine or altar space dirty or overly-cluttered, and it should be cleaned on a regular basis.

If you are performing a ritual or any devotional activities with others, thanking them by name and wishing them well in their departures, whether with hugs or handshakes, and whether with standardized language or spontaneous expressions, should certainly be a part of the proceedings. Always try to remember that the ways in which we treat our fellow humans, both in ritual and outside of it, are just as important as the ways in which we relate to our deities. If you wish for courtesy and favor to be shown to you, then do not fail to demonstrate courtesy, good manners, and favor towards others. The gods certainly do not demand this of everyone, but I am quite assured that they notice and appreciate it when it is done!

Devotio Antinoo,
Conclusion:
What is "*Devotio*"?

The entirety of this book has proceeded before now without delving at all into the meaning of the Latin word *devotio*. It has been assumed all along that *devotio* is the transparent root of the English term "devotion," and that what devotion entails is obvious. In actuality, this is not the case.

It may, however, be useful first to examine what the English term means and how it is usually understood. "Devotion" in English carries the meanings of profound dedication; consecration; earnest attachment to a person, cause, or ideal; assignment or appropriations to any purpose (e.g. devoting one's time or wealth to someone or something); or, in the specific context of religion, a religious observance, or a form of prayer or style of worship, often for specialist usage. All of these meanings certainly apply to the larger project of *Devotio Antinoo*, devotion to Antinous, but also to the present book, its purpose, and the activities described therein and the texts which exemplify such devotion.

A Sanskrit concept that is quite prevalent in modern Hinduism is often how devotion is understood in modern polytheist contexts: that concept is *bhakti*, which is often translated as "devotion," but which more accurately means "participation." The creation of relationship and a sense of belonging, both with one's community of fellow devotees, but also with the being who is the target of one's devotions, is quite essential in understanding *bhakti*. It comes from roots meaning "to share in," "to belong to," and "to worship," and a similar root gives the term *bhajan*, a devotional song or chant to a deity. Indeed, this style of devotion, and *bhajan* and *kirtan* singing, have had a profound influence on my own spiritual practices, and a great deal of the hymnody given in the present volume! *Bhakti*, however, also covers further semantic ground, and includes the intense love one feels for a

451

deity, the bliss derived from immersion in this love, and even in some contexts, intense and exclusive devotional feelings toward only one deity. As a polytheist outside of the Hindu tradition, I do not find the latter concern to be necessary or applicable to my own experience—intense love and devotion for one deity leads to intense love and devotion for many of them. In a polytheist framework, like that of ancient Egypt, Greece, and Rome, no deity arises in a vacuum and is not in some manner connected to one or more other deities, and the same is true of heroes, honored ancestors, and many other divine beings. So, with the exception of the exclusivistic shades of meaning that can be implied with the term, *bhakti* is a useful concept in imagining modern polytheist devotion generally speaking, and in understanding it in the particular context of Antinous and the works presented in the present volume.

While *devotio* was used in medieval Latin Christian contexts with much the same meaning as it has in English today, as discussed above—in addition to the many comparable manners in which it is similar to *bhakti*, in terms of dedication and particular spiritual practices done in association with a deity, saint, or other supernatural being in order to foster personal relationships between the human worshipper and the divine being/s concerned—the original meaning of *devotio* in ancient Rome was much different. *Devotio* could carry the meaning of consecrating or devoting, but also cursing, or even enchantment or incantation. *Devotio* is a verbal noun derived from the verb *devoto, devotare*, meaning "to consecrate" or "to devote to death," and/or the verb *devoveo, devovere*, meaning "to consecrate," "to devote to a god or to death," "to curse or execrate," "to enchant or bewitch," or "to give up." Its past participle as a substantive, *devotus/a/um*, includes the meanings "a devoted person," "an accursed person," "someone attached to another person," or a "faithful follower."

It would have been good to have known this from the start, perhaps, then...!?!

In the particular context of Antinous' life and death, *devotio* has a quite specific meaning. In the *Historia Augusta*, there is the suggestion (among several possibilties given) that Antinous' death was a willing sacrifice on behalf of Hadrian—a *devotum*.[633] Suc an expiatory sacrifice was not unknown in Roman practices. While I find this possibility not only unlikely, but sensationalistic, and even very specifically homophobic (since it often is accompanied by the suggestion that Antinous knew his time in the sun was coming to an end, and he would never live down that he was the Emperor's "love-slave," and therefore suicide under the appearance of heroic sacrifice was far preferable to living longer),[634] nonetheless the specific usage of this terminology in relation to Antinous' death begs a number of questions that need to be addressed at present.

First, let me make the following matter entirely clear: the older meanings of any word, or older understandings of any concepts, aren't necessarily truer or better than modern ones. As a reconstructionist organization, the Ekklesía Antínoou looks backward for inspiration, and for direct sources on many matters relating to Antinous, Hadrian, syncretism, and the religions and cultures of Greece, Rome, and Egypt; however, it also recognizes—entirely in line with reconstructionist methodologies, despite many erroneous suggestions to the contrary by poorly informed groups and individuals—that we live in the present, we function within our own semantic and cultural spectrums the best and most logically, and no matter how well we may understand the past on its own terms, we do not live in it. The Ekklesía Antínoou is a religious group of the twenty-first century, not the second century, and though we honor Antinous as a god, a hero, and a *daimon* as people did from the second through sixth centuries of late antiquity, nonetheless even our understandings of the ancient world's understandings are modern, and not necessarily accurate in replicating every detail or nuance that was recognized in the past. Nor should they even attempt to be, because it is impossible to do so!

Before addressing these matters of *devotio* in the ancient sense, however, their connection to the death of Antinous, and the possible

---

[633] Royston Lambert, *Beloved and God: The Story of Hadrian and Antinous* (New York: Viking, 1984), pp. 130-142 (esp. 134); Daniel Ogden, *Greek and Roman Necromancy* (Princeton: Princeton University Press, 2001), p. 198.

[634] This is the viewpoint adopted in Dylan Bickerstaffe, "Death in the Nile: The Birth of Ancient Egypt's Last God," *KMT: A Modern Journal of Ancient Egypt* 19.2 (Summer 2008), pp. 74-82.

implications of these for the modern devotee of Antinous, there is another matter to address. There is a building conflict, which is apparent but often overstated, which suggests that modern pagan and polytheist groups will soon experience a clash between devotional or "congregational" members and mystical or "initiated" members. Just as many major religions worldwide have specialists who are ritual and institutional functionaries, but also "religious" who have devoted their lives to intense service of their deities, but likewise they also have a lay population that takes place in regular worship and seasonal activities, but may not be primarily religious in their overall lives, or they may have some dedication but due to the other demands of jobs, families, and so forth, they do not have the ability to devote as much mental or spiritual space, time, and energy to spiritual matters. Many modern forms of paganism were started in the last five or six decades as initiatory traditions intent on imparting particular mysteries to individuals who aspired to spiritual adepthood. However, many modern pagans and polytheists are more interested in the cultural aspects of paganism, the communal atmosphere, and of simply being a part of such a vibrant and interesting religious movement as modern paganism and polytheism happens to offer, without a desire to become initiated into a particular tradition. Indeed, this is exactly how things functioned in the ancient world: not everyone in Athens was an initiate of Eleusis. Therefore, a split between what has been called the "devotional" and the "mystical" has been proposed as a major problem that will impact the development of paganism and polytheism in the years to come.

From my viewpoint—biased though it may be—this set of concerns is entirely artificial. Taking a cue from the *bhakti* movement, which is a popular and widespread phenomenon amongst modern Hindus, and has been for the past five or six centuries, there need be no automatic distinction between these two elements of mysticism and devotion. If "mysticism" is direct contact with deities, then true devotion depends upon it; and if "devotion" is simply being a part of a community, spiritual lineage, or religious tradition, then that "participation" (the most accurate meaning of *bhakti*) is a kind of mysticism and connection to something wider and larger than oneself in itself. In my own mind and understanding, despite some occultists and magical practitioners, as well as other modern pagans and polytheists, having opinions that are quite to the contrary, I think that there is no difference between true devotion and true mysticism.

While that debate and its intricacies could be enlarged upon further, for now let us leave it at that, and move on to the more pressing matter of Antinous' *devotio* as it relates to death.

To have a devotion to Antinous in the modern world does not, by any means, suggest that one will *die for him*. However, questions like "What will you die for?" are the fodder of so many discussions of religion, particularly with Christians and Muslims, that demonstrate that their unswerving "faith" and the necessity of such fervent "belief" is the *sine qua non* of "true religion," without which any religious activity is simply an ineffectual hobby at best, and a self-deluded quagmire at worst. This kind of construction highlights the differences between the creedal religions (of which Christianity and Islam are the only full examples), which are based on belief, and the religions of practice, conduct, and experience, as paganism and polytheism in both their ancient and modern forms happen to be.

This is not to suggest that religions of belief do not have practices to follow, conduct to be concerned with, or an experiential basis. Likewise, it isn't that there aren't beliefs involved in religions of practice, conduct, and experience—indeed, in terms of polytheism, thinking that any of the matter of the worship of or engagement with the gods is a worthwhile concern at all is a belief in itself! But, in such experiential, practical religions, the particularity of one's beliefs are not the main issue of focus; nor are the creedal religions as often concerned with practice or experience as they are with the beliefs about certain experiences (including which ones are valid) and the beliefs underlying certain practices being of primary concern. But with these general differences in mind, we can examine how an experiential and practical relgious framework like polytheism works in terms of such suggestions on what is and is not "worth dying for."

While the notions of "belief" and "faith," both of which are often used as synonymous in creedal religious frameworks (and which have even been used as synonyms for "religion" itself), are prone to many different possible definitions than the ones used most commonly, the idea that belief is an assumption about an aspect of reality that is accepted as true despite lack of definitive evidence is highly problematic from the viewpoint of an experiential religion. No one would expect acceptance of the existence of any of the gods in the context of a religions of experience like polytheism unless there was some experience on the part of an individual of that reality of the god or gods concerned. It would be likewise with many other things that some people say they would be willing to die for: no one "dies for love" because it is a beautiful idea, they tend to offer to die for it because they have experienced it directly (endless romantic pop songs to the contrary!). The suggestion, therefore, that one must die on behalf of their belief in a deity is ridiculous; but, if someone was willing to die on behalf of their admitted and acknowledged experience of a deity, their *gnosis* of such a divine being's reality, that would be another matter entirely. No one should die on behalf of what they believe in, from the polytheist experiential-practical viewpoint, but people are entirely free to die on behalf of what they *actually know*.

Belief in Antinous (or, indeed, in any deity) is not required of anyone in a polytheist framework, and therefore the regulation of belief is not in the interests of the Ekklesía Antínoou, nor of any polytheist individual or organization in relation to their particular deities, because there is no suggestion that it is "necessary for salvation" to have such beliefs. I would argue that this is one reason why polytheistic religions are, in many respects, superior to certain dominant creedal religions, because in the very pluralistic world we currently inhabit (and which has been the only actual reality on earth since humans first lived on it), this represents the best strategy for fostering peace, mutual respect, and cooperation between peoples of all nations, languages, backgrounds, and every other division and disctinction possible amongst humans—including religion and sexual orientation. But, this lack of focus on belief is also why polytheist groups instead focus on practice rather than on belief, because practice leads to experience, and the richness and development of one's experience generally leads to greater manifestation of virtue, ethics, and good conduct, and thus doing so is good for society more widely speaking.

456

It has often been said that creedal religions focus upon orthodoxy, "right belief/teaching," whereas practical and experiential religions focus on orthopraxy, "right practice." While this is true to some extent, the reality has tended to not be orthopraxy, but instead polypraxy—different communities developed their own unique traditions, and within those there was also room for individual variation and catering to personal preferences. And yet, some basics in terms of practice tend to be more widespread than others. The personal identity of deities makes it that much more important to pay attention to specifics like their names and their proper pronunciations, their natural, symbolic, and mythic associations, the attested practices that have proven successful in eliciting their attention or gaining their favor, and the texts which are used traditionally in relation to them, as well as many other possible practical concerns. However, this reality is no barrier to those matters of personal preference—both on the parts of a human devotional community and a given deity—expanding or developing further over time, either. It is obvious that conceptions of deities have changed over time, as is apparent in ancient texts from different periods but the same general culture or geographic area that are concerned with the same deity or cult site. Just as humans are known to do, individually as well as societally, the gods adapt, change, and evolve, both of their own volition and due to the shifting pressures of the environment and the conditions of the world at any given moment.

Devotion to the gods, and to Antinous in particular, therefore, is an ongoing project, and not one that has been exhausted by the pages of this book. It will continue to develop, not only in my own personal practices and engagements with Antinous, but also in the traditions of the Ekklesía Antínoou, in devotion to Antinous more widely, and throughout all of human history while the name of Antinous of Bithynia is still known and recognized as divine.

By taking up the task of devotion to Antinous willingly and of one's own accord, possibly with the assistance of the instruments presented in the present book, I hope that you will come to a greater knowledge of the god through direct experience, a greater integration in your own person, a greater realization of your own divine nature, and a greater ability to deal with the difficulties as well as a greater appreciation of the beauties which this beautiful world might present to you.

The greatest challenge and test of one's convictions is not whether or not one's *devotio Antinoo* will propel one to die for Antinous. Instead, the greatest reward for one's *devotio Antinoo* will be the experience of **_living with Antinous_**.

Index

Androklos 77, 135

anemone 367

Angels in America 53

Angerona 155

Angeronalia 155

"*Animula Vagula Blandula*" 50, 411-413

Ann Arbor, Michigan 296

Antaura 85

Antimachus 408

Antinoan Mysteries 291, 416-417

Antinoan Petition 74-81

Antinoë 239, 240-241, 330, 375

Antinoeia 131

Antinoeion 350

Antinoeios 131, 369, 372-373

Antinoöpolis (also Antinoë, Antenon, Antina, Adrianopolis, Besantinoë, Besantinopolis, Sheikh-'Ibada) 10, 32, 48, 52-53, 125, 129, 135-136, 138, 142, 151, 154-155, 167, 211, 239, 246, 267, 269, 286, 354, 358, 360, 366, 374, 388-405, 406, 407n573, 415, 420, 426

Antinous, *passim*

Antinous the Liberator 34, 62, 64, 69, 86, 93-96, 99, 101, 125, 152, 177, 180, 231-233, 267, 440

Antinous the Lover 34, 63, 64, 68, 93, 95, 133, 181, 231-233

Antinous the Navigator 34, 63, 64, 69, 93, 95, 97-101, 122, 162-163, 180, 231-233, 440

Antiochus 345

Antium 400n564

Antonine Emperors/Dynasty 44, 102, 118, 120-121, 125, 157, 296, 331

Antoninianus of Aphrodisias 32

Antoninus Pius, 78, 125, 129, 140-141, 146, 164, 173, 274, 311, 338n474, 363, 402, 403, 408

Anubis 150, 167, 240, 276, 391, 394, 418

Aparktias 383; see also Boreas

Aphrodite 132-133, 138, 149, 166, 206, 310, 316, 328n462, 348; see also Venus

Apideus (*deme*) 398

Apis (Bull) 76, 134, 180, 240, 398

Apis (king) 345

Appia Annia Regilla 78, 127, 294, 295-297, 299, 300, 307-308, 310-314, 320, 323

Appius 307, 313

apples 27, 127, 434

Apollo, Apollon 10, 25n7, 31-32, 49, 77, 106-107, 135, 138, 139, 142, 156, 166-167, 168-169, 171-172, 180, 197, 200, 202, 206, 208, 211, 217, 223, 226, 231-233, 307, 310, 363, 369, 375, 386, 399, 400

Apollo the Wolf-God 45

Apollodorus of Damascus 105

Apolloneion 432

Apollonieus (*deme*) 400

Apollonius (citizen) 403

Apollonius of Tyana 400n564

Apologia Prima 406

Apologeticus 406

Apta 410

Aquarius 40, 121

Aquila 10, 40, 45, 94, 95, 98, 100, 122, 141, 162-163, 170

Arab, Arabian 87, 396

Arakhne 128

Arascids 341

Araujo, Gwen 78

Arbeia 140

Arbor Day 140-141

Arcadia, Arcadian 9, 56, 62, 97, 99, 124, 133, 136, 160, 180, 182-183, 200, 207, 209, 225, 239, 241, 255, 263, 330n475, 399, 416-417, 428n618

Arch of Constantine 33, 46, 133, 135, 198, 370

archigalli 130

Area 394, 395

Areopagos 308, 313

Ares 316; see also Mars

Aretalogia Antinoi 97-101

arête 97

Arete 329n468

Arius (citizen) 401

Argeiphontes 76

Argus 76n135, 202, 209, 372

Argos, Argives 364

Aristaios 33, 76, 142

Aristeides 369

Aristogeiton 78

Aristokrates 303

Aristotimos, T. Flavius 31, 388

Aristotimos (oracle, *Mystes Antinoou*) 3, 291

Arkas 133, 226, 241, 399

Arrian of Nikomedia 138, 199-205, 225, 275, 382-384, 388

Arsinoite 401, 430

Artemis 51, 85, 133, 136, 141-142, 170, 180, 185, 226, 236, 305, 312, 329n466, 397, 398; see also Diana

Artemisios (*deme*) 397

ash tree 221

Asia, Asia Minor 26, 32, 130, 135, 193-194, 199, 294, 329n464, 385-386

Asiatikos Lanptreus 304

Asklepios 13, 25n7, 76, 119, 205, 237, 308, 315, 400

Asklepios (*deme*) 400

Assyrians 369

Astarte 149

asteroids 40, 45, 154

astrology 44-45, 122, 153-154, 343, 370, 400, 421

Astros 34

Atalanta 205

Athamantidian 385

Athanasius of Alexandria 406

atheists 11

Athena 128, 312, 315-316, 329n466, 398; see also Minerva

Athenaeum 419

Athenaeus of Naukratis 42, 50, 154, 230, 370-373

Athenagoras the Athenian 406

Athenais (also occasionally Panathenais, daughter of Herodes Attikos) 126, 294, 300, 308

Athenais (*phyla*) 397

Athenaios 303

Athenius Sextus Lateranus 221

Athens 9, 28, 51, 105, 136, 145, 173, 235, 286-287, 294, 297, 300-301, 308, 311-314, 316, 319, 343, 368, 369, 373, 382, 397, 398, 419, 454

Attic Nights 297-298

Attica 255

Attikos Azerieos 315

Attikos Bradua 294-295, 301, 311

Attis 76, 129, 130

Augurinus 221

Augustine of Hippo 407

Augustus (Octavian) 121, 400

Aulus Gellius 296-298

Aurelia Eudaemonis 403

Aurelian (emperor) 156, 404, 405

Aurelius Alexander 428

Aurelius Ammonius 403

Aurelius Hier...(?) 405

Aurelius Ptollion 403, 404

Catholicism, Catholics 11, 12, 75, 242, 276

cats 27

cattle 132, 135, 187, 220

celandine 373

Celsus 406

Celtic 11, 48, 118n173, 134, 198, 448

Cephisus River 235

Cerberus 150, 180, 237, 366, 386n545

Ceres 122, 128, 137, 156, 165-166, 173, 324-328, 337-338, 400, 419, 437; see
    also Demeter

Chaeremon 430

Chalkis 31

chariots 131, 144, 172, 223, 296, 404, 405

Charon 150

chickens 27, 422

China, Chinese 122, 374

Chios 386

Chnoubis 86, 91, 149

chocolate 27

Choreios 76, 208, 427

Christianity, Christians 10, 33, 66, 82, 85, 116, 215-216, 276, 374, 396, 397,
    406-409, 414, 415, 421-422, 452, 455

Christianity, Social Tolerance, and Homosexuality 31

Christmas 75

Christopher, St. 276

Chronicon Paschale 406

Chronicorum 406

Chryseros 303

Cicero 48, 445

Circle of Dionysos 80

Circus Maximus 130

Claudia Damo Synamate 343, 344, 346

Claudius Quintianus 430

Claudius Ptolemy 396

Clement of Alexandria 406

Cobain, Kurt 131

Cocidius 141, 170

coinage, coins 18, 29, 31, 32, 132, 154, 207, 213-214, 275, 286, 328n460

colors 29, 391

Colossoi of Memnon 53, 152-153, 159, 342-346

Columbia 332

Come As You Are Coven 80

Coming Forth By Day 52, 71-73

468

Diana 12, 25, 32, 51, 66, 78, 93, 95, 99, 101, 133, 143, 171-172, 193-194, 197, 219, 227-229, 268, 329, 374, 377; see also Artemis
Dían Cécht 232
Diann, Lucinda 3
Diarmaid Úa Duibhne 199
Didymus 401-403
Dies Caniculares 142, 171, 185, 225
Dies Divae 120, 286
Dies Natalis Antinoi 25, 27, 53, 66, 117, 153-154, 160, 268, 377, 378, 380, 381, 431-432
Dies Natalis Dianae 25, 50, 66, 143-144, 171-172, 377, 380, 381
Dies Sancti Ignoti 135
Dies Sanctorum Omnium 147
Dietrichson, Dr. L. H. S. 42
Diocletian 374, 376, 388, 397, 415
Diogenes (Cynic philosopher) 369
Diogenes (official) 376
Dionysantinous 375
Dionysia (Oxyrhynchite woman) 430-431
Dionysian artists 103, 427
Dionysieus (*deme*) 398
Dionysios (archon) 303
Dionysius of Alexandria 207, 212, 385-387, 388
Dionysos 10, 12, 25n7, 26, 29, 30-31, 34, 35, 53, 62, 76, 104, 127, 131, 137, 142, 145, 156, 161, 167-168, 180, 208, 211, 231-233, 236, 263, 269-270, 302, 314, 321, 369, 375, 398, 399, 417, 424, 427, 440, 442; see also Bacchus
Dionysos: Archetypal Image of Indestructible Life 53
Dionysus: Myth and Cult 53
Dioscorus of Aphrodito 407n573
Dioskouroi 122, 137, 138, 143, 295, 384, 400; see also Castor and Pollux, Kastor and Polydeukes
Dioskurios (*deme*) 400
Disciplina, Disciplina Augusta 139-140, 169, 213-218, 329
Divae, Divi 5, 14, 59, 119, 120, 123, 128-129, 139-140, 157, 165, 274, 278-293, 324-334, 340-346, 415, 448
dogs 21, 27, 50, 70, 104, 111, 112, 124, 134, 137, 167, 171, 184-185, 200, 244, 386; see also hounds
dolphins 195
Domitia Lucilla 312
Domitia Paulina 140, 374, 399, 418
Domitian (emperor) 418
Domitianos 308

470

472

474

476

Jove/Iove 291, 293; see also Jupiter, Zeus

Judaea 106, 141

Judaism 66, 82, 116, 416, 421-422

Julia Balbilla 14, 53, 145, 152-153, 159, 212, 250, 255, 259-265, 275, 329, 342-346

Julian "the Apostate" (emperor) 415, 418-419

Julius Caesar 12, 140, 185, 274, 357n502, 400

Julius Fidus Aquila 425

Julius Varianus 430

Juno 324, 328, 400; see also Hera

Jupiter 40, 45, 78, 124, 137, 397, 400; see also Jove/Iove, Zeus

Justin Martyr 406

Juturna 120

kabbalah, kabbalistic 41

Kadmos 312, 400

Kaisarios (*deme*) 400

Kallimachus 3

Kallineikos 304

Kalliope 159

Kallisto 133, 225

Kalliteknios (*deme*) 398, 403

kalokagathia 277

kami 273

Kapitolieus (*deme*) 397

Karneios 29

Kasianos 303

Kastor and Polydeukes 77, 122, 143, 237, 295, 400; see also Castor and Pollux, Dioskouroi

Kato Souli 302, 304

Kaunos 386

Kekrops 311, 316

Kemetic 1

Kephisia 303, 304, 307, 309, 313

Kerényi, Karl 48, 51, 53, 208

Kershaw, Kris 45

Keryx 311

Kessler, Dieter 350

kharis 217, 348-349

Khemenou 352

Kinar 78

kirtan 37, 451

Kleitor 399

486

Oseirantinous 32, 209, 325, 391, 403
Osiris 10, 12, 32-33, 38, 52, 76, 148-149, 151, 167, 175, 180, 209, 232, 240, 252-253, 256-257, 260-262, 264, 273, 295, 350-355, 359, 362, 391-392, 399
Otto, Walter 53
Ourania 349
Ouranos 360
ouroboros 282, 283
Ovid 119, 121, 128, 137, 325n457, 442
oxen 137
Oxyrhynchus 67, 153-154, 160, 182, 198, 230, 239, 291, 371, 374, 377, 403-405, 428, 430-432
Oxyrhynchus Papyri 13, 374, 428, 430, 431
O-Zone 40

Paganalia 121
paidika 382, 407-409
Palatine 184
Palestina 220
Pallas 128
Palmyrian 425
Pan 10, 77, 119, 124, 180, 182-183, 223, 241
Panantinous 182-183, 375, 428
Pancrates/Pachrates 9, 40n58, 50, 148, 212, 230, 250-265, 275, 370-373, 375, 393n554
Pannonia 288, 410, 416, 417
Panthea 149, 175
PantheaCon 3, 17n4, 26, 70, 184, 250
Pantheon 46, 54, 266-267
Pantheus 141
Paparizou, Elena 39
Papiri della R. Universita di Milano 367
Paphlagonia 124
papyrus 36
Parentalia 123
Pares 132
Parilia 132
Paris 31-33
Parnassus (Mount) 223
Parrhasios 45, 241, 399
Parrhasios (deme) 399
Parthia 340, 418
Pastor, Ben 52

488

494

496

About the Author

P. Sufenas Virius Lupus is a founder of the Ekklesía Antínoou—a queer, Graeco-Roman-Egyptian syncretist reconstructionist polytheist group dedicated to Antinous, the deified lover of the Roman Emperor Hadrian and related divine figures—as well as a contributing member of the Neos Alexandria group, and a practicing Celtic Reconstructionist polytheist in the *filidecht* and *gentlidecht* traditions of Ireland (with further devotions to Romano-British, Gaulish, and Welsh deities), and a devotee of several divine ancestors and land spirits in the area of western Washington state. Lupus also occasionally participates in Shinto, Buddhist, and Hindu spiritual activities.

To date, Lupus' work has appeared in the Bibliotheca Alexandrina devotional anthologies for Artemis, Hekate, Isis and Serapis, Zeus, Pan, Thoth, and the Near Eastern deities, with further forthcoming work to appear in the devotional volumes for Persephone, the Dioskouroi, and Hephaistos, as well as others. Lupus is also in the process of co-editing a devotional anthology on cynocephalic deities for Bibliotheca Alexandrina, as well as an anthology on queer magic for Megalithica. Lupus' essay, fiction, and poetry have also appeared in *Datura: An Anthology of Esoteric Poeisis*, ed. Ruby Sara (Scarlet Imprint, 2010), *Spirit of Desire: Personal Explorations of Sacred Kink*, ed. Lee Harrington (Mystic Productions Press, 2010), and *Etched Offerings: Voices from the Cauldron of Story*, ed. Inanna Gabriel and C. Bryan Brown (Misanthrope Press, 2011). As you can imagine, many more pieces are in the works, and will appear in the future, if all goes well...

Lupus appears yearly at PantheaCon over President's Day in San Jose, CA, and also runs public rituals in the greater Seattle area. Lupus also writes regularly on Antinous-related subjects at the Aedicula Antinoi blog (http://aediculaantinoi.wordpress.com/), and contributes a bi-weekly column to Patheos.com's Pagan Portal called "Queer I Stand."

500

The Syncretisms of Antinous

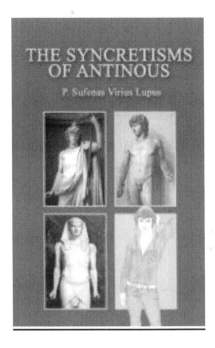

The Syncretisms of Antinous is an in-depth exploration of Antinous' relationship to other gods and heroes of the Greek, Roman, and Egyptian pantheons, both in antiquity and in later centuries. Antinous, the deified lover of the Roman Emperor Hadrian (117-138 CE), was syncretized to a large number of deities and heroes in his ancient cultus, and the process didn't stop when that cultus ended in the fifth century. Archaeologists, scholars, artists, and admirers of male beauty continued to link him to a great many figures from Greek, Roman, and Egyptian mythology. In this book, you will find out about the familiar as well as the more obscure syncretisms of Antinous, from Hermes to Herakles, Dionysos to the Dioskouroi, Apollon to Apis, Adonis to Attis, Pan to Poseidon, Achilleus to Aristaios, Endymion to Eunostos, Eros to Echmoun, and many more! You will also find resources to guide you in getting to know these syncretisms further, and ideas for devotional practices based upon them.

$20. ISBN 1456300458   http://www.createspace.com/3493936

Coming soon from
THE RED LOTUS LIBRARY

All-Soul, All-Body, All-Love, All-Power: A Trans Mythology
A new exploration, in poetic myth, of Trans and Gender-Variant deities.

Studium Antinoi: The Doctor's Notes, Volume Two Studies in theology and ethics, both new and from P. Sufenas Virius Lupus' old website, Aedicula Antinoi.

Something To Do: A Pagan Experiential Praxis Theology An argument for pagan theology in general from a radical perspective, and on the value of experiential, personal, and local polytheist religion.

Liber Dies Antinoi An in-depth detailing of the Ekklesía Antínoou calendar and the *Sancti*, formatted for use as a "book of days."

The Triads of Antinous A gnomic text for ease in understanding theological shorthand for Antinous and within Ekklesía Antínoou practice.
COMING IN 2012!
For More Information, see
http://aediculaantinoi.wordpress.com/the-red-lotus-library/

Nysa Press was founded to publish the writings of H. Jeremiah Lewis and help promote the revival of Greco-Egyptian polytheism today. His books explore ancient history, literature, philosophy, mythology and the contemporary worship of the Greek and Egyptian deities.

From the Satyr's Mouth: Wit and Wisdom from an Opinionated Polytheist [ISBN: 1453643249]

In ancient Greece, satyrs were famed for their mocking criticism of societal conventions. H. Jeremiah Lewis brings that same spirit to a discussion of contemporary Pagan life and values in this latest collection of essays. Prepare to be challenged, informed, annoyed and hopefully entertained!

The Balance of the Two Lands: Writings on Greco-Egyptian Polytheism [ISBN: 1442190337]

This collection of essays explores the long history and contemporary manifestations of Greco-Egyptian polytheism. It provides overviews of the system, information on theology, ethics, and the afterlife, as well as material on domestic worship, ritual forms, and the basics needed to begin practicing the religion today.

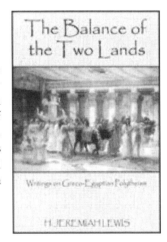

Nysa Press was founded to publish the writings of H. Jeremiah Lewis and help prom ote the revival of Greco-Egyptian polytheism today. His books explore ancient history, literature, philosophy, mythology and the contemporary worship of the Greek and Egyptian deities.

Echoes of Alexandria: Poems and Stories [ISBN: 1442190396]

This volume of poetry and short stories celebrates the author's undying love for the incomparable city of dreamers and the immortal gods and famous historical figures who once walked Alexandria's fabled streets. Included are hymns that have been used in actual worship, imaginative retellings of ancient stories, and modern myths set down for the first time.

Gods and Mortals: New Stories of Hellenic Polytheism [ISBN: 1449931294]

These are the stories of Hellenismos today. What it feels like to recognize the presence of the gods around you. To discover the mystery of the divine, the power of love, the joy of life, the pangs of grief, the loneliness that comes with belonging to a minority faith. You can read about ancient Greek religion in academic tomes - but none will tell you what it's like from the inside. For that, you must hear our stories, in our own words. Stories of gods and mortals.

504

Ecstatic [ISBN: 1463534655]

Who is Dionysos? There are as many answers to this enigmatic question as there are people asking it. For a significant portion of his life H. Jeremiah Lewis (perhaps better known by his religious name Sannion) has struggled to understand the ways and nature of this elusive ancient Greek deity of wine, vegetation, madness, drama, liberation and much else besides. In the course of his study and explorations he has produced an immense body of writing which has been gathered together in this unique volume for the first time ever. In addition to learning about Dionysian history, mythology, symbolism, and methods of worship both ancient and modern, the reader will gain a first-hand glimpse of what it's like to know and love a god as strange as Dionysos. Of special interest to Dionysians and occultists, this volume sees the first publication anywhere of a new oracular system involving the myths, symbols and associations of Dionysos with a concise explanation of how to use it.

For more information, see
http://www.thehouseofvines.com/nysapress.htm

BIBLIOTHECA ALEXANDRINA

To help promote the revival of traditional polytheistic traditions, Bibliotheca Alexandrina is publishing a series of volumes dedicated to the ancient Gods of Greece, Egypt and surrounding regions. Each volume contains essays, poetry, short fiction, rituals, artwork, et cetera focused on a particular divinity or group of divinities. These anthologies are a collaborative effort drawing on the combined resources of the modern Hellenic, Kemetic and broader polytheist communities, in the hope that we can come together to praise the Gods and share our diverse understandings, experiences and approaches to the divine. All of the proceeds from these books go to help promote the worship of the Gods, either by bringing out further volumes or through donation to charitable causes in Their names.

For more information, see
http://www.neosalexandria.org/publishing.htm

Current Titles from the Bibliotheca Alexandrina include:

Written in Wine: A Devotional Anthology for Dionysos
The Phillupic Hymns by P. Sufenas Virius Lupus

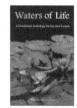

Unbound: A Devotional Anthology for Artemis
Waters of Life: A Devotional Anthology for Isis and Serapis

Bearing Torches: A Devotional Anthology for Hekate

From Cave to Sky: A Devotional Anthology for Zeus

Out of Arcadia: A Devotional Anthology in Honor of Pan

Anointed: A Devotional Anthology for the Deities of the Near and Middle East

The Scribing Ibis: An Anthology of Pagan Fiction in Honor of Thoth

And Coming Soon:

Devotional anthologies for Persephone, Hephaistos, the Dioskouroi, Cynocephalic Deities, Hermes, Athena, Virgin Goddesses, Polytheist Science Fiction, and more!

Coming Soon from Misanthrope Press

Etched Offerings
Voices From the Cauldron of Story

An anthology of Pagan fiction

With an Introduction by:

Including stories by:

R. S. Bohn

P. Sufenas Virius Lupus

Cory Thomas Hutcheson

and Llewellyn author
Kenny Klein

S. J. Tucker

Misanthrope Press

508

Did You Like What You Read?

If you enjoyed this book, you might also like...

Sekhem Heka by Storm Constantine
ISBN: 978-1-905713-13-4 /MB0114
£12.99/$21.99 paperback
Drawing upon her experiences in Egyptian Magic and the energy healing systems of Reiki and Seichim, Storm Constantine has developed this new system to appeal to practitioners of both magic and energy healing.

Women's Voices in Magic edited by Brandy Williams
ISBN 978-1-905713-39-4 /MB0139
£11.99/$20.99 paperback
The essays in this book explode gender stereotypes and survey the spectrum of women's experiences in magic. Women are witches, but also ceremonial magicians, Satanists and sex magicians. Women dream, use intuition and make magical tools but they also argue, create ritual, and fiercely contest their right to achievement

Dancing With Spirits by Denny Sargent
ISBN 978-1-905713-52-3/MB0146
£10.99/$19.99 paperback
An intellectual but accessible 'travel guide through the history and fun reality of the most important Shinto and Buddhist festivals of Japan, featuring entertaining first-hand accounts of wild revels like Tanabata and Setsubun.

Ogam by Erynn Rowan Laurie
ISBN 978-1-905713-02-8/MB0110
£13.99/$22.99 paperback
An explanation of the history of ogam, with an introduction to each of the ogam and their origins and divination layouts. There's plenty more to the magic of ogam than divination, and Ogam: Weaving Word Wisdom makes it quite clear that if you thought you knew everything about ogam--you're in for a big surprise!

Talking About the Elephant edited by Lupa
978-1-905713-24-0/MB0125
£11.99 $20.99 paperback
Modern pagans draw from a variety of cultural wells. All too often the effects of this borrowing are ignored in lieu of "spiritual development". This book promotes constructive communication about issues surrounding cultural appropriation in neopaganism. The 19 essays cover a multitude of practices and topics.

Graeco-Egyptian Magic by Tony Mierzwicki
ISBN 978-1-905713-03-7/MB0103
£12.99 $21.99 paperback
Stemming from years of study this book outlines a daily practice involving planetary Hermeticism, drawn from the original texts and converted into a format that fits easily into the modern magician's practice.

Shades of Faith edited by Crystal Blanton
ISBN 978-1-905713-69-1 / MB0151
£10.99 $19.99 paperback
An anthology that addresses some of the challenges, stereotyping, frustrations, talents, history and beauties of being different within the racial constructs of typical Pagan or Wiccan groups.

Ecstatic Ritual by Brandy Williams
ISBN 978-1-905713-25-7 /MB0111
£10.99 $19.99 paperback
From ancient to modern times, people have looked to sexuality to aid them in connecting with the Divine.This book offers the reader clear, concise exercises and ritual forms which comprise a full understanding of sacred and magical sexuality.

Find these and the rest of our current lineup at http://www.immanion-press.com

Made in the USA
San Bernardino, CA
29 August 2014